THE
Rock & Roll Film
ENCYCLOPEDIA

D1537418

THE
Rock & Roll Film
ENCYCLOPEDIA

John Kenneth Muir

APPLAUSE THEATRE & CINEMA BOOKS

An Imprint of Hal Leonard Corporation

New York

The Rock & Roll Film Encyclopedia
By John Kenneth Muir
Copyright © 2007 John Kenneth Muir
All rights reserved

Cover design by Mark Lerner. Book design by Pearl Chang. All photos courtesy of Photofest.

Library of Congress Cataloging-in-Publication Data:

Muir, John Kenneth, 1969-
    The rock & roll film encyclopedia / by John Kenneth Muir.
        p.   cm.
    Includes bibliographical references and index.
    ISBN-13: 978-1-55783-693-9 (pbk.)
    ISBN-10: 1-55783-693-0 (pbk.)
1. Rock films--United States--Encyclopedias. I. Title. II. Title: Rock and roll film encyclopedia.
PN1995.9.M86M84 2007
791.43'657--dc22   2006103377

Applause Theatre & Cinema Books (an imprint of Hal Leonard Corporation)
    19 West 21st Street
    Suite 201
    New York, NY 10010
    Phone: (212) 575-9265
    Fax: (212) 575-9270
    Email: info@applausepub.com
    Internet: www.applausepub.com

Applause books are available through your local bookstore, or you may order at www.applausepub.com or call Music Dispatch at 800-637-2852

Sales & Distribution

North America:
    Hal Leonard Corp.
    7777 West Bluemound Road
    P. O. Box 13819
    Milwaukee, WI 53213
    Phone: (414) 774-3630
    Fax: (414) 774-3259
    Email: halinfo@halleonard.com
    Internet: www.halleonard.com

Europe:
    Roundhouse Publishing Ltd.
    Millstone, Limers Lane
    Northam, North Devon EX 39 2RG
    Phone: (0) 1237-474-474
    Fax: (0) 1237-474-774
    Email: roundhouse.group@ukgateway.net

With love for my father Kenneth Muir—the man who introduced me to Joan Jett.

Contents

ACKNOWLEDGMENTS IX

ONE GREAT ROCK SHOW
An Introduction to The Rock & Roll Film Encyclopedia

XI

A NOTE ON FORMAT

XVII

THE ENCYCLOPEDIA
A-Z

I

CONCLUSION
Don't Look Back...
321

THE TOPS (AND BOTTOMS...)
of the Rock Film Genre

323

ENDNOTES 333

SELECTED BIBLIOGRAPHY 337

INDEX 341

Acknowledgments

My humble thanks to June Clark, my rock'n'roll agent…for making this book come to life
(and also for suggesting some interesting rock titles!)
Also, my gratitude to Kevin Flanagan, a fine writer and research assistant who
stepped up to the plate and wrote a half-dozen entries in a timely fashion
when I had to contend with various medical crises.

My sincere appreciation goes to the interviewees who aided me
in shedding light on their superior rock efforts.
This list includes Allan Arkush, Kent Beyda, Martin Davidson, Gloria Gifford,
Albert Magnoli, Pete Smokler, and Lewis Teague.

I must also thank my supportive "back-up singers" at Applause.
As always, this dream team "has my back," but never more so than now.
Michael Messina is a prince among publishers, a friend
and a bastion of good taste (and knowledge on the subject matter).
As always, he's been the better angel of my nature…and a 24-hour party person.
Also, Pearl Chang has designed a gorgeous book, and
editor Brian Black once more has marshaled his vast expertise in fact-checking
and cleaning the manuscript. Party on dudes!
Lastly, special thanks to Brad Smith, my rock 'n' roll archivist!

THIS ENCYCLOPEDIA

SHOULD BE READ LOUD

(at Maximum Volume...)

ONE GREAT ROCK SHOW

An Introduction to the Rock & Roll Film Encyclopedia

This encyclopedia to fifty years of rock movies (1956–2005) is submitted in accordance with the wisdom, philosophy, and spirit of a venerated rocker named Dewey Finn, the protagonist portrayed so memorably by actor Jack Black in the 2003 Richard Linklater comedy *The School of Rock.*

In the Oracle's own well-chosen words: *"One great rock show can change the world..."*

The preceding proverb is not merely optimistic, it happens to be true.

Consider, for instance, the case of Michael Wadleigh's Academy Award–winning documentary, *Woodstock* (1970), the living record of the August 1969 rock festival. This cinematic enterprise proved to rapt audiences that 1.5 million young rock music-lovers from the Age of Aquarius could dwell together in peace and harmony at a get–together the size of a modern metropolis for seventy-two hours, despite mud slides, pounding rain...and long lines for the portable toilets. There was no hate. No violence. Only rock music (and, a few recreational drugs).

Though the festival itself was attended by over a million, that impressive number pales in comparison to the breadth of the movie's reach. How many millions, over how many generations, have viewed the documentary *Woodstock* and marveled at the piece; at the accomplishment it chronicles; or found themselves inspired by its example? And, in how many cultures and foreign lands has this occurred?

Again, just *one good rock show can change the world...*

Contemplate next the example of *Rock Around the Clock* (1956) an effort from the prehistoric days of rock 'n' roll history (back in the Eisenhower era, for goodness sake).

Featuring Bill Haley and His Comets and their trademark titular tune (which had also served as the theme song to the Glenn Ford melodrama *The Blackboard Jungle*), this movie so enthused and entranced audiences of its day that some teens reportedly raised a ruckus during some matinees.

For many of those adolescent viewers (who are now in their sixties), this experience in a movie theatre represented their first encounter with a larger world, and with a new and radical form of music. Like *Woodstock*, *Rock Around the Clock* changed the world too, and reportedly no less a figure than England's Queen Elizabeth II requested a personal screening.

Considering that (perhaps apocryphal) tale, one wonders how the Queen, or any Head of State may have been altered by that particular and singular rock show.

In truth, one can never accurately calculate just how many people have been touched and forever changed by their first cinematic brush with the likes of Elvis Presley (in *King Creole*, 1958, perhaps), or The Beatles in *A Hard Day's Night* (1964). Or even Bill and Ted's Wyld Stallyns, who—through their most triumphant rock compositions—have ushered in a new golden age of peace and prosperity on Earth.

Whoa! Wait a minute! That didn't really happen…

Yet the glorious thing about Dewey Finn's "great rock show" theorem is that perhaps, *just perhaps*, it could happen.

After all, music is often termed "the universal language." Music bridges ethnic differences, leaps over language barriers, and can overcome lines of racial divide. It's the one thing every human being anywhere on Earth can experience and internalize without the interference or stratifications of class, wealth, or country of origin.

As for rock music, it is specifically and eternally the music of *youth*; the melody of rebellion, experimentation, and—importantly—*potential*. Since youth represents the future (especially in movies), each great rock show boasts the power to forever alter the course of our collective tomorrow.

The point of this rumination on the so-called Dewey Finn Postulate remains simple. For over half a century, rock 'n' roll music and the technological art form of movies have combined to create some of the greatest and most beloved movies of our time. In the process of doing so, perhaps some of these memorable silver-screen rock shows—efforts such as *Don't Look Back* (1967), *Gimme Shelter* (1970), *Tommy* (1975), *Pink Floyd: The Wall* (1982), *Purple Rain* (1984) and *Metallica: Some Kind of Monster* (2004)—HAVE actually changed the world too.

Indeed, this alchemy has been magical and, on occasion, miraculous. Rock music and cinema fit hand-in-glove; they go together like—well—chocolate and peanut butter. Over the years, rock 'n' roll and cinema have shared a complex, give-and-take, multifaceted relationship.

As the decades have passed, the face and form of rock movies have changed with the times; reflecting and often forecasting each new age or trend. The fifties introduced films like *Don't Knock the Rock* (1956), which were careful to appear morally valuable, and assured parents that this new fangled "*jungle music*" would not debauch the decade's youth or transform them into juvenile delinquents.

The 1960s came, and rock movies quickly became the voice of the counterculture, in efforts as diverse as the cinema verité *Don't Look Back* (1967), *Head* (1968), and *Alice's Restaurant* (1969).

The 1970s first saw cynicism in the Watergate age and then unfettered escapism and the rise of the blockbuster (following *Jaws*, 1975 and *Star Wars*, 1977). The rock efforts of the 1970s reflected the zeitgeist of the time; in a word: *disco*. Multiplexes filled with titles like *Saturday Night Fever* (1977) and The Bee Gees' *Sgt. Pepper's Lonely Hearts Club Band* (1978).

Reagan's conservative Eighties came (with yuppies included!) and the wide availability of cable TV and the ubiquitous, powerful nature of the boob tube gave rise to MTV and the new short form of "music videos," which forever impacted how cinematic artists crafted rock movies. *Flashdance* (1983) and *Footloose* (1984) are just two examples of this new aesthetic.

The independent film movement of the 1990s democratized film production, making it cheaper and expanding the once-limited playing field of Hollywood for new and original voices. The VHS/DVD revolution and birth of the World Wide Web suddenly meant that years and years of rock films—previously missing in action—could be resurrected to form the gestalt of home entertainment libraries.

At the same time, movies picked up on a new and exciting trend in rock music: Seattle grunge and alternative rock. Movies such as *Slaves to the Underground* (1997) and the documentary *Kurt & Courtney* (1998) diagramed these new perspectives.

By the dawn of the new millennium, the popular TV series *American Idol* and a slew of other so-called reality programs like MTV's *The Real World* again changed how rock movies were crafted, granting endeavors such as *Metallica: Some Kind of Monster* (2004) a brand new (and sometimes shocking) level of intimacy.

Notice that this text keeps mentioning *rock movies*, but at this point, the intrepid reader may rightly be wondering what, precisely, constitutes a rock film, or "the genre?" Let's begin that discussion with the basics: a brief definition of rock music itself.

"When we use rock as a noun or adjective to describe music," writes Michael Campbell and James Brody in their book, *Rock and Roll: An Introduction*, "we imply a certain sound, or range of sounds. It is not classical, or folk, or pop, or jazz, or country. It is rock. We expect loud guitars, up-front rhythms...rough-edged vocals." [1]

Then these selfsame writers go on to conclude. "Without question, a lot of rock music has none of these qualities." [2]

A-ha!

So even on this relatively simple front, there's not likely to be a consensus of how to define Rock (let alone Rock movies!). Thus, for the purpose of this book, films that involve rock music, but also disco, rhythm & blues, soul, and pop are *all* included in the mix. These related formats may boast elements or ingredients of rock music—or may simply be closely related siblings, but in any case, there's a "genetic" similarity between forms worth charting.

That only leaves one more form to worry about: hip hop or rap. After much soul searching, I've concluded that the expansive body of hip hop films (from *Beat Street*, 1984, to *Get Rich or Die Tryin'*, 2005) and hip-hop performers in the cinema (L.L. Cool J, Ice Cube, Ice-T, Vanilla Ice, etc.) precludes the possibility of adequately covering it in what is primarily intended to be a text concerning rock. A powerful, expressive art form, hip-hop is also too important historically and culturally, I'd wager, to gaze at in half-measures. So let's save rap for another day, and perhaps another manuscript (*The Hip-Hop Movie Encyclopedia*? Any takers?), and concentrate instead on rock and its closer brethren.

Now that it is understood what kind of music will be included, one must gaze at how it is featured in the medium of film to determine and define the parameters of a "rock genre." Quite frankly, there's a wide variety of film types that feature either rock music or rock practitioners, and as many of these types as possible are included in this book.

First, there are nonfiction films or documentaries (usually in the cinema verité or direct cinema mold), that chronicle rock concerts or festivals. *Woodstock* falls into this category, but so do a whole host of films: *Monterey Pop* (1967), *Don't Look Back* (1967), the terrifying *Gimme Shelter* (1970), George Harrison's *Concert for Bangladesh* (1971), *The Last Waltz* (1978), and so on.

Another critical category in the genre involves movie soundtracks. Many films over the decades have utilized rock songs to generate feelings of nostalgia or to just engender fun. Films with rock soundtracks (like *American Graffiti*, 1973, or *Dirty Dancing*, 1987) thus represent fair game too.

Then there are those films that star authentic rock 'n' roll stars. *The Hunger* (1983) stars David Bowie, *Desperately Seeking Susan* (1984) features Madonna, *Purple Rain* (1984) spotlights Prince, and the Beatles headline all their own films. These also find coverage within these pages.

In addition, there are films about the very *subject* of rock music and the rock world themselves, carefully-crafted fictional narratives about imagined performers. *This Is Spinal Tap* (1984), *Rock Star* (2001), and *Prey for Rock & Roll* (2003) are just a few examples of this particular format.

Finally, one must not neglect or forget the rock operas and movie musicals of yesteryear, the music-based films such as *Phantom of the Paradise* (1974), *Tommy* (1975), *The Rocky Horror Picture Show* (1975), and *Pink Floyd: The Wall* (1982), which in some fashion deploy rock 'n' roll in an operatic style to transmit critical portions of a narrative; and usually with stunning, avant-garde imagery.

Each of these film styles encompasses what I have termed the "rock genre" and fits within the purview of this encyclopedia.

In addition to important movies reflecting these various stripes, this work takes the extra step of identifying the rock movie's *conventions and trends*. This is critical, especially now, at this juncture, since there are fifty years of backstory and history to consider and weigh. What thematic elements or stock characters bind the diverse rock-film genre together? What components do these films have in common? That's this text's bailiwick too.

Hopefully, the reader will find this comprehensive approach a valuable one that respects and honors the Dewey Finn ethos. Yet let's not get carried away, either. There's also ample opportunity in this survey merely to enhance the enjoyment of these films, to experience good memories or even a few laughs.

In the latter regard, this introduction closes with the important words of another oracle in rock lure, The Who's Roger Daltrey.

In the documentary *The Kids Are Alright* (1979), the star of *Tommy* notes that "*rock 'n' roll has never ever stood dissecting and inspecting at close range. It doesn't stand up. So shut up!*"

In honor of that particular statement, this book will not get carried away with dissecting or inspecting.

But I won't shut up just yet, either.

So let's rock!

A NOTE ON FORMAT

The entries contained in the following encyclopedia fall roughly into three categories or types. These are: *films* (of which over two hundred are surveyed), *genre conventions*, and *the rock movie hall of fame*, which gazes briefly at an individual rocker who has had significant impact on film.

The film entries themselves come labeled with a variety of descriptors (ten to be exact), for benefit of easy reference. Why categorize films in this fashion? In particular, because the genre of the rock movie encompasses so many varieties of filmmaking styles and sub-groups. The following key may prove helpful:

Entry Legend

(ANIM) This indicates that the rock film in question is either an animated film (a cartoon) or features an animated interlude. *Yellow Submarine* (1968) is an example of the former, *Pink Floyd: The Wall* (1982) the latter.

(BIO-PIC) These films are the ostensible "true life" stories or biographies of famous rock stars. Examples: the story of Jim Morrison in *The Doors* (1991) or Tina Turner in *What's Love Got to Do With It* (1993).

(CAMEOS) This descriptor indicates that the film in question features a bit by a rock star. Cameos appear frequently in rock movies, so this descriptor arises often.

(DOC) An abbreviation for documentary. Many of the finest films in rock history are chronicles of live events, whether it be the Woodstock festival in *Woodstock* (1970), The ill-fated Altamont concert in *Gimme Shelter* (1970), or the final performance of The Band in Martin Scorsese's *The Last Waltz* (1978).

(ELVIS) In all caps in honor of the King of Rock 'n' Roll. Elvis films include not just the pictures he starred in, both fictional (*King Creole*, 1958, *Kid Galahad*, 1962, *Wild in the Country*, 1962, and documentary (*Elvis: That's the Way It Is*, 1970), but those films which feature Elvis as a subject matter, including the fantasy *Heartbreak Hotel* (1988) or *Finding Graceland* (1998).

(FIC BAND) An abbreviation indicating that the rock film in question features rock as a subject, and in particular, a fictional band (or performer) as its central character. *This Is Spinal Tap* (1984) concerns a fictional band, for instance; Bette Midler's *The Rose* (1979) a fictional performer.

(HORR) Simply rock horror, an unholy blending of the rock format with the scary movie. Surprisingly, there are more of these than you might imagine, including *The Hunger* (1983) and *Trick or Treat* (1986).

(MUS) An indication that the rock movie is actually a "break-out into song"–style musical. Some examples of this form are *Grease* (1978), *Hair* (1979), and *Hedwig and the Angry Inch* (2001).

(REAL ROCKER) This descriptor points out that a rock star appears in a *featured* role in the film. For instance, Mick Jagger stars in *Performance* (1970), or Bob Dylan in *Pat Garrett & Billy the Kid* (1973).

(SNDTRK) Finally, a number of famous films, including *American Graffiti* (1973) fall under this category. Simply put, sndtrk simply means that the film being surveyed extensively features rock music on the soundtrack. One tune, (like Aerosmith performing a tune during one montage in *Armageddon*, 1998), does not a soundtrack make.

As readers will quickly detect, rock movies are genuine genre blenders, and many of the film entries feature more than one of the preceding abbreviations.

For instance, Prince's *Graffiti Bridge* (1990) stars an authentic rock star (REAL ROCKER), includes break-out-into-song moments like a traditional movie musical (MUS), and concerns the trials and tribulations of a fictional performer, "The Kid," thus being a (FIC BAND) movie. See how easy that is?

Finally, in terms of entry length and general content, I subscribe to absolutely no established rule or regulation. To paraphrase a thought from *Metallica: Some Kind of Monster*, "*this is a rock 'n' roll book…I don't want fucking rules.*"

Uniformity and conformity are the long-time enemies of rock 'n' roll, and in honor of that spirit, I've decided to be rebellious. Some entries feature first-person interview material, others feature critical remarks, some are plainly descriptive, some are lengthy, and some are brief.

"*Don't accept the old order,*" The Sex Pistols demand in *The Filth and The Fury* (2000), and with that edict in mind, let's begin.

A-Z

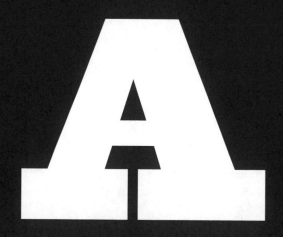

(is for *The Apple*)

ABBA: The Movie (1977)(DOC)(MUS)

STARRING: Anni-Frid Lyngstad (Anni-Frid); Benny Andersson (Barry); Bjorn Ulvaeus (Bjorn); Agnetha Faltskog (Agnetha); Robert Hughes (Ashley Wallace); Tom Oliver (Bodyguard/Taxi Driver); Stig Anderson (Manager); Bruce Barry (Boss).

FILM EDITORS: Lasse Hallstrom, Malou Hallstrom, Ulf Neidemar. DIRECTORS OF PHOTOGRAPHY: Jack Churchill, Paul Onorato. WRITTEN BY: Robert Caswell, Lasse Hallstrom. PRODUCED BY: Stig Anderson, Reg Grundy. DIRECTED BY: Lasse Hallstrom. M.P.A.A. RATING: G. RUNNING TIME: 96 minutes.

Shot in part during the ABBA's Australian tour in the spring of 1977, this unusual rock film melds a fictionalized narrative with video-like dream sequences as well as documentary-style concert and backstage footage of Sweden's most popular group.

Directed by Lasse Hallstrom, who later presided over a mainstream Hollywood career helming films such as *What's Eating Gilbert Grape?* (1993), *The Cider House Rules* (1999), and *Chocolat* (2000), *ABBA: The Movie* debuted in select American theatres right after Christmas in 1977 and coincided with the release of the band's fifth album, *ABBA: The Album.*

The film's fictionalized narrative finds an Australian reporter named Ashley tasked by his boss, Barry, to secure a "dialogue" with "*the most popular group*" in the world during its stay Down Under. Ashley makes several attempts to get up close and personal with ABBA, but is rebuffed until he happens to meet ABBA's *manager*, played by Stig Anderson. A last-minute happy ending sees Ashley getting

his piece on the air in the nick of time.

A strange fusion of reality and fiction, *ABBA: The Movie* presents many trademark ABBA tunes in a variety of colorful settings. "Dancing Queen" is recorded on stage in concert to glorious, rousing effect, while "The Name of the Game" is featured in a fantasy sequence resembling an early music video.

Other tunes that appear in the film include "Tiger" and such ABBA classics as "Fernando," "Waterloo," and "Mamma Mia."

(DVD) This effort was just recently released in the U.S. on DVD in March 2006 after long being unavailable on the home entertainment market.

Absolute Beginners (1986)(MUS)(CAMEOS)

STARRING: Eddie O'Connell (Colin); Patsy Kensit (Suzette); David Bowie (Vendice Partners); James Fox (Henley of Mayfair); Ray Davies (Arthur); Eve Ferret (Big Jill); Anita Morris (Dido Lamont); Lionel Blair (Harry Charms); Steven Berkoff (The Fanatic); Sade (Athene Ducannon).

FILM EDITORS: Michael Bradsell, Gerry Hambling, Richard Bedford, Russell Lloyd. DIRECTOR OF PHOTOGRAPHY: Oliver Stapleton. BASED ON THE NOVEL BY: Colin MacInnes. SCREENPLAY BY: Richard Burridge, Christopher Wicking, Don Macpherson. MUSIC ARRANGED AND CONDUCTED BY: Gil Evans. CHOREOGRAPHY: David Toguri. Executive Producers: Nik Powell, Al Clark, Tobert Devereux. PRODUCED BY: Stephen Woolley, Chris Brown. DIRECTED BY: Julien Temple. M.P.A.A. RATING: PG-13. RUNNING TIME: 108 minutes.

Set in London of 1958 during a moment in history when *"the teenage miracle reached full bloom,"* director Julien Temple's (**see: *The Great Rock 'n' Roll Swindle, The Filth and the Fury***) ambitious *Absolute Beginners* is a 1980s musical adaptation of the cult novel by Colin MacInnes (1914–1976).

The novel (and indeed, the film) concern the beginnings of the so-called Mod youth culture in London, as well as the race riots in Notting Hill during the late 1950s. Temple's ambitious and occasionally impressive film boasts an overabundance of visual style and is an enjoyable feast for the eyes, but remains rather dry and remote from a narrative perspective. Temple cut his teeth directing music videos for the likes of Bowie, Culture Club, and The Rolling Stones, so he boasts the capacity to turn musical set-pieces into dazzling standalone sequences…a talent which comes in handy here.

Absolute Beginners stars Eddie O'Connell as Colin, a young photographer who has fallen head-over-heels for the beautiful Suzette (Patsy Kensit), an up-and-coming fashion designer, just as the Age of Rock commences in a neon-lit London. However, Suzette shuns Colin and marries an older, more professionally-established man (James Fox) to advance her career. As Colin attempts to win back Suzette, racial tensions in his neighborhood burn white-hot courtesy of a supremacist hate group called "White Defense" which advocates deporting all Blacks.

Jerry Lee Lewis' "Great Balls of Fire" gets an unusual airing in this setting, sung by the leader of the fascists while his piano burns in the street.

The flip side of this racism is that Black Culture, while despised by such segregationist forces, is simultaneously responsible for the music and fashion growing increasingly popular among the youngsters of England. In fact, Kensit performs an African jungle dance ("Bongo Rock") at a fashion show alongside a group of shirtless black men, scandalizing the crusty high-class set in attendance.

Cut by some of the finest talents in England (including Alan Parker's regular editor, Gerry Hambling, **see: *The Commitments, Fame***), *Absolute Beginners* reaches its pinnacle during a magnificently-orchestrated number which finds Colin arriving at home and lamenting his life there to the tune of "Landlords and Tenants." The entire house (with all its rooms) is depicted in one glorious, living frame as each tenant goes about his or her business in isolation, individually choreographed.

Another knockout musical number occurs at roughly the one-hour point, with David Bowie dancing atop a giant typewriter and pertinently querying: *"Why am I so exciting?"* The sultry Sade (of "Smooth Operator" fame) also *cameos* in the film, along with The Kinks' Ray Davies.

Although it's set at the fascinating epoch when—according to the film—*"this teenage thing is getting out of hand,"* and teenagers were becoming a major economic force (thus causing the burgeoning popularity of rock), *Absolute Beginners* still features a strange flatness and dullness about it that Temple never quite licks. The film ends with a race riot, which may be historically appropriate since the advent of rock is tied inexorably to the civil rights movement of the 1960s, but a musical hardly seems the place for it.

Films in Review's Louise Stanton opined that Temple's film is "not the absolute mess it could have been," and that the "humor and entertainment throughout most of the picture save *Absolute Beginners* from souring completely in its awkward, somber moments."[1] This is a fair assessment of a film more worthy of study than it is enjoyable to view.

On a historical note, *Absolute Beginners* reportedly suffered financing problems during production, and on at least one occasion this resulted in a temporary stop to shooting. The next musical spectacle to be shot entirely in London was Kenneth Branagh's *Love's Labour's Lost* (2000), which came some fourteen years later.

Bowie performs "Absolute Beginners" and Slim Gaillard sings "Selling Out" in the film; and other tunes featured include "Having it All" and "Riot City." The original music is by Gil Evans.

DVD Available on DVD.

AC/DC: Let There Be Rock

(1982)(DOC)

STARRING: Bon Scott, Angus Young, Malcolm Young, Phil Rudd, Cliff Williams.

FILM EDITOR: Mariette Levy Novion. DIRECTOR OF PHOTOGRAPHY: Jean-Francis Gondre. PRODUCED AND DIRECTED BY: Eric Dionysus and Eric Mistler. M.P.A.A. RATING: PG. RUNNING TIME: 98 minutes.

This is the filmed account of a live AC/DC 1980 concert in Paris. The Australian hard-rock group is captured on stage performing a dozen tunes, including "Dog Eat Dog,"

"Go Down," "Let There Be Rock," "Live Wire," "Highway to Hell," "Overdose," "Shot Down in Flames," and "Sin City."

The film's musical material is interspersed with several backstage interviews and footage of the band preparing for the performance. *Let There Be Rock* was lensed prior to the death of Bon Scott, AC/DC's lead singer, and he's revealed onscreen here—appearing well on his way to death's door. Which, according to *Newsday*, was "attributed to acute alcohol poisoning."[2] That's believable since when questioned about what makes him special, Scott tellingly notes that he's a "special drunkard" who "drinks too much."

Writing for *The New York Post*, Ed Naha described this concert film as "boring" and noted that "Basically, it's a '*let's set up*, *let's drink*, *let's play some more*,' flick that never really tells you much about the band except that they seem high a lot and have a hard time keeping their pants up onstage."[3]

Although that quotation may be a perfect rock 'n' roll epitaph, it's not a particularly happy one…

DVD Not available on DVD as of this writing.

Airheads (1994)(FIC BAND)(SNDTRK)

STARRING: Brendan Fraser (Chazz); Steve Buscemi (Rex); Adam Sandler (Pip); Chris Farley (Wilson); Michael McKean (Milo); Judd Nelson (Jimmie); Amy Locane (Kayla); Michael Richards (Doug); Joe Mantegna (Ian).

FILM EDITOR: Stephen Semel. DIRECTOR OF PHOTOGRAPHY: John Schwarzman. WRITTEN BY: Rich Wilkes. PRODUCED BY:

Mark Burg, Robert Simonds. DIRECTED BY: Michael Lehmann. M.P.A.A. RATING: PG-13. RUNNING TIME: 92 minutes.

The director behind the black-comedy *Heathers* (1989) and the Bruce Willis bomb *Hudson Hawk* (1991), Michael Lehman, returned to comedic terrain with *Airheads*, a mid-1990s comedy concerning the world of heavy metal rock. This film stars Brendan Fraser, Steve Buscemi and Adam Sandler as the members of a rock band amusingly called The Lone Rangers. Having failed to make it big in the cutthroat music industry, The Lone Rangers arm themselves with water pistols (which resemble real weaponry) and take over a local metal radio station in hopes of forcing the station to broadcast their tape.

The hapless would-be rock-terrorists attempt to control the hostages, including the put-upon DJ, Ian (Mantegna) and an evil station manager (*This Is Spinal Tap*'s Michael McKean), but things go awry when one hostage, Doug (Michael Richards, *Seinfeld*'s Kramer) escapes in the vent shaft and notifies the police of the crisis. The police soon circle the building, escalating the situation. Another big problem for The Lone Rangers emerges, however. Their only surviving demo tape is far from the station in the hands of Chazz's former girlfriend (Amy Locane), and they must retrieve it.

If this synopsis makes the film sound silly, so be it. *Airheads* is a fun movie packed with stupid, broad humor; and yet it has a winning way. Not all critics agreed, however, and the film received decidedly mixed reviews.

At *The Austin Chronicle*, Marc Savlov wrote that instead "of playing up the inherently silly, goofy nature of heavy metal, he, director Lehmann, sinks to its level, offering nothing more than an occasional chuckle and some ratty old combat boots."[4]

Mike La Salle at *The San Francisco Chronicle* offered an alternate viewpoint, noting that *Airheads* "celebrates the purity and completeness of rock 'n' roll fanaticism, implying that it can be a healing thing, or at least a great way of embracing life."[5]

Airheads spotlights a strong, pulsing metal track, including performances by White Zombie ("Feed the Gods"), Anthrax ("London"), Primal Scream ("Rocks"), The Ramones ("We Want the Airwaves"), and Aerosmith ("Jamie's Got a Gun").

The Lone Rangers also perform their own ditty in the triumphant finale, entitled "Degenerated."

DVD Available on DVD.

Alice's Restaurant (1969)

(REAL ROCKER)(CAMEOS)

STARRING: Arlo Guthrie (Arlo); Pat Quinn (Alice); James Broderick (Ray); Michael McClanathan (Shelly); Tina Chen (Mari-Chan); Kathleen Dabney (Karin); Seth Allen (Evangelical); Joseph Boely (Woody). M. Emmet Walsh (Group W. Sargeant).

FILM EDITOR: Dede Allen. DIRECTOR OF PHOTOGRAPHY: Michael Nebbia. SCREENPLAY BY: Venable Herndon, Arthur Penn. ORIGINAL MUSIC BY: Arlo Guthrie. PRODUCED BY: Hillard Elkins, Joe Manduke. DIRECTED BY: Arthur Penn. M.P.A.A. RATING: R. Running time: 111 minutes.

Arlo (Arlo Guthrie) considers an ass of a different stripe after a run-in with mule-headed local police in the rambling *Alice's Restaurant* (1969).

A post–*Bonnie & Clyde* (1967) Arthur Penn directed this rambling but entirely pleasant effort based on the eighteen-minute Arlo Guthrie "talking blues" song "Alice's Restaurant Massacre," which was first released on Guthrie's 1967 debut album.

The song and the movie both concern a strange true-to-life event in which a likeable young hippie named Arlo—a fellow with a nasty "*habit of getting arrested*"—experiences a run-in with the law on Thanksgiving Day 1965 for illegally dumping garbage in Great Barrington, Massachusetts. Arlo's nemesis is an overzealous officious police officer, William Obanheim—a man who actually plays himself in the film! (Reportedly so no one else would have the opportunity to portray him as a fool).

Chicago Sun-Times critic Roger Ebert awarded the film four stars upon its release in November 1969 and accurately termed *Alice's Restaurant* "a relaxed, unstudied portrait of some friends, and some months in their lives, and some births, deaths and marriages."[6] That pretty well sums up the loosey-goosey atmosphere.

The film also serves as a coming of age tale about the *Vietnam War* era and caustically depicts Guthrie's surreal experiences both at college and with a military draft board. However, some of the action also occurs at the Stockbridge, Massachusetts restaurant run by Alice and her husband Ray, who have also purchased a local church, "a *place to be the way we want to be, at last,*" as one character notes.

Alice's Restaurant smoothly captures both the hippie ethos and the mainstream anti-hippie prejudice rampant in America at the time of the film's release, a time when authorities hated "long-hairs" with a passion. One nice musical montage, however (to the tune of "Amazing Grace"), visually reveals how Alice's church shares more in common with "good" churches than parishioners in other, more traditional houses of God would care to admit. The visuals, tied together by the music, puts all the churches on the same playing field.

Despite a mostly positive stance on the quasi-commune culture, Penn's film also subtly begins to hint at a slow-dawning dissatisfaction with the hippie lifestyle, what Irish poet Johnny Byrne (author of the chronicle *Groupie*) memorably termed "the wake-up after the hippie dream." In particular, the film unearths in Alice a kind of melancholy and unhappiness over the lifestyle she and Ray have selected (one of sexual freedom). Since the film came out in 1969, this element is ahead of its time by at least three or four years.

Pete Seeger appears in *Alice's Restaurant* as himself, and Joni Mitchell's "Song to Aging Children" underlines a touching scene at a graveyard, but *Alice's Restaurant* is remembered, appropriately, for the song which inspired it.

Today, it would seem that few mainstream audiences have patience for such a loose, wild narrative, but *Alice's Restaurant* skillfully and sensitively captures the hippie age (including the questioning of *authority;* which is here depicted as bureaucratic buffoons and silly law enforcement officials).

(DVD) Available on DVD.

Almost Famous (2000) (FIC BAND)

STARRING: Billy Crudup (Russell Hammond); Frances McDormand (Elaine Miller); Kate Hudson (Penny Lane); Jason Lee (Jeff Bebe); Patrick Fugit (William Miller); Zooey Deschanel (Anita); Philip Seymour Hoffman (Lester Bangs).

FILM EDITORS: Joe Hutsching, Saar Klein. DIRECTOR OF PHOTOGRAPHY: John Toll. PRODUCED BY: Ian Bryce, Cameron Crowe. WRITTEN AND DIRECTED BY: Cameron Crowe. M.P.A.A. RATING: R. RUNNING TIME: 122 minutes.

The new millennium started off strong, giving the world one of its finest (fictional) backstage rock musicals of recent vintage, director Cameron Crowe's autobiographical feature *Almost Famous.*

Based on the filmmaker's personal experiences as a teen journalist working for *Rolling Stone*, this is an effort filled with nostalgia, humor, and even some genuine pathos.

Costing approximately $60 million to produce, *Almost Famous* was cast in the year 1999, and many young actors auditioned for the role of the lead character, a semi-fictionalized, youthful version of the director. The sensitive, expressive (and very young-seeming) Patrick Fugit won the coveted role.

Set in the year 1973, *Almost Famous* (originally titled *Untitled*) dramatizes the tale of a precocious whip-smart teenager named William Miller (Fugit), the Crowe surrogate, as he wins the writing gig from a *Rolling Stone* editor, the legendary and much-storied real-life figure Lester Bangs (Philip Seymour Hoffman). His mission: to tour with a rock band on the verge of becoming famous, called Stillwater.

On the lengthy road trip, William befriends the band's up-and-coming star vocalist, Russell (Billy Crudup) and falls in love with a "band aid" (meaning a groupie) named Penny Lane, played with fetching charm by a barely-legal Kate Hudson. While learning important life lessons, William must also contend with his worrying mother at home, played by Frances McDormand. She checks in with William periodically just to make sure he isn't doing any drugs.

Stillwater performs on stage throughout *Almost Famous*, and several concert performances are highlighted. The film boasts wall-to-wall classic tunes on the soundtrack, including "Sparks" by The Who, "America" by Paul Simon and Art Garfunkel, and even "The Chipmunk Song."

Almost Famous's most charming and recognizable moments—now virtually the movie's trademark—occur on the band's tour bus (**see: The Bus**) as the passengers (including Stillwater) spontaneously break into a stirring, sing-along performance of Elton John's "Tiny Dancer." The unfettered joy engendered by this scene is wonderful to behold, and a high-water mark for recent rock films.

Unfortunately, *Almost Famous* tanked at the box office, though Hudson and McDormand were nominated for Oscars. Even as audiences stayed away, critics raved about the dedicated effort. "Not since *A Hard Day's Night* has a movie caught the thrumming exuberance of going where the music takes you," suggested *Rolling Stone*, which also concluded "*Almost Famous* is a winner because Crowe dares to wear his heart on his sleeve."[7]

Stanley Kauffmann at *The New Republic* suggested that

"Crowe unreels his story neatly, Hoffman proves again that he is an odd and true talent, and Crudup does all that is humanly possible—almost superhumanly—possible to give the guitarist individuality and depth."[8] *Newsweek*'s David Ansen noted simply and accurately that Crowe's movie "gives off the warm glow of mercy."[9]

DVD Available on DVD.

Alone in the Dark (1982)(HORR)

STARRING: Jack Palance (Colonel Frank Hawkes); Donald Pleasence (Dr. Leo Bain); Martin Landau (Preacher); Dwight Schultz (Dr. Daniel Potter); Erland Van Lidth (Ronald "Fatty"); Deborah Hedwell (Nell); Lin Shaye (Receptionist).

FILM EDITOR: Arline Garson. DIRECTOR OF PHOTOGRAPHY: Joseph Mangine. PRODUCED BY: Robert Shaye. WRITTEN AND DIRECTED BY: Jack Sholder. M.P.A.A. RATING: R. RUNNING TIME: 92 minutes.

Director Jack Sholder's horror/slasher effort (no relation to the 2005 film by Uwe Bolle starring Christian Slater) is actually social commentary disguised as a genre film. It involves a group of insane mental patients called "voyagers" played by Martin Landau, Jack Palance, and Erland Van Lidth. They escape from a facility called The Haven (run by a wacko, weed-smoking Donald Pleasence) and terrorize the family of their new psychiatrist Dr. Potter, played by *The A-Team*'s Dwight Schultz.

Early in the film, key characters attend a concert by a rock band memorably named The Sick Fucks. This outfit sings a tune called "Chop Up Your Mother" and the audience responds by play-hacking invisible victims with fake meat cleavers.

Alone in the Dark is a meditation on the idea of violence-obsessed 1980s American society, and "death"-obsessed rock music like this is apparently Exhibit A. During the coda, one of the escaped psychopaths, Hawke (Palance), also attends a rock concert where he is greeted as a conquering hero. In the topsy turvy world of Ronald Reagan's 1980s, where "winnable" nuclear war is possible, ketchup is termed a vegetable, and the Commander-in-Chief suggests poor people are homeless "by choice," this killer isn't the sick exception to the rule, he's the norm!

Other Sick Fucks tunes that appear in *Alone in the Dark* include the happily titled "Rock or Die," "Take Me to the Bridge," and "Insects Rule My World."

DVD *Alone in the Dark* is not currently available on DVD; though some 1980s-era VHS editions can still be located through second-hand venues.

American Graffiti (1973)(SNDTRK)

STARRING: Richard Dreyfuss (Curtis); Ron Howard (Steve); Paul Le Mat (John Milner); Charlie Martin Smith (Terry the Tiger); Candy Clark (Debbie); Mackenzie Phillips (Carol); Cindy Williams (Laurie); Wolfman Jack (Disc Jockey); Bo Hopkins (Joe); Harrison Ford (Falfa); Suzanne Somers (Blonde in T-Bird).

FILM EDITORS: Verna Fields, Marcia Lucas. DIRECTOR OF PHOTOGRAPHY: Haskell Wexler. WRITTEN BY: George Lucas, Gloria Katz, Willard Huyck. PRODUCED BY: Francis Ford Coppola. CO—PRODUCER: Gary Kurtz. DIRECTED BY: George Lucas. M.P.A.A. RATING: PG. RUNNING TIME: 118 minutes.

Before director George Lucas forever altered the film-going world (and pop-culture landscape) with his block-buster space fantasy *Star Wars* (1977), the young talent co-wrote and directed *American Graffiti*, a delightful and frequently amusing paean to the sub-culture of "cruisin'," a uniquely American teen ritual involving fast cars, weekends, good tunes, hamburger joints and girlfriends. Cruising as a teen preoccupation probably lasted for just a few short years (coming right before the *Vietnam War* escalated and British rock music invaded America with The Beatles), but this effort brings everything into focus.

Lucas referred to his film—which is filled wall-to-wall with a classic-rock soundtrack—as a "musical montage" and secured funding from Universal to make it based on Francis Ford Coppola's involvement as a producer.

American Graffiti cost less than $1 million to produce and was shot during the summer of 1972 in just under a month on location, including San Rafael and Petaluma, California. Unexpectedly, the film nonetheless became a huge hit, eventually grossing more than $100 million worldwide. Nominated for five Academy Awards, including in the coveted "best film" category, *American Graffiti* also introduced a whole new generation of stars to American movie audiences including Harrison Ford, Cindy Williams, Suzanne Somers, Candy Clark, Mackenzie Phillips, and Richard Dreyfuss.

Perhaps more importantly, *American Graffiti* captures a sense of nostalgia about late 1950s and early 1960s rock 'n' roll (**see: Camelot**). The soundtrack practically bursts with great tunes from that period, including Frankie Lymon's "Why Do Fools Fall in Love?", The Flamingos' "I Only Have Eyes For You," Flash Cadillac's "At the Hop," The Platters' "The Great Pretender," and Bill Haley and His Comets' hit "Rock Around the Clock," which had been used to such dramatic effect in *Blackboard Jungle* (1956) some seventeen years earlier.

Fats Domino's "Ain't That a Shame," "Love Potion #9" by The Clovers, and "Surfin' Safari" by the Beach Boys also inform important scenes, and for many filmgoers, *American Graffiti* indeed presented the soundtrack of their lives, a time of innocence in American history before the Vietnam War and Kennedy assassination.

American Graffiti's story occurs during one long night (in 1962) as a diverse group of teen friends forge fateful decisions about their future. Kurt (Richard Dreyfuss) contemplates whether he should leave town to attend college and then encounters (briefly) a dream girl driving a Thunderbird, played by Suzanne Somers. Steve (Ron Howard) and Laurie (Cindy Williams) debate staying together or breaking up, and come to a surprising decision. Meanwhile, the ultra-cool Milner (Paul Le Mat) drives around all night in his souped-up car with a young teenager (Mackenzie Phillips) while Terry the Tiger (Charlie Martin Smith) attempts to "make it" for the first time with a lovely girl named Debbie (Candy Clark).

In and of itself, this synopsis may not sound like an earth-shattering tale, but *American Graffiti* concerns transition; it's a film about chapters closing and new ones beginning. The American age of innocence passes like the end of a long summer here, as each character heads off

Cruisin' in Camelot. Left to right it's Candy Clark, Charles Martin Smith, and Ron Howard starring in George Lucas's paean to innocence ended, *American Graffiti*.

into the future and unknown destinies. This is significant, because what *American Graffiti* charts is the first "teenage" generation (the generation of Elvis Presley) broaching adulthood and attempting to fashion a new identity for itself.

At the same time, the success of *American Graffiti* also proved that the self-same generation was now a potent economic force at the box office, and in a mood to reminisce about its formative years and past history. *Entertainment Weekly* listed *American Graffiti* as one of America's one hundred most popular films (landing at slot ninety-one) because it "caught the exact moment in '60s history when baby boomers began to lose their innocence," and the magazine also praised "the brilliant ensemble cast and sharp writing."[10]

Not coincidentally, the year after *American Graffiti* bowed in theatres, a TV show set in the 1950s, *Happy Days*, premiered on ABC (starring Ron Howard again!) and evoked many of the same themes as *American Graffiti*. For its first season, ABC also utilized "Rock Around the Clock" as the show's theme song.

A much less successful sequel to *American Graffiti*, called *More American Graffiti* followed in 1979. It reunited much of the cast, save for Dreyfuss and Somers.

(DVD) Available on DVD.

American Hot Wax (1978)

(BIO-PIC)(CAMEOS)

STARRING: Tim McIntire (Alan Freed); Fran Drescher (Sheryl); Jay Leno (Mookie); Laraine Newman (Louise); Chuck Berry, Jerry Lee Lewis, Screamin' Jay Hawkins.

FILM EDITORS: Ronald Fagan, Melvin Shapiro. DIRECTOR OF PHOTOGRAPHY: William A. Fraker. WRITTEN BY: John Kaye, Art Linson. PRODUCED BY: Fred T. Gallo, Art Linson. DIRECTED BY: Floyd Mutrux. M.P.A.A. RATING: PG. RUNNING TIME: 91 minutes.

This now-obscure rock treasure is a biography or so-called "bio-pic" of Alan Freed (Tim McIntire), the once-famous Cleveland disc jockey who in the mid-to-late 1950s introduced American teenagers to legendary treasures like Louisiana's Jerry Lee Lewis. This is how author David Shirley described the legendary Freed in his book, *The History of Rock and Roll*:

"A former classical musician with a talent for stirring up controversy, Freed had first become interested in rock 'n' roll while working for the radio station WJW in Cleveland, Ohio, in the early 1950s. By the time he signed with New York's WINS in 1954, Freed had become a total convert to the new form of music. With the station's support, he organized a number of huge music shows in New York featuring record-setting crowds and an impressive list of rock 'n' roll and rhythm and blues stand-outs."[11]

Such efforts also earned Freed the enmity of organized religion, concerned parents, and even law enforcement on occasion. Unfortunately, the rebellious (and perhaps even heroic) Freed also became involved in a payola scandal which ultimately destroyed his career and reputation, and his absence paved the way for new talents such as Dick Clark.

American Hot Wax, Freed's story, features performances by some great artists of the 1950s including Chuck Berry ("Reelin' & Rockin'"), Screamin' Jay Hawkins' ("I Put a Spell on You"), and Jerry Lee Lewis, the talent behind "Great Balls of Fire" and "Whole Lotta Shakin' Goin' On."

Long before his hosting gig *The Tonight Show*, a young Jay Leno co-stars in the film.

DVD Sadly, *American Hot Wax* has never been released on DVD or in VHS formats.

American Pop (1981)(FIC)(ANIM)

STARRING (THE VOICES OF) Ron Thompson, Mary A. Small, Jerry Holland, Lisa Jane Pesky, Jeffrey Lippa, Roz Kelly.

FILM EDITOR: David Ramirez. MUSIC ADAPTATION AND ORIGINAL MUSIC BY: Lee Holdridge. WRITTEN BY: Ronni Kern. EXECUTIVE PRODUCERS: Richard R. St. Johns, Maggie Abbott. PRODUCED BY: Ralph Bakshi, Martin Ransohoff. Animated and DIRECTED BY: Ralph Bakshi. M.P.A.A. RATING: R. RUNNING TIME: 95 minutes.

The history of American popular music from jazz to crooners rock 'n' roll to disco to New Wave is charted in Ralph Bakshi's breathtaking and sizzling animated effort, *American Pop*. The film commences in Russia under the czars, and traces the escape of one family to America, taking succeeding sons from vaudeville and World War I right up to the 1980s (which is depicted in the film as a kind of modern-day Hell on Earth).

There are four central characters in *American Pop*, and each one is featured in a vignette. First comes Jaacov (a rabbi), then Zalmie (an entertainer who dies in World War I), third Benny (a jazz pianist), fourth Tony (a 1950s "open road" rocker who battles drug addiction), and finally Tony's son, Pete, a cocaine dealer who hits it big on the pop scene in the 1980s.

In each case, real-life music is utilized symbolically to represent the talents of the family members. For instance, Tony's hit that sweeps him into the music industry is "Night Moves," by Bob Seger and the Silver Bullet Band. Other tunes that appear in the film are "As Time Goes By," "You Send Me," and Cole Porter's "Anything Goes." Rock fans will find the latter part of the film particularly enjoyable as it focuses on the genre, and features a performance of "Purple Haze" by an animated Jimi Hendrix.

American Pop has been perpetually derided in some corners because the film's animation is based on the now obsolete process of rotoscoping, meaning that live-action actors are traced over and rendered animated. However, today this film is simply an example of its context and time period, and therefore quite interesting historically. The film's point, which survives despite what many complain is a primitive technique, is simply that art and music arise from struggle. *American Pop* also sees art (and music) as a continuum, and therefore places old fashioned "classic" music on equal standing with new-fangled, techno-rock, depicted in the "Devil With a Blue Dress On" number, which includes material that appears computer-generated or like a hologram.

American Pop weaves a fascinating tapestry of American popular music and artfully reminds viewers that every exciting new trend in music is born of something before. That knowledge puts rock music in an interesting context. One only wishes the film could be updated today to include the disappointing "next generation" form, which is toothless Jessica Simpson, Britney Spears, corporate bubble gum rock. But even that would make an interesting coda to a century of American pop.

(DVD) Available on DVD.

Americathon (1979)(REAL ROCKER)(CAMEOS)

STARRING: John Ritter (President Roosevelt); Harvey Korman (Monty); Fred Willard (Vanderhoff); Peter Riegert (Eric); Meat Loaf (Roy); Elvis Costello (Earl of Manchester); Howard Hesseman (Margolis); Jay Leno (Larry); George Carlin (Narrator).

FILM EDITOR: John C. Howard. DIRECTOR OF PHOTOGRAPHY: Gerald Hirschfeld. WRITTEN BY: Phil Proctor, Peter Berman, Neal Israel, Monica Johnson. PRODUCED BY: Joe Roth. DIRECTED BY: Neal Israel. M.P.A.A. RATING: PG. RUNNING TIME: 86 minutes.

This is the (supposedly humorous) story of a man who attains the Presidency based on a family name, and who, once ensconced in the Oval Office, presides over the bankruptcy of America. No, it's not *The George W. Bush Story*, it's the tale depicted in the "futuristic" political parody, *Americathon* (set in the far-flung year of 1998).

The film stars John Ritter as President Chet Roosevelt,

who—in realizing the country's financial insolvency—organizes a telethon to raise money for the U.S.A.

Harvey Korman performs "My Life" in this tepid comedy, but rock fans may be more interested in Elvis Costello's "(I Don't Want to Go) To Chelsea," and "Crawling to the U.S.A." Eddie Money is also present on the soundtrack ("Get a Move On"), as is the Beach Boys tune "It's A Beautiful Day."

Meat Loaf, fresh off his 1977 hit record "Bat Out of Hell" is also on hand for the national festivities, as is *WKRP in Cincinnati*'s Doctor Johnny Fever himself, Howard Hesseman, and—again—a very young, pre-*Tonight Show* Jay Leno.

(DVD) This film is not currently available on DVD, and there doesn't seem to be any great demand to resurrect it.

Animation (GENRE CONVENTION) Over time, the

rock genre has witnessed cartoon interludes in live-action films and also featured full-bore animated movies. The fusion of cartoons and music may have started with *Fantasia* (1940), but as always, rock performers and directors have taken matters to the next level.

Yellow Submarine (1968) is a "Mod" odyssey by The Beatles, a fairy tale pitting the Fab Four against Blue Meanies, and the production is one of animated rock's undisputed landmark efforts. In 1981, Ralph Bakshi also dramatized the history of rock 'n' roll and other musical forms in the animated (rotoscoped) *American Pop*, a film that audaciously morphed the genre's greatest guitarist,

Jimi Hendrix, into a strutting cartoon (to the tune of "Purple Haze").

Too bad he didn't get a Saturday morning cartoon show, too.

Other notable rock films have gone the interlude route in lieu of total animation. In *The Great Rock 'n' Roll Swindle* (1980), the Sex Pistols appear as cranky-looking animated characters time and time again. In the misbegotten Olivia Newton-John musical vehicle *Xanadu* (1980), the muse and her lover, Sonny (Michael Beck) spend time together for a spell as fish in the ocean and as tweeting little birdies.

There is terrifying animation spotlighting devouring plants (and hungry vaginas) in Alan Parker's *Pink Floyd: The Wall* (1982), as well as some disturbing Nazi-inspired cartoon imagery (with soaring eagles representing the icons of a new, Fourth Reich cult, and so forth).

Why have animation and rock movies shared such a deep and continuous relationship over the years? Well, by its very nature, rock 'n' roll creates images in the mind of the listener; and those images aren't always based on a consensus reality (meaning they can be psychedelic). Perhaps this symbiosis has occurred because animation can readily (and relatively cheaply) reveal worlds not available to the live-action film; ones where monsters can be depicted in all their horrific glory, and pretty music can cause flowers to sprout (as in *Yellow Submarine*).

The Apollo Theatre (GENRE CONVENTION)

One of the most famous and important live venues in rock movie history, located at 253 W. 125TH Street in Harlem, New York, this predominantly African-American theatre has witnessed the ascent of many a great rock artist.

The Apollo has been featured in several rock 'n' roll films including *The Buddy Holly Story* (1978), which noted that Holly and his Crickets represented the first white act to play the auditorium, the fictional *The Five Heartbeats* (1991), and the Tina Turner bio-pic *What's Love Got to Do With It?* (1993).

The Apple (1980)(MUS)

STARRING: Catherine Mary Stewart (Bibi); George Gilmour (Alphie); Grace Kennedy (Pandi); Allan Love (Dandi); Joss Ackland (Mr. Topps); Vladek Sheybel (Boogalow); Ray Shell (Shake).

FILM EDITOR: Alain Jakubowicz. DIRECTOR OF PHOTOGRAPHY: David Gurfinkel. WRITTEN BY: Menahem Golan. PRODUCED BY: Menahem Golan, Yoram Globus. DIRECTED BY: Menahem Golan. M.P.A.A. RATING: PG. RUNNING TIME: 90 minutes.

In the distant and futuristic year of 1994, two innocents from the town of Moosejaw, Bibi (Catherine Mary Stewart) and Alphie (George Gilmour) participate in a televised singing competition of global popularity (no, not

American Idol, but the *World Vision Song Contest*).

After the show, these babes in the wood retain the services of the world's most famous agent, Mr. Boogalow (Vladek Sheybel), who also happens to be the Devil. Boogalow seduces Bibi into signing away her soul with promises of pop fame and fortune, but Alphie experiences a vision of Hell, realizes the danger, and rescues Bibi from Boogalow's grasp.

Then, Alphie and Bibi flee the celebrity spotlight to live in a park with aging hippies, where they wait expectantly for the return of Mr. Topps (Jesus Christ or perhaps God Himself). Topps does indeed arrive (in a flying car, no less) and ushers in a glittery Judgment Day. He carries all the hippies off of Earth to a "new place," this time without the Devil's ministrations.

That's the plot of *The Apple*, perhaps one of the worst and most bizarre films ever produced. The film opens with a wacky, "futuristic" television concert wherein the performing band is dressed in silver and steel and space age head gear. Behind the scenes, a computer room monitors the audience's pulse, excitement, and tension, a new kind of TV ratings. *"We just scored over one hundred and fifty heart beats!,"* an enthused technician reports giddily.

From that odd opening, which accurately forecasts the success of singing contests like *American Idol*, the film goes into a strange cautionary tale about evil agents and their plans for corporate domination. For instance, Boogalow's most successful band is called Bim, and very shortly all of his talent pool is forced to wear "Bim Marks," a new product fashion line (facial stickers).

Later, the U.S. government gets into the act and legislates universal physical exercise for its citizenry, as well as mandatory wearing of Bim Marks. *"Prepare for the national Bim Hour,"* an Orwellian voice declares, *"Exercises designed for your health and peace of mind! The National Fitness Program is watching you!"*

Okay, so admittedly this is fun material and it's true that corporations have exerted ever more power on who actually gets to become a pop star, but *The Apple*, despite these inventive flourishes, is one relentlessly cheesy film, especially by the time that Bibi (the Kelly Clarkson of this movie) and Alphie (the Justin Guarini) seek to escape their fame with refugees from the 1960s, *"commonly known as hippies."* The strange climax with counter-culture hippies following God into the sky (during a rock 'n' roll rapture) is either bizarre inspiration or a low-water mark for rock operas, depending on one's point of view.

One more pearl of wisdom from *The Apple*, this one to aspiring pop stars: *"First you sell it, then you make it. That's marketing."*

How true. Maybe this movie isn't so crazy after all. Nonetheless, despite any piddling merits, in the summer of 2006 *The Onion AV Club*'s Nathan Rabin named *The Apple* one of "the six movies that helped kill disco," terming it so "relentlessly trippy that it makes recreational drug use redundant."

DVD *The Apple* is available—in all its cheesy glory—on DVD.

Authority (GENRE CONVENTION) *"There used to be a way to stick it to the man. It was called rock 'n' roll,"* declares Dewey Finn, the teacher and oracle in Richard Linklater's *The School of Rock* (2003).

In rock 'n' roll movies, authority is *the enemy*. The rock-movie aesthetic requires that all symbols of authority be destroyed, ridiculed and humiliated, and that stance is carried over into genre movies.

Authority can be represented by suck-up students such as hall monitors or jocks (*Rock 'n' Roll High School; Detroit Rock City; Trick or Treat*), mothers who don't "get" rock (*South Park: Bigger*, *Longer*, and *Uncut*; *Detroit Rock City*), men of God (*The Buddy Holly Story*, *Footloose*), and the representatives of the press (*The Doors*).

Even Elvis Presley's films, which are lightweight and charming rather than strident, evidence a strong dislike for authority. *Follow That Dream*, *It Happened at the World's Fair* and *Speedway* push hard against government officials in the Highway Department, Welfare Office, and the IRS, respectively.

Note this well: it is an absolute requirement of the rock movie form that a protagonist strike a blow against foolish figures of authority, and this facet of the genre can even be seen in films that feature a rock soundtrack, including *American Graffiti*. There, cruisin' kids pull a stunt on the officious Office Holstein, destroying his patrol car.

Simply stated, if authority ain't questioned or threatened, it ain't a rock movie.

(is for Beach Party Movies)

Baby Snakes (1979)(DOC)

STARRING: Frank Zappa, Adrian Belew, Tommy Mars, Terry Bozzio, Kerry McNabb, Ron Delsener, Bruce Bickford, Rob Leacock, Ed Mann, Chris Martin, Klaus Hundsbichler, Fancy the Poodle, Mrs. Pinky's Larger Sister, Roy Estrada, New York's Finest Crazy Persons, Bill Harrington, Patrick O'Hearn, Phil Parmet, Peter Wolf, Dick Pearce, Angel, Janet Planet, Donna U Wanna, Phil Kaufman, Tex Abel, Dale Buzzio.

FILM EDITOR: Klaus Hindsbichler. CINEMATOGRAPHERS: Dick Pearce, Phil Parmet, Rob Leacock. ANIMATION: Bruce Bickford. MUSIC: Frank Zapa. WRITTEN, PRODUCED, AND DIRECTED BY: Frank Zappa. M.P.A.A. RATING: R. RUNNING TIME: 166 minutes.

Frank Zappa (1940–1993) was a true rock original, and his strange documentary (released by Zappa himself during the final year of the disco decade) makes that point in spades. This very long film (although there's also a ninety-minute version floating out there on VHS) features scads of concert footage from Zappa's Halloween concert at the Palladium Theatre in New York in 1977. It also takes time to reveal Zappa in a recording/editing studio, toiling on a strange Claymation project and enthusiastically directing voice actors.

Lanky, laconic, and—truth be told—a tad creepy, Zappa was part rock star, part performance artist, part comedian and all showman, and *Baby Snakes* reveals every shade of his abundant talent. It's not a film for the faint of heart, consisting as it does of incomprehensible images that flash by so fast some audiences will seize. The film also features far too lengthy footage of Claymation cre-ations morphing into different ghoulish forms. This seems to last an eternity. There's also a running joke with an inflatable doll, and an interview with an animator who tells a pointless shaggy-dog story that ends with the words "*then the dope wore off.*"

Baby Snakes was made at a time when Zappa was having trouble with Warner Bros. (**see: Record Company**) and a supportive fan at his concert displays a sign reading "*Warner Brothers Sucks.*" By the time the film is over, weird animation has been displayed, Zappa has done some shtick about God's three early mistakes (creating Man, Woman, and Poodle) and, with some degree of exhaustion, one may come to agree with the words of the put-upon drummer in his band:

"*This show has pushed me past the brink of what I can physically withstand,*" he says. Indeed!

DVD Available on DVD.

Back to the Beach (1987)

(SNDTRK)(CAMEOS)

STARRING: Frankie Avalon (Frankie); Annette Funicello (Annette); Lori Loughlin (Sandi); Tommy Hinkley (Michael); Connie Stevens (Connie); Paul Reubens (Peewee Herman); Bob Denver (Bartender); Alan Hale (Bartender's Buddy); Don Adams (Harbor Master); Jerry Mathers (Judge).

FILM EDITOR: David Finfer. DIRECTOR OF PHOTOGRAPHY: Bruce Surtees. WRITTEN BY: Peter Krikes, Steve Meerson, Christopher Thompson. STORY BY: James Komack, B.W.L. Norton, Bruce Kirschbaum. PRODUCED BY: Frankie Avalon,

Annette Funicello, Frank Mancuso, Jr. M.P.A.A. RATING: PG. RUNNING TIME: 92 minutes.

This is a beach party movie reunion, set two decades after the last film in the Frankie Avalon/Annette Funicello cycle (**see: Beach Party Movies**), the 1965 effort *How to Stuff a Wild Bikini.* Here Annette (forty-five years old) and Frankie (pushing fifty) attempt to recapture some of their teenage glory with the help of writers Peter Krikes and Steve Meerson, who had already succeeded with an "Over The Hill Gang Rides Again" blockbuster from a 1960s property, *Star Trek: The Voyage Home* (1986).

The plot finds Frankie as an unfulfilled used car sales-man and wife Annette as a Stepford Wife–like homemak-er (who, because of Funicello's popularity as a Skippy spokesman, seems obsessed with peanut butter). The cou-ple is also saddled with an angry, cynical "punk" son. They all head to Malibu to visit Frankie and Annette's daughter (Lori Loughlin), who is secretly bedding down with her boyfriend and wants to keep that fact secret from her old fashioned, stuck-in-the-Sixties parents.

Once back at the beach, the sanctity of the Frankie and Annette relationship is threatened by the presence of Connie Stevens as Connie. While beach bums and punks fight it out for supremacy on the beach, a surfing contest is proposed and Frankie, "The Big Kahuna," comes out of retirement to win it.

Back to the Beach is loaded with appearances (**see: Cameos**) by past-their-prime TV stars from the 1960s (including Bob Denver from *Gilligan's Island,* Don Adams from *Get Smart,* and Jerry Mathers from *Leave It to Beaver*),

but the film remains funny because it replaces the original films' sense of innocence with 1980s-style cynicism. Frankie and Annette haven't changed, but the world they inhabit is vastly different, and so many of the jokes really stick. This is a delicate alchemy that the *Brady Bunch* films of the later 1990s also forged. The end result is that the innocence of the old days reflects badly on modern times, which are revealed to be commercial, crassly overhyped, and cynical.

Rising star Peewee Herman makes a cameo in *Back to the Beach* (as does O.J. Simpson), and steals the show with his performance of "Surfin' Bird." Meanwhile, Connie, Annette, and Frankie vocalize for the appropriately titled "Some Things Never Change."

Harvey Lembeck, who played the "Rats" gang leader Eric Von Zipper in the original beach party films passed away in 1982, five years before *Back to the Beach,* and his presence as that goofy villain is perhaps the one thing that would have made this silly picture an even-more welcome treat for fans of the original material.

ⅅⅤⅅ Available on DVD.

Backbeat (1994) (BIO-PIC)

STARRING: Sheryl Lee (Astrid); Stephen Dorff (Stu); Ian Hart (John Lennon); Gary Bakewell (Paul); Chris O'Neill (George); Scot Williams (Pete Best); Kai Wiesinger (Klaus); Jenifer Ehle (Cynthia).

FILM EDITOR: Martin Walsh. DIRECTOR OF PHOTOGRAPHY: Ian Wilson. SCREENPLAY BY: Iain Softley, Michael Thomas, Stephen

Ward. EXECUTIVE PRODUCER: Nik Powell. PRODUCERS: Finola Dwyer, Stephen Woolley. DIRECTED BY: Iain Softley. M.P.A.A. RATING: R. RUNNING TIME: 100 minutes.

This is the based-on-a-true-story tale of the late Stuart Sutcliffe, the legendary "fifth" Beatle who left the soon-to-be Fab Four just as it was becoming famous in the early 1960s. By his own admission, he was *not much of a bass player* and was in the band *for a laugh*. Also, he had no desire to be famous.

Backbeat follows this fascinating figure, Stu (Stephen Dorff) and the other Beatles from Liverpool in 1960 to a period playing strip clubs in Germany in 1961, up until Stuart decides to leave the band and become a painter instead. Tragically, he dies a young man during a brain hemorrhage (in spring, 1962) in the arms of his beloved girlfriend, photographer Astrid (Sheryl Lee). Thus Stu never even witnesses the Beatles reach their apex of success, and the film ends with Astrid turning her back on a cheering clapping crowd at a Beatles performance. Along the way, *Backbeat* also very subtly suggests that there may have been a homosexual attraction between Lennon and Sutcliffe. (For more information on Lennon's sexual orientation, see *The Hours and Times*, 1991).

Movies about The Beatles are a dime a dozen (*I Wanna Hold Your Hand*, 1978, *Beatlemania*, 1981), yet *Backbeat* is a dynamic and interesting film, in part because it focuses on a period in the band's history that has not been illuminated very often on the silver screen. This is the time in the group's career when the band played American rock like "Good Golly, Miss Molly" instead of their own remarkable compositions. Still, the music in the film is rip-roaring good, and at times rousing.

"When the group finally launches into the ascending 'ahhhs' of 'Twist and Shout,'" *Entertainment Weekly*'s Owen Gleiberman wrote, "it has the effect of a pop-culture nova: For the first time, their energy is united with beauty, and a revolution is born."[12]

Some critics have argued that *Backbeat* is a relatively minor film and that it's emphasis is all wrong, focusing on a man who is, essentially, a footnote in history. However, the famous mop-top look of The Beatles, this film establishes, began with Astrid and Stu. Also, Stu's story is a reminder that not everyone is cut out to be, nor wants to be, a rock star. Stu clearly didn't have the drive of the others, and Paul McCartney is depicted in this movie in less than objective terms, always pushing, always driving for the group to be better. It's those qualities, however, that made The Beatles what they ultimately became.

(DVD) Available on DVD.

Backstage Antics (GENRE CONVENTION)

Since rockers are supposed to flout authority, they often misbehave and prove themselves very bad boys and girls. Accordingly, many films have depicted backstage antics that reveal the band in a new light.

Nigel Tufnel revealed as a prima donna, for instance, in *This Is Spinal Tap*, when he complains about the sandwiches served to him before a show in Chapel Hill, North Carolina.

In the classic *A Hard Day's Night* (1964), The Beatles reinforce their image as fun-loving, smart, quippy (but essentially harmless) youngsters by playing backstage with fake beards and noses, as well as make-up.

Not all backstage antics are funny, however. In the Tina Turner bio-pic, *What's Love Got to Do With It?*, Ike Turner arrives backstage before Tina's comeback show and threatens her with a gun. She reveals her strength, however, and carries on.

Bad Fathers (GENRE CONVENTION) Authority is the persistent nemesis in the rock movie genre, but authority is often personified in the ultimate establishment figure: the *Bad Father*.

Berger's dad in the musical *Hair* (1979) will only come to the aid of his desperate son if Berger trims his long hair. John Lithgow plays a repressive reverend in *Footloose* (1984), one who has successfully banned rock 'n' roll and dancing from his "wholesome" community. Ted "Theodore" Logan's dad in *Bill & Ted's Excellent Adventure* (1989) wants to send his rocker son to a military academy in Alaska!

In *The Five Heartbeats* (1991), Choir Boy's dad (also a man of the cloth) objects to his son's participation in a Motown Group. And, in both *Tommy* (1975) and *Pink Floyd: the Wall* (1982), it is the death of a father, an absent father, that sets Tommy and Pink down troubling roads.

In 2005's *Walk the Line*, Johnny Cash's dad, played to perfection by Robert Patrick, wishes that his young son Johnny would have died in an accident with a saw blade rather than Cash's older brother, who would have become a reverend. (Notice the connection between *Bad Fathers* and Christianity?)

What's the fix for a "bad father?" Well, 1988's fantasy *Heartbreak Hotel* has the right idea. There, a boy captures kindly and loving Elvis Presley to play "house" with his family for a time...

Battle of the Bands (GENRE CONVENTION) Winning this commonly seen movie contest could change the entire world, as *Bill & Ted's Bogus Journey* (1991) reveals. If Bill and Ted can win the fourth annual battle of the bands in San Dimas in that particular film, their group, Wyld Stallyns, will usher in a whole new era of peace and prosperity for the human race!

The Battle of the Bands is a cliché that also shows up in the climax of the cheapie monster/slasher flick *Neon Maniacs* (1986), and more recently, in Richard Linklater's delightful comedy *The School of Rock* (2003).

In the latter film, Dewey Finn (Jack Black) grooms a bunch of pre-adolescent students to win the contest, and in the process beat the band that tossed Dewey out. The Battle of the Bands also appears as a plot point in the John Landis sequel, *The Blues Brothers 2000* (1998).

Be My Guest (1965) (FIC BAND)

STARRING: David Hemmings (Dave Martin); Steve Marriott (Ricky); John Pike (Phil); Andrea Monet (Erica); Ivor Salter (Herbert); Diana King (Margaret); Joyce Blair (Wanda).

FILM EDITOR: Sidney Stone. DIRECTOR OF PHOTOGRAPHY: Basil Emmott. WRITTEN BY: Lyn Fairhurst. PRODUCED AND DIRECTED BY: Lance Comfort. M.P.A.A. RATING: UR. RUNNING TIME: 82 minutes.

Currently unavailable in the U.S. on DVD or other home video formats, this British film involves a young rock band (led by David Hemmings) that rescues a family coastal hotel from financial doom.

Jerry Lee Lewis (**see:** *Great Balls of Fire,* 1989) appears in the film and sings "My Baby Loves Nobody But Me." The score also includes the titular effort "Be My Guest." Marshall Crenshaw's outstanding guide book from 1994, *Hollywood Rock*, calls the project "contrived" but also "reasonably well-handled."[13]

Beach Party Movies (GENRE CONVENTION): Beach or beach party movies were a genre unto themselves in the mid-1960s. Produced by exploitation kings at American International Pictures, these teen-themed films were shot in Malibu and usually starred ex-Mouseketeer Annette Funicello and crooner Frankie Avalon, who was pushing thirty by the end of the fad's run.

The Beach Party movies pitted clean, wholesome, healthy (and scantily clad) American youth against the evil, leather jacketed forces of motorcyclists, or "Rats." Often in the films, the bad guys were led by Harvey Lembeck's inept Eric Von Zipper, who was reportedly a spoof on Marlon Brando's character in *The Wild One* (1953). Von Zipper learned the mystical power to paralyze people by giving them "the finger," but often found in these films that he could only really paralyze himself.

Jody McCrea was the series' second-tier star and always played the same type of pleasant surfer dude. He was named "Bonehead," "Big Lunk," and other sad monikers, but in essence he was the beach party's all-around nice guy (though none too bright).

The Beach Party movies tended to be light on plot, heavy on teen romance, and buttressed by past-their-prime stars such as Boris Karloff, Buster Keaton, Vincent Price, and Basil Rathbone, all of whom presented the product line a veneer of respectability to the older generation. Many times, fanciful elements were brought to the beach, including Martians, ghosts, witch doctors, and, on one notable occasion, a fetching mermaid played by Marta Kristen (**see:** *Beach Blanket Bingo*).

Each beach party movie also came replete with a cool 1960s rock score by the likes of the Del-Tones, The Hondells, and The Kingsmen.

The beach movie cycle ran hot from 1963 to 1966 and included seven films, including *Beach Party, Muscle Beach Party, Bikini Beach, Pajama Party*, the most famous of the bunch: *Beach Blanket Bingo, How to Stuff a Wild Bikini*, and *The Ghost in the Invisible Bikini*.

Other studios retaliated against the popular series with knockoffs, and after twenty years, Annette and Frankie reunited for a comedy called *Back to the Beach* (1987).

Beach Ball (1965)(MUS)(CAMEOS)

STARRING: Edd Byrnes (Dick); Chris Noel (Susan); Robert Logan (Bango); Aron Kincaid (Jack); Mikki Jamison (Augusta); Don Edmunds (Bob).

FILM EDITOR: Jack Woods. DIRECTOR OF PHOTOGRAPHY: Floyd Crosby. WRITTEN BY: David Malcolm. PRODUCED BY: Gene Corman, Bart Patton. DIRECTED BY: Lennie Weinrib. M.P.A.A. RATING: UR. RUNNING TIME: 83 minutes.

Diana Ross and the Supremes (singing "Surfer Boy") appear in this knock-off of the popular 1960s Beach Party movies. The Four Seasons, The Righteous Brothers, The Walker Brothers, and The Hondells also contribute performances in a film involving a hot-rod show in Long Beach, California.

DVD Despite such high-profile acts, this film is not currently available on DVD and was not available for review.

Beach Blanket Bingo (1965)(MUS)

STARRING: Frankie Avalon (Frankie); Annette Funicello (Dee Dee); Deborah Walley (Bonnie); Harvey Lembeck (Eric Von Zipper); John Ashley (Steve); Jody McCrae (Bonehead); Marta Kristen (Lorelei); Linda Evans (Sugar Kane); Don Rickles (Big Drop); Paul Lynde (Bulletts); Earl Wilson (Himself); Buster Keaton (Himself).

FILM EDITORS: Fred Feitshans, Eve Newman. DIRECTOR OF PHOTOGRAPHY: Floyd Crosby. WRITTEN BY: William Asher, Leo Townsend. PRODUCED BY: James H. Nicholson, Samuel Z. Arkoff. DIRECTED BY: William Asher. M.P.A.A. RATING: UR. RUNNING TIME: 97 minutes.

Beach bum teenagers Dee Dee (Annette Funicello) and Frankie (Frankie Avalon) tangle again with their nemesis, Eric Von Zipper (Harvey Lembeck), while learning to sky dive from hot-to-trot Bonnie (Deborah Walley) and hunky Steve (John Ashley) in this, the fifth film of the "beach" cycle of the 1960s.

Meanwhile, Frankie and Annette also befriend a new rock sensation, Sugar Kane (Linda Evans), who is being ruthlessly promoted by her snide manager, Bullets (Paul Lynde). At the same time, Bonehead (Jody McCrea) falls in love with a beautiful mermaid Lorelei (Marta Kristen).

Although these films are essentially harmless, the humor in *Beach Blanket Bingo* hasn't aged well, and all the shtick with Eric Von Zipper today appears particularly lame. Also, Linda Evans gives a dazed, vapid performance that makes one wonder how she ever went anywhere in the film industry, but more to the point, how she could ever be a "rock sensation." The future star of TV's *Dynasty*, sleepy and sullen throughout. Otherwise, it's business as usual at the beach as Bonnie and Steve threaten to ruin the perfect union represented by Frankie and Annette.

The most enjoyable subplot in *Beach Blanket Bingo* involves gorgeous (and often bikini-clad) Marta Kristen as the mermaid Lorelei. Unlike, Evans, Kristen (who would later star on the TV series *Lost in Space*) has real charisma

Where's the suntan lotion?

Left to right: Dee Dee (Annette Funicello), Frankie (Frankie Avalon), and Sugar Kane (Linda Evans)

contemplate life on the beach in *Beach Blanket Bingo* (1965).

and screen presence, and her scenes with McCrae (playing the character unfortunately named Bonehead) boast a genuine sweetness and innocence.

The saddest element of *Beach Blanket Bingo* (besides the ridiculous script, that is), may be the great Buster Keaton's presence in a supporting role, punching himself out and performing silent film antics that stopped being funny decades earlier. He looks like a sad old man. Don Rickles doesn't fare much better with his on-the-nose stand-up comedy routine, which rightly suggests Frankie Avalon is too old to participate in such nonsense.

The film perks up slightly near the climax with its keystone cops fast-motion finale and nod to *The Perils of Pauline* (1914), but most of the tunes in the film are downright forgettable. "Beach Blanket Bingo" opens the film and is sung by the young ensemble, and Frankie and Annette share a nice duet (against rear-projected dusk) to "I Think, You Think." Linda Evans contributes the bland "New Love" and The Hondells sing "Cycle Set."

Next up in the series: *How to Stuff a Wild Bikini* (1966). (DVD) Available on DVD.

The Beach Boys: An American Band (1985)(DOC)(CAMEOS)

STARRING: Brian Wilson, Dennis Wilson, Carl Wilson, Mike Love, Al Jardine, Bruce Johnston.

FILM EDITOR: Mark Cole/David Fairfield. DIRECTOR OF PHOTOGRAPHY: John Toll. WRITTEN BY: Malcolm Leo. PRODUCED BY: Bonnie Peterson, Leo Peterson. DIRECTED BY: Malcolm Leo. M.P.A.A. RATING: PG-13. RUNNING TIME: 103 minutes.

In 1983, US President Ronald Reagan's hapless Secretary of the Interior, James G. Watt (later indicted by a Federal grand jury on eighteen counts of perjury and obstruction of justice), caused a national hullabaloo by banning the all-American band, The Beach Boys, from performing at the annual July 4TH Independence Day celebration on the National Mall at the Capitol. Watts went on record stating his parochial belief that rock concerts could attract "*an undesirable element.*"

The Beach Boys?! An undesirable element?!

Naturally, middle-America blanched at such an accusation…and President Reagan and First Lady Nancy intervened to make sure The Beach Boys were on the docket.

This colorful and absorbing 1985 documentary film was released post-Watt controversy and after the death of band member Dennis Wilson in 1983. It utilizes interviews, TV appearances and concert material to paint a portrait of a band that is literally as American as apple pie. Formed in 1961, the Beach Boys have produced several number one singles and are members of the Rock and Roll Hall of Fame. Among their memorable albums are *Surfin' Safari* (1962), *Surfin' U.S.A.* (1963), *Surfer Girl* (1963) and *Little Deuce Coupe* (1963).

The Beach Boys: An American Band has been accused in some circles of glossing over the negative in favor of myth-building, and indeed, this "official" chronicle has much in common with *The Who: The Kids Are Alright* (1979) and *U2: Rattle and Hum* (1988), both of which also promise "access" but keep darker and more scandalous material at arm's length.

All your favorite Beach Boys tunes are accounted for here, including "Surfin' U.S.A.," "God Only Knows" (also heard in *Boogie Nights*, 1997), "Good Vibrations," and "Fun, Fun, Fun."

DVD Available on DVD.

Beach Party (1963) (MUS)

STARRING: Bob Cummings (Bob); Dorothy Malone (Marianne); Frankie Avalon (Frankie); Annette Funicello (Dee Dee); Harvey Lembeck (Eric Von Zipper); Eva Six (Ava); John Ashley (Ken); Jody McCrea (Deadhead); Dick Dale and the Del Tones.

FILM EDITOR: Homer Powell. DIRECTOR OF PHOTOGRAPHY: Kay Norton. WRITTEN BY: Lou Rusoff. PRODUCED BY: Samuel Z. Arkoff, James H. Nicholson, Lou Rusoff. DIRECTED BY: William Asher. M.P.A.A. RATING: UR. RUNNING TIME: 101 minutes.

This is the first, though not the best, of American International's wildly successful beach movies starring Frankie Avalon and Annette Funicello, who—amusingly—are billed in *Beach Party* behind the grown-up, Bob Cummings.

Nonetheless, this William Asher effort sets the tone for all the wacky hijinks to follow. The film introduces the gang menace, Eric Von Zipper (Lembeck), as well as Jody McCrea's Deadhead, perhaps the best (and most sweetly) enacted character in the series.

Beach Party's plot—such as it is—finds trouble brewing between Frankie and Dee Dee. Frankie wants to *ahem* go further in their romantic relationship (meaning have sex), and when she won't comply, he tries to make her jealous by throwing himself at built-like-a-brick-shithouse Ava (Eva Six). Meanwhile, anthropologist Bob (Cummings) is busy studying the dating rituals of the surfer set and wants to see how Frankie will react to a jealousy trap, so he starts making eyes at Dee Dee.

See how needlessly complicated this all gets?

Anyway, before the day is done, Avalon and Funicello reconcile and sing the titular song "Beach Party." Avalon also sings "Don't Stop Now," while Funicello has a sweet moment with "Treat Him Nicely." Between pie fights and other silly gags, Dick Dale and the Del Tones show up and offer "Secret Surfing Spot" and "Surfin' and Swingin'."

DVD Available on DVD.

Beatlemania (1981) (MUS)

STARRING: David Leon (John Lennon); Mitch Weissman (Paul McCartney); Tom Teely (George Harrison); Ralph Castelli (Ringo Starr).

FILM EDITOR: King Baggot. PRODUCED BY: David Klebs. DIRECTED BY: Joseph Manduke. M.P.A.A. RATING: PG. RUNNING TIME: 86 minutes.

"*The Music! The Magic! The Total Experience!*," the poster art for this film boldly shouted. *Beatlemania* is a cinematic tribute to the Fab Four starring look-a-likes playing The Beatles (hence the famous tag "*Not The Beatles, But An Incredible Simulation*," which has become something of a running joke in pop culture.)

Beatlemania is an adaptation of the once-popular stage production of the same name. Here, the history of the Beatles is vetted chronologically, with music from each period charting the group's development. Like the stage show, this movie is actually a "multimedia" experience wherein images of events from the 1960s flash on-screen throughout. It's a nostalgia trip and one that features over two dozen songs, including ones from the Beatles' pre-fame cover band days ("Let's Twist Again"), their meteoric rise ("I Wanna Hold Your Hand"), and their later, more daring original age ("Eleanor Rigby").

DVD The film is not available on DVD at this time.

The Beatles (ROCK MOVIE HALL OF FAME) An

incredible and trail-blazing rock 'n' roll act second only to Elvis Presley in the rock movie Valhalla. The Beatles—or the Fab Four—as they are sometimes termed, have influenced everything from the shape and form of American rock music to teenage haircuts.

This mop-topped foursome from Liverpool—the vanguard act most directly responsible for the so-called British music invasion—consisted of John Lennon, Paul McCartney, Ringo Starr, and George Harrison. It's a testament to each that all of these talents went on to impressive solo careers (both cinematically and musically) even after the act broke up. Yet, it's for the magic time they spent together before the eyes of the world that

makes them a beloved group.

In 1964, Richard Lester's *A Hard Day's Night* introduced the Beatles on the silver screen. Their first movie was bracing; a non-stop, black-and-white assault on the senses packed with puns, in-jokes, self-reflexivity, wacky humor, and, perhaps most importantly, a string of great songs, including "Can't Buy Me Love," "She Loves You," and "All My Lovin'."

The film's French New Wave approach (accenting the surreal and absurd) served the self-reflexive story well, and found the four musicians rushing madly around London (and usually being mobbed) while preparing to perform on a live TV broadcast. Director Lester staged each song as an individual set piece (like music videos in the 1980s), and *A Hard Day's Night* thus remains one of the most influential rock films ever produced.

A sophomore (and some insist sophomoric) effort called *Help!* made the scene in 1965. This Beatles' film is a strange spy spoof that reflects the popularity of the James Bond films of the early 1960s. *Help!* was also directed by Lester and focuses in part on the hapless (but charming) Ringo, here haunted by a weird cult. The enterprise didn't meet with the same level of critical and audience success as the earlier venture, perhaps because *Help!* seemed so far-fetched.

The Beatles bounced back, however, with another landmark production. In 1968 came an animated production, the dazzling *Yellow Submarine*. This beautiful (and trippy) cartoon found the Fab Four (rendered in animated form) transported to the magical land of Pepper to combat joy-

The Fab Four (Paul, George, Ringo, and John) take the stage—and silver screen—as one of cinema's most beloved rock acts.

killing creatures known as "The Blue Meanies." This was the band's "mod" odyssey, and a brilliant, timeless fairy tale.

The 1970s saw the arrival of The Beatles' final film as a group. *Let it Be* is a documentary that charts the recording sessions leading up to The Beatles' break-up. Yoko Ono (long believed the cause of the split) is on the scene by now, and the film reveals some of the tensions bedeviling the group (particularly between Paul and George). Still, *Let It Be* ends strong, culminating in a spirited and impromptu rooftop performance.

Although The Beatles disbanded and the members went their separate ways, in a very real way, the Beatlemania craze never really ended.

In 1978, Robert Stigwood produced The Bee Gees vehicle *Sgt. Pepper's Lonely Hearts Club Band*, a disco-era musical that featured only Beatles tunes. The same year also saw the release of a wacky Robert Zemeckis comedy, *I Wanna Hold Your Hand*, which concerned four crazed female fans doing anything—and I mean anything—to get close to The Beatles' during their performance on *The Ed Sullivan Show*.

The year 1981 saw an adaptation of the popular stage show, *Beatlemania*, a production which gazed back nostalgically at the bygone heyday of the Fab Four, employing lookalikes as the band members.

As late as the 1990s, filmmakers still carry an obsession with this influential group. *Backbeat* (1991) recounts the story of the legendary "fifth" Beatle, who quit the group before it hit big. The black-and-white art picture, *The Hours and Times* (1991) speculates about John Lennon's

sexual orientation and a fling with the band's manager in Barcelona in 1963.

Although John Lennon was tragically gunned down by a madman in New York City in 1980, the surviving Beatles continued to participate in films through the decade.

Paul McCartney composed and performed (with Wings) the theme song to the first Roger Moore James Bond flick, *Live and Let Die* (1973) and later starred in his own musical-based film, *Give My Regards to Broad Street* (1984).

Ringo Starr guested in the Who documentary *The Kids Are Alright* (1979) to interview the late Keith Moon, as well as the aforementioned *Give My Regards to Broad Street*, and even starred in a wacky prehistoric comedy called *Caveman* (1981).

George Harrison was a critical mover and shaker behind *The Concert for Bangladesh* (1972), which also featured Ringo Starr on drums; he passed away in 2001.

In rock film history the Beatles represent camaraderie, comedy, and free-spirited, youthful fun. Their imitators are legion (including the carefully manufactured knockoff group, The Monkees). But no one ever did what they did as well as the Beatles. Each of their films represents a pioneering step in cinematic style, whether it be the black-and-white New Wave (*A Hard Day's Night*), satire (*Help!*), counterculture animation (*Yellow Submarine*) or concert performance (*Let It Be*).

Even The Sex Pistols took a crack at Beatles-like cinematic material in their own version of *A Hard Day's Night*, *The Great Rock 'n' Roll Swindle* (1980).

The Beatles have been mentioned frequently in film (including the Bond movie *Goldfinger*, 1964), and widely parodied (in the TV production called *The Rutles: All You Need is Cash*, 1978).

The Beatniks (1960) (FIC BAND)

STARRING: Tony Travis (Eddy Crane); Karen Kadler (Iris); Peter Breck (Moon); Bob Wells (Chuck); Sam Edwards (Red); Joyce Terry (Helen Tracy); Charles Delaney (Harry Bayliss); Martha Wentworth (Nadine).

FILM EDITOR: Harold White. DIRECTOR OF PHOTOGRAPHY: Murray Deatley. WRITTEN BY: Paul Frees, Arthur Julian. PRODUCED BY: Edward Heite. DIRECTED BY: Paul Frees. M.P.A.A. RATING: UR. RUNNING TIME: 78 minutes.

This is a strangely compelling and cheap-jack B production from rock 'n' roll's early days. The film's most significant drawback is that it has been badly mistitled. There are no counterculture proto-hippies on hand at all; no men in berets and goatees reading poetry or the like. Instead *The Beatniks* focuses squarely on hoodlums and greasers.

The Beatniks is the story of a poor slob named Eddy Crane (Tony Travis), the leader of a gang of juvenile delinquents. After robbing a convenience store with his buddies, he returns to their hang-out joint, Nadine's Diner and has a chance encounter with Hollywood agent Harry Bayliss (Charles Delaney).

This rep hears Eddy sing "Leather Coats" to his girl Iris by the juke box and immediately decides to sign him as a talent. Eddy, who's spent his whole life as a "nothing" sees this opportunity as his big chance for success, but his lunatic, destructive friends want only to party and be anti-social, threatening his climb to the top. A night of drinking at the Hollywood Inn leads to one crime after another, and even, ultimately, to murder.

Eddie falls in love with Bayliss' secretary, a girl with bleach blond hair and painted eyebrows, named Helen Tracy (Joyce Terry). She grooms him for success, and Eddy appears on the teen-centric (fictional) TV series "Rocket to Stardom" where he becomes an immediate sensation, even getting a record deal. But again, his friends—led by the psychotic Moon (Peter Breck)—just won't let him go legit. Every time he thinks he's out, they pull him back in.

Although the film's title indicates a desire to capitalize on the fresh (1958) Beatnik movement (a development of the Beat Generation), *The Beatniks* focuses more closely on gangs, and one young man's attempt to break out of a lifestyle that will ultimately lead him to jail. The ad lines screamed "*Hollywood Hoodlums on a Rock 'n' Roll Rampage!*" and "*Living by Their Code of Rebellion and Mutiny*," but frankly the film isn't that inflammatory.

Still, viewers may find themselves unprepared for the level of involvement they feel with Eddy as he tries to break free of those who want nothing better for him than what they already have. It's a classic rags-to-almost-riches story, and against one's better judgment, it works.

The Beatniks main claim to modern-day fame may be its appearance on TV's *Mystery Science Theatre 3000* in the early days of Joel Hodgson. There, Joel and the 'bots (Servo and Crow) also complained that the movie really has nothing to do with beatniks.

DVD Available on DVD.

Beavis and Butthead Do America (1995) (ANIM)(SNDTRK)

STARRING (THE VOICES OF): Mike Judge, Bruce Willis, Demi Moore, Cloris Leachman, Robert Stack.

FILM EDITORS: Gunter Glinka, Terry Kelly, Neil Lawrence. WRITTEN BY: Mike Judge, Joe Stillman. PRODUCED BY: Abby Terkuhle. DIRECTED BY: Mike Judge, Yvette Kaplan. M.P.A.A. RATING: PG-13. RUNNING TIME: 81 minutes.

This movie is a spin-off from the popular animated MTV television series of the early nineties. In the hallowed tradition of Wayne and Garth and Bill and Ted, Beavis and Butthead are two semi-literate, semi-civilized teenage adolescent boys who grunt and giggle a lot while they enjoy their favorite leisure activity: sitting on a filthy sofa eating junk food and watching music videos. Importantly, Beavis and Butthead are unrepentant heavy metal fans, and they enjoy rocking out (occasionally holding up their hands and wagging their heads).

Beavis and Butthead Do America picks up where the TV series left off. One sad day, Beavis and Butthead discover that their TV set has been stolen, which is about the worst thing that could ever happen to them. They thus embark

on a life-changing cross-country road trip to recover their property and return to their chosen lifestyle.

Along the way, however, the duo encounters the FBI, President Clinton, and—out west in the desert—two aging, pot-bellied roadies (for Motley Crue) who prove to be the boys' parents. Beavis also reprises a favorite alter-ego from the TV program, "Cornholio!"

On the hard-rocking soundtrack: "Walk on Water" by Ozzy Osbourne, "Snakes" by No Doubt, "The Lord Is a Monkey" by the Butthole Surfers (great name, huh?), And "Gone Shootin'" by AC/DC.

DVD Available on DVD.

The Big Chill (1983) (SNDTRK)

STARRING: Tom Berenger (Sam Weber); Glenn Close (Sarah Cooper); Jeff Goldblum (Michael Gold); William Hurt (Nick Carlton); Kevin Kline (Harold Cooper); Mary Kay Place (Meg); Meg Tilly (Chloe); Jo Beth Williams (Karen).

FILM EDITOR: Carol Littleton. DIRECTOR OF PHOTOGRAPHY: John Bailey. WRITTEN BY: Lawrence Kasdan, Barbara Benedek. PRODUCED BY: Michael Shanberg. DIRECTED BY: Lawrence Kasdan. M.P.A.A. RATING: R. RUNNING TIME: 105 minutes.

Oh, those poor, aging yuppies…

This is a self-indulgent 1960s nostalgia trip made in the 1980s and concerning a group of angsty professional thirtysomethings who gather for a reunion after the funeral of an old friend (a corpse played by Kevin Costner). All the characters are upwardly mobile baby boomers who've sold out the ideals of their youth, the 1960s, and are now going through midlife crises; trying to hold onto their fleeting youth any way they can. Invariably, this means swapping sexual partners or dating women half their age.

A high point of *The Big Chill*, other than a superb ensemble cast, is the 1960s era, Motown-heavy soundtrack. Indeed, Kasdan's film may owe its success not to his navel-gazing screenplay or even the fine actors, but rather to the amazing rock hits that underpin several of the scenes and actually add life and meaning to the self-indulgent material. On its release, many critics compared *The Big Chill* unfavorably to John Sayles' *Return of the Secaucus 7* (1980), yet it was *The Big Chill* that became a kind of boomer touchstone, and the great soundtrack is the reason why.

On the soundtrack: The Rolling Stones ("You Can't Always Get What You Want"), Aretha Franklin "([You Make Me Feel Like a] Natural Woman"), The Rascals ("In The Midnight Hour"), Percy Sledge ("When a Man Loves a Woman"), Creedance Clearwater Revival ("Bad Moon Rising"), The Beach Boys ("Wouldn't It Be Nice"), The Temptations ("My Girl"), Smokey Robinson ("Tracks of My Tears"), and Marvin Gaye ("I Heard It Through The Grapevine").

DVD Available on DVD.

Bikini Beach (1964) (SNDTRK)(MUS)

STARRING: Frankie Avalon (Frankie/Potato Bug); Annette (Dee Dee); Martha Hyer (Vivian); Don Rickles (Big Drag); Harvey Lembeck (Von Zipper); John Ashley (Johnny); Jody McCrae (Deadhead); Stevie Wonder (Himself) Keenan Wynn (Harvey Huntington Honeywagon).

FILM EDITORS: Fred Feitshans, Eve Newman. DIRECTOR OF PHOTOGRAPHY: Floyd Crosby. WRITTEN BY: William Asher, Robert Dillon, Leo Townsend. PRODUCED BY: Samuel Z. Arkoff, Jack Nicholas, Anthony Carras. DIRECTED BY: Willam Asher M.P.A.A. RATING: UR. RUNNING TIME: 99 minutes.

For a time in the mid-1960s, American International Pictures (AIP) was really pounding out these beach party films like they were coming off an assembly line somewhere in Hollywood. *Bikini Beach* arrived in theatres in 1964 just as the British rock invasion (courtesy of the Beatles) was taking hold in America. Naturally, the beach party movies had to comment on this threatening trend, and so here Avalon not only plays Frankie, but a twin of sorts, the mop-topped Brit named "Potato Bug" who speaks with a daft accent and has a thing for Annette.

But Potato "Jolly Good!" Bug is only point one on this triangular axis of beach-bound evil. The gang must also contend with its usual nemesis, Harvey Lembeck's Eric Von Zipper, as well as Keenan Wynn's evil land developer (who comes replete with a monkey sidekick named Clyde).

Bikini Beach adds drag racing (or rather, hot-rodding) to the mix for distraction's sake (as *Beach Blanket Bingo* would later involve skydiving), but this is another film with no real drama, no real suspense, and no truly funny jokes. The music is okay though.

Stevie Wonder (here called "Little Stevie Wonder," by the way) gets a "Happy Feeling" while the Avalon/Funicello duet this time is "Gimme Your Love." The Pyramids are also on hand to sing "How About That," and the whole cast works its way through "Bikini Beach." (DVD) Available on DVD.

Bill & Ted's Excellent Adventure

(1989)(FIC BAND)

STARRING: Keanu Reeves (Ted "Theodore" Logan); Alex Winter (Bill S. Preston, Esquire); George Carlin (Rufus); Terri Camilleri (Napoleon); Dan Shor (Billy the Kid); Tony Steedman (Socrates); Rod Loomis (Sigmund Freud); Al Leong (Genghis Khan); Jane Wiedlin (Joan of Arc); Robert V. Barron (Lincoln); Clifford David (Beethoven).

FILM EDITORS: Larry Bock, Patrick Rand. DIRECTOR OF PHOTOGRAPHY: Timothy Suhrstedt. WRITTEN BY: Chris Matheson, Ed Solomon. PRODUCED BY: Scott Kroopf, Michael S. Murphey, Joel Soisson. DIRECTED BY: Stephen Herek. M.P.A.A. RATING: PG. RUNNING TIME: 90 minutes.

At San Dimas High School, Valley Boys Ted "Theodore" Logan (Keanu Reeves) and Bill S. Preston Esq. (Alex Winter) care more about their rock 'n' roll band, Wyld Stallyns, than passing their high school history course. To them, Napoleon is a "*short dead dude*," Joan of Arc is "*Noah's wife*," and Caesar is a "*salad dressing dude*." Contrarily, they *are* concerned that they need guitarist Eddie Van Halen to make a video for their band. "*In time our band will be most triumphant*," they predict.

Ultimately, Bill and Ted are granted one last chance to succeed in history class, and must prepare an oral presentation in one day. If they fail, much more is on the line than a diploma: Ted's Dad plans to send him away to mili-

tary school in Alaska!

Out of the blue, a time-traveler named Rufus (George Carlin) arrives in San Dimas to avert this crisis. He takes the boys through time in a phone booth (Doctor Who, where are you?) and gives them first-person contact with the likes of Napoleon, Beethoven, Genghis Khan, Joan of Arc, Billy the Kid, Abraham Lincoln, and Sigmund Freud. The boys bring these dignitaries "back to the future" to help them with their critical project.

Why is Rufus bothering with two teenage dolts? Because—in the future of 2688—the lyrics of Bill & Ted's ("*the two great ones*") rock band, Wyld Stallyns, have made the planet Earth a peaceful utopia ("*The air is clean, the water is clean, even the dirt is clean,*" Rufus reports). Bill & Ted are worshiped by the masses as the historical figures who brought truly "excellent" living to the planet. So, with the help of the historical figures, Bill & Ted manage to pass history and save the future.

This 1989 comedy reflects and perhaps reinforced the way a generation of kids spoke (well ahead of Wayne and Garth, even). *Bill & Ted's Excellent Adventure* is a rock film in spirit because it acknowledges the first rule of wise man Dewey Finn: A good rock show can change the world. Here, the air-guitar strumming Bill & Ted will ultimately use rock music to bring peace and prosperity to mankind and make a better tomorrow. Though, first, they have to learn to play the guitar.

What's amusing about the film is the manner in which the duo relates everything to their love of rock music. In medieval England, they don suits of armor and quip "heavy metal!" When told of a torture device called an "iron maiden," they evidence delight, because they're thinking of the band. Finally, the "air guitar," Bill and Ted's favorite gesture becomes the salute of the future age. There's nothing "bogus" about that.

DVD Available on DVD.

Bill and Ted's Bogus Journey

(1991)(FIC BAND)(SNDTRK)

STARRING: Keanu Reeves (Ted); Alex Winter (Bill); William Sadler (Grim Reaper); Joss Ackland (Chuck de Nomolos); George Carlin (Rufus).

FILM EDITOR: David Finfer. DIRECTOR OF PHOTOGRAPHY: Oliver Wood. WRITTEN BY: Chris Matheson, Ed Solomon. PRODUCED BY: Scott Kroopf. DIRECTED BY: Pete Hewitt. M.P.A.A. RATING: PG. RUNNING TIME: 93 minutes.

This sequel to the 1989 teen hit finds "dudes" Bill & Ted (the architects of man's peaceful future) imperiled by a renegade from the future (Joss Ackland) who despises everything the "triumphant" fellas stand for. He sends back to the 1990s robot duplicates of Bill & Ted to kill the duo and destroy the peaceful timeline. Unfortunately, the evil twins succeed, and Bill & Ted find themselves in Hell dealing with the Grim Reaper (William Sadler). This disaster couldn't have come at a worse time, either, because Bill and Ted's rock band, Wyld Stallyns is competing in an all-important *battle of the bands*. If the band don't win that fourth annual competition in San Dimas (and see their music broadcast worldwide), mankind is doomed.

In every way funnier and more accomplished than the 1989 original, the very disarming *Bill & Ted's Bogus Journey* culminates with a performance by Wyld Stallyns, and the Grim Reaper himself even joins the band as the bassist. Another member (or members?) is the strange creature "Station," the greatest scientist in the universe (who helpfully mans the bongos). During one very funny moment in the afterlife Ted and Bill also take the opportunity to quote lyrics from Poison's "Every Rose Has Its Thorn" when asked about the meaning of life.

Original rock music composed for the film includes the triumphant "God Gave Rock and Roll to You Too," "Battle Stations," and "Shout It Out." The film ends with newspaper headlines revealing how one good rock show has changed the Earth. Wyld Stallyns on tour brings peace to the Middle East and causes crops to grow in the Midwest.

Party on, dudes!

DVD Available on DVD.

Billboard magazine (GENRE CONVENTION)

An institution. This long-lived American magazine has chronicled the rise and fall of many a rock act on its "*Billboard* Hot 100" chart, a popularity gauge it began in the year 1958...just as rock was sizzling.

In the rock film, close-ups of slots on the *Billboard* chart have become a cliché, a shorthand to establishing the meteoric rise (and sometimes catastrophic fall) of a particular act.

The *Billboard* close-up appears in Robert Townsend's *The Five Heartbeats* (1991) and during the climb of the One-ders (or Wonders) in Tom Hanks' *That Thing You Do!* (an ascent that finds the act hopping from number ninety-three to seventy one, to forty-nine, to twenty-one, to number seven).

In the Jerry Lee Lewis bio-pic, *Great Balls of Fire* (1989), Jerry (Dennis Quaid) watches with increasing tension as his new song "High School Confidential" slips on the *Billboard* chart from thirty four to seventy-eight, all the way down to ninety seven.

A *Billboard* cover also heralds the arrival of a new sensation in *Sgt. Pepper's Lonely Hearts Club Band* (1978) and highlights the age of Wyld Stallyns in *Bill & Ted's Bogus Journey* (1991).

As late as 2005, *Walk the Line,* which finds a Johnny Cash tune racing up to number fourteen, features this rock film convention.

Blackboard Jungle (1955)(SNDTRK)

STARRING: Glenn Ford (Rick Dadier); Anne Francis (Ann); Louis Calhern (Jim Murdock); Margaret Hayes (Lois Hammond); John Hoyt (Mr. Warnecke); Sidney Poitier (Miller); Vic Morrow (Artie West); Richard Kiley (Josh Edwards); Emile Meyer (Mr. Halloran); Paul Mazursky (Emmanuel Stocker); Jamed Farah (a.k.a. Jamie Farr) (Santini).

FILM EDITOR: Ferris Webster. DIRECTOR OF PHOTOGRAPHY: Russell Harlan. SCREENPLAY BY: Richard Brooks. BASED ON THE NOVEL BY: Evan Hunter. PRODUCED BY: Pandro S. Berman. DIRECTED BY: Richard Brooks. M.P.A.A. RATING: Approved. RUNNING TIME: 101 minutes.

"We in the United States are fortunate to have a school system that is a tribute to our communities and to our faith in American youth. Today, we are concerned with juvenile delinquency—its causes and its effects. We are especially concerned when the delinquency boils over into our schools. The scenes and incidences depicted here are fictional. However, we believe that public awareness is a first step toward a remedy of any problem. It is in this spirit and with this faith that *Blackboard Jungle* was produced."

With those portentous words begins *Blackboard Jungle,* an American film that has long carried the distinction of being the world's first so-called rock 'n' roll movie.

However, this description is somewhat of a misnomer since there is no rock band, no rock music, and no mention at all, in fact, of that "devil's music" sweeping the land in the body proper of the movie. Instead, the melodramatic film merely opens with a rock theme song, "Rock Around the Clock" performed by Bill Haley and His Comets (a tune first recorded in late 1952). The movie and the song both became hits together, though the movie actually warns against just the kind of teen rebellion that the song represents.

In *Blackboard Jungle,* World War II vet Rick Dadier (Glenn Ford) takes a new job teaching high-school English, only to run into a class of juvenile delinquents which includes a young Sidney Poitier, Vic Morrow, Paul

A punk named Artie (Vic Morrow) threatens Mr. Dadier (Glenn Ford) while Miller (Sidney Poitier)

looks on in a tense scene from *Blackboard Jungle* (1955), widely considered the "first" rock 'n' roll movie.

Mazursky, and Jamie Farr! The kids in the class call Dadier "Daddy-O" and openly challenge him for dominance in the classroom. All the while, at home, Mr. Dadier's very pregnant wife, Ann (Anne Francis) suffers extreme anxiety about her husband's safety (and also fidelity, since rumors of an affair with another teacher start to circulate). The kids continue to spiral out of control (and in one infuriating scene destroy the record album collection of Richard Kiley's math teacher), but in the end, Dadier earns the respect of his students, especially after a climactic knife fight involving Morrow's character.

Fifty-one years after its release, *Blackboard Jungle* appears stilted and overly theatrical and preachy in its depiction of semi-literate teen monsters threatening to overturn the prized status quo. There's one scene where a car overturns on a busy avenue and narrowly misses Ford and Francis, thereby indicating that 1950s America is a "war zone" and that juvenile delinquents are the combatants.

Today we all realize that rock music didn't bring civilization to its knees or throw America into barbarism, but the film clearly demagogues the issues of teens and their "new" culture. It plays to audience fears of teenagers, even if it ends on a happy note, but notably one where the establishment triumphs; assimilating youth with the lure and economic power of a good education.

So *Blackboard Jungle* gets an "A" for it's theme song and early acknowledgment of rock as a new presence in the American public square, even if the script and overdramatic acting renders it a hair below "C" level. Also, this movie adopts the perspective of an authority figure

(teacher), not rebels, so it's not really much of a rock film in the final analysis.

(DVD) Available on DVD.

Blame It on the Night (1984)(FIC BAND)

STARRING: Nick Mancuso (Chris Dalton); Byron Thames (Job Dalton); Leslie Ackerman (Shelly); Richard Bakalyan (Manzini); Rex Ludwigh (Animal).

FILM EDITOR: Tony Lombardo. DIRECTOR OF PHOTOGRAPHY: Alex Phillips Jr. WRITTEN BY: Mick Jagger, Len Jenkin, Gene Taft. PRODUCED AND DIRECTED BY: Gene Taft. M.P.A.A. RATING: PG-13. RUNNING TIME: 85 minutes.

In this nearly-forgotten obscurity (co-written by icon *Mick Jagger*), the thirteen-year old adolescent son (Byron Thames) of a popular rock god (Nick Mancuso) meets his free-wheeling father for the first time following the unexpected death of his mother. The star takes the boy with him on *the road* (and away from his beloved military school), and the generation gap causes issues for them. Until, that is, they learn to laugh at love again.

Ironically, the problem in *Blame It on the Night* is not a conservative father and a rebellious son as is usually the case in rock movies, but rather the reverse. The boy is uptight and rigid, and the Dad is too loose for words.

Blame It on the Night had a very limited release (just over two hundred theatres) when it debuted in November 1984, and consequently made very little money.

(DVD) Not available on DVD.

Blue Hawaii (1961)(ELVIS)(MUS)

STARRING: Elvis Presley (Chad Gates); Joan Blackman (Maile Duval); Angela Lansbury (Sarah Lee Gates); Pamela Kirk (Selena); Darlene Tompkins (Patsy).

FILM EDITOR: Terry Morse. DIRECTOR OF PHOTOGRAPHY: Charles Lange, Jr. WRITTEN BY: Allan Weiss, Hal Kanter. PRODUCED BY: Hal B. Wallis. DIRECTED BY: Norman Taurog. M.P.A.A. RATING: UR. RUNNING TIME: 102 minutes.

I know the purists will quibble at this assessment, but I prefer my Elvis films with a healthy dose of rebellion and a bit of kinkiness. Presley's best films, including *King Creole* (1958), *Kid Galahad* (1962), and *Follow That Dream* (1962) give Elvis something meaty to play, whether it be angst, lust, or naïvete. His films grow tedious (and then later, insipid) when The King's just supposed to be a "regular guy" be-bopping between willing ladyfriends.

Again, at the risk of angering the faithful, Elvis movies are also better when he has fewer numbers to perform (again, I'm thinking *Kid Galahad*, *Wild in the Country,* and *King Creole*), because the narrative isn't fractured so often.

Which brings us to Elvis' eighth film, *Blue Hawaii*. It was a big hit, both as a film and as a soundtrack, but—to be brutally honest—nothing of consequence or real interest happens in it. Elvis plays Chad Gates, a guy returning to Hawaii from a stint in the Italian Army. He returns to hang out as a beach bum, but must contend with his domineering mother, played by Angela Lansbury. Chad evades employment in his father's business and goes to work for a tourist company instead. Along the way, he sings a lot of songs, and romances Joan Blackman. The location photography in *Blue Hawaii* is non-stop gorgeous, and it's no wonder Elvis returned twice more to Hawaii (for *Girls! Girls! Girls!* and *Paradise, Hawaiian Style*). But jeez, Elvis, how about throwing in a narrative?

Among the songs in *Blue Hawaii*: "Blue Hawaii," "Almost Always True," "Aloha Oe," "No More," the memorable and stirring high point, "Can't Help Falling in Love," "Rock-a-Hula Baby," "Moonlight Swim," "Hawaiian Sunset" and "Hawaiian Wedding Song."

(DVD) Available on DVD.

The Blues Brothers (1980)

(FIC BAND)(CAMEOS)

STARRING: John Belushi (Jake Blues); Dan Aykroyd (Elwood Blues); James Brown (Reverend James); Cab Calloway (Curtis); Ray Charles (Ray); Aretha Franklin (Mrs. Murphy).

FILM EDITOR: George Folsey, Jr. DIRECTOR OF PHOTOGRAPHY: Stephen M. Katz. WRITTEN BY: John Aykroyd and John Landis. PRODUCED BY: Robert K. Weiss. DIRECTED BY: John Landis. M.P.A.A. RATING: R. RUNNING TIME: 133 minutes.

"Who do you think you are, The Beatles?" Steve Lawrence asks in this outrageous comedy, an effort that evidences a real love of the rock movie form (not to mention rampant glee in the *destruction of property*).

Brothers Jake (John Belushi) and Elwood (Dan Aykroyd) get out of jail and visit their old orphanage only to learn it owes money on back taxes and could be shut down. Accepting a *"mission from God,"* the brothers decide

They're on a mission from God. Elwood (Dan Aykroyd) and Jake (John Belushi)

Blues in John Landis's demolition derby, *The Blues Brothers* (1980).

to assemble their old band, put on a show, and save the orphanage. Roughly, that's the plot skeleton for John Landis' amazing *The Blues Bothers*, an endlessly quotable demolition derby of a movie that involves everything from car crashes to neo-Nazis and entertaining rock/blues performances.

Shot on location in Chicago, this is John Landis' big-budget extravaganza, based on the old *Saturday Night Live* skit by Belushi and Aykroyd. However, unlike many films based on *SNL* material, *The Blues Brothers* never wears out its welcome, even at its considerable running time. There's probably never been another movie like it; one that so brilliantly and ably pits action scenes against musical performance and yet remains funny throughout. Some of the elaborately planned and executed chases (and crashes) in the film provoke gasps of awe, and the performances by the likes of Ray Charles ("Shake a Tail Feather"), Aretha Franklin ("Think"), Fats Domino ("I'm Walkin'"), and James Brown ("The Old Landmark") are stirring. They'll make your first want to tap your feet, then get up and dance.

Some of the high points in the film include Cab Calloway performing "Minnie the Moocher" in white tux at the Palace Hotel, trying to stall for time when the Blues Brothers are late for their own show; the Blues Brothers, mistaken for the "Good Ole Boys" at Country Bob's Bunker and singing the theme song to *Rawhide* behind a chicken wire barrier; and the full-fledged musical number (with dancers populating the streets) at Ray's Music Exchange.

After *The Blues Brothers*, Landis had a bad run of things in Hollywood (going on trial for the fatal accident on the set of *Twilight Zone: The Movie*, 1983), and, of course, John Belushi died of an overdose in March 1982. Thus *The Blues Brothers* represents a kind of shining moment in both careers. For a big budget movie (and it must have cost a bloody fortune destroying all those automobiles) this is a strangely quirky and individual film. In its zeal to destroy property and belief that rock music can save the day, *The Blues Brothers* proves one of the most consistently delightful efforts of 1970s genre pictures. Give it an extra star if you grew up with it.

(DVD) Available on DVD.

The Blues Brothers 2000 (1998)

(FIC BAND)(CAMEOS)

STARRING: Dan Ayrkoyd (Elwood Blues); John Goodman (Mack); Joe Morton (Cap); Nia Peeples (Elizondo); Kathleen Freeman (Mother Mary Stigmata); J. Evan Bonifant (Buster Blues); Erykah Badu (Queen); B.B. King (Malvern).

FILM EDITOR: Dale Beldin. DIRECTOR OF PHOTOGRAPHY: David Herrington. WRITTEN BY: Dan Aykroyd, John Landis. PRODUCED BY: Dan Aykroyd, Leslie Belzberg, John Landis. DIRECTED BY: John Landis. M.P.A.A. RATING: PG-13. RUNNING TIME: 123 minutes.

Evidence you can't go home again. And more so, that you probably shouldn't even try. The mind boggles at the state of mind that would permit this ill-advised sequel to go forward. One half of the famous Blues Brothers, John

Belushi, died a full fifteen years before this sequel, so really, what's the point? The virtuoso original film was a product of its time (an age when car crashes were a common sight in mainstream movies) and a high point for everyone involved (meaning John Landis, Belushi and Dan Aykroyd). So why on Earth sully the memory of that achievement with a witless follow-up?

Welcome to the age of "brand name" movies and nostalgia rock.

The plot of *Blues Brothers 2000* is a sad retread of the original's formula. There's a release from prison (only this time, Elwood learns that Jake's dead); a visit to a wrist-smacking nun; another "*mission from God*" (this time to reassemble the group, win a *battle of the bands*, and thereby and save a childrens' hospital); some run-ins with the cops, a few brushes with evil (not neo-Nazis, but the Russian mafia and a right-wing gun group); and, of course, the requisite musical numbers. Wilson Pickett, Eric Clapton, B.B. King, Isaac Hayes, and Bo Diddley all show up, but it is the returning Aretha Franklin who steals the show with her rendition of "R.E.S.P.E.C.T."

Adding insult to injury, J. Evan Bonifant plays a little kid "blues brother" (in a role originally designed for Macauley Culkin). If dancing kids in sunglasses and a retread plot are your thing, you might like this.

(DVD) Available on DVD.

The Bodyguard (1992)

(SNDTRK)(REAL ROCKER)

STARRING: Kevin Costner (Frank Farmer); Whitney Houston (Rachel Morran); Gary Kemp (Sy); Bill Cobbs (Bill Devaney); Ralph Waite (Herb).

FILM EDITOR: Donn Cambern. DIRECTOR OF PHOTOGRAPHY: Richard A. Harris. WRITTEN BY: Lawrence Kasdan. PRODUCED BY: Kevin Costner, Lawrence Kasdan, Jim Wilson. DIRECTED BY: Mick Jackson. M.P.A.A. RATING: R. RUNNIING TIME: 130 minutes.

Pop star Whitney Houston starred as an imperiled rock star in this early 1990s mega-hit. Kevin Costner (in an early Julius Caesar-style haircut) plays the bodyguard trying to protect her from harm but ultimately falling in love with her. The film involves a spectacular onstage set piece set to the tune of Whitney's power ballad "Queen of the Night."

Other tunes on the soundtrack include Houston belting out the film's big radio hit, "I Will Always Love You," as well as "I Have Nothing," "I'm Every Woman" (which served as Oprah Winfrey's theme song), "Jesus Loves You," and "Run to You." Joe Cocker contributes a theme song and Lisa Stansfield adds "Someday (I'm Coming Back)."

The Bodyguard's soundtrack sold a whopping seventeen million copies on the film's release.

(DVD) Available on DVD.

Jon Bon Jovi (1962–)(ROCK MOVIE HALL OF

FAME) This New Jersey boy and rock-and-roller has made good at the movies, serving as the romantic lead in such efforts as *Moonlight and Valentino* (1995) and Edward Burns' melancholy *No Looking Back* (1998).

Like many icons of rock, Bon Jovi has also found a comfortable niche in the *horror* genre. He starred as a vampire hunter in *John Carpenter's Vampires: Los Muertos* (2002) and as a libidinous English professor suspected of murder at a private school in the 2005 slasher film, *Cry_Wolf*.

Bon Jovi's hard-driving tunes have been heard in rock movies for two decades, including Paul Schrader's *Light of Day* in 1987 ("Only Lonely"), Kevin Smith's *Jay and Silent Bob Strike Back* in 2001 ("Bad Medicine"), and *Rock Star* in 2001 ("Livin' on a Prayer"). Outside of the rock genre, his tunes have been spotlighted in films as diverse as *Armageddon* (1998), *Edtv* (1999), and *Charlie's Angels: Full Throttle* (2003).

Boogie Nights (1997)(SNDTRK)(MUS)

STARRING: Mark Wahlberg (Eddie Adams/Dirk Diggler); Burt Reynolds (Jack Horner); John C. Reilly (Reed Rothchild); Julianne Moore (Amber Waves); Heather Graham (Rollergirl); Don Cheadle (Buck Swope); Luiz Guzman (Maurice); Philip Seymour Hoffman (Scotty J.); William H. Macy (Little Bill); Thomas Jane (Todd); Melora Walters (Jesse); Ricky Jay (Kurt); Robert Ridgeley (The Colonel); Alfred Molina (Rahad); Philip Baker Hal (Floyd Gondoli).

FILM EDITOR: Dylan Tichenor. DIRECTOR OF PHOTOGRAPHY: Robert Elswit. PRODUCED BY: Paul Thomas Anderson, Lloyd Levin, John S. Lyons, Joanne Sellar. WRITTEN AND DIRECTED BY: Paul Thomas Anderson. M.P.A.A. RATING: R. RUNNING TIME: 156 minutes.

Paul Thomas Anderson's searing (and often humorous) look at the porno film industry of the 1970s and early-1980s (the burgeoning age of video-tape) captures the whole vibe of that era through its canny use of period rock music. Later in his career, particularly in his second sortie, *Magnolia* (1999), Anderson would select original compositions (by rocker Aimee Mann) to support his complex narrative, but here he provides a soundtrack for the ages, one loaded with all the great hits of the disco decade and the beginning of the Reagan era.

The story of Dirk Diggler's (*Rock Star's* Mark Wahlberg) rise and fall in the porn industry is punctuated by The Emotions' "Best of My Love," Melanie's roller-skating masterpiece "Brand New Key," Eric Burdon's "Spill the Wine," Marvin Gaye's "Got to Give It Up (Part I)," "Machine Gun" by The Commodores, "Magnet and Steel," performed by Walter Egan, "Ain't No Stopping Us Now," performed by McFadden and Whitehead, Night Ranger's classic "Sister Christian," and The Beach Boys' "God Only Knows."

Late in *Boogie Nights*, Dirk Diggler also attempts to transcend his porno experience by becoming a rock star him-self. In a troubled (and very funny) *recording studio session*, he records the dreadful tunes (by his buddy Reed Rothchild) "Feel the Heat" and "He Will Rock You." Ultimately, they have trouble taking possession of the master tapes because they can't afford to pay for them (they've spent all their dough on cocaine).

Paul Thomas Anderson never fails to weave music bril-liantly into the tapestry of his films, and while *Boogie Nights* visually apes Martin Scorsese's oeuvre (particularly a scene involving a mirror from *Raging Bull*, 1980) as well as Brian De Palma's (*Dressed to Kill*, 1980) penchant for long, unbroken tracking shots, Anderson's choices for the soundtrack skillfully reveals character, expresses mood, and wraps the audience up in an overwhelming and emo-tional sense of nostalgia.

 Available on DVD.

human roles. For instance, Bowie essayed the role of a predatory punk vampire in Tony Scott's *The Hunger* (1983) and a goblin king in the muppet movie, *Labyrinth*, both to good impact.

Bowie, who is also one of the wealthiest British rock stars, has been no stranger to serious, dramatic movie roles, either. He earned critical hosannas for his role as a captured soldier in the prison camp/war movie *Merry Christmas, Mr. Lawrence* (1983), and also appeared as Pontius Pilate in Martin Scorsese's controversial *The Last Temptation of Christ* (1989).

Bowie songs have underpinned scenes in the oeuvre of David Lynch (*Lost Highway*, 1997), David Fincher (*Seven*, 1995), Danny Boyle (*Trainspotting*, 1996), and more. The actor has also appeared in cameos in Julien Temple's *Absolute Beginners* (1986), *Twin Peaks: Fire Walk With Me* (1992) and the Ben Stiller comedy *Zoolander* (2000).

David Bowie (1947–   )(ROCK MOVIE HALL OF FAME)

Of all the rock 'n' roll movie stars, perhaps none has revealed more versatility on screen than David Bowie. This Brixton-born native is not only the central figure of the glam-rock era, but the poster boy for androgyny. Using this quality to his advantage, Bowie played a strand-ed alien in Nicolas Roeg's *The Man Who Fell to Earth* (1976), a reflection, perhaps of his space-age alter ego, Ziggy Stardust. Bowie's strange (but attractive) looks also granted the talent a sense of authenticity in other non-

Break-up (GENRE CONVENTION)

As inevitable as death and taxes in the rock 'n' roll movie.

In virtually every movie about a fictional (or authentic) band, the group splits up, either permanently or in time for a last reel reunion.

In *The Buddy Holly Story* (1978), *This Is Spinal Tap* (1984), *Light of Day* (1987), *The Doors* (1991), *The Five Heartbeats* (1991), *That Thing You Do!* (1996), *Rock Star* (2001), *Metallica: Some Kind of Monster* (2004), and beyond, there's a messy break-up involving one or more of the band members walking away in a huff. Since being in a rock band has often been termed the equivalent of a marriage, it's no wonder there have been so many silver-screen divorces.

The Bride (1985)(REAL ROCKER)(HORR)

STARRING: Jennifer Beals (Eva); Sting (Baron Frankenstein); Anthony Higgins (Clerval); Clancy Brown (Viktor); David Rappaport (Rinaldo); Alexei Sayle (Magar); Phil Daniels (Bela); Veruschka (Countess); Quentin Crisp (Dr. Zahlus); Cary Elwes (Josef); Tim Spall (Paulus); Geraldine Page (Mrs. Baumann); Ken Campbell (Pedlar); Guy Rolfe (Count); Andrew De La Tour (Priest); Tony Haygarth (Tavern Keeper); Jack Birkett (Blind Man); John Sharp (Bailiff).

FILM EDITOR: Michael Ellis. DIRECTOR OF PHOTOGRAPHY: Stephen H. Burum. WRITTEN BY: Lloyd Fonveille. PRODUCER: Victor Drai. DIRECTED BY: Franc Roddam. M.P.A.A. RATING: PG-13. RUNNING TIME: 119 minutes.

The arrogant Baron Frankenstein (Sting) creates a mate for his monster (Clancy Brown)—Jennifer Beals (star of *Flashdance*, 1983). But the good doctor wants the lovely and innocent young woman for his own sick sexual desires, in this mid-1980s variation on the Frankenstein theme.

There's no rock music in *The Bride*, but Franc Roddam's film does boast a starring performance by Sting as the glacial doctor, and the presence of a post-*Flashdance* Beals also makes it a rock 'n' roll twofer.

(DVD) Available on DVD.

Bring on the Night (1985)(DOC)

STARRING: Sting, Miles Copeland, Branford Marsalis, Omar Hakim, Darryl Jones, Kenny Kirkland.

FILM EDITOR: Robert K. Lambert, Melvin Shapiro. DIRECTOR OF PHOTOGRAPHY: Ralf D. Bode. PRODUCED BY: David Manson. WRITTEN AND DIRECTED BY: Michael Apted. M.P.A.A. RATING: PG-13. RUNNING TIME: 97 minutes.

This 1980s-era documentary by Michael Apted gazes at a week or so in the life of Sting, ex-lead for The Police, as he launched a solo career and formed a new band. This movie finds the talent toiling in Paris with Branford Marsalis on sax, Kenny Kirkland on keys, Omar Hakim on drums, and Darryl Jones on Bass.

The album they're all developing and rehearsing is *The Dream of the Blue Turtles* (which went on to sell three million copies in the U.S.), and *Bring on the Night* alternates concert performance with rehearsals and interviews.

Surprisingly, Sting comes off as thoroughly humorless in the film, and live-wire Marsalis steals the show right out from under him. *Bring on the Night* also features such rock-movie conventions as the *press conference*, the *manager* (here, a tyrannical Miles Copeland), and the *recording session*.

During the course of the film, Sting also sees his son born, which is certainly a twist on formula.

Tunes in this Sting feature include "Burn for You," "Fortress Around Your Heart," "Consider Me Gone," and "Bring on the Night."

(DVD) Available on DVD.

Bubba Ho-tep (2002)(ELVIS)(HORR)

STARRING: Bruce Campbell (Elvis Presley/Sebastian);
Ossie Davis (President Kennedy); Ella Joyce (Nurse);
Bob Ivy (Bubba Ho-Tep).

FILM EDITORS: Scott Gill, Donald Milne. DIRECTOR OF
PHOTOGRAPHY: Adam Janeiro. STORY BY: Joe R. Lansdale.
WRITTEN BY: Don Coscarelli. PRODUCED BY: Don Coscarelli,
Jason R. Savage. DIRECTED BY: Don Coscarelli. M.P.A.A.
RATING: R. RUNNING TIME: 92 minutes.

A low-budget treasure with a very limited theatrical
release, and one of the greatest (and most unlikely)
movies about The King of Rock ever produced. *Bubba
Ho-tep*'s director, Don Coscarelli, couldn't afford to pay
for any Elvis tracks (or use any footage of Elvis, either),
but this deficit hardly matters, since the helmer of
Phantasm (1979) has assembled a sentimental, silly, and
exciting cult classic.

Bruce Campbell (of *Evil Dead*, 1982, fame) stars as an
elderly Presley. Only nobody believes he's really Elvis at
all; they believe he's an Elvis impersonator named
Sebastian. In fact, Campbell is the real thing, and (as
depicted in flashbacks), years earlier gave up fame and fortune to live as an "everyman." But now Elvis is a senior citizen, he has cancer on his penis(!) and is living in a run-
down nursing home in Texas after breaking a hip. One of
his fellow wards in the home is a black man (Ossie Davis)
who believes that he is actually President Kennedy and
that Lyndon Johnson "dyed" him black so no one would
ever find him. He has even decorated his room to resemble the Oval Office.

Into this strange world unexpectedly arrives an evil and
murderous Mummy, an Egyptian soul-sucker who is turning the old folks' home into a killing field. Elvis Presley
and President Kennedy strike back, mounting a defense
against the monster before it's too late.

Bubba Ho-tep is graced by Bruce Campbell's affectionate
and true performance (one of the cinema's finest Elvis
portrayals) And even though the plot might sound like a
joke, the film treats the King with compassion and dramatizes his humanity. What would a senior citizen Elvis look
and sound like? How would he feel about his career?
About Priscilla? The Colonel? Lisa Marie? Remarkably,
Bubba Ho-tep answers those questions with wit, and allows
the viewer to get inside The King's thoughts by grace of a
clever, literate voice over from Campbell.

Elvis Presley has officially become one of America's pop
culture gods, and *Bubba Ho-tep* tacitly acknowledges that
fact, transforming the Boy from Memphis into the Old Man
from Texas; the one who is still a black-belt karate expert
and ready to fight for our country's cherished values.
ⒹⓋⒹ Available on DVD.

The Buddy Holly Story (1978)(BIO-PIC)

STARRING: Gary Busey (Buddy Holly); Don Stroud (Jesse);
Charles Martin Smith (Ray); William Jordan (Riley); Fred
Travalena (Madman Mancuso); Dick O'Neill (Sol).

FILM EDITOR: David Blewitt. DIRECTOR OF PHOTOGRAPHY:
Stevan Larner. Source material from BUDDY HOLLY, HIS LIFE

Elvis has entered the building. Director Don Coscarelli (left) with star Bruce Campbell (right)—playing Presley—on the set of *Bubba Ho-tep* (2002).

AND MUSIC by John Goldrosen. SCREENPLAY BY: Robert Gittler. PRODUCE BY: Freddy Bauer. DIRECTED BY: Steve Rash. M.P.A.A. RATING: PG. RUNNING TIME: 117 minutes.

Steve Rash's bio-pic about Buddy Holly made a young, pre-crazy Gary Busey a rising star to watch, but it's also a splendid evocation of the late 1950s, and the societal fear that rock 'n' roll was a "threat" to the nation's "morals." A preacher in the film notes with intolerance that "*there is a new form of music—if you can call it music—that is as un-Christian and un-American as anything we have had to face in the last fifty years.*" Given such hyperbole, it's no wonder that so much of rock history involves flouting and humiliating authority. How else can you deal with such crazies like these?

The Buddy Holly Story commences in Lubbock, Texas in 1956 as a young local celebrity, Holly (Busey) shocks fans of his radio show—as well his parents and the local minister—by playing that so-called "*jungle music,*" rock 'n' roll. After getting his tune "That'll Be the Day" played on the radio by Madman Mancuso, Buddy Holly's star rises. Although his band The Crickets has some internal problems, the artist nonetheless breaks all sorts of barriers by serving as producer of his own album, proving to be the first white act to ever play a gig at the Apollo Theatre, and marring a Latino.

Despite his success (and even a comparison by an impressed violinist to Beethoven), Holly can't escape his fate, and the film ends just before the tragic flight that would take the life of Ritchie Valens, The Big Bopper, and Lubbock's hero.

Along the way in the film, there's the requisite *Ed Sullivan Show* appearance, a rock movie cliché, and much ado over the band's *break—up* (another convention), but most of all the film revels in Holly's music, which includes "Peggy Sue," "Maybe Baby," and "It's So Easy." Overall the film is pleasant, the period details carefully observed, and Busey certainly nails his character. However, at points there seems to be some essential element of drama missing.

In films such as the *The Doors* (1991) or *Walk the Line* (2005), icons like Jim Morrison and Johnny Cash have their own crises and demons to overcome. Their fate, the audience feels, is in their own hands. Buddy Holly seems far more centered and placid than most rock stars. He doesn't want to leave home to go on tour, and it turns out there is good reason. The film ends on a freeze frame, and there's some sadness because he is, essentially, the victim of circumstance by dying in a plane crash.

Although early on, Buddy wrestled with men of the cloth and the disapproval of his own parents, by film's end he is facing no character crisis, so much of the film seems mild and pleasant rather than searing and involving.

But oh yeah, Gary Busey is fantastic in the film. As Vincent Canby aptly suggested in *The New York Times*, "The movie is really a one-man show. It's Gary Busey's galvanizing solo performance that gives meaning to an otherwise shapeless and bland feature length film…"[14]

DVD Available on DVD.

The Bus (or Road Trip) (GENRE CONVEN-

TION) An essential ingredient of a good rock movie is the tour bus scene, one in which members of the band reveal their softer, more intimate side on the yawning highways of America. In *This Is Spinal Tap*, the band is depicted on the road and relaxing on the tour bus (playing video games and canoodling with groupies) when David St. Hubbins shows off the fuzzy sweatshirt knitted for him by his girl-friend Jeanine.

In *Almost Famous* (2000), the members of Stillwater spontaneously break into a rendition of Elton John's "Tiny Dancer." In the oddest tour bus film, *Spice World* (1997), the Spice Girls have transformed their vehicle into a home away from home and a James Bond–style control room/headquarters.

A tour bus to "nowhere" also shows up briefly in the Sex Pistols mock-doc, *The Great Rock 'n' Roll Swindle* (1980), and Ike Turner's bus puts in an appearance in the Tina Turner bio-pic, *What's Love Got to Do With It?* (1993).

A tour bus also shows up in *The Who* documentary *The Kids Are Alright* (1979).

(is for *The Commitments*)

Camelot (a.k.a. The Age of Innocence)

(GENRE CONVENTION) A wide variety of rock films are set in the years 1962–1963, a time seen by many scholars (and entertainers) as "the end of an era," or an "Age of Innocence." This was the era immediately preceding the Kennedy assassination, but also the British music invasion. Also, the Vietnam conflict had not yet escalated to become the conflagration that would divide America.

Accordingly, many filmmakers have selected this span for their rock films in an attempt to capture that spirit of American innocence. It's the epoch of *American Graffiti* (1973), *Dirty Dancing* (1987), *Shag: The Movie* (1989), and even John Waters' *Hairspray* (1988), to name but a few.

Ironically, in the case of *Hairspray*, the ever-needling Waters flouts conventional wisdom and finds not much cause for romance or nostalgia. Instead, his film punctures the "aura" of innocence many folks associate with that period in our history and deals plainly instead with segregation and racism.

Cameos

(GENRE CONVENTION) Another requirement of the rock film genre is the sudden, unexpected appearance of a legitimate rock star for a cameo or clip. A movie can be humming along normally and then— boom—an icon appears briefly, holds center stage with a "bit," and then disappears as the narrative resumes. It's just a salute to the rock brotherhood, but it's another convention of the form.

Meat Loaf and Alice Cooper appear in *Wayne's World* (1992), and Aerosmith in that film's sequel, *Wayne's World 2* (1993).

Frankie Avalon cameos as the "Teen Angel" in *Grease* (1978).

Gene Simmons and Ozzy Osbourne cameo in *Trick or Treat* (1986).

Linda Ronstadt cameos in *FM* (1979).

Morris Day and the Time cameo in *Jay and Silent Bob Strike Back* (2001) and Deborah Harry appears briefly in *Roadie* (1980).

Non-rock stars, but cultural icons Jack Nicholson and Dennis Hopper cameo in The Monkees' *Head* (1968), and on and on, and Nicholson returns to the rock form as "The Specialist" in Ken Russell's *Tommy* (1975).

Frankly, it's not really a rock film if someone famous doesn't show up for a minute or two so the other stars can genuflect and insist "We're not worthy! We're not worthy!"

Can't Stop the Music (1980)(BIO-PIC)(FIC)

STARRING: The Village People; Valerie Perrine (Samantha); Bruce Jenner (Ron White); Steve Guttenberg (Jack Morrell); Paul Sands (Steve); Tammy Grimes (Channing); June Havoc (Helen Morell); Barbara Rush (Norma White); Altovise Davis

(Alicia Edwards); Marilyn Sokol (Lulu); Leigh Taylor-Young (Claudia Walters); Jack Weston (Benny).

FILM EDITOR: John F. Burnett. DIRECTOR OF PHOTOGRAPHY: Bill Butler. WRITTEN BY: Bronte Woodward, Allan Carr. PRODUCED BY: Allan Carr, Jacques Morali, Henri Belolo. DIRECTED BY: Nancy Walker. M.P.A.A. RATING: PG. RUNNING TIME: 123 minutes.

Hailed by its makers as the *"musical extravaganza that starts the 1980s," Can't Stop the Music* (which also boasted an ad-line that threatened *"once it begins, you can't stop the music"*) is a cinematic cavalcade of movie cheese, campy humor, and slapstick schtick.

The film purports to tell the story behind the creation of The Village People, one of the most popular groups of the late 1970s and early 1980s. A record store employee named Jack Morell (Steve Guttenberg) gets a record deal unexpectedly, but has no band to record his stuff so he quickly assembles a diverse group to sing his trademark tunes. Along with his scatter-brained roommate, Samantha (Valerie Perrine), Jack finds talented singers one-by-one, including an American Indian, a construction worker, a policeman, and a cowboy, among others. From the opening scene, which finds Guttenberg roller skating through a record store and then on the streets of Manhattan, (see: *Roller Boogie*) to the tune of "Sound of the City," to the closing number, "Can't Stop the Music," which finds the screen awash in a blizzard of glitter, this is one strange movie.

Budgeted at $15 million and originally called *Discoland—Where The Music Never Stops*, this vehicle for The Village People was directed by Nancy Walker, popularly known by TV audiences as the Bounty Towel spokeswoman. The film was a huge bomb upon release, but upon closer inspection today one has to give The Village People their props for so blatantly selling audiences a gay-themed film without audiences or critics really figuring it out.

For instance, it isn't difficult to detect that many of the tunes in the film boast wicked double-meanings and double entendres involved with homosexuality. For "YMCA," all the men in the film, including Bruce Jenner, visit a locker room and spy on naked men there. Then as the song continues, the number is staged on exercise bikes, in a sauna, a shower, and so forth. The Busby Berkeley–style number inevitably focuses on attractive men adorned only in Speedos.

Another number, called "Milk Shake"…well, I'll leave an interpretation of that one to your imagination.

My point is simply this: even though the movie is unredeemably bad, kudos to The Village People for not compromising their identity. The movie is ridiculous, campy, and over the top, but at least it's not a betrayal of the fan base, and that's commendable, isn't it?

Can't Stop the Music's biggest flaw is that at 123 minutes, it's overlong, and the material designed as comedy simply isn't that funny. Maybe a more genuinely biographical approach would have served the band better than this effort, which in essence is a farce.

Perhaps *New York Times* critic Janet Maslin said it best when she wrote: *"Can't Stop the Music* is a movie with its

Even if you want to, you *Can't Stop the Music* (1980). Steve Guttenberg (left), Valerie Perrine (center), and Bruce Jenner (right) enthusiastically suffer the indignities of the Village People movie.

own ice cream flavor, which is duly plugged during the course of the so-called story…The Village People, for whom the movie is more or less a vehicle, perform lively songs and try less successfully to act."[15]

Jacques Morali is responsible for the score here, and the songs include "YMCA," "Magic Night," "Liberation," "I Love You to Death," "Milk Shake," "Give Me a Break," "Sophistication," and "Sound of the City."

A camp treasure, *Can't Stop the Music* is currently available on DVD and really, everybody should see it at least once. Especially if *The Apple* isn't in stock.

(DVD) Available on DVD.

Celebration at Big Sur (1971)(DOC)

STARRING: Joan Baez, David Crosby, Mimi Fariña, Joni Mitchell, Graham Nash, John Sebastian, Neil Young.

FILM EDITOR: Johanna Demetrakas. DIRECTOR OF PHOTOGRAPHY: Baird Bryant. PRODUCED BY: Carl Gottlieb. DIRECTED BY: Baird Bryant, Johanna Demetrakas. M.P.A.A. RATING: PG. RUNNING TIME: 82 minutes.

"It happened one weekend by the sea…"

This is the concert film made from the 1969 Big Sur Folk Festival. Smaller than *Woodstock* (1970), and less memorably filmed and fashioned (with fewer resources) than that watershed event, this effort nonetheless features some terrific tunes.

Joni Mitchell sings "Woodstock," John Sebastian does "Red Eye Express" Joan Baez belts out "Song for David," and Crosby, Stills, Nash & Young perform "Suite: Judy

Blue Eyes." The movie ends with the whole slate singing "Oh Happy Day."

Everyone did it for "the sheer love of it," as the tagline reminds viewers and there's really something wonderful about that.

Sadly, though *Celebration at Big Sur* is often remembered in the same breath as *Monterey Pop* (1967) and *Woodstock* itself, it remains unreleased on DVD and the VHS version is long out of print. That said, the film occasionally plays on television.

Change of Habit (1969)(ELVIS)(MUS)

STARRING: Elvis Presley (Dr. John Carpenter); Mary Tyler Moore (Sister Irene Hawkins); Jane Elliot (Sister Barbara); Leora Dana (Mother Joseph); Edward Asner (Moretti).

FILM EDITOR: Douglas Stewart. DIRECTOR OF PHOTOGRAPHY: Russell Metty. WRITTEN BY: Eric Bercovici, John Joseph, James Lee, Richard Morris, S.S. Schweitzer. DIRECTED BY: William Graham. M.P.A.A. RATING: G. RUNNING TIME: 93 minutes.

This Elvis Presley vehicle boasts one humdinger of a plot. To get the obvious out of the way first, the change of "habit" of the title refers to the traditional uniform of the Catholic nun. Accordingly then, the movie concerns Mary Tyler Moore as a nun named Sister Irene who literally goes undercover (sans habit) to the bad part of town to assist the godly efforts of the King.

No, not Jesus Christ, Elvis Presley!

Presley plays a Good Samaritan children's doctor (with mutton chop sideburns and a bad haircut, no less). The duo soon bonds over an autistic child, and love is in the air. But wait a second! Should Sister Irene (Moore) love J.C. (the messiah) or John Carpenter (the doctor who tends to the poor)?

The once and future TV star gets plenty of time to mull it all over as Elvis sings "Let Us Pray," "Change of Habit," "Rubberneckin'," and "Have a Happy." Many critics saw this Elvis flick as a more substantive one than previous efforts, but they must have had in mind *Harum Scarum*. This one can't hold a candle to *King Creole*.

(DVD) Available on DVD.

Christine (1983)(HORR)(SNDTRK)

STARRING: Keith Gordon (Arnie); John Stockwell (Dennis); Alexandra Paul (Leigh); Robert Prosky (Darnell); Harry Dean Stanton (Junkins); Christine Belford (Regina Cunningham); Roberts Blossom (Le Bay); William Ostrander (Buddy); David Spielberg (Mr. Casey); Malcolm Danare (Moochie).

FILM EDITOR: Marion Rothman. DIRECTOR OF PHOTOGRAPHY: Donald M. Morgan. BASED UPON THE NOVEL BY: Stephen King. SCREENPLAY BY: Bill Phillips. PRODUCED BY: Richard Kobritz. EXECUTIVE PRODUCERS: Kirby McCauley, Mark Tarlov. DIRECTED BY: John Carpenter. M.P.A.A. RATING: R. RUNNING TIME: 110 minutes.

Stephen King's best-selling novel about a 1958 Chevrolet Fury with an evil mind of its own was turned into this 1983 film by horror maestro John Carpenter (that name keeps reappearing, doesn't it?). *Christine* finds young Arnie (Keith Gordon) buying the old junker and restoring her to

cherry condition. But there's a strange bond between bullied teenager and his car, and soon the car is killing his enemies at school.

Christine commences on the assembly line in Detroit with the malevolent car's unusual origin. Carpenter utilizes a 1950s rock score throughout the film both for ironic and funny purposes. "Bad to the Bone" by George Thorogood and the Destroyers (*"On the day I was born, I was bad to the bone"*) informs the first scenes, as Christine kills two auto workers.

Later, when Christine flattens fat old garage owner Mr. Darnell between her seat cushions and the dashboard, the radio blares "Bony Maroni" by Larry Williams, a song about a skinny girl. When Dennis (John Stockwell), the film's protagonist, attempts unsuccessfully to break into the hell car, the soundtrack responds with "Keep a Knockin'" by Little Richard (*"I hear you knockin', but you can't come in"*).

To dramatize Arnie's enduring love for *Christine*, Carpenter selects "We Belong Together" (*"I'll forever love you, for the rest of my days"*). Finally, after Christine's "death," her immortality is suggested when Carpenter chooses "Rock 'n' Roll is Here to Stay" by Danny and the Juniors, which establishes that rock 'n' roll music, like *Christine* herself, *"will never die."*

"It was meant to be that way, though I don't know why..."

(DVD) *Christine* is available on DVD.

Chuck Berry: Hail! Hail! Rock 'n' Roll! (1987)(DOC)

STARRING: Chuck Berry, Ingrid Berry, Eric Clapton, Bo Diddley, Don Everly, Phil Everly, Etta James, John Lennon, Julian Lennon, Jerry Lee Lewis, Little Richard, Roy Orbison, Keith Richards, Linda Ronstadt.

FILM EDITOR: Lisa Day. DIRECTOR OF PHOTOGRAPHY: Oliver Stapleton. PRODUCED BY: Stephanie Bennett, Chuck Berry. DIRECTED BY: Taylor Hackford. M.P.A.A. RATING: PG. RUNNING TIME: 120 minutes.

This is a fascinating rockumentary about one of rock's most admired performers and writers. The occasion for the movie is Berry's sixtieth birthday, and there's a star-studded tribute concert held at St. Louis's Fox Theatre (in October 1986).

Taylor Hackford (*The Idolmaker*, 1980, *Ray*, 2004) is the director, and he fills the film with rehearsal footage, performances from the concert and plenty of archival footage, notably a duet with the late John Lennon (on *The Mike Douglas Show* in the mid-1970s) in which the ex-Beatle likened Berry to a poet.

There are plenty of solicitous interviews from the likes of Bruce Springsteen that attempt to play up Berry's acknowledged greatness. Yet more genuinely interesting is the relationship between the program's musical director, a frazzled Keith Richards (of the Rolling Stones), and a combative Berry, who doesn't seem to enjoy the process of prepping for the concert.

The performances range from extraordinary (Eric Clapton, "Wee Wee Hours," Linda Ronstadt, "Back in the U.S.A.," and Etta James, "Rock and Roll Music", to merely ordinary (Julian Lennon's duet with Berry to the tune of "Johnny B. Goode").

However, be forewarned, if you're more interested in the personal side of Berry's career, meaning his brushes with the law and prison, and his rumored affection for "groupies," this will disappoint. Even his wife, who appears in an interview, seems hamstrung and unwilling to talk specifics on pain of death. Hackford does attempt to explore the personal side of Berry's rock journey, so give him credit for trying; but Berry cuts him off frequently, keeping everything on a professional but therefore distancing plateau.

Still, *Chuck Berry: Hail! Hail! Rock 'n' Roll* is an amazing chronicle of a man whom many critics consider the true King of Rock.

DVD Available on DVD.

Circular Logic (GENRE CONVENTION) Wherein a rocker/musician attempts to say something meaningful and deep, but only succeeds in confusing the audience, and usually himself.

In *This Is Spinal Tap*, for instance, the band members make their immortal remark about the fine line separating "stupid and clever." Even the very title of a Tap song exhibits circular thinking: "Tonight I'm Gonna Rock You, Tonight."

Going back to the Bob Dylan documentary, *Don't Look Back*, Dylan utters a variety of bizarre and nonsensical (but sometimes pretentious) statements for the record.

For example, Dylan observes that he will "become insane if he becomes insane"; he opines that "There are no ideas in *Time* magazine. There's just facts…Every word has its little letter and its big letter." And after one disturbing incident involving a hurled drinking glass, the artist reports that, "I don't care who did it. I just want to know who did it."

Similarly, in *The Last Waltz*, Rick Danko of The Band comments on an upcoming performance serving as "a celebration of the beginning of the end of the beginning," further displaying the propensity in rock towards tail-chasing logic.

Lars Ulrich, the drummer for Metallica, asks in Joe Berlinger's *Some Kind of Monster*: "Where does the record start? Where does it end?"

Later the same talent also opines that the band has created "aggressive music without negative energy." Right.

Clambake (1967)(ELVIS)(MUS)

STARRING: Elvis Presley (Scott Heyward/Tom Wilson); Shelley Fabares (Dianne Carter); Will Hutchens (Tom Wilson/Scott Heyward); Bill Bixby (James); Gerry Merrill (Sam); James Gregory (Duster); Suzie Kaye (Sally); Angelique Pettyjohn (Gloria).

FILM EDITOR: Tom Rolf. DIRECTOR OF PHOTOGRAPHY: William Margules. WRITTEN BY: Arthur Brown Jr. PRODUCED BY: Arthur Gardner, Arnold Laven. DIRECTED BY: Arthur H. Nadel. M.P.A.A. RATING: UR. RUNNING TIME: 100 minutes.

Unfortunately, another Elvis time-waster. In this not-so-rockin' film supposedly set in Miami (though it looks like the actors never got off the Hollywood lot…), the son of a millionaire, Scott Heyward (Presley), switches places with a lowly hotel water-skiing teacher (Hutchens). Why? The tender soul just isn't sure that people love him for his personality and not his money, fast cars and other expensive toys.

To distill this lightweight effort down to the essentials: Bill Bixby plays Elvis' nemesis; Shelley Fabares his romantic prize; and the final battle involves a speed boat race and a new but unstable chemical fuel (devised by Elvis, no less).

On the song count, Elvis sings a half dozen or so forgettable tunes. These are (drum roll, please): "Clambake," "A House That Has Everything," "Confidence," "Hey, Hey, Hey," "Who Needs Money," "You Don't Know Me," and "The Girl I Never Loved."

A peanut-butter and banana sandwich to the reader who can explain what the title *Clambake* actually has in common with the narrative. This Elvis movie is so dull it seems to bend time itself, making the minutes pass by at a mind-numbing crawl.

(DVD) Clambake—the movie the fast-forward button was invented for—is currently available on DVD.

The Commitments (1991)(FIC BAND)

STARRING: Robert Arkins (Jimmy Rabbitte); Michael Aherne (Steven Clifford); Angeline Ball (Imelda Quirke); Maria Doyle (Natalie Murphy); Dave Finnegan (Mickah Wallace); Bronogh Gallagher (Bernie); Johnny Murphy (Joey "The Lips" Fagan); Andrew Strong (Deco Cuffe); Colm Meaney (Mr. Rabbitte).

FILM EDITOR: Gerry Hambling. DIRECTOR OF PHOTOGRAPHY: Gale Tatersall. WRITTEN BY: Dick Clement, Ian La Frenais, Roddy Doyle. BASED ON THE NOVEL BY: Roddy Doyle. EXECUTIVE PRODUCERS: Armyan Bernstein, Tom Rosenberg, Souter Harris. PRODUCED BY: Roger Randall-Cutler, Lynda Myles. DIRECTED BY: Alan Parker. M.P.A.A. RATING: R. RUNNING TIME: 119 minutes.

In the inspiring and funny *The Commitments*, a young man named Jimmy (Robert Arkins) attempts to rise above his working-class roots and assemble the world's hardest working band. He has a vision for the group too: they will only play soul music. After extensive, sometimes comical auditions, he settles on two musician buddies, a singer who only really comes to life when he's drunk (Andrew Strong), the trumpeteer named Joey 'the Lips" (Johnny Murphy) and two very good-looking Commitment-ettes as background singers.

The Commitments follows the all-too-brief rise and fall of this band, self-described *"overnight assholes."* They travel to gigs in their "Mr. Chippy" concession-stand truck, and their first show is at a roller skating rink. Before long, that rock 'n' roll demon, *sex*, shows its face and begins to interfere with the music. Jimmy must watch helpless as the Commitments self-destruct and all his work is for naught. If only Wilson Pickett, who was supposed to have jammed with the group on one big night, had shown up…

This movie by Sir Alan Parker is a fun, rollicking effort, that—in contrast to many rags-to-riches stories—focuses on failure, not success. *"I've achieved nothing,"* Jimmy notes at one point, and meditates on whether or not failure is "poetry" or a "pisser." Success, he concludes, would have been so predictable.

What enlivens *The Commitments* is not just the wonderful performances of the Irish cast and the script's welcome sense of humor, but the electric performances of the band itself. The toe-tapping soundtrack includes "Mustang Sally," "Take Me to the River," "Chain of Fools," "The Dark End of the Street," "Destination Anywhere," "Try a Little Tenderness," "Treat Her Right," "Mr. Pitiful," "In the Midnight Hour," and "Slip Away," among others.

Sir Alan Parker remembers some of the technical innovations of the film: "Most film music from *Singin' in the Rain* to MTV uses pre-recorded tracks and vocals which are played back as the camera takes up different positions with the artists miming," he explains. "I wanted to capture the reality of the rehearsals and performing by recording the vocals live on set. This is very difficult, as modern film requires different angles to be covered and a constant soundtrack is needed in order for the finished, edited scene to match cut-by-cut."

"We used a new system of out-of-phase speakers which enables us to play the pre-recorded constant backing tracks at maximum volume on-set to give us a live-performance atmosphere for the vocalists to sing to," he continues.

"Each vocal was then recorded live onto a twenty-four-track recorder that was on-set with us. Because of the out-of-phase speakers, the vocals could be recorded cleanly, as they were filmed for re-mixing later. This allowed us the technical precision needed for a complicated cut, but gave us the truth, energy and spirit of a live performance. It also enabled us to interweave dramatic dialogue with songs. Again we were only able to do this because they were singing directly into visible microphones."

(DVD) Available on DVD.

The Compleat Beatles (1984)(DOC)

STARRING: Malcolm McDowell (Narrator); IN ARCHIVAL FOOTAGE: George Harrison, John Lennon, Paul McCartney, Ringo Starr. ALSO FEATURING: Marianne Faithful, Lenny Kaye, Chuck Berry, Bill Haley, Mick Jagger, Richard Lester, George Martin.

FILM EDITOR: Pamela Page. DIRECTORS OF PHOTOGRAPHY: Nick Hale, Peter Schnall, Djura Adnjic, Joel King. WRITTEN BY: David Silver. PRODUCED BY: Stephanie Bennett. DIRECTED BY: Richard Montgomery. M.P.A.A. RATING: UR. RUNNING TIME: 119 minutes.

This is a thorough and dedicated documentary (based on a book of essays regarding the Fab Four) that studies the full breadth of The Beatles experience, gazing at archival footage, photographs, press kits, and featuring interviews, clips of TV appearances, and the like.

The Compleat Beatles traces the development of this famous group from Lennon and McCartney's childhood days in Liverpool all the way up to the release of the album *Let It Be*, which came after the break up of 1969–70.

The film also finds time to remember The Beatles' earlier incarnations (The Quarrymen, anyone?). The movie features the band's managers too (Bill Harry, Brian Epstein) and includes information on music producer George Martin.

At barely two hours in length, it's difficult to make the claim that this is the "complete" anything, but *The Compleat Beatles*—boosted by great narration from Malcolm McDowell—does a terrific job of hitting all the basics and covering in broad terms the career of the most influential rock band in history.

Writing for *The New York Post*, Ira Mayer determined that serious "Beatle fans may have legitimate gripes with *The Compleat Beatles*—there are a number of misrepresentations of scenes from the career of the Fab Four," but likewise noted that "apart from these, the film is entertaining and exceptionally well-crafted."[16] *Newsday*'s Wayne Robins concurred with the former sentiment and described *The Compleat Beatles* as "a thorough, intelligent and entertaining chronological history of that profoundly influential pop music group."[17]

The film also contains a commendable focus on the music, and the ways that The Beatles' sound changed over time, so that's also a welcome feature.

(DVD) Not currently Available on DVD.

The Concert for Bangladesh (1972)(DOC)

STARRING: Eric Clapton, Bob Dylan, George Harrison, Billy Preston, Leon Russell, Ravi Shankar, Ringo Starr, Klaus Voorman, Badfinger, Allan Beutler, Jesse Ed Davis, Chuck Findley, Marlin Greene, Jeanie Green, Jo Greene, Jim Horn, Delores Hall, Kamala Chakravarty, Jackie Kelso, Jim Keltner, Claudia Lennear, Lou McCreary, Ollie Mitchell, Don Nix, Don Preston, Carl Radle, Alla Rakah.

FILM EDITOR: Howard Lester. CINEMATOGRAPHERS: Sol Negrin, Richard Brooks, Fred Hoffman, Tohru Nakamura. PRODUCERS: George Harrison, Allen Klein. DIRECTED BY: Saul Swimmer. M.P.A.A. RATING: UR. RUNNING TIME: 96 minutes.

This 1972 UNICEF fundraiser for war refugees from Bangladesh begins at a *press conference*, as ex-Beatle George Harrison explains the importance of helping. After that brief interlude, the film cuts to the stadium concert as a throng of fans gather. Harrison introduces the concert to the screaming admirers, beginning with a set of Indian music featuring Ravi Shankar on the sitar. Before starting, Shankar urges the audience to be patient during his set, while waiting for their favorite "stars."

After the Indian interlude, George Harrison takes center stage, Ringo Starr and Jim Keltner behind him at the drums, Eric Clapton at the guitar, and Leon Russell and Billy Preston at the piano. Their set includes "Jumpin' Jack Flash" (by the Rolling Stones), and "Here Comes the Sun." In some songs, archival film clips of starving, emaciated people in Bangladesh are intercut with the music.

George Harrison remains on stage to support Bob Dylan, the next headline artist. Dylan performs "A Hard Rain's a Gonna Fall" and "Blowin' in the Wind" before the concert is through.

DVD Available on DVD.

Alice Cooper (1948–   )(ROCK MOVIE HALL OF FAME) One of rock's most enduring and talented legends, the imposing Alice Cooper (born Vincent Damon Furnier) is the son of a minister and hails from Detroit. He changed his name to Alice Cooper (which had been the name of his band in the early 1970s) and has been going non-stop ever since. He's known for his black eye makeup (which grants an ominous, menacing look) and long black hair.

In film, this rocker has made a name for himself by embracing the horror genre. Cooper starred as a murderous homeless street-walker in the John Carpenter flick *Prince of Darkness* (1987), and perhaps even more notably appeared as Freddy Krueger's abusive father in *Freddy's Death: The Final Nightmare* (1991).

Cooper's weakest horror credit may be *Monster Dog* (1985), which saw the star essay the role of a rocker named "Vince" with a familial werewolf problem. In that film, he even sang a few tunes, including "Identity Chrises"[sic].

Also in the horror genre, Alice Cooper has composed and performed a number of important theme songs. In 1986, he contributed "He's Back (The Man Behind the

Mask") to *Friday the 13th Part VI: Jason Lives!* In 1989, Cooper performed the tune "No More Mr. Nice Guy" for Wes Craven's *Shocker*, which had been the film's original title.

Even Cooper's crowd-pleasing cameo in *Wayne's World* (1992) boasts a horror angle since the rocker performs on stage a tune called "Feed My Frankenstein."

Outside of the horror genre (though not far outside), Cooper has portrayed villains like cult-leader Father Sun in the Bee Gees vehicle *Sgt. Pepper's Lonely Hearts Club Band* (1979), and also supplied original tunes to *Roadie* (1980) and *Class of 1984* (1982). He also appeared in *Roadie*.

Cooper's composition "School's Out" may be the most utilized teenage anthem in film history. It has appeared in no less than half a dozen films including *Rock 'n' Roll High School* (1979), Richard Linklater's *Dazed and Confused* (1993), Ben Stiller's *Reality Bites* (1994), Wes Craven's *Scream* (1996), *The Faculty* (1998), and Julien Temple's *The Filth and the Fury* (2000).

Cover Art (GENRE CONVENTION) Rock album covers are often a source of contention or strife in genre films.

To wit: "Smell the Glove" by Spinal Tap arrives sans cover art of any kind whatsoever. Or lettering. Or identifying marks for that matter. "*None more black*," Nigel Tufnel famously says, and he's dead right.

In *The Five Heartbeats* (1991), the all-African-American doo-wop group is confronted with a ludicrous album cover giving no indication that the record arrives from black recording artists. This is an attempt to help their music "cross over" to whites. The cover art instead reveals a white family at a beach in a car; with a heart around them.

In *The Gate* (1987), liner notes on a Sacrifyx album cover provide the clue to defeating diminutive demon soldiers from another dimension.

In *Xanadu* (1980), Sonny (Michael Beck) actually works as a cover album artist, painting covers for billboards. It's in that milieu that he spies his muse, Olivia Newton-John, for the second time in one day.

Coyote Ugly (2000) (SNDTRK)

STARRING: Piper Perabo (Violet Sanford); Adam Garcia (Kevin O'Donnell); John Goodman (Bill); Maria Bello (Lil); Izabella Miko (Cammie); Tyra Banks (Zoe); Bridget Moynahan (Rachel); Melanie Lynskie (Gloria).

FILM EDITOR: William Goldenberg. DIRECTOR OF PHOTOGRAPHY: Amir Mokri. WRITTEN BY: Gina Wendkos. PRODUCED BY: Jerry Bruckheimer, Chad Omar. DIRECTED BY: David McNally. M.P.A.A. RATING: PG-13. RUNNING TIME: 100 minutes.

In her review for *Coyote Ugly* at Salon.com, critic Stephanie Zacharek opined: "If you're planning to see the Jerry Bruckheimer–produced *Coyote Ugly* just to get an eyeful of leggy beauties dancing across a whiskey-slick bar top, you should know that this is really a prudish, glassy-eyed movie about dreams coming true in the heart of the cold, cold city. Really. In that sense, *Coyote Ugly* may be the most disappointing movie of the summer: I went in hoping for shameless exploitation and all I got was a handful of crappy Diane Warren songs. It just doesn't get grimmer than that."[18]

I don't think I can add much to that description.

To offer a tad more detail, this film (which was rumored to have undergone an uncredited re-write by indie director Kevin Smith) concerns a 21-year-old Jersey Girl named Violet (Piper Perabo) who heads to New York City in hopes of becoming a successful songwriter. To make ends meet after renting an apartment, she gets a job at the new night club called "Coyote Ugly," populated by hot women who tend bar, dance, and wait tables. Lil (Maria Bello) owns the establishment, and gives Violet a shot. But Violet never gives up her dream of getting her demo tape into the right hands and becoming a big success.

There are two reasons for *Coyote Ugly* to exist. One is to feature gorgeous, athletic women romping and stomping. The second is to give those romping and stomping women a marketable soundtrack. In addition to the aforementioned Diane Warren songs (which are actually voiced by LeAnn Rimes, not Perabo), the soundtrack is practically overripe with rock tunes. Sugar Ray's "Fly," Sybersound's "I Will Survive," Snap's "The Power," Def Leppard's "Pour Some Sugar on Me," "Lenny Kravitz's "Fly Away," Uncle Kracker's "Follow Me," Kid Rock's "Cowboy," Billy Idol's "Rebel Yell" and even the Elvis Presley standard "Can't

Help Falling in Love" all make their duly appointed rounds. Not surprisingly, the film's soundtrack cracked *Billboard*'s top-forty album chart during the film's release. Mission accomplished.

ⅅⅤⅅ Available on DVD.

Critters (1986)(HORR)(FIC BAND)

STARRING: Dee Wallace Stone (Mrs. Helen Brown); M. Emmet Walsh (Sheriff Harve); Billy Green Bush (Jay Brown); Scott Grimes (Brad Brown); Nadine Van der Velde (April Brown); Don Opper (Charlie McFadden); Lin Shaye (Sally); Billy Zane (Steven Elliot); Ethan Phillips (Jeff Barnes); Terence Mann (Johnny Steele); Michael Lee Gogin (Warden Zanti).

FILM EDITOR: Larry Bock. DIRECTOR OF PHOTOGRAPHY: Tim Suhrstadt. SPECIAL CRITTER EFFECTS: Chiodo Brothers Productions. MUSIC: David Newman. "POWER OF THE NIGHT" WRITTEN BY: Terrence Mann, Richie Vetter, PERFORMED BY: Terrence Mann. STORY BY: Domonic Muir. SCREENPLAY BY: Domonic Muir. EXECUTIVE PRODUCER: Robert Shaye. PRODUCED BY: Rupert Harvey. DIRECTED BY: Stephen Herek. M.P.A.A. RATING: PG-13. RUNNING TIME: 86 minutes.

Another 1980s horror film with a rock 'n' roll edge, *Critters* is the story of malevolent alien fur balls called "Crites." These escaped convicts (created by the Chiodo Brothers) come to Earth to wreak havoc in a small town called Grover's Bend, and are pursued by two shape-shifting bounty hunters.

One of the bounty hunters adopts the form of Earth's most popular rock star, hairband leader Johnny Steele

(Terrence Mann). Steele is seen in the film performing his video for the hit single "The Power of the Night."

In one of the film's most wicked jokes about small-town Kansas, none of Grover's Bend's denizens recognize the world-famous celebrity.

(DVD) Available on DVD.

Cry-Baby (1990)(MUS)

STARRING: Johnny Depp (Cry-Baby Walker); Amy Locane (Allison Vernon-Williams); Susan Tyrrell (Ramona); Iggy Pop (Belvedere); Ricki Lake (Pepper); Traci Lords (Wanda); Stephen Mailer (Baldwin); Darren E. Burrows (Milton); Polly Bergen (Mrs. Vernon-Williams); Patricia Hearst (Wanda's Mom); David Nelson (Wanda's Dad); Troy Donohue (Hatchet's Father); Mink Stole (Hatchet's Mother); Kim McGuire (Hatchet Fac); Willem Dafoe (Guard).

FILM EDITOR: Janice Hampton. DIRECTOR OF PHOTOGRAPHY: David Insley. EXECUTIVE PRODUCERS: Jim Abraham, Brian Grazer. WRITTEN AND DIRECTED BY: John Waters. M.P.A.A. RATING: PG-13. RUNNING TIME: 86 minutes.

"*Juvenile delinquents are everywhere! Right here in this community!,*" an authority figure frets in John Waters' popular low-budget effort, a glorious and knowing tribute to the late 1950s and early 1960s and the bygone era of juvenile delinquent teen films like *The Beatniks* (1960).

Waters' pseudo-musical film focuses on Cry-Baby Walker (Johnny Depp), a gang leader of "The Drapes" in Baltimore, a fella who likes his women "*bad, not cheap*" and wants to date the respectable Allison Vernon-Williams (Amy Locane). Unfortunately, her square (and mean) boyfriend, Baldwin (Stephen Mailer) doesn't cotton to the idea of competition and does everything in his power to destroy Cry-Baby, a sensitive soul whose trademark is a single tear on his cheek. Cry-Baby is an orphan, you see, whose father was the nefarious Alphabet Murderer (who bombed places in alphabetical order) and met his fate in the electric chair.

After a rumble in the park one night (which ends with Cry-Baby's prized motorcycle aflame), Cry-Baby Wilson is sentenced to a Juvenile Hall, The Maryland School for Boys, until he turns twenty-one. There a malevolent prison guard (Willem Dafoe) lords it over the inmates, until a climactic run on the facility by Allison and her mother frees this already free spirit. Matters of the heart are settled by a drag race and a dangerous (and amusing) game of chicken between Cry-Baby and Baldwin.

Cry-Baby is an amusing and campy retro rock treasure that opens in humorous fashion with high school students of all stripe and denomination (including the terrifying Hatchet Face, Kim McGuire), receiving polio shots via terrifying-looking injections. The film then moves to the story at hand, with Depp portraying a pseudo-Elvis Presley figure with a snarl familiar to fans of the King. During a performance at the Jukebox Jamboree, Cry-Baby even sings an Elvis-esque number "King Cry-Baby," which features the telling, though perhaps apocryphal lyrics: "I am the King."

The era of air raid drills, "duck and cover" and innocent teenagers is remembered fondly and humorously here. In one funny sequence, the naïve Allison asks Cry-Baby as they French kiss: "*I won't get mononucleosis, will I?*" Waters appears to have special fun staging his film's over-the-top prison sequences. It may not be "Jailhouse Rock," but *Cry—Baby* comes to life with such crowd-pleasing, prison-related tunes as "Please, Mr. Jailer" and "In the Jailhouse Now."

Although adults in the film fear Cry-Baby and lament his antisocial behavior and this "*scary vision of today's youth*," the audience that grew up with juvenile delinquent films will certainly find much to enjoy here. Some have compared *Cry-Baby* to a low-rent version of the popular film (and Broadway musical), *Grease* (1978), but *Cry-Baby* boasts Waters' telltale anarchic spirit. Therefore, his film is wicked and wild, not merely romantic or nostalgic.

More tunes on the soundtrack include: "Sh-Boom," "Bunny Hop," "Teardrops Are Falling," and "High School Hellcats." All the performers in the film, it should be noted, lip-synch rather than actually sing; but *Cry-Baby* is so much anarchic fun, you'll hardly care.

DVD Available on DVD.

(is for *Don't Look Back*)

DJ (GENRE CONVENTION) A critical stock-character in the rock movie canon.

Disc jockeys are often powerful allies to rockers (and teens). They often represent the voice of democracy (the voice of the people), and in history, they played a real role in bringing rock music to the masses. Considering this accomplishment, it's no wonder that they are often depicted as sages and wise men.

Alan Freed in *American Hot Wax* (1978) is known as "the father of the rock" because he used his power (and public platform) to disseminate rock religion to a generation of teens. In 1973's George Lucas venture, *American Graffiti*, Wolfman Jack serves the same purpose, but also supplies wise guidance to Richard Dreyfuss in their face-to-face meeting.

In *Trick or Treat* (1986), Gene Simmons passes along the last album of heavy-metal god Sammi Curr to a kid named Rag Man, and almost destroys the prom in the process, so he's not a particularly positive role model. But those disc jockeys in *FM* (1978) sure are: they go on a kind of non-stop rant of civil disobedience to prevent "the man" (the U.S. Army) from using their rock station to run recruitment ads. Power to the people!

A rebellious disc jockey, Happy Harry Hard-On (Christian Slater) gives angsty teens a voice in Allan Moyle's *Pump Up The Volume* (1990), and the "Lone Rangers" seize a radio station and force Joe Mantegna's

disc jockey to play their demo tape in *Airheads* (1994).

Daddy-O (1958)(MUS)

STARRING: Dick Contino (Phil/Daddy-O), Sandra Giles (Jana); Bruno Vo Sota (Sidney); Gloria Victor (Marcia); Jack McClure (Bruce).

FILM EDITOR: Harold White. DIRECTOR OF PHOTOGRAPHY: Perry Finnerman. WRITTEN BY: David Moessinger. PRODUCED BY: Elmer C. Rhodes, Jr. DIRECTED BY: Lou Place. M.P.A.A. Rating: UR. Running time: 74 minutes.

Ready to enter the thrilling world of "*Hot Blondes, Souped-Up Rods, and Espionage?*"

Were it not for those jokesters on *Mystery Science Theatre 3000*, this 1958 juvenile delinquent/rock film would probably have gone the way of all flesh and disappeared off the face of the Earth. Instead, thanks to the popular TV show, a brand-new generation has become acquainted with this Dick Contino vehicle, a low-rent Elvis-type film involving a truck driver who falls for a blonde femme fatale (Sandra Giles) and inadvertently gets mixed up in the drug trade thanks to his new job as a night club singer.

Though he's supposed to be a teenager, Contino appears to be about 45, and wears his trousers so high one wonders how his lungs can breathe. For thrill's sake there's a drag race in Griffith Park, and every now and then Contino (allegedly an accordionist) horrendously belts out tunes such as "Angel Eyes" and the immortal "Rock Candy Baby."

DVD For some reason, Daddy—O still awaits its release on DVD; to be discovered all over again...

Dance Contest (GENRE CONVENTION) This rock

movie convention shares something in common with the battle of the bands. It's another field of battle, another arena in which teens and young people can compete to see who's best. And, of course, it also involves rock music.

Tony Manero (John Travolta) finds an upscale partner to dance in a disco contest at Brooklyn's 2001 Odyssey in *Saturday Night Fever* (1977). The prize is $500 and Tony wins, but he gives back the money and the trophy because he feels the contest was rigged; that a Latino dancing couple actually won.

In *Hairspray* (1988) and *Shag: The Movie* (1989), dance contests also figure prominently in the climax. (As it does in *Roller Boogie*, 1979, though there the dance contest is on roller skates.)

As late as *Dirty Dancing 2: Havana Nights* (2004), the dancing contest was resurrected to provide the film an exciting denouement.

Dazed and Confused (1993)(SNDTRK)

STARRING: Jason Landon (Randall 'Pink' Floyd); Rory Cochrane (Ron); Wiley Wiggins (Mitch); Sasha Jenson (Don); Adam Goldberg (Mike); Michelle Burke (Jodi); Matthew McConaughey (David); Joey Lauren Adams (Simone); Ben Affleck (Fred).

FILM EDITOR: Sandra Adair. DIRECTOR OF PHOTOGRAPHY: Lee Daniel. PRODUCED BY: Sean Daniels, James Jacks, Richard Linklater. WRITTEN AND DIRECTED BY: Richard Linklater. M.P.A.A. RATING: R. RUNNING TIME: 103 minutes.

A large ensemble cast including several future stars (including Matthew McConaughey, Parker Posey and Ben Affleck) is a highlight of Richard Linklater's comedic time capsule of the 1970s.

Dazed and Confused involves the high-school set of the Bicentennial year, as Texan adolescent students smoke dope, drink, fight, play games, haze underclassmen, and generally waste time. It's a loving evocation of the "malaise days" of the disco decade, buoyed by a clever script and its fine young cast. In essence, this is *American Graffiti* updated to focus not on Camelot, but the glory days of Gerald Ford and Jimmy Carter.

The film owes much of its success to its eclectic (and apparently expensive) constellation of seventies-era tunes. *Dazed and Confused* features more than two dozen compositions from the day of Whip Inflation Now (WIN) buttons, including "Sweet Emotion" (Aerosmith), "School's Out" (Alice Cooper), "Fox on the Run" (Sweet), "Cherry Bomb" (The Runaways), and "Summer Breeze" (Seals & Crofts).

DVD Available on DVD.

The Decline of Western Civilization (1981)(DOC)

STARRING: The Alice Bag Band, Black Flag, The Circle Jerks, Fear, Germ, X, Catholic Discipline.

FILM EDITOR: Charlie Mullin. DIRECTOR OF PHOTOGRAPHY: Steve Conant. PRODUCED BY: Jeff Prettyman, Penelope Spheeris. DIRECTED BY: Penelope Spheeris. M.P.A.A. RATING: R. RUNNING TIME: 100 minutes.

All together now: the title of this cult film is meant *ironically*. Director Penelope Spheeris (who shot two more films in this series and also the crowd pleaser *Wayne's World*, 1992) helmed this 1981 independent documentary to cast a light on the Los Angeles punk scene and clearly doesn't *really* believe that punk is contributing to the end of civilization. It's almost the opposite, actually.

The Decline of Western Civilization instead charts "*the revolution of music, the rise of a culture,*" and the movie remains a great artifact of its day (1979–1980), in part because no filmmaker had ever explored this particular territory before.

Some historians (and some punk rockers) have argued that *The Decline of Western Civilization* sensationalizes the life-style; that it's really about Spheeris' career ambitions not punk, and that it doesn't accurately reflect their punk aesthetic. Some have also accused Spheeris of "staging" particularly sequences, or giving a false impression through editing (cutting to an audience from one show during a performance at a different one).

To be fair, virtually every documentary film "fudges" things in ways like that. Take another look at *Don't Look Back* (1967) and you'll see Dylan "acting" throughout. Or Scorsese's *The Last Waltz* (1978) and you can detect the "myth-making" in action. To a large degree, every documentary is a reflection of the filmmaker's point-of-view, and *The Decline of Western Civilization* is no exception. And, it is unfailingly superb at what it does. Really, one can't help but admire a production in which song lyrics are translated via subtitles, as though punk rock is a foreign language.

The Decline of Western Civilization also proves unfailingly compelling as Spheeris' camera follows seven bands through rehearsal sessions, concert performance, and life itself. Some of the stories revealed here are heartbreaking, some are bizarre and others will rock you back on your heels.

For example, Darby Crash, who appears in the film, died months after the documentary was completed.

Black Flag performs "Revenge." The dreadful Alice Bag Band performs "Gluttony." The film also features "I Don't Care About You" by Fear, and X's appropriately titled "We Are Desperate." If you can find a video copy, see this movie; it is well worth tracking down. *Part II* (1998's *The Metal Years)* and *Part III* (1998) are also both out-of-print efforts, and ones which feature more familiar stars (such as Steven Tyler, Alice Cooper, Gene Simmons, Ozzy Osbourne, Poison), but it is the original *Decline* which captures the uneasiness, aggression, and revolutionary aspects of punk's early days.

(DVD) Not released on DVD. Old VHS copies can be found at exorbitant prices through secondhand resources.

Desperately Seeking Susan

(1985)(REAL ROCKER)(SNDTRK)

STARRING: Rosanna Arquette (Roberta); Aidan Quinn (Dez); Robert Joy (Jim); Mark Blum (Gary Glass); Laurie Metcalf (Leslie); Will Patton (Wayne Nolan); Madonna (Susan); John Turturro (Ray).

FILM EDITOR: Andrew Mondshein. DIRECTOR OF PHOTOGRAPHY: Edward Lachman. WRITTEN BY: Leora Barish. PRODUCED BY: Sarah Pillsbury, Midge Sanford. DIRECTED BY: Susan Seidelman. M.P.A.A. RATING: PG-13. RUNNING TIME: 104 minutes.

Madonna's big screen acting debut is a mistaken identity/trading places "comedy" set in New York. Bored suburban housewife Roberta Rosanna (Rosanna Arquette) follows the personal ads with obsessive focus, and comes upon one that strikes her fancy.

It reads: "*Desperately Seeking Susan. Keep the faith. Tuesday, 10:00 a.m. Battery Park, Gangway 1. Love Jim.*"

Roberta makes that rendezvous and begins to shadow Susan, a fly-by-the-seat-of-her-pants free spirit who has unknowingly stolen a pair of rare Egyptian earrings.

When Roberta is bonked on the head during a confrontation with the real thief of those earrings (Will Patton), she forgets her suburban life and husband (Gary Glass) and thinks she is Susan, the object of her obsession.

As "Susan," Roberta falls for hunky Dez (Aidan Quinn), and gets a job in a magic show. Meanwhile, Susan tracks down Roberta's husband and enjoys the suburban lifestyle of Fort Lee, New Jersey for a time. Everything finally rights itself at the magic club, as the stolen earrings are recovered, the thief is apprehended, Roberta leaves her dullard husband and stays with Dez, and Susan goes on her merry, anti-authority ways with boyfriend Jim.

Too long by about twenty minutes and burdened by a plot that was old in the 1930s, *Desperately Seeking Susan* is nonetheless a 1980s *cause celebre*. Madonna doesn't make a particularly strong impression as an actress, though millions of obsessed teenage girls of the time followed her every move and behavior (hence the Eighties trend of the Madonna Wannabe).

For a comedy, *Desperately Seeking Susan* isn't particularly funny, either, but the film was nonetheless the right vehicle at the right time to propel Madonna to greater heights. Overall, critics received the film warmly. Michael Musto at *Saturday Review* called *Desperately Seeking Susan* a "clever comedy of errors deftly directed by Susan Seidelman...The actors are so good that all the absurd plot twists seem to make perfect sense,"[19] and *Time*'s Richard Schickel termed the Madonna effort a "farcically fizzling movie that bursts with youthful high spirits yet still treats you like a functioning adult."[20]

On the film's soundtrack is Madonna's "Into the Groove," "(The Shoop Shoop Song) It's In His Kiss" by Betty Everett, Iggy Pop singing "Lust for Life," and Aretha Franklin belting out "Respect."

(DVD) Available on DVD.

Destruction of Property (GENRE CON-

VENTION) You can't really make a good rock movie unless your stars destroy personal property. It's a rule. And, it clearly establishes the *anti—authority* credentials of the damager.

In *The Who: The Kids Are Alright*, a montage is featured during which drummer Keith Moon ransacks a hotel room. The same film also reveals the band's propensity to smash guitars (and even totals up the cost to The Who for this destructive tic).

In D.A. Pennebaker's *Monterey Pop* (1968), Pete Townshend is back to his guitar-destroying tricks, but is one-upped by Jimi Hendrix who, following a performance of "Wild Thing," sprays fuel on his guitar and then sets it aflame.

In *Walk the Line* (2005), an angry Johnny Cash (Joaquin Phoenix) rips apart a bathroom, tugging a sink basin right out of the wall.

In *Don't Look Back* (1967), somebody who doesn't want to fess up (allegedly Joan Baez) is responsible for throwing a drinking glass out a window and angering Bob Dylan.

In both *Pink Floyd: The Wall* (1983) and *The Doors* (1991), rock stars (fictional character Pink and Jim Morrison, respectively), make wreckages of their hotel rooms, a seeming rite of passage for this demographic.

Detroit Rock City (1999)(SNDRTK)(CAMEOS)

STARRING: Edward Furlong (Hawk); Giuseppe Andrews (Lex); James DeBello (Trip); Sam Huntington (Jam); Melanie Lynskey (Beth); Nick Scotti (Kenny); Shannon Tweed (Amanda Finch); Miles Dougal (Elvis); Ron Jeremy (Emcee); Natasha Lyonne (Christine); Lyn Shay (Mrs. Bruce) and KISS—Gene Simmons, Paul Stanley, Ace Frehley, Peter Criss.

FILM EDITORS: Mark Goldblatt, Peter Schink. DIRECTOR OF PHOTOGRAPHY: John R. Leonetti. SCREENPLAY BY: Carl V. Dupre PRODUCERS: Gene Simmons, Barry Levine, Kathleen Haase. EXECUTIVE PRODUCERS: Brian Witten, Michael De Luca. DIRECTED BY: Adam Rifkin. M.P.A.A. RATING: R. RUNNING TIME: 95 minutes.

Four high school students in the 1970s—Hawk (Edward Furlong), Lex (Giuseppe Andrews), Trip (James DeBellow) and Jam (Sam Huntington)—will do absolutely *anything* (even strip down and beat each other up to appear the victims of crime) to attend a KISS rock concert in Detroit in this modern (and unofficial) updating of *Rock 'n' Roll High School*.

The film's central notion—that of a life-changing concert—isn't the only familiar element here; there is also a pair of comedic hall monitors who serve as a symbol of *authority* to overcome. The Ramones' "Blitzkrieg Bop" appears on the soundtrack of *Detroit Rock City*, and even more reminiscent of that Arkush film, a critical plot element here is a radio contest/giveaway for concert tickets. Also, Mark Goldblatt worked as an editor on both films.

Although an uncredited "homage" to a classic of the genre, Adam Rifkin's raucous film remains a high-flying hoot. *Detroit Rock City* opens with several glimpses of 1970s icons (Charlie's Angels, Jimmy Carter, the Fonz) and thus falls into the category of modern rock-nostalgia: evidencing a romanticism for the halcyon days when popular KISS merchandise included posable action figures, and rock competed with its evil twin brother, disco.

In one of the film's wittiest and silliest moments, Rifkin's camera cuts to a "tongue cam," adopting the perspective of Gene Simmon's oversized tongue and gazing out through the singer's mouth into the concert audience. That's a little *mise en scène* you don't see everyday.

Shots like this ramp up the fun aspects of the film. And in a word, that's precisely what this movie is. *Fun*. According to *Billboard*: "Furlong, Andrews, De Bello, and especially Huntington are all decent players and very likeable characters. For the inner teen in you, *Detroit Rock City* is a rocking good time. Like KISS, it's all good fun as long as one does not take it too seriously." [21]

Among the tunes on the soundtrack: "Ladies Room," "Shout it Out," "I Stole Your Love," and "Love Gun," all from KISS. From The Ramones comes the aforementioned "Blitzkrieg Bop" and "I Wanna Be Sedated." AC/DC's "Highway to Hell," The Sweet's "Fox on the Run," "Boogie Shoes" by KC and the Sunshine Band, and C.W. McCall's "Convoy" all contribute to the film's disco decade vibe.

Detroit Rock City also casts "Mom," not a *Bad Father,* as a villain. Here, it's Lyn Shaye as Mrs. Bruce, who heads the organization Mothers Against Music of KISS. And like the John Lithgow character in *Footloose*, Mrs. Bruce sees rock music as an affront against Jesus. Rebelling against Mrs. Bruce's authority, her son actually loses his virginity in a church.

(DVD) Available on DVD.

Dirty Dancing (1987)(SNDTRK)

STARRING: Jennifer Grey (Baby); Patrick Swayze (Johnny Castle); Jerry Orbach (Dr. Jake Houseman); Cynthia Rhodes (Penny); Jack Weston (Max).

EDITOR: Peter C. Frank. DIRECTOR OF PHOTOGRAPHY: Jeff Jur. WRITTEN BY: Eleanor Bergstein. PRODUCED BY: Linda Gottleib. DIRECTED BY: Emile Ardolino. M.P.A.A. RATING: PG-13. RUNNING TIME: 100 minutes.

Nobody puts Baby in a corner!

This is the 1987 sleeper film that made Patrick Swayze a household name. It stars a pre-plastic surgery Jennifer Grey as Baby, a seventeen-year old Jewish girl who spends the summer of 1963 in the Catskill Mountains at a resort with her family.

Once there, Baby falls in love with dark and dangerous Johnny Castle (Swayze), a man-in-black dance instructor. Over the course of the summer, Baby learns to dance and with Johnny's help, even to perform (when his regular partner suffers a botched abortion and needs time to recover). Baby's buttoned-down father, the late Jerry Orbach, objects to Johnny on principle (and also thinks he got his partner pregnant), but it proves to be a summer no one will ever forget.

At the time of its release, critics despised *Dirty Dancing* but audiences loved it and turned the film into a blockbuster. The film's soundtrack is loaded with a nostalgic rock'n'roll soundtrack. "Be My Baby" (The Ronettes), "Big Girls Don't Cry" (Frankie Valli and the Four Seasons), "Some Kind of Wonderful" (The Drifters), and "These Arms of Mine" (Otis Redding) are just a few of the non-original tunes on the soundtrack.

New tunes for the film include "She's Like the Wind," sung by Patrick Swayze and "(I've Had) The Time of My Life," performed by Bill Medley and Jennifer Warnes. (DVD) Available on DVD.

Dirty Dancing 2: Havana Nights (2004)(SNDTRK)

STARRING: Diego Luna (Javier Suarez). Ramola Garai (Katey Miller); Sela Ward (Jeannie Miller); John Slattery (Bert Miller); Jonathan Jackson (James Phelps); Patrick Swayze (Dance Instrutor).

FILM EDITOR: Luis Colina, Scott Richter. DIRECTOR OF PHOTOGRAPHY: Tony Richmond. STORY BY: Kate Gunzinger, Peter Sagal. WRITTEN BY: Boaz Yakin, Victoria Arch. PRODUCED BY: Lawrence Bender, Sarah Green. DIRECTED BY: Guy Ferland. M.P.A.A. RATING: PG-13. RUNNING TIME: 86 minutes.

"While the other girls were dancing to Elvis and dreaming about prom dates, I was dreaming of college and reading Jane Austen…"

With those evocative words (transmitted in voice over) begins *Dirty Dancing: Havana Nights*, the long-delayed sequel to the 1987 sleeper which grossed over $100 million at the box office. The follow-up film is very much a case of too little too late. By the time it was released (seventeen full years after the original) the pop culture zeitgeist had long since moved on to other things.

This handsomely produced 2004 movie is actually a prequel to the original film, not a sequel, since it is set in 1958 Cuba (pre-Castro; pre-revolution) and the original occurred in 1963. This film finds a nice American family moving to Havana (though the film was shot in Puerto Rico) and a teenage daughter, Katey (Garai) falling for a handsome Cuban waiter, Javier (Diego Luna).

This duo must overcome racial as well as political barriers to dance together, and Patrick Swayze makes an appearance (looking tired), to provide some advice. "*If you can't move through your fear and connect with yourself, there's absolutely no way you are going to connect with your partner,*" he advises.

Naturally, Katey and Javier start dancing at a hopping night club nearby (filled with sweaty Cubans perpetually grinding hips), and make plans to win an all-important *dance contest*. Dressed in black again, Swayze helpfully asks "*Who's gonna enter the big dance contest?*" as the plot creaks from hackneyed point to point.

Dirty Dancing: Havana Nights also features performances of "You Send Me" (Sam Cooke) and "Do You Wanna Dance?" (Bobby Freeman), but even the rock score isn't as memorable the second time around. For old time's sake, there's also a snippet of "(I Had) The Time of My Life." (DVD) Available on DVD.

Dogs in Space (1987)(BIO-PIC)(REAL ROCKER)

STARRING: Michael Hutchence (Sam); Saskia Post (Anna); Nique Needles (Tim); Deanna Bond (The Girl); Tony Helou (Luchio); Chris Heywood (Chainsaw Man); Peter Walsh (Anthony); Laura Swenson (Clare); Adam Briscomb (Grant).

FILM EDITOR: Jill Bilcock. DIRECTOR OF PHOTOGRAPHY: Andrew de Groot. PRODUCED BY: Glenys Rowe. DIRECTED BY: Richard Lowenstein. M.P.A.A. RATING: R. RUNNING TIME: 103 minutes.

Richard Lowenstein directed this apparently semi-autobiographical peek at the Melbourne punk rock scene in the late 1970s (particularly the summer of 1979, when pieces of the falling satellite Skylab were crashing in Western Australian towns).

Dogs in Space involves daily life in a weird commune-type house, where the various inhabitants experience strange lives, and come and go. One of the denizens is Sam, the lead singer of a group called "Dogs in Space," who externally lives the lifestyle not only of rock, but sex (with his girlfriend, Anna), and drugs (ditto; heroin). Sam is played by the late Michael Hutchence, the lead singer for the popular 1980s rock group INXS.

Other denizens in the house include a hippie couple, an engineering student, and a girl who happens to drop by and stick around for a while, and Lowenstein visits with each in a roving, almost Robert Altman-esque fashion. The film comments on David Bowie fans, features an overdose, and gazes at the self-obsessed Sammy, who doesn't quite live the "punk" scene as closely as others believe (he's a bit of a poser).

Dogs in Space is underscored by a number of rock tunes, and includes performances by Iggy Pop ("The Endless Sea," "Dogfood"), Gang of Four ("Love is Like Anthrax"), and the late Hutchence ("Rooms for the Memory," "Dogs in Space").

DVD Not Available on DVD.

Don't Look Back (1965)(DOC)

STARRING: Bob Dylan, Joan Baez, Donovan, Alan Price, Albert Grossman, Bob Neuwirth, Tito Burns, Derroll Adams.

CINEMATOGRAPHERS: Howard Alk, Jones Alk, Ed Emshwiller, D.A. Pennebaker. PRODUCED BY: Albert Grossman, John Court, Leacock-Pennabaker, Inc. WRITTEN AND DIRECTED BY: D.A. Pennebaker. M.P.A.A. RATING: UR. RUNNING TIME: 95 minutes.

"I feel like I've been through some kind of thing," Bob Dylan admits near the closing of D.A. Pennebaker's seminal *Don't Look Back*. Thanks to the director's cinema verité (or direct cinema) approach to the material, which stresses the concepts of life unfolding unrehearsed and live sound recording, rapt audiences will feel much the same way.

This documentary finds a young, wild-maned Dylan on his London tour of 1965 as he plays venues such as the Sheffield City Hall and the Royal Albert Hall. Many scenes find him hanging out with friends Joan Baez and Alan Price (**see: O Lucky Man!**) in a hotel room, and clashing with the press in a series of *press conferences*.

In these situations, the short-tempered Dylan is confronted with a series of stupid questions ("Do you care about people, really?," "Do young people understand what

Bob Dylan (left) and D.A. Pennebaker (right) prepare to shoot *Don't Look Back (1967)*, a cinema verité documentary of Dylan's British tour.

you're saying?," "Have you read the Bible?") and he tends to respond in hostile fashion, denigrating *Time* magazine and newspapers along the way. He feels that they don't publish the "plain truth," which to him is "a tramp vomiting" into the sewers. Later in the film, a science student attempts to interview the musician, and Dylan reveals a cruel streak by putting the young man down for a cringe-worthy five minutes.

Don't Look Back also gives the rock film one of its most fascinating *managers* in producer Albert Grossman. The camera watches as he verbally abuses a hotel manager when a problem with noise is reported by the patrons near Dylan's room. Later, Grossman sits in an office and ruthlessly plays the BBC against Granada TV, trying to raise Dylan's fee.

Don't Look Back opens with the famous shot of Dylan standing at the foreground of an alley flashing large cards with lyrics from "Subterranean Homesick Blues," and that's the only part of the film that appears to be overtly staged. The rest appears spontaneous and true (a gift of the form), though many critics over the years have suggested that Dylan isn't simply "being," but rather "acting" for the cameras (which puts him in the same class as Madonna in *Truth or Dare*).

On the liner notes for the laserdisc release of *Don't Look Back*, this is what Pennebaker had to say on that topic:

"It may not be so much about Dylan because Dylan is sort of acting throughout the film. And that's his right. He needs some protection in a sense against the process. But I think what you do find out a little bit is the extraordinary

pressure of having to go out and be absolutely perfect on call. That is, he had to fill a house. It wasn't just enough that he had to have every seat booked, he had to have standees. He had to be extraordinary where most of us settle for just being adequate."[22]

Pennebaker may have a valid point, but it also seems that the true Dylan sneaks through at points. He's a great talent, but like so many of us, insecure. The film reveals subtly how Dylan feels threatened and jealous of a competitor, Donovan. It also shows how seriously he takes his responsibilities. When there's a problem in the hotel and a drinking glass is thrown out a window, he interrogates his suitemates ruthlessly, understanding that the press will inevitably blame him for the infraction.

Also, the film makes clear the idea that the press doesn't know what to make of him. Some writers consider him a "poet, not a pop singer" while some see him as the latest "thing," the next Beatles sensation, and others attempt to pigeonhole him as an "anarchist." One senses that with Dylan, these labels are not only meaningless but actually offensive.

Cinema-verité filmmaking is especially efficacious at capturing the feeling that "you are there," and in *Don't Look Back*, the ubiquitous cameras capture everything from *stagecraft* disasters (a microphone that fails during a performance), to crazy fans (there's one screaming aficionado who won't get off the hood of Dylan's car...even when it's moving), to moving performances of Dylan tunes such as "Subterranean Homesick Blues," "The Times They Are A-Changin'," "Love Is a Four Letter Word," and "It's

Alright, Ma (I'm Only Bleeding"). The end result is a warts-and-all documentary and a gaze at greatness. This is a remarkable chronicle of a time, a place, and an icon. (DVD) Available on DVD.

Don't Knock the Rock (1956)

(MUS)(SNDTRK)

STARRING: Alan Dale (Arnie Haines); Patricia Hardy (Francine MacLaine); Alan Freed (Himself); Fay Baker (Arlene McLaine); Jana Lund (Sunny Everett); Pierre Watkin (Mayor); Bill Haley and his Comets, Little Richard, The Applejacks.

FILM EDITORS: Paul Borotsky, Edwin H. Bryant. DIRECTOR OF PHOTOGRAPHY: Benjamin Kline. WRITTEN BY: James B. Gordon, Robert E. Kent. PRODUCED BY: Sam Katzman. DIRECTED BY: Fred F. Sears. M.P.A.A. RATING: UR. RUNNING TIME: 84 minutes.

It's "*the Newest, Biggest Rock 'n' Roll Movie of All!*" This is the follow up to *Rock Around the Clock* (1956) and the story of rock star Arnie Haines (Alan Dale), who returns home to his sleepy little town for the summer only to run smack into the brick wall of intolerant *authority*, represented by the town mayor (Pierre Watkin), a man who has banned rock following a riot because he believes the music is a bad influence.

With the help of famous DJ Alan Freed (**see: *American Hot Wax***), Arnie arranges for a benefit dance that will show everyone, parents and local officials alike, that rock music is nothing to fear. To that ends, Bill Haley and His Comets arrange to play at the event, as does Little Richard.

Don't Knock the Rock is the second film featuring Haley and Freed together and comes replete with lip-synched performances of the titular tune "Don't Knock the Rock." This tune plays over the main credits (Haley and his Comets) and then in the body of the film, performed by star Dale.

Don't Knock the Rock is also the film that introduced Little Richard, and here the talent goes wild with his renditions of "Tutti Fruiti" and "Long Tall Sally." The Treniers are also on hand for the festivities, as are The Apple Jacks. (DVD) Not currently available on DVD.

The Doors (1991)(BIO-PIC)(CAMEOS)

STARRING: Val Kilmer (Jim Morrison); Meg Ryan (Pam Morrison); Kyle MacLachlan (Ray Manzarek); Frank Whaley (Robby Krieger); Kevin Dillon (John Densmore); Michael Wincott (Paul Rothschild); Michael Madsen (Tom Baker); Billy Idol (Cat); Dennis Burkley (Dog); Kathleen Quinlan (Patricia); Mimi Rogers (Photographer); Paul Williams (Himself); Crispin Glover (Andy Warhol).

FILM EDITORS: David Bremer, Joe Hutshing. DIRECTOR OF PHOTOGRAPHY: Robert Richardson. MUSIC PRODUCER: Paul A. Rothchild. WRITTEN BY: J. Randal Johnson, Oliver Stone. EXECUTIVE PRODUCERS: Mario Kassar, Nicholas Clamos, Brian Grazer. PRODUCED BY: Bill Graham, Sasha Haarari, A. Kitman Ho. DIRECTED BY: Oliver Stone. M.P.A.A. RATING: R. RUNNING TIME: 138 minutes.

Oliver Stone, the auteur behind *Platoon* (1986) and *JFK* (1991) turned from matters of national import to a matter of rock history with his sprawling, two-and-a-half hour

Jim Morrison bio-pic from 1991, *The Doors*. Although members of the Doors have quibbled with some of Stone's choices (and some facts presented in the film) the effort is an engaging, epic production headlined by a strutting Lizard King in the person of Val Kilmer (**see:** *Top Secret*). Kilmer eerily resembles Morrison in both form and voice and to this day his work here represents his finest film performance.

Stone's film commences in the New Mexico desert in 1949 (to the strains of "Riders on the Storm") as little Jim Morrison witnesses a terrible car accident and sees the bloodied survivors, including an Indian (Floyd Crow Westerman) with dead, hollowed eyes. After this unusual and portentous prologue, the film jumps to Venice Beach in 1966, where Morrison is an insecure young adult courting the lovely and supportive Pam (Meg Ryan), "the one" he believes can serve as his muse.

He then attends UCLA Film School and is a failure because he makes pretentious, bombastic student films that raise the ire of his film professor (Stone, in a cameo). The student films do serve their purpose, however, since they hook up Morrison with Ray (Kyle MacLachlan), his partner in The Doors. Ray appreciatively sees the Morrison films as "*non-linear,*" "*poetic,*" "*everything art stands for.*" Together, they embark on self-styled creative journey, with Robby Krieger and John Densmore, to "*make the myths,*" to swing open "*the doors of perception.*" Hence the name of the group. To put it in another way, the group soon becomes a latter-day international phenomenon just like The Beatles did several years earlier.

The Doors also focuses on the making of the group's most popular hit, "Light My Fire," noting that the original lyrics came from Robby (Frank Whaley), not Morrison. Stone's camera then follows the band to the blazing desert where each musician samples peyote and—in a trippy, self-important scene (set to the group's "The End")—Morrison once again encounters the Indian from earlier in the film, who represents both death and his spirit guide.

The Doors' fame next takes the young men from American television exposure (**see:** *The Ed Sullivan Show*), where Morrison refuses to compromise the lyrics to "Light My Fire," to the Andy Warhol/New York scene.

As the Sixties become the Seventies, Morrison becomes ever more befuddled and destroyed by his dependance on booze and drugs. He becomes abusive to Pam, and self-destructive. Before long he's so addled he can't maintain an erection and requires odd stimulation (including the drinking of human blood) to get it on with his wiccan mistress (a fetching Kathleen Quinlan).

Anyone with half-a-brain and a passing familiarity with the Doors' story will know where all this is leading, but *The Doors* lumbers messily (but compellingly) towards Jim Morrison's death in a Parisian bathtub in 1971. The film ends with a shot of Morrison's grave, an obscure little corner of earth soiled by graffiti. It's an inauspicious ending for a modern-day poet, but *The Doors*, despite its girth and sloppy pacing, makes plain the idea that Morrison lived his whole life with a sense of inadequacy; it was this belief that he was somehow a pretender that led him to destroy himself and the ones he loved.

Poignant and never less than visually stunning, *The Doors* remains a rock-film masterpiece, warts and all. Like it's subject matter, it feels bloated and over-important at times, a train wreck of monumental proportions, but hey, that's just form echoing content.

Stone skillfully captures the age of The Doors with his trademark attention to detail and obsessive focus. Rock movie fans looking for conventions of the format will recognize the *press conference*, the *destruction of property* and other clichés; but this familiarity with the tropes hardly matters when the soundtrack is so alive and delightful, and takes audiences back to the heyday of a classic group. The score includes: "Hello, I Love You," "Break on Through," "Light My Fire," "The End," "Love Me Two Times," "Back Door Man," "Touch Me," and "People Are Strange," all sung by Kilmer.

(DVD) Available on DVD.

Drop Dead Rock (1995)

(FIC BAND)(REAL ROCKER)(CAMEO)

STARRING: Shoshani Ami (Bonnie); Ian Maynard (Spazz-O); Chelsea Parks (Holly); Adam Ant (Dave Donovan); Deborah Harry (Thor).

FILM EDITING: Susan Graef. DIRECTOR OF PHOTOGRAPHY: David Hausen. WRITTEN BY: Adam Dubin, Ric Menello. PRODUCED BY: David L. Bushell. DIRECTED BY: David Dubin. M.P.A.A. RATING: PG. RUNNING TIME: 93 minutes.

This is an obscure and derivative comedy filled with scattershot jokes, that will be familiar to longtime fans of horror movies.

Here, a hopeless garage-style band called "Hindenburg" hatches a wacky scheme to get famous. They decide to kidnap the fading rock star Spazz-O (Ian Maynard) and make him listen to their music. It's sort of a rock version of Scorsese's *The King of Comedy* (1983). Unbeknownst to the daft members of Hindenburg, Spazz-O is already endangered, because he's worth more dead to his evil agent (real rocker Adam Ant) and his ex-porn-star wife, played by Chelsea Parks. Deborah Harry has an extended cameo playing a record company executive (and recovering alcoholic).

On the soundtrack: the immortal "Inseminator."

(DVD) Not Available on DVD.

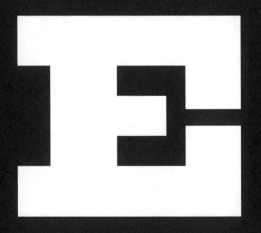

(is for *Eddie and the Cruisers*)

Easy Rider (1969)(SNDTRK)

STARRING: Peter Fonda (Wyatt/Captain America); Dennis Hopper (Billy/Billy The Kid); Antonio Mendoza (Jesus); Phil Spector (Connection); Jack Nicholson (George); Sabrina Scharf (Sarah).

FILM EDITOR: Donn Cambern. DIRECTOR OF PHOTOGRAPHY: Laszlo Kovacs. WRITTEN BY: Peter Fonda, Dennis Hopper, Terry Southern. PRODUCED BY: Peter Fonda, William Hayward, Bert Schneider. DIRECTED BY: Dennis Hopper. M.P.A.A. RATING: R. RUNNING TIME: 94 minutes.

Billy (Dennis Hopper), George (Jack Nicholson), and Captain America (Peter Fonda) tour America in the counterculture masterpiece, *Easy Rider*.

An odyssey across the highways and back roads of America; a motorcycle flick; a drug trip movie; a counterculture film. A film that defines a generation. And one that protests against a country that used to be great, but now?—*not so much*. Dennis Hopper's directorial debut, *Easy Rider* is all these things and much more.

It's the simple (but well-told) story of two guys on bikes, "Captain America" (Peter Fonda) and Billy (Dennis Hopper), and their journey from Los Angeles to Mardi Gras. Their *road trip* takes this duo to a commune, a whorehouse, and ultimately into a close encounter with bigotry, and finally, death.

A young, devilishly grinning Jack Nicholson appears in the film too in the role that made him a star. He plays likeable George, a drunken lawyer and all around great guy (the film's everyman), who comes, alas, to a bad end.

In fact, all the heroic *dramatis personae* come to a bad end in this film; and the explosive conclusion scared Yankees away from the South for years.

A high-water mark of the personal 1960s cinema (and replete with trippy location footage set at a Louisiana graveyard), *Easy Rider* remains famous for its soundtrack, which so brilliantly captured the thrill of the open highway.

Among the memorable tunes, "The Pusher" and "Born to Be Wild" by Steppenwolf, "If Six Was Nine" by the Jimi Hendrix Experience, "It's Alright Ma (I'm Only Bleeding)" written by Bob Dylan and performed here by Roger McGuinn, and "The Ballad of Easy Rider," also by McGuinn.

(DVD) Available on DVD.

If you want to make a rock movie,

stage at least one scene on this guy's show. It's the ubiquitous Ed Sullivan.

The Ed Sullivan Show (GENRE CONVEN-

TION) This variety show shot at CBS-TV Studio 50 in New York ran from 1948 to 1971, and was known originally as "Toast of the Town." The series, which aired Sunday nights at 8:00 p.m., is important in the annals of rock history because the program and its host were early and frequent supporters of the genre.

In 1955, Bill Haley and His Comets appeared on this CBS series and many scholars consider this billing the first example of rock 'n' roll on television.

On September 9, 1956, Elvis Presley appeared on *The Ed Sullivan Show* for the first time (though it was hosted that night by Charles Laughton and still titled *Toast of the Town*). The program reeled in over 60 million viewers.

Elvis returned to the show for two further appearances, and in one, Ed Sullivan gave Presley his explicit blessing, thus taking some wind from the sails of disapproving parents who feared the King's gyrating pelvis.

When The Beatles appeared on the Sullivan show on February 9, 1964, the ratings again proved stellar. Later, acts such as The Doors (September 17, 1967) and The Rolling Stones were also introduced to a vast swath of middle America through Mr. Sullivan's auspices.

Given *The Ed Sullivan Show*'s importance in rock history, it's only natural that several films, especially those based on real rockers, would feature bands appearing on the program.

Robert Zemeckis' *I Wanna Hold Your Hand* (1978) concerns The Beatles' first appearance, as a group of teenage girls comedically attempt to acquire tickets for the show.

In Oliver Stone's bio-pic *The Doors*, a controversial real-life incident is re-staged. In particular, Jim Morrison (played by Val Kilmer) refuses to change the sexually suggestive lyrics of "Light My Fire" (specifically the phrase "girl, we couldn't get much *higher*) to accommodate TV's standards and practices, and reportedly made an enemy of Sullivan in the process.

Sullivan has been portrayed on film frequently by actor Will Jordan, who essayed the role of the popular host in *The Buddy Holly Story* (1978), *I Wanna Hold Your Hand* (1978), *The Doors* (1991), the TV-movie *Elvis* (1979), and the non-rock film, *Down with Love* (2003).

"I remember seeing Elvis on *Ed Sullivan*," describes *Rock 'n' Roll High School* director Allan Arkush. "I thought it was really exciting. He was terrific. But when I saw The Beatles I was already in high school, and *that* galvanized the entire school. That's all anybody could talk about the next day."

Eddie and the Cruisers (1983)

(FIC BAND)

STARRING: Michael Paré (Eddie Wilson); Ellen Barkin (Maggie Foley); Tom Berenger (Frank Ridgway); Joe Pantoliano (Doc Robbins); Matthew Laurance (Sal Amato); Helen Schneider (Joann Carlino); David Wilson (Kenny Hopkins); Michael Antunes (Wendell Newton).

FILM EDITOR: Priscilla Nedd. DIRECTOR OF PHOTOGRAPHY: Fred Murphy. ORIGINAL MUSIC: John Cafferty. SCREENPLAY BY: Martin Davison and Arlene Davidson. BASED UPON THE NOVEL BY: P.F. Kluge. EXECUTIVE PRODUCERS: Rich Levine, James L. Stewart. PRODUCED BY: Joseph Brooks, Robert K. Lifton. DIRECTED BY: Martin Davidson. M.P.A.A. RATING: PG. RUNNING TIME: 92 minutes.

A rock 'n' roll movie classic from the eighties, *Eddie and the Cruisers* —which critic Kevin Cahillane described as "alternately rollicking and melancholy,"[23]—is another example (like *Rock 'N' Roll High School* and *This Is Spinal Tap*) of a film that failed financially in its original release, but very soon developed a devoted following.

"Yes, *Eddie* became what is called a cult film," director Martin Davidson agrees. "I usually think that relates to films that didn't make enough money."

The director recalls how he became involved in the project that came to prove so popular. "I optioned [the novel], with my own financing, which was a big risk for me. I wrote it and adapted it to the screenplay, and fortunately I made a deal with a company called Time-Life that went into the film business."

Unfortunately, Time-Life also quickly went *out* of the film business.

"They closed the doors on us. After two movies that didn't make a lot of money, they just shut the doors and everybody was sent home," Davidson remembers. "However, I just got incredibly lucky. I went out to dinner within a couple of nights after that—and I was still devastated—and I ran into a friend of mine, who had been a secretary on the first movie I ever made She had always been very nice to me, and I hadn't seen her in years. There she was in this restaurant, and she said to me '*What are you doing?*' And I said, '*Oh, you caught me at a bad time, I just had my picture pulled out from under me. Time-Life just shut down.*'"

This old acquaintance took Davidson's script for *Eddie and the Cruisers* back to her business partners, and very soon, a deal was tendered with Davidson slotted to make the film for $6 million. "Never in my life had I had an experience like this," Davidson reveals. "Usually for me making a movie is a struggle that takes a year or a year-and-a-half and you have every kind of disappointment you could possibly ever experience, like the one at Time-Life. I was set for a journey, and now in forty-eight hours someone was telling me they were going to put up the money."

"It was a company called Aurora," Davidson details. "It was two guys who had worked at Disney and decided they wanted to produce movies. They went out kind of like Tupperware salesmen, house by house throughout the country, and people were throwing dinner parties and these two guys came in to do their dog and pony act and said they were going to make three movies and they needed $18 million."

The three movies Aurora made were *The Secret of NIMH* (1982), *Heart Like a Wheel* (1983), and Davidson's *Eddie and the Cruisers*.

Now that Davidson had backing, the director was intent on making a good movie, and to that end, imbued *Eddie and the Cruisers* with a *Citizen Kane*–style story structure (**see:** *Velvet Goldmine*).

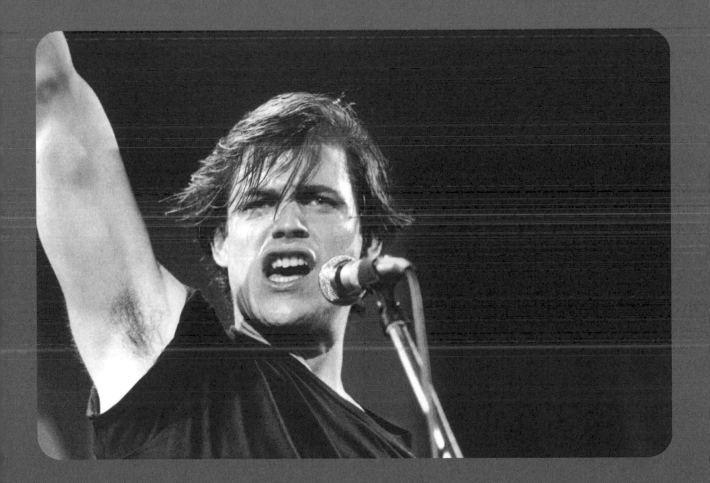

Rock on! It's the enigmatic (and inscrutable) Eddie Wilson

(charismatic Michael Paré) of *Eddie and the Cruisers* (1983).

"That was the intent of it. That was the conceit. When I decided to write the screenplay, which is a little different from the novel, I used the *Citizen Kane* structure. That was in my head: *the search*. The whole use of the Ellen Barkin character going back in history. That whole experience of a reporter who goes back and says, 'What does it all mean?'"

Settling on this format was an easy decision compared to the next one. To wit: How do you make a fictional band come to life, with authentic songs that sound like they could be legitimate hits?

"Who are Eddie and the Cruisers? What do they sound like? What does the hit 'On the Dark Side' sound like?" Davidson asks rhetorically, making his case.

"I worked with this guy Kenny Vance on *Eddie and the Cruisers*. He was one of the original Jay and the Americans. So he came by to see me and showed me his scrapbook and the places they performed, the car they drove around in, and how they transported their instruments. He told me stories and I would incorporate whatever I could into the script, and I just adored this guy Kenny Vance. I asked him if he would come in and help me do the music for the picture, and he was thrilled to do that. He said to me, '*Describe the band. What is the music? Are the actors actually going to do the singing?*'

"I said '*most probably not. From what I'm seeing I can't find four different guys, put 'em together in the amount of time I have and hope they can not only act, but sing.*'"

"Again, he said, '*Describe to me what the sound is.*' And the best I could do is say the following: the band members met in high school and they probably sang in the school hallways and under train trestles and in the auditorium, wherever they could find themselves a good echo. They didn't write original compositions, or anything, so they were doing cover songs.

"I said, '*The sound I hear is Dion and the Belmonts, like 'Runaround Sue.*' So it starts out that they are Dion and the Belmonts. That's who Eddie really is. Then the group evolves and Eddie decides he wants to do something special; he falls in love with the lyrics but he can't write the lyrics, so he needs the Tom Berenger character, the word man. He knows he needs someone to give him the poetry he hears in his head but can't put down on paper."

"At this point he's Jim Morrison and The Doors," Davidson suggests. "They're after a sound that may be ahead of its time, that has poetry, and the lyrics mean more. So Dion becomes Jim Morrison. And, I said '*We shouldn't lose sight of the idea that they are in fact and always will be a Jersey bar band. That's where they perform. It isn't for huge concerts.*'"

"The only thing I could think of was Bruce Springsteen and the E Street Band. That's the epitome of rock 'n' roll, Jersey rock bands. So I said '*Find me something that gives me those three groups, then we'll have Eddie and the Cruisers.*'"

"Kenny laughed and said, '*I'll go do that boss.*' And I said '*I'm serious. That's the sound. I don't know how else to describe it for you.*'"

Tasked with a seemingly impossible mission, Vance actually came back with just the band Davidson had imagined.

"We were getting close to rehearsals, and we were in

Cherry Hill, New Jersey when Kenny calls me up from Manhattan. He says, '*I've got the band for you. And I said, you have it? Send them here!*' He said, '*I can't do that. They're a Providence, Rhode Island band. They're performing at midnight. I'll fly up from New York and you fly up from Philadelphia and I'll meet you there.*' And I said, '*You're crazy. I'm not going to fly, I'm exhausted.*' And he said, '*I already have the airline, call these people and they'll get you there in an hour and get you home after the show.*' He said, '*Marty, this is it!*'

Davidson relented and with about five cohorts flew a Lear jet up to Providence. "It was one of those strange nights with fog, and we landed at a small airport and there appeared an old Lincoln like the one JFK was shot in. It pulled up with some long-haired roadie behind the wheel, right there on the tarmac. And he said, '*Come on, hop in, we've got an hour.*' And I said, '*We've got an hour drive?*' And he said, '*Yeah, they're waiting for you.*' It was about 11:00 p.m.

"What he didn't tell me was that we were 100 miles away. So we were *flying*. We were going a 100 miles-an-hour in this foggy, strange night in this old Lincoln with seven of us in the car, and we got to this out of the way bar somewhere outside of I-don't-know-where Providence. There must have been five hundred cars there at midnight on a weeknight. We walked in and the whole house was waiting for us. And the band wouldn't go on until we got there."

"It was John Cafferty and the Beaver Brown Band," Davidson reveals. "They came out and I looked at them and it was almost the exact makeup of the guys we had

written into our script, right down to our black saxophone player. So we come in, the show starts, and I go crazy. I can't believe what I'm hearing, I just loved these guys. {After the show] I went backstage and I said '*I want you to be the sound of Eddie and the Cruisers,*' and they were thrilled. Over the course of the next month, they came back to Jersey with me and we made the deal with them."

After shooting the movie, which stars Michael Paré, there was a scheduling glitch, however, and a movie that had been intended for a summer release (before Labor Day) was consigned to the no-man's land of late September, when the primary audience (teenagers) would be back in school."

Not surprisingly, *Eddie and the Cruisers* bombed.

"It did absolutely no business," Davidson relates. "They pulled it from the theatres after three weeks. And they pulled all the ads after one week. That was the end of that. I forgot about it basically. It broke my heart, because I thought we had a picture that would play and it did nothing."

But the last chapter hadn't been written yet. "Then July 4TH weekend comes seven months later, and I get a call from this fellow at CBS Records, which released the soundtrack album, and he says '*Do you have any idea what's going on with your movie?*' And I said, '*No, what do you mean?*' And he said, '*It's going through the roof. It's been on HBO for a week, and it's unbelievable.*'

"He says, '*Let me give you an example: when the picture opened we were selling about 5,000 records a week. We sold about 50,000 records all together. We're gonna sell 50,000 records tomorrow! We're going to sell 100,000 this week*."

"We sold three million albums over the course of HBO's play dates," says Davidson, "which only showed me that if they had released the picture theatrically [in the summer]—given it a chance—it would have hit. One of our songs, nine months after the film opened, "On the Dark Side" became the number one song in the country. That's the sadness about the picture. It is a cult film, but it's a cult film based on television, on cable, on DVD sales, and on record sales. That picture should have been a theatrical success. There was an audience for it. People still watch it and still tell me about it.

"A lot of people discover it, and it seems more real today," Davidson considers. "I remember when people saw the movie, they would say, 'Was there really a group called *Eddie and the Cruisers?*' and they weren't sure if there was a group. Now if they hear 'On the Dark Side,' they say, '*I remember that, that really was number one.*' But it was number one *twenty* years ago, not *forty* years ago. The fiction has become a reality."

That reality is that *Eddie and the Cruisers* is a fascinating mystery filled with some great music, enthusiastically performed. The *Citizen Kane*-structure grants the film an epic feel, the feel of a legend, and Paré is dynamic and charismatic as the lead singer. This is one of those minor rock-movie miracles; a film that has stood the test of time and outlived its own historical context (and theatrical failure). DVD Available on DVD.

Eddie and The Cruisers II: Eddie Lives! (1989)(FIC-BAND)(SNDTRK)

STARRING: Michael Pare (Eddie Wilson/Joe West); Marina Orsini (Diane); Bernie Coulson (Rick Diesel); Matthew Laurance (Sal Amato); Michel Rhoades (Dave Pagent); Anthony Sherwood (Hilton).

WRITTEN BY: Charles Zev Cohen, Rick Doehring. PRODUCED BY: Wendy Grean, William Stuart. DIRECTED BY: Jean Claude-Lord. M.P.A.A. RATING: PG-13. RUNNING TIME: 104 minutes.

This is the 1989 theatrical sequel to the hit *Eddie and the Cruisers*, and an unnecessary one at that. The film finds the rock star Eddie Wilson (Michael Paré, again) back in the saddle, performing under a different name with a different band, in Montreal. But things get complicated for the rugged rocker when those pesky "Season in Hell" tapes again raise a popular ruckus and Eddie's identity is once more a hot topic. Jean Claude-Lord directs the flick.

"I was offered Two but I wanted no part of it. I thought it was absurd. I don't like sequels," original director Martin Davidson says about *Eddie Lives!* "And then the people who were making the sequel were not the producers of the [original] movie, the two guys from Aurora. They had sold the rights. The Scotti Bros. released the album and they had a deal with CBS Records, but it [the movie] came out on the Scotti Bros. label. They considered themselves to be music mavens. They called me in and asked me if I'd come in and talk about it [the sequel]."

"They wanted me to write it and direct it, but basically they were going to show me how to *really* make a movie.

The head brother had a home in Paris and he wanted Eddie to go to Paris, and asked if I would write the script set in Paris. And I said, '*Rock 'n' Roll in Paris? No, I don't see that.*' I could see London, because that's where the music went to after Eddie, with The Beatles and the Stones. And he said '*What about Johnny Holiday?*' And I said '*Gimme a break, maybe you should do this without me.*'

In addition to Paré, Matthew Laurance also returned for the follow-up.

"Everybody called me basically to see if it was okay with me that they do it. I said, 'By all means. It's your livelihood, if you want to do it, go do it,'"Davidson reports. "They all came to my house and asked me to do it with them, and I didn't want to be a part of it.

"It opened on a Friday afternoon, and my wife and I went to see it." But what Davidson saw on screen shocked him. "They had stolen a lot of footage. They had taken a number of scenes out of *Eddie and the Cruisers* that were in this movie, the sequel, without paying for them or anything. It was the strangest experience to see all these people and film I had actually shot in this other movie that someone else did with a totally different sensibility. I think they shot the whole picture in Canada."

Probing a little deeper into the Eddie mystique, Davidson provides a very good argument why a sequel was unwarranted. "I had no answer to "Rosebud" [the answer to whether Eddie was alive; and why he had stayed out of the spotlight]. I just wanted it to live on. I wanted the memory to live. I wanted you to *not* know. I wanted it to be vague; the whole Jim Morrison idea of '*Is he alive, did he kill himself?*' That's rock 'n' roll lure and legend. I thought the more mystery I can attach to this, the better off I'll be.

"When you get the answer, you're usually disappointed. That's why I didn't want to give it to you," Davidson laughs. "If you can get people walking out of the theatre and they can go get coffee and say '*Well, what do you think?*'...you have made a movie. That's all you can ask for; that the characters have a life that goes beyond the end."

(DVD) Eddie and the Cruisers II has not yet had an official DVD release in the U.S., though it has played on HBO in 2006.

Eegah! (1962)(HORR)

STARRING: Arch Hall Jr. (Tom Nelson), Marilyn Manning (Roxy); Richard Kiel (Eegah); William Watters (Robert Miller).

FILM EDITOR: Don Schneider. DIRECTOR OF PHOTOGRAPHY: Vilis Lapenieks. WRITTEN BY: Arch Hall Sr., Bob Wehling. PRODUCED AND DIRECTED BY: Arch Hall Sr. M.P.A.A. RATING: UR. RUNNING TIME: 90 minutes.

A classic bad movie and yet another one resurrected for the modern pop culture by *Mystery Science Theatre 3000*.

This low-budget effort stars Richard Kiel (later the steel-toothed assassin Jaws in *The Spy Who Loved Me*, 1976, and *Moonraker*, 1979) as a prehistoric man, Eegah, who wanders out of his cave in the desert near Palm Springs, California one night and abducts both a scientist (William Watters) and his daughter, a comely lass named Roxy (Marilyn Manning). This turn of events requires that budding guitar hero Tommy (Arch Hall, Jr.) save the day. But in between rescue chores in the desert, the 16 year-old star gets to belt out a rock tune or two with his band, the "Archers."

Their most infamous song is "Nobody Lives on the Brownsville Road," which Tommy performs at a hotel pool the night Eegah comes down from the desert to steal his girl.

Earlier in the picture, Tommy also sings "Vicki" poolside while Roxy cavorts in the water in her brand-new bathing suit.

(DVD) Available on DVD.

Elvis (1935–1977)(ROCK MOVIE OF HALL OF FAME)

Quite simply, Elvis Aaron Presley is the one, true King of Rock 'n' Roll. Although other notable talents in the 1950s matriculated to the screen before he did (namely Bill Haley in *Rock Around the Clock*, 1956), this charming, charismatic, and ruggedly handsome Southern performer is nonetheless considered the first major rock star in history, and definitely the first rock-movie star.

Born in Tupelo, Mississippi in 1935, Elvis unveiled his first rock album when he was still under twenty years old. By the time Elvis was just twenty-one, he had a number one hit in "Heartbreak Hotel" under his belt. By 1957, at 22, the King's career in Hollywood had commenced in earnest. His freshman film was the Civil War era epic *Love Me Tender* (1956), which had been hastily re-titled to take advantage of Presley's burgeoning popularity.

Following that successful initiative, Elvis appeared in over two dozen films in the following fifteen years. Not all these efforts were good choices, but Presley routinely left business decisions in the hands of his controversial manager, Colonel Tom Parker.

Reportedly, Presley lost the lead role in *West Side Story* (1960), a major movie musical directed by the great Robert Wise, due to Parker's lack of foresight. The Colonel apparently preferred that his most famous client appear in mostly innocuous romantic dramas that featured some light singing and dancing. Nothing too scandalous to inflame the masses.

Accordingly, the Elvis Presley movie canon is not necessarily highly regarded among critics, and that's because various films tend to blunt the King's wicked edge. The artist was universally famous for wriggling his pelvis and hips, and gyrating at fast speed, so much so that his body motions were considered scandalous. Yet in his movies, Elvis rarely performs his most famous or popular, "sexual" moves. His movies are very much a case of Presley de-fanged.

Instead, many of Elvis' pictures find him playing a "white bread" character, a bland, mainstream American protagonist (usually with very basic, heartland-sounding names such as Deke Rivers, Mike Edwards, Vince Everett, Mike Windgren, and Danny Fisher). Early on, a workable formula was cemented for these films, and after that nobody tampered with it. Even when it begged for change.

The first part of that successful formula involves Elvis' relationship and interaction with children. In a number of films, including *Girls! Girls! Girls!* (1962), *Paradise, Hawaiian Style* (1966) and especially *It Happened at the World's Fair* (1963), Elvis is deliberately teamed on-screen for a time with cute-as-a-button children. He sings to that child, dances with him or her, and generally proves to audiences he is a responsible and decent fellow. In other words, the message to parents was—*you can trust Elvis with your children*. Don't fear the Pelvis.

The other element in the Elvis formula finds the fickle King forced to choose between two women of vastly different personal qualities. One woman is always a sexually-knowledgeable, almost feral *femme fatale* who appeals to the King's lusty, naughty side. The other woman is a virtual innocent (and usually blond), a "good girl" who would make a fine wife to bring home to mother.

In *King Creole* (1958), Elvis is forced to choose between the hot to trot, sexually-ravenous Carolyn Jones and the sweet five-and-dime waitress, a blond named Nellie (Dolores Hart). Here, the *femme fatale* conveniently dies, making Elvis' choice a *fait accompli*.

Similarly, in *Fun in Acapulco* (1963), Elvis must select from a kindly (but gorgeous) foreign heiress played by Ursula Andress and a powerful, aggressive female bullfighter, Dolores (Elsa Gardenas). The latter undergoes a last-minute personality alteration and proves to be mean to Elvis, so again, his choice is clear. This was also the dynamic in *Girls! Girls! Girls!* (featuring bad girl Stella Stevens and good girl Laurel Goodwin), as well as other Presley pictures.

In all his films, Elvis' protagonists prove to be quite versatile. He always played a man capable of virtually any feat, including racing cars (*Speedway*, 1968,), flying helicopters (*Paradise, Hawaiian Style*), boxing (*Kid Galahad*, 1962) and cliff-diving (*Fun in Acapulco*). And yet there's always time to sing too. This may be why many Elvis fans see the man as something of a superhero or messianic figure. Like James Bond, there's nothing this idol can't do.

Even considering the dramatic range of these professions, Elvis' characterizations boil down to two basic character-types. He could play a rebellious sort (*King Creole, Wild in the Country*, 1961) or a basically harmless stud, singing and dancing his way through life (*Clambake*, 1967, *Paradise, Hawaiian-Style*).

Despite his films' narrative and pacing flaws, Elvis was—contrary to many opinions—a pretty good actor; and one who could hold the screen seemingly by force of an unearthly, remarkable charisma.

Elvis played comedy well in *Follow That Dream* (1967), and convincingly nursed psychological wounds in *Wild in the Country*. Few people remember this today, but Elvis could also express dynamic passion, particularly in his earlier work like *Jailhouse Rock* (1957) and the aforementioned *King Creole*. It's just a shame he never was in better, more involving films.

By the latter days of his film career, Elvis began to succumb to the ridiculous story lines he was forced to vet, and by appearances, seemed to give up; merely walking through roles.

An example of this characteristic comes in *Harum Scarum* (1965) which sees the King portray a matinee idol abducted by Arabs in an exotic Middle East country, forced to become an assassin. It was an utterly ridiculous plot, but at least it made use of Elvis' physicality. He was always convincing in a fight (Elvis had a black belt in karate), just as he was in romancing the ladies.

Another commonality: Elvis' films tend to feature a harmless secondary male lead, a good-looking guy who isn't quite handsome enough to actually threaten the King's superiority. Bill Bixby (*Speedway*) and Gary Lockwood (*It Happened at the World's Fair*) occasionally filled out these "best friend" roles.

By the 1970s, Elvis had successfully put his middling film career behind him and went whole hog into the documentary format instead. Fitter and more dynamic than ever, he released a terrific concert film entitled *Elvis: That's the Way It Is* in 1970, and later *Elvis on Tour* (1972).

The King died tragically young, in August 1977. His untimely passing was mourned by fans across the globe, and yet Elvis' impact on the film world would still be felt for years—even decades—to come.

Elvis Presley impersonators have appeared in films including *Honeymoon in Vegas* (1992), and the Kurt Russell/Kevin Costner crime adventure *3000 Miles to Graceland* (2001).

Presley has also appeared as a fantasy figure in the sweet Chris Columbus comedy, *Heartbreak Hotel* (1988) and a messiah of sorts in *Finding Graceland* (1998). An aging Elvis, played by horror icon Bruce Campbell, even battles a soul-sucking mummy in a nursing home in Don Coscarelli's *Bubba Ho-tep* (2002).

Elvis has also appeared as a character in a variety of rock biographies. In *Great Balls of Fire* (1989), Elvis appears competitive with Jerry Lee Lewis, and tells him (on the eve of being shipped out to West Germany), that the title of Rock King falls to him. In 2005's *Walk the Line*, it is Elvis, according to the film, who first introduces "The Man in Black," Johnny Cash to amphetamines.

Many of Elvis' films were produced by Hal B. Wallis, and featured the Jordanaires supplying back-up vocals. Norman Taurog was a frequent director.

In 1981, *This is Elvis* was released with the blessing of the Presley estate. This is a pseudo-documentary featuring actors "playing" Elvis at various ages. Some critics, including Pauline Kael, quibbled with the technique of mixing ham-handed fictionalized "scenes" with authentic footage.

Considering his multiple appearances in biographies, horror pictures, fantasies, and comedies, it's fair to state that no other rock star has matched the impact of Elvis Presley. His moniker "King" turns out not to be an exaggeration at all.

Elvis on Tour (1972)(DOC)(ELVIS)

STARRING: Elvis Presley, James Burton, Joe Esposito, Glen Hardin, Charlie Hodge, The Stamps.

FILM EDITORS: Bert Lovitt, Martin Scorsese, Ken Zemke.
CINEMATOGRAPHERS: Michael A. Brown, David Myers.
WRITTEN, PRODUCED AND DIRECTED BY: Robert Abel, Pierre Adidge. M.P.A.A. RATING: G. RUNNING TIME: 93 minutes.

Martin Scorsese was one of the editors on this impressive chronicle, which nabbed a Golden Globe Award for best documentary. The footage of Elvis (looking slightly heavier than in his previous concert film, *Elvis: That's the Way It Is*) in front of a live (and enthusiastic) audience is taken from his tour across Texas, Virginia, Ohio, and North Carolina in 1971.

Some of The King's performances here are cut to montages (using split screens and other stylistics) from his many films, a technique which makes an emotional impact—and could make you nostalgic for the likes of *It Happened at The World's Fair* or his other work.

Elvis sings over two dozen songs, including covers of "Proud Mary," "Johnny B. Goode," and "Bridge Over Troubled Water." He also sings his most famous hits including "Love Me Tender" and "Blue Suede Shoes," and adds some fresh material too, including "An American Trilogy" and "Burning Love."

All in all, this is quite a good concert film, and it represents Elvis' final screen appearance. There's some behind-the-scenes stuff and footage of Elvis going back and forth from car to venue to dressing room and the like, but it's for his on-screen performances that this film is remembered.

DVD Available on VHS.

Elvis: That's the Way It Is (1970)
(DOC)(CAMEOS)(ELVIS)

STARRING: Elvis Presley, Richard Davis, Joe Esposito, Joe Guercio, Charles Hodge, Felton James, Millie Kirkham, Jerry Scheff.

FILM EDITOR: Henry Berman. DIRECTOR OF PHOTOGRAPHY: Lucien Ballard. PRODUCED BY: Dale Hutchinson, Herbert F. Solow. DIRECTED BY: Denis Sander. M.P.A.A. RATING: PG. RUNNING TIME: 97 minutes

This is the modified DVD version of the original 1970 documentary. This edition removes much of the material from the old theatrical version (which no longer remains in print). What's lost? In particular, many interviews with enthusiastic and occasionally obsessive fans. This revamped version of *Elvis: That's The Way It Is* instead accents Elvis' concert performances rather than background detail and interviews.

This concert film is actually culled from several concerts (half a dozen, to be precise) Elvis gave to adoring crowds during his gig at the International Hotel in Las Vegas in 1969. The films reveals some rehearsals too with his back-up artists, but in essence, this is Elvis in his come-back phase, re-booted, tanned, rested and ready to go (no scripted hokiness to spoil things, thank goodness).

Elvis flashes his trademark charm and plays lightly with the crowd, humbly joking about live-audience jitters. Ever likeable, Elvis sings a number of tunes, including early material such as "Hound Dog."

Other tunes in the film: "Sweet Caroline," "Can't Help Falling in Love With You," "That's All Right, Mama," "Blue

Suede Shoes," "Mystery Train," "Suspicious Minds," "In the Ghetto," "Love Me Tender," and "All Shook Up." In all, Elvis sings over twenty songs, some of which didn't appear in the original 1970 release but were re-inserted after lost footage was recently found.

Don't go in expecting this to be the ultimate behind-the-scenes documentary on Elvis, because, quite frankly, that animal doesn't exist. This is all about showmanship, and about Elvis getting past the baggage of weak Hollywood films that saddled him with bubble gum soundtracks. The King looks fine on stage, and his energy level is high.

(DVD) Available on DVD.

Empire Records (1995)(SNDTRK)

STARRING: Anthony La Paglia (Joe); Maxwell Caulfield (Rex Manning); Debi Mazar (Jane); Rory Cochrane (Lucas); Johnny Whitworth (A.J.); Robin Tunney (Debra); Renée Zellweger (Gina); Liv Tyler (Corey Mason); Ethan Randall (Mark); Brendan Sexton (Warren); James Wills (Eddie); Tobey Maguire (Andre).

FILM EDITOR: Michael Chandler. DIRECTOR OF PHOTOGRAPHY: Walt Lloyd. WRITTEN BY: Carol Heikkinen. PRODUCED BY: Arnon Milchan, Michael Nathsonson, Alan Richie, Tony Ludwig. DIRECTED BY: Allan Moyle. M.P.A.A. RATING: PG-13. RUNNING TIME: 91 minutes.

"*They're selling music, but not selling out*," blared one ad-line for this 1995 comedy from Allan Moyle, the director of *Times Square* (1980) and *Pump Up the Volume* (1990).

Empire Records is somewhere in the middle range of that trifecta, a goofy but not entirely unamusing Clinton-era teenage comedy about a group of young record store employees who work for Joe (Anthony La Paglia) an understanding boss who has been resisting a corporate take-over by an evil chain called "Music Town Records," an outfit with stringent rules including a dress code (no revealing outfits) and code of conduct (no chewing gum). Unfortunately, Joe's good efforts have been undercut by the odd bird named Lucas (Rory Cochrane), a troubled young employee who steals Joe's money after closing one night and gambles it all ($9,104) in an attempt to make more money to prevent the takeover.

The next day, Joe is livid to learn what has occurred, but that's only the beginning of his troubles. Each of the employees at Empire Records has chosen this day to undergo his or her own personal teen crisis.

Debra (Robin Tunney), who has shorn her locks in a bid to look like Sinead O'Connor, is a dark, lonely teen obsessed with suicide, and she's "tired of being invisible."

Gina (a young Renée Zellweger) is a slut who will sleep with anyone but in truth feels bad about herself.

Liv Tyler (daughter of Aerosmith's Steve Tyler) plays Corey Mason, a smart college-bound girl who occasionally takes uppers to stay on top of things and is nursing a major league crush on rock star Rex Manning...who just happens to be coming to Empire Records for a book signing that very day!

A.J. (Johnny Whitworth), an aspiring artist, has been bitten by the love bug and is smitten with Corey. He just can't tell her how he feels…until he works up the courage.

Finally, Ethan Randall (**see:** *That Thing You Do!*, 1996) plays an all-around dork named Mark who likes to hop around the store listening to hard heavy metal.

These various and sundry personal failings and issues come to light in a day that will see friendships questioned, destroyed and rebuilt. In the final act, the record store gang bands together one more time to save Empire Records from the evil corporation (**see: Authority**). Accordingly, the movie climaxes with true love triumphant as Corey and A. J. finally admit their feelings and get together, and as Gina takes the lead in a rock band and performs from the ledge of the store while jubilant customers of Empire Records dance in the streets below (an interesting allusion to the finale in the botched *Times Square*).

Fans of musicals will note that Renée Zellweger performs the closing song "Sugar High" well before she took the lead role in the Academy Award–winning *Chicago* (2002).

With so many well-timed character epiphanies, *Empire Records* feels like a pilot for a sitcom that never was. The performances are wildly variable too, with Tyler, Zellweger and La Paglia acquitting themselves well. Cochrane and Randall, however, give over-the-top, oddly mannered, and theatrical performances that don't fit well with the material.

Empire Records' greatest claim to fame is its mid-1990s soundtrack, which indeed rocks. It includes "Video Killed the Radio Star" by The Buggles, "Crazy Life" by Toad the Wet Sprocket, "Romeo & Juliet" by Dire Straits, "Candy" and "Liar" by The Cranberries, and "If You Want Blood (You've Got It)" by AC/DC.

Empire Records has recently become a staple of HBO and is on TV virtually every day of the week. Still, it features at least one great line. Robin Tunney (a star of Fox-TV's *Prison Break*) voices this thought: "I went to rock 'n' roll heaven and I wasn't on the guest list." How's that for teen angst?

DVD Empire Records is available on DVD, but don't bother: it'll be on TV again tomorrow.

The Endless Summer (1966)

(DOC)(SNDTRK)

STARRING: Mike Hynson, Robert August, Bruce Brown (Narrator).

FILM EDITOR: Bruce Brown. CINEMATOGRAPHERS: Bruce Brown, Philip Akin, George Greenough, Bob Richardson. WRITTEN AND DIRECTED BY: Bruce Brown. M.P.A.A. RATING: UR. RUNNING TIME: 97 minutes.

How many kids grew up harboring fantasies of becoming surfers after this timeless, beautifully-shot surfing (long board) documentary hit the scene?

It's difficult to imagine, but *The Endless Summer* was first released over forty years ago, and yet still hasn't been topped. Even today—despite a little goofy humor and some politically-incorrect antics set-up specifically for the camera—this remains the definitive surfing movie. Shot on a shoestring budget of $50,000 filmmaker Bruce Brown films two accomplished young surfers on his 16mm cameras as they literally go around the world in search of the elusive perfect wave. Part travelogue, part sports film, *The Endless Summer* is all classic.

"*One day of the year, it's summer somewhere in the world*," the ad-line for *The Endless Summer* reminded viewers, and the film boasts vignettes set in Senegal, Ghana, Cape Town, Australia, and New Zealand.

Although the narration by Brown seems woefully naïve today, the film has lost none of its visual power and beauty. What makes this effort a rock film is its dedicated soundtrack by The Sandals, which includes the theme song "Endless Summer," "Wild as the Sea," "Driftin'," "Outer Wave," "Lonely Road," ""Out Front," "Decoy," and "6 Pack." There's a whole generation that can't separate rock from surfing, and this movie is the primary reason why that happened.

Although a sequel was produced in 1994 by Brown, this original documentary is the one that made history.
ⅅⅤⅅ Available on DVD.

F

(is for *The Filth and the Fury*)

Fame (1980)(MUS)

STARRING: Irene Cara (Coco); Lee Curreri (Bruno); Laura Dean (Lisa); Antonia Franceschi (Hilary); Albert Hague (Mr. Shorofsky); Gene Anthony Ray (Leroy); Paul McCrane (Montgomery); Debbie Allen (Mrs. Grant).

FILM EDITOR: Gerry Hambling. DIRECTOR OF PHOTOGRAPHY: Michael Seresin. WRITTEN BY: Christopher Gore. PRODUCED BY: David De Silva, Alan Marshall. DIRECTED BY: Alan Parker. M.P.A.A. RATING: R. RUNNING TIME: 134 minutes.

Originally known as *Hot Lunch* and featuring music by Michael Gore, Alan Parker's buoyant musical (with a screenplay by Christopher Gore) focuses on the High School of the Performing Arts in New York City, and the loves and labors of the students who attend it for four tumultuous years.

All the stock "theatre" types one expects in backstage musicals like this one attend *Fame*'s school but are rendered up-to-date for the fast-paced 1980s. There's the dedicated musician/prodigy Bruno (Lee Curreri), shy-girl Doris (Maureen Teefy), proud African-American dancer Leroy (Gene Anthony Ray), the token homosexual, Montgomery (Paul McCrane), the haughty ballerina, Hilary (Antonia Franceschi), and the singer Coco (Irene Cara).

Despite stereotypes, this dynamic film skillfully represents the new realities of its age, including a deeper concentration on realistic teen issues of the time, including drugs and sex. Though some critics at the time of release saw the film as campy or over the top, especially with its quasi-spontaneous dance numbers spilling over into city streets or threatening the cafeteria, it nonetheless rang true with its target audience (mostly teenage girls).

Fame instantly became the favorite movie of every aspiring teenage dancer and singer in America, and the film was a substantial enough hit to generate a TV series spin-off in 1982 that saw Curreri and Ray stay back as students, and Debbie Allen and Albert Hague return in their roles as instructors. The series was a big hit too, and lasted for five seasons before cancelation.

"I know we started a fashion in leg warmers around the world," notes director Parker. "It's interesting that '*Fame*'-type schools have opened all over the world. The film was about the flip side of the American dream. It was as much about failure as success. The TV series made me puke, but it was a big hit in sixty-odd countries in syndicated television."

Among *Fame*'s hard-driving tunes in addition to the hit song of the same name, are "Red Light," "Hot Lunch Jam," "Out Here on My Own," and "I Sing the Body Electric." DVD Available on DVD.

Family Ties (GENRE CONVENTION) In the 1980s, the "kids" on the popular NBC sitcom *Family Ties* (1982–1989) tried their hand at rock 'n' roll movies. Michael J. Fox starred in *Light of Day* (1987) with Joan Jett. Justine Bateman, who played Mallory on the long-lived sitcom, starred in *Satisfaction* (1988) with Julia

Roberts. Neither film performed well at the box office, but at least Tina Yothers didn't join the act.

Fictional Bands (GENRE CONVENTION) The
bread-and-butter of rock movies. Although real bands appear in cameos and documentaries, filmmakers who want to "say" something about the rock aesthetic often decide to use fictional bands or performers so as to avoid litigation. Indeed, a regular joy of the rock film is guessing which real act the fictional band is based on. This parlor game has been going in regards to *This Is Spinal Tap* for over twenty years.

Over the years, Hollywood has created wonderfully memorable fictional acts. The messiahs known as Wyld Stallyns (*Bill & Ted's Excellent Adventure*), the one-hit Wonders (*That Thing You Do!*), the all-girl Clamdandy (*Prey for Rock & Roll*), the legendary Eddie and the Cruisers, those stars from the heyday of Motown, The Five Heartbeats, even *Garage Days'* popular Sydney band Sprimp are just a few examples.

You've also got The Lone Rangers (*Airheads*, 1991), The Juicy Fruits (*Phantom of the Paradise*, 1974), The No Exits (*Slaves to the Underground*, 1997), The Sleez Sisters (*Times Square*, 1980), The Angry Inch (*Hedwig and the Angry Inch*, 2001), Stillwater (*Almost Famous*, 2000), The Strange Fruits (*Still Crazy*, 1998), The Fabulous Stains (*Ladies and Gentlemen: The Fabulous Stains*, 1981) Hindenburg (*Drop Dead Rock*, 1995), The Hunzz (*Light of Day*, 1987), and more.

A mangy bunch? Nah, the bands that dreams are made of!

54 (1998)(SNDTRK)(CAMEOS)

STARRING: Ryan Phillippe (Shane O'Shea); Neve Campbell (Julie Black); Salma Hayek (Anita); Breckin Meyer (Greg); Mike Myers (Steve Rubell); Sela Ward (Billie).

FILM EDITOR: Lee Percy. DIRECTOR OF PHOTOGRAPHY: Alexander Gruszynski. WRITTEN BY: Mark Christopher. PRODUCED BY: Richand N. Gladstein, Polly Hall, Ira Deutchman. DIRECTED BY: Mark Christopher. M.P.A.A. RATING: R. RUNNING TIME: 100 minutes.

First-time feature director Mark Christopher had his film, *54*, eviscerated by Miramax after a disastrous preview screening, but this look at the Manhattan nightlife from the late 1970s-to-early 1980s at the infamous Studio 54 still captures the decadence and excess of the age.

Ryan Phillippe stars as Shane O'Shea, a New Jersey boy who is willing to do anything (including dole out sexual favors) to make his way up the ladder at the club and become a bartender. Salma Hayek is his friend and an aspiring singer, Greg (Breckin Meyer) her husband and a drug dealing thief. Perhaps the best (and most daring) performance in the film comes from a post–*Wayne's World* Mike Myers as 54's gay owner, Steve Rubell.

The world of Studio 54 (described in the film as "*one big bender with business cards*") is memorably portrayed as a glittery cocaine wonderland, and Rubell finds to his dismay that his belief that "old labels and prejudices don't apply anymore" is but wishful thinking. The party ends after an IRS raid takes down the careless Rubell, and after an abortive love triangle between Anita, Shane, and Greg (a subplot that was heavily cut).

On the soundtrack of this effort, a poor man's *Boogie Nights* (1987): Mary Griffin's "Knock on Wood" (the movie's introductory number in the club), "Love Machine" by The Miracles, "Heaven Must Have Sent You" by Bonnie Pointer, and Blondie's "Heart of Glass."

Available on DVD in a slightly different cut than the theatrical version, with several sexual scenes re-inserted. Still, there's some hot stuff missing here (including a filmed ménage à trois), making a provocative and promising picture feel disjointed and disappointing instead of stimulating.

(DVD) Available on DVD.

The Filth and the Fury (2000)

(DOC)(CAMEOS)

STARRING: Paul Cook, Steve Jones, Glen Matlock, Johnny Rotten, Sid Vicious (archival footage).

FILM EDITOR: Niven Howie. PRODUCED BY: Anita Camarata, Amanda Temple. DIRECTED BY: Julien Temple. M.P.A.A. RATING: UR. RUNNING TIME: 108 minutes.

This documentary is legendary punk band The Sex Pistols' response to the 1980 film *The Great Rock 'n' Roll Swindle*, which allegedly related manager Malcolm McLaren's view more closely than the band's perspective on things.

The director of both features is Julien Temple (**see:**

Absolute Beginners), and his second go-round with The Sex Pistols consists primarily of archival documentary footage from films such as *D.O.A.*, *Punk Rock: The Movie*, and other seventies efforts (including his previous *Swindle*). Johnny Rotten, Steve Jones, Glen Matlock and Paul Cook also appear for fresh sit-down interviews, but with their faces shielded by darkness, ostensibly to protect their mature identities. Their stories complement the documentary footage and serve as a kind of running commentary on the band's history.

An impressive aspect of *The Filth and the Fury* is Temple's insistence on including background material. He doesn't merely start the film with the formation of the group. Instead, there's a lengthy interlude that looks at the band's context; specifically at London in the mid-1970s. "*The Old Way was clearly not working,*" one of the Pistols suggests, and 1976 is called (over footage of *Richard III*, 1955) "*the summer of*" England's "*discontent.*"

To transmit this notion, Temple cuts to frightening shots of social upheaval in the streets, and refuse piled ten feet high due to a lengthy garbage workers strike. It was this world which gave rise to punk; a world that had essentially failed to deliver to the working class much of what the Labour Party had promised since World War II.

The film then follows the protean Sex Pistols through roster changes (adding Sid Vicious in 1977), problems with manager McLaren, who specialized in sex-fetish rubber wear, and protests by religious organizations. On one occasion, the camera cuts between The Sex Pistols waggling on stage and Christian protesters outside the venue, singing "Silent Night." At first, the band is shunned by the mainstream culture ("*We're like some contagious disease*," Cook notes), but later—and disappointingly—the mainstream assimilates punk rock and the group until their ratty clothes and antisocial behavior is "*absorbed back into the system.*"

The Filth and The Fury spends some time (beginning at about the one-hour point) describing the fatal relationship between Sid Vicious and Nancy Spungeon (see also: *Sid and Nancy*). The other members of the band considered her a "dark cloud" and did everything they could to get rid of her (including dangling her out of a hotel room window by her ankles), but failed.

In heartbreaking terms, a period interview with Vicious reveals his demons. "*I don't want to be a junkie my whole life,*" he says. "*I don't want to be a junkie at all.*" Even more devastatingly, as the film closes, an interviewer asks Sid where he wants to be, following Nancy's murder. "*Under the ground*" he replies without a hint of pretension or sarcasm. Sadly, Vicious would soon be granted his wish.

The Filth and The Fury's final thought is that "only the fakes survive," setting The Sex Pistols in the rarified strata of rockers who never bowed to the old ways…even when it might have saved lives.

Marc Bolan and Billy Idol appear briefly in the film, and *The Filth and the Fury* is loaded with The Sex Pistol standards: "God Save the Queen," "Anarchy in the U.K.," "Pretty Vacant," "EMI," and "No Feelings."

(DVD) Available on DVD.

Finding Graceland (1998)

(SNDTRK)(ELVIS)

STARRING: Harvey Keitel (Elvis); Johnathan Schaech (Byron Gruman); Bridget Fonda (Ashley); Gretchen Mol (Beatrice Gruman); John Aylward (Sheriff Haynes); Susan Traylor (Maggie).

FILM EDITOR: Luis Colina. DIRECTOR OF PHOTOGRAPHY: Elliot Davis. STORY BY: Jason Horwitch, David Winkler. WRITTEN BY: Jason Horwtich. PRODUCED BY: Cary Brokaw. DIRECTED BY: David Winkler. M.P.A.A. RATING: PG 13. RUNNING TIME: 106 minutes.

Revealing the King's seeming permanence in the pop-culture firmament, a crop of Elvis Presley fantasy pictures have sprung up over the last few decades that gaze at the icon in a variety of ways.

There's been Elvis as suburban Daddy-ideal (*Heartbreak Hotel*, 1988), Elvis as monster-fighter (*Bubba Ho-tep*, 2004) and this picture, *Finding Graceland*, which is plainly Elvis as Christ-figure and messiah.

Finding Graceland involves a young man, Byron (Johnathan Schaech) still smarting from the death of his wife Beatrice (Gretchen Mol). In mourning, he drives the endless by-ways of the country in his 1959 Cadillac convertible (which is missing its driver's-side door). One day, en route from New Mexico to Memphis, he picks up a most strange hitchhiker, a man who insists he's the real deal, Elvis Presley (Harvey Keitel).

This film was produced by Priscilla Presley herself, so don't expect any untoward revelations about the King.

Instead, it's a kind of religious hagiography as this beatific King—returning home to Graceland on the anniversary of "his death"—helps Byron conquer his personal demons. Along the way, a Marilyn Monroe impersonator also appears, played by Bridget Fonda. It's interesting to compare a "definite" imposter with a "suspected" or possible one (Elvis), but the film doesn't make obvious comparisons or belabor the issue.

Finding Graceland is simultaneously silly and touching, and reveals how Americans have, in some sense, elevated Elvis Presley beyond the realm of rock singer, beyond the realm of celebrity and propped him firmly amongst the constellations as a Saint.

Elvis is present on the soundtrack too ("If I Can Dream," "Long Black Limousine," "One Night," and "Rip It Up," and so are Joe Cocker ("Wayward Soul"), Mark Campbell ("Suspicious Minds"), and Marc Cohn ("Walking in Memphis").

This is likely required viewing for fans of Elvis. Especially the ones who still believe He Walks Among Us. (DVD) Available on DVD.

First Marriage (GENRE CONVENTION) These

are the ones that don't count, at least in rock movies. In *Great Balls of Fire* (1989) and *Walk the Line* (2005) for instance, Jerry Lee Lewis and Johnny Cash find true love only after leaving behind their first nuptial arrangements. Sometimes it just works out that way.

The Five Heartbeats (1991)(FIC BAND)

STARRING: Robert Townsend (Duck); Michael Wright (Eddie); Leon (J.T.); Harry J. Lennix (Dresser); Tico Wells (Choir Boy); Chuck Patterson (Jimmy); Harold Nicholas (Sarge); Diahann Carroll (Eleanor Potter); Hawthorne James (Big Red).

FILM EDITOR: John Carter. DIRECTOR OF PHOTOGRAPHY: Bill Dill. MUSIC BY: Stanley Clarke. WRITTEN BY: Robert Townsend, Keenan Ivory Wayans. PRODUCED BY: Loretha C. Jones. DIRECTED BY: Robert Townsend. M.P.A.A. RATING: R. RUNNING TIME: 120 minutes.

This is the fictional rags-to-riches story of The Five Heartbeats, an all-black rock band that confronts racism, drugs, and interpersonal strife during its rise "all the way to the top" and subsequent fall, from 1965 to 1972 and beyond.

Sensitive Duck (Robert Townsend) is the group's writer, a man inexperienced with the ladies and overshadowed by his womanizing brother, J.T. (Leon), who sings in the act. Eddie is The Five Heartbeats' lead singer and his story arc takes him from success to drug addiction, alcoholism and petty crime to redemption. Another member of the band, Choir Boy (Tico Wells), must deal with his reverend father, who thinks rock is "evil" and condemns him for being a part of it.

Although Townsend's film is notably good-intentioned, *The Five Heartbeats* is also overlong and predictable as the band goes through all the rock film stereotypes, from the band break-up (over a girl, naturally; **see: *The Yoko Factor*)**, to its depictions of the "spiral," the man who loses

THE Rock & Roll Film ENCYCLOPEDIA

everything because he can't handle success. It's all been vetted numerous times before, and the ending, which sees the group reunited at a backyard barbecue, hardly inspires.

However, what distinguishes *The Five Heartbeats* from many rock films is the way it acknowledges the black experience in America, even for celebrities. In one telling scene, the members of the band and their manager, Jimmy (Chuck Patterson—who gives the film's finest performance) attempt to make a record deal with a white executive. He promptly tells them that he likes the music, but he already has a group their music would be perfect for. Suddenly, a group of beach-blond white boys in Letterman sweaters are then marched into the office, where they proceed to sing a sanitized version of "black" music. This scene reveals what black artists were up against, and also how white musicians appropriated so much of the African-American sound to win popular acclaim.

Another scene in the film finds the band stopped by a group of prejudiced Southern law-enforcement officials who force them to sing to prove that they really are part of a band. It's a humiliating moment, and Townsend stages it well, with agonizing close-ups to reveal how—even with a number-one single—blacks in the South in the 1960s were treated as second class citizens.

One memorable and telling scene finds the band seeing their first album cover and learning, to each member's horror, that it gives no indication the band is black. Instead, a "safe" white family is shown frolicking in the ocean within the perimeter of a heart icon. The record promoter tries to explain that this color-neutral cover will provide the band "crossover" appeal, and one of The Five Heartbeats rightly complains that white bands never have to worry about crossing over, so why should they?

In moments like these, *The Five Heartbeats* proves a memorable film, but it would have benefitted from tighter editing. That said, many of the performances are positively rousing, particularly a duet sung by Robert Townsend and Tressa Thomas, playing Duck's sister.

(DVD) Available on DVD.

Flashdance (1983)(SNDTRK)

STARRING: Jennifer Beals (Alex Owens); Michael Nouri (Nick Hurley); Sunny Johnson (Jeanie); Kyle Heffner (Ritchie); Lee Ving (Johnny C).

FILM EDITOR: Walt Mulconery, Bud Smith. DIRECTOR OF PHOTOGRAPHY: Don Peterman. WRITTEN BY: Tom Hedley, Joe Eszterhas. PRODUCED BY: Jerry Bruckheimer, Don Simpson. DIRECTED BY: Adrian Lyne. M.P.A.A. RATING: R. RUNNING TIME: 95 minutes.

"What a Feeling!"

This is Adrian Lyne's contemporary fairy tale (aimed directly at teenage girls), and a film filled with sound and fury—and energy to spare. According to critic Archer Winston, it's a movie "fresh enough to be eye-opening and familiar enough to be popular too,"[24] the perfect blockbuster equation.

Flashdance depicts the high-voltage tale of a welder by

day, exotic dancer by night, Alex (played by Jennifer Beals), who desires to attend a prestigious ballet school and also hook-up with Mr. Right in the person of Michael Nouri. In plain description, with a few tweaks, this could be the plot of *The Red Shoes* (1948), or any "Star Is Born"-type film wherein a protagonist battles big odds to achieve an impossible dream.

However, *Flashdance* is more frankly sexual than any old-fashioned Hollywood film. One number, "He's a Dream," involves a dancer dousing herself in water on stage, while not wearing much. Also, the musical numbers are dazzling, brilliantly cut, and fast-paced (like music videos), and embody the spirit of dance in a new way.

Though a nervous Paramount Studios reportedly sold a quarter of its stake in *Flashdance* before the film's release, it nonetheless went on to become a monster hit. The soundtrack sold more than 500,000 copies in the first two weeks of release, the film's musical numbers (especially the one with the splashing water) were parodied endlessly, and Jennifer Beals' casual fashions in the film, including a ripped off-the-shoulder sweatshirt, became required gear for a generation of youngsters.

In 2003, twenty years after *Flashdance*, Jennifer Lopez shot a video for her song, "I'm Glad," that recreated shot-for-shot in fetishistic fashion, the climactic audition from *Flashdance*, thus acknowledging it as a classic.

On the popular soundtrack: "Romeo," "Manhunt," "He's a Dream," "Seduce Me Tonight," "Flashdance/What a Feeling."

DVD Available on DVD.

FM (1978) (SNDTRK)

STARRING: Michael Brandon (Duggan); Eileen Brennan (Mother); Alex Karras (doc); Cleavon Little (Prince of Darkness); Martin Mull (Eric Swann); Cassie Yates (Laura); SPECIAL CONCERT APPEARANCE: Linda Ronstadt, Jimmy Buffett.

FILM EDITOR: Jeff Gourson. DIRECTOR OF PHOTOGRAPHY: David Myers. WRITTEN BY: Ezra Sacks. PRODUCED BY: Rand Holston. DIRECTED BY: John Alonzo. M.P.A.A. RATING: PG. RUNNING TIME: 104 minutes.

This nearly forgotten comedy from the disco decade gazes at the wacky goings-on at a silly radio station (and no, I don't mean *WKRP in Cincinnati*). Instead, its 711 FM, QSKY on your dial, broadcasting out of Los Angeles. There, a group of unruly DJs including "Doc" (Alex Karras), "Mother" (Eileen Brennan), and the Prince of Darkness" (Cleavon Little) team up with the feisty station manager, Duggan (Michael Brandon) to prevent management from broadcasting Army recruiting ads on their pure rock station. First, though, they have to steal a Linda Ronstadt and Jimmy Buffett concert out from under their competitor on the dial, K-LAX.

When the station owners won't budge on the Army ad, the staff at QSKY rebels. It locks itself into the building and won't go off the air. Before long, the street outside the station is overrun by supportive fans and the police department, and civil disobedience is the order of the day. Basically, it's a battle against corporate interests (**see: Authority**) so the team can preserve the station for the listeners, so they "can keep the station" just as they "want it."

All's well that ends well, but the film is oddly paced and strangely constructed, since all the character crises are resolved offscreen. First Mother wants to quit, but then she returns without explanation. Duggan and Laura (Cassie Yates) are supposed to be in love, but the audience never really sees much of them courting. Instead, the film just ends with them together. It's all a hodgepodge, and even though the soundtrack includes Queen's "We Will Rock You," the only thing *FM* will do is bore you.

Also on the better-than-expected soundtrack: Steely Dan ("FM," "Do It Again," "FM Reprise"), The Eagles ("Life in the Fast Lane"), Billy Joel ("Just the Way You Are"), James Taylor ("Smiling Face"), REO Speedwagon ("Riding the Storm Out"), Foghat ("Slow Ride"), Linda Rondstadt ("Tumbling Dice," "Love Me Tender"), Foreigner ("Cold as Ice," "Feels Like the First Time"), and Jimmy Buffet ("Livingston Saturday Night").

(DVD) Available only on VHS.

Follow That Dream (1962)(MUS)(ELVIS)

STARRING: Elvis Presley (Toby Kwimper); Arthur O'Connell (Pop); Anne Helm (Holly); Joanna Moore (Alisha Claypoole); Simon Oakland (Nick); Jack Kruschen (Carmine); Alan Hewitt (H. Arthur King); Roland Winters (Judge).

FILM EDITOR: William B. Murphy. DIRECTOR OF PHOTOGRAPHY: Leo Tover. SCREENPLAY BY: Charles Lederer. BASED ON THE NOVEL Pioneer, Go Home by: Richard Powell. PRODUCED BY: David Weisbart. DIRECTED BY: Gordon Douglas. M.P.A.A. RATING: UR. RUNNING TIME: 109 minutes.

For my money, *Follow That Dream* ranks among the top-three finest Elvis films (along with *Kid Galahad* and *King Creole*) ever produced. This adaptation of the Charles Lederer novel *Pioneer, Go Home* finds a makeshift family of down-on-their-luck homesteaders, the Kwimpers, staking a claim on unoccupied beach side land in Florida and running afoul of both overreaching government bureaucracy and local gangsters who want to run them off.

Elvis is at perhaps his most charming playing Toby, a rube who has sworn off women, but remains ever loyal to his wise father, Pop (Arthur O'Connell). Anne Helm portrays Holly, an orphan living with the Kwimpers, and who makes a splendid romantic foil for Elvis. For once, this is a romantic relationship that seems to boast genuine sparks. *Follow That Dream* even ends in uplifting fashion with Elvis arguing for the rights of his family in court, routing an evil welfare officer (Joanna Moore) and an officious Supervisor of State Highways.

Much of *Follow That Dream* relies on bumpkin or redneck humor, as Elvis plays a character of "total naïvete" who counts multiplication tables when tempted by women. He also takes the job of sheriff to protect his family from rowdy gamblers in a trailer casino set up next to their home, but evidences no sense of danger on the job. Presley's screen presence here is laid-back, charming, and natural. He's not striving to be anything other than a good ole boy and the winning performance anchors the film in a pervading sense of good humor.

Follow That Dream's anti-government message, that "the spirit of the pioneer...is still functioning today," is pure

Rock 'n' Roll: rebelling against authority and those who would force Americans to live just one certain way. Here, the Kwimper unit, consisting of an old man, his son, and four orphans, is every bit as much a family as any "traditional" one.

There are fewer Elvis musical numbers to interrupt the narrative in *Follow That Dream*, but every song is a winner, from the titular "Follow That Dream" and "Sound Advice" to "I'm Not the Marrying Kind," "What a Wonderful Life" and the romantic "Angel," which is sung to Helm following the family reunion in the court room. Although the movie exhibits suspicion and hostility toward lawyers, psychologists, the government and more, *Follow That Dream* never actually feels mean. Instead, Elvis dishes out good homespun wisdom with an infectious charm that reminds one of...Bill Clinton! Seriously, watching this film (and particularly Elvis arguing his case in court), you'll wonder if the two "Bubbas" weren't actually separated at birth. This is an appropriate contemplation, since in some corners President Clinton is disparagingly known as the nation's first rock 'n' roll president.

(DVD) Available on DVD.

Footloose (1984)(SNDTRK)

STARRING: Kevin Bacon (Ren McCormack); Lori Singer (Ariel Moore); John Lithgow (Reverend Moore); Dianne Wiest (Mrs. Moore); Christopher Penn (Willard); Sarah Jessica Parker (Rusty).

FILM EDITOR: Paul Hirsch. DIRECTOR OF PHOTOGRAPHY: Ric Waite. WRITTEN BY: Dean Pitchford. PRODUCED BY: Lewis J. Rachmil, Craig Zadan. DIRECTED BY: Herbert Ross. M.P.A.A. RATING: PG. RUNNING TIME: 107 minutes.

If you spend too much time thinking about it, you're bound to conclude that the 1980s—in some fashion—played as a full-blown rerun of the 1950s. The 1950s had avuncular (meaning *old*) two-term President Eisenhower in the oval office; the 1980s two-term avuncular President Reagan. Both decades saw conservative ethos reign supreme too, especially in regards to rock music. In the fifties, it was the cause of juvenile delinquency, according to the religious right. In the 1980s, according to the Moral Majority, rock was delivering nothing less than Satanic messages to American youth. Really—in either decade—this was the same intolerant schtick.

So it's no surprise then that *Footloose*, released in the mid-1980s, actually feels a lot like one of those older 1950s rock movies wherein kids (or musicians) must convince skeptical authority figures (judges, parents, men of the cloth, you name it) that rock music is not a force to be feared. It's *Don't Knock the Rock* for the Izod-and-leg-warmer set. Everything old is new again.

Allegedly based on a true story about a town with a

public dancing ban in Oklahoma (Elmore City), *Footloose* recounts the journey of a rebellious teenager from Chicago named Ren (Kevin Bacon) who moves to the Midwest burg of Bomont only to find that a restrictive ordinance has banned all dancing. It's straight out of *The Twilight Zone*, and this sticks in Ren's craw, in no small partly because the senior prom is coming up.

So, with the help of the town minister's daredevil daughter, Ariel (Lori Singer), Ren attempts to set things straight. John Lithgow plays the Bible-thumping minister (a classic *Bad Father*) who has it in for dancing and rock music but whose cold heart unconvincingly (and rather inexplicably) melts at just the right point.

Rock movies are always about fighting unreasoning *authority*, and that's the theme of *Footloose* too. The film made a star out of Kevin Bacon, though for years he was reportedly embarrassed by his "teen idol" status. In the scenes wherein Ren "cuts loose" with abandon, it's fairly obvious that the twentysomething Bacon has been replaced by a more coordinated dance double.

Still, *Footloose* is a Generation X touchstone (don't knock it!) and filled wall-to-wall with Eighties-brand rock. Kenny Loggins offers up the theme song, "Footloose," Denise Williams performs the rousing "Let's Hear it For the Boys," Bonnie Tyler is "Holding Out for a Hero" and John Cougar tells us when it "Hurts So Good." Yes indeed, it's "Almost Paradise" (by Eric Carmen), Eighties-style! *Footloose* had a second life as a 1998 Broadway musical as well.

ⓓⱽⒹ Available on DVD.

Fubar (2002)(SNDTRK)

STARRING: Paul Spence (Dean); David Lawrence (Terry); Gordon Skilling (Farrell); Tracey Lawrence (Trixie); Sage Lawrence (Chastity).

FILM EDITORS: Jerome Canon, Michael Dowse. DIRECTOR OF PHOTOGRAPHY: Michael Dowse. WRITTEN BY: Michael Dowse, David Lawrence, Paul Spence. PRODUCED BY: Michael Dowse, David Lawrence, Melanie Owen, Paul Spence. DIRECTED BY: Michael Dowse. M.P.A.A. RATING: R. RUNNING TIME: 76 minutes.

A favorite with the Sundance Film Festival set, this low-budget but lively and funny import from Canada concerns a (fictional) documentary filmmaker (Gordon Skilling) investigating the lives and habits of two mullet topped, beer guzzling, hockey-loving head bangers Dean (Paul Spence) and Terry (David Lawrence).

The title *Fubar* is an acronym for "*Fucked Up Beyond All Recognition*," a common state of mind for these fellas. A mockumentary lensed in Calgary in the spirit and tradition of *This Is Spinal Tap*, *Fubar* nonetheless distinguishes itself as an unusual entry in the field. To wit, a variation in the expected (and by now, rote) mockumentary format finds one of the hard rockers, Dean, unexpectedly diagnosed with cancer in a most tender spot. This painful reckoning concerning testicular cancer manages to spark the last portions of the film with an unexpected degree of humanity and pathos, and manages to illuminate the whole head banger culture and aesthetic in unique fashion.

Unlike many rock films, *Fubar* makes note of the way that youngsters (headbangers or not) use pop culture to avoid facing maturity and responsibilities. Then again, sometimes music is the only thing that makes adulthood (and reality) livable.

Not all critics were so favorably impressed however. *The Guardian Unlimited* stated (rather uncharitably) in 2004 that *Fubar* "purports to be an inept documentary, directed by a smug college-educated filmmaker who dies in an accident during its making. In fact, *Fubar* is a spoof, an inept, unfunny mockumentary. I can think of few films so totally lacking in purpose or interest."[25]

On *Fubar's* soundtrack: "Run for the Hills" by Iron Maiden. *Pass the pilsener…*

(DVD) Available on DVD.

Fun in Acapulco (1963)(ELVIS)(MUS)

STARRING: Elvis Presley (Mike Windgren); Ursula Andress (Margharita); Elsa Gardenas (Dolores); Paul Lukas (Maximillian Dauphin); Larry Donasin (Raoul); Alejandro Rey (Moreno).

FILM EDITOR: Stanley E. Johnson. DIRECTOR OF PHOTOGRAPHY: Daniel L. Fapp. MUSIC NUMBERS STAGED BY: Charles O'Curran. MUSIC: Joseph Lilley. WRITTEN BY: Allan Weiss. PRODUCED BY: Hal B. Wallis. DIRECTED BY: Richard Thorpe. M.P.A.A. RATING: PG. RUNNING TIME: 90 minutes.

Elvis plays Mike Windgren, a talented young singer in Acapulco who has imposed an exile on himself following a tragedy in America. Turns out Mike is from the "Flying Windgrens," a popular trapeze act, and during one fateful show, Mike's brother was killed. Now, Windgren boasts a terrible fear of heights, and while singing at a hotel, also gets a job as a lifeguard so he can contemplate the nearby high diving board, and eventually conquer his fears.

In the meantime, Mike also sings at the club El Torito's and finds himself romantically linked with two lovers: Dolores (Elsa Gardenas), the local female bullfighter, and a former duchess, Margharita played by Ursula Andress. Mike's rival for each's affections is the arrogant Moreno (Alejandro Rey), an athletic cliff diver. The film culminates with Mike conquering his fear and jumping from a high cliff himself.

Fun in Acapulco is so clichéd and familiar that one can almost hear the gears squeaking as, in *Girls! Girls! Girls!* Elvis Presley finds himself torn between two women, facing a bitter rival, and (as in the later *Speedway*) boasting a friendly relationship with a child, here his "manager," Raoul (Larry Donasin). It is odd, however, that *Fun in Acapulco* saddles the King with a psychological neurosis (fear of heights), and tragic backstory (amusingly about his history as a circus performer). The film cuts to several ominous shots of a diving board at one point, and the attempt at creating a psychological trauma is almost laughable.

Also, the musical numbers in *Fun in Acapulco* strangely lack punch and are undistinguished. "Fun in Acapulco" is here, but the best effort might be Elvis' song to Gardenas, "Bullfighter Was a Lady" by Sid Tepper and Roy C. Bennett. Another tune, "El Toro," also focuses on bullfighting.

The strangest thing about *Fun in Acapulco* is the all-too-neat wrap-up at the end. Dolores the bullfighter suddenly has a change of character at the end and becomes mean, thus snuggling up to Elvis' rival, the cliff diver played by Alejandro Rey. This last-minute conversion to evil grants Elvis' Mike the opportunity to focus on Ursula Andress' character, who wants to marry him so she and her father, a former duke now turned hotel chef, can become American citizens. The film also ends with the suggestion that Mike will adopt his resourceful manager, Raoul, who has the film's best scene: a moment in a hotel room where, using the telephone and his own resourcefulness, he bargains up Mike's singing fee by pitting all the local hotels against one another.

(DVD) Available on DVD.

(is for *Gimme Shelter*)

THE *Rock & Roll Film* ENCYCLOPEDIA

Garage Days (2002)(SNDTRK)

STARRING: Kirk Gurry (Freddy); Maya Stange (Kate); Pia
Miranda (Tanya); Russell Dykstra (Bruno); Brett Stiller (Joe);
Chris Sadrinna (Lucy); Martin Csokas (Shad Kern).

FILM EDITOR: Richard Learoyd. DIRECTOR OF PHOTOGRAPHY:
Simon Duggan. WRITTEN BY: David Warner, Alex Proyas,
Michael Udesky. PRODUCED BY: Topher Dow, Alex Proyas.
DIRECTED BY: Alex Proyas. M.P.A.A. RATING: R. RUNNING
TIME: 105 minutes.

An anomaly in the canon of director Alex Proyas (*The
Crow*, 1994 and *Dark City*, 1998). This is no dark futuristic
fantasy, but rather the earthbound tale of a wannabe rock
band struggling to make it big in the music scene of
Sydney, Australia. Sex, drugs, and rock 'n' roll play
important parts in the story as Freddy (Kirk Gurry) pursues fame for his band…which has never even played a
real gig. The secret to success may be recruiting sleazy
band *manager* Shad Kurn (Martin Czokas), but the band
also needs to raise money for a demo tape.

Relationships among the band members is fragile, and
one rocker is struck by mental illness in what *The
Hollywood Reporter* termed "a very flimsy story."[26] Director
Proyas brings perhaps too much style and flair to a film
that might have benefitted from a more grounded
approach (like 2003's *Prey for Rock & Roll*). That said, the
surprising climax of this film makes it worth a viewing.
There's also a memorable section of the film called "Fun
with Drugs."

On the *Garage Days* soundtrack is an eclectic mix of old

and new from the likes of D4 ("High Voltage"), Roxy
Music ("Love Is the Drug"), Rhombus ("Ghost Town"),
"That's Entertainment" (The Jam), and—for the end cred-
its—Tom Jones' "Help Yourself."
(DVD) Available on DVD.

The Gate (1987)(HORR)

STARRING: Stephen Dorff (Glenn); Louis Tripp (Terry); Christa
Denton (Al); Kelly Rowan (Lori Lee).

FILM EDITOR: Rit Wallis. DIRECTOR OF PHOTOGRAPHY: Thomas
Vamos. MUSIC: Michael Hoenig. WRITTEN BY: Michael Nankin.
PRODUCED BY: Johnny Kemeny. DIRECTED BY: Tibor Takacs.
M.P.A.A. RATING: PG-13. RUNNING TIME: 85 minutes.

Like Charles Martin Smith's *Trick or Treat* (1986), this is
another mid-1980s horror film that draws an explicit connection between Death Metal Music and Satanism and
horror. In the film, best friends Glenn (a very young
Stephen Dorff) and Terry (Louis Tripp) dig up a hole in the
former's backyard, excavating a gateway to Hell which
teems with miniature stop-motion demons.

All of Terry's knowledge about demonology amusingly
comes from a rock band called Sacrifyx that the character
enjoys (and listens to when his father isn't home).

Terry references an album cover and liner notes in
which the band warns about Satanism. After this one
album (and this explicit warning) however, the members
of the band died in a plane crash.

Notice that the spelling of Sacrifyx is reminiscent of Styx.
(DVD) Available on VHS.

Get Back! (1991)(DOC)

STARRING: Paul McCartney, Linda McCartney, Robbie McIntosh, Hamish Stuart, Chris Witten, Paul Wickens.

FILM EDITOR: John Victor-Smith. DIRECTORS OF PHOTOGRAPHY: Jordan Cronenweth, Robert Paynter. MUSIC: Paul McCartney, John Lennon. PRODUCED BY: Philip Knatchbull, Henry Thomas. DIRECTED BY: Richard Lester. M.P.A.A. RATING: PG. RUNNING TIME: 90 minutes.

A chronicle of McCartney's celebrated 1989–1990 World Tour, this concert film combines footage from several dates and strings it into one somewhat seamless set list. Played like a career retrospective by a very streamlined band, the film showcases great songs ranging from early Beatles, through Wings, and up to McCartney's then-contemporary pop. This is the last film directed by Richard Lester (*A Hard Day's Night*), giving it the strange distinction of acting both as a return to the spotlight for one artist and a parting statement by another.

Musically the film is fine, but several aspects of the surrounding production detract from its ultimate worth. The lapses in time and space give the film a kind of vertigo, and it seems that a document culled from one concert would have been better in the end. There are some moments of residual 1980s cheeseiness, including stage hydraulics, very ham-fisted video montages that are implicitly meaningful but atypically amateurish, and a wide array of dated fashions. The most straight-ahead presentation comes on "Yesterday," which captures an introspective McCartney singing from the heart. Crowd-pleasers like "Band on the Run" and "Hey Jude" prove as infectious as ever. Reputedly, the April 1990 show in Rio de Janeiro from this tour holds the Guinness World Record for most paid attendees at a stadium concert, boasting over 184,000 fans.

In the final analysis, fans of The Beatles and Lester are best serviced by their previous collaborations. Though some great directors are able to skillfully articulate through concert films (Martin Scorsese's *The Last Waltz*, 1978), others (Lester in this instance, or Lindsay Anderson with his detrimentally modified *Wham! In China*, 1985) are better advised to create for a less controlled and conventional genre.—Kevin Flanagan. DVD Available on DVD.

Get Crazy! (1983) (MUS)(SNDTRK)

STARRING: Malcolm McDowell (Reggie Wanker); Allen Garfield (Max Wolfe); Daniel Stern (Neil Allan); Gail Edwards (Willy Loman); Miles Chapin (Sammy Fox); Ed Begley, Jr. (Colin Beverly); Stacey Nelkin (Susie); Billy Henderson (King Blues); Lou Reed (Auden); Robert Picardo (O'Connell).

FILM EDITOR: Kent Beyda. DIRECTOR OF PHOTOGRAPHY: Thomas Del Ruth. WRITTEN BY: Danny Opatoshu, Henry Rosenbaum, David Taylor. PRODUCED BY: Hunt Lowry. DIRECTED BY: Allan Arkush. M.P.A.A. RATING: R. RUNNING TIME: 92 minutes.

Get Crazy, according to its editor, Kent Beyda, is a "lost movie," one that "sort of fell between the cracks," despite its strong cast. "It's got Malcolm McDowell and Lou

Reed, and Daniel Stern in the cast…and a, lot of musical numbers," he remembers.

Director Allan Arkush adds some further details about the film and it's plot. "It was [set on] New Year's Eve at a rock 'n' roll show. It was a way also of presenting all kinds of music under the guise of a concert, and lampooning the concert business and recreating some of the experiences I had, in the business. So we had a Muddy Waters kind of character, and that was done by Bill Henderson, [and] there was a Rod Stewart/Mick Jagger English aging pop star character, played by Malcolm McDowell."

"In order to get it made," Arkush continues, "I had to mutate it more into like an *Airplane* style comedy. That's what was popular at the time. That's how it got made."

However, as Arkush soon found out, his movie was never intended to see the light of day or remain in the public eye.

"The company that made it decided that the best thing to do about it was take a tax loss and make more money, like in *The Producers*. So they did everything possible to make it lose money. They would have a critics screening and then not screen it," he recalls. "Or they would announce it was opening in a city and then not open it. Or they would release it without the stereo track. It was a horrible, horrible experience."

"Later on, a year or so later, I met someone who had invested in it, a tax shelter guy, and he filled me in on how they ripped us off. The company that made it went through various owners and was taken over at various times by different people, so ultimately no one knows [who owns the movie]."

"MGM called me up a couple of years ago and found the negative," Arkush explains, "but they couldn't find the sound. Until they do, I don't think there will ever be a re-issue of it."

Until that eventuality, researchers have to do with critical estimations of the picture Elliott Stein noted: "Allan Arkush's antic comedy, *Get Crazy* (1983), fully of goofy, cartoonish gags about a New Year's Eve rock concert where everything goes wrong, gets everything right. McDowell, in a supporting role, steals the show as Reggie Wanker, a preposterous, burned out rock star with a padded basket, clearly a take off on Mick Jagger."[27]

Kevin Thomas at *The Los Angeles Times* described Arkush's effort as "90 infectious minutes of non-stop mayhem and music, an exuberant, affectionate satire of the zany world of rock. It's sharp, fast and funny, a refreshingly modest and unpretentious summer entertainment, chock full of gags."[28]

(DVD) Not Available on DVD.

The Ghost in the Invisible Bikini (1966)(MUS)

STARRING: Tommy Kirk (Chuck); Deborah Walley (Lili Martin); Quinn O'Hara (Sinistra); Jesse White (J. Sinister Hulk); Harvey Lembeck (Eric Von Zipper); Nancy Sinatra (Vicki); Basil Rathbone (Reginald Ripper); Boris Karloff (The Corpse).

FILM EDITORS: Fred R. Feitshans, Eve Newman. DIRECTOR OF PHOTOGRAPHY: Stanley Cortez. WRITTEN BY: Louis M. Heyward, Elwood Ullman. PRODUCED BY: Samuel Z. Arkoff,

James A. Nicholson. DIRECTED BY: Don Weis. M.P.A.A. Rating: UR. RUNNING TIME: 82 minutes.

This is American International's sad last gasp in the once-popular genre of beach party movies. Franchise stars Annette Funicello and Frankie Avalon sat this one out (though Harvey Lembeck returns as Eric Von Zipper), and the new stars were bland Tommy Kirk and Deborah Walley.

The Ghost in the Invisible Bikini's story involves two ghosts (the great Boris Karloff and Quinn O'Hara) attempting to keep their old mansion out of the hands of evil sinister real estate developer Hulk (Jesse White), while the kids from the beach stay in the "haunted house."

Nancy Sinatra sings "Geronimo," and The Bobby Fuller Four put in an appearance with "Make the Music Pretty" and "Swing a Ma Thing." The series death-knell (as if the other entries weren't bad enough!).

DVD Available on DVD.

G.I. Blues (1960)(ELVIS)(MUS)

STARRING: Elvis Presley (Tulsa McLean); Juliet Prowse (Lili); Robert Ives (Cookie); James Douglas (Rick); Leticia Roman (Tina); Sigrid Maier (Marla); Arch Johnson (Sgt. McGraw).

FILM EDITOR: Warren Low. DIRECTOR OF PHOTOGRAPHY: Loyal Griegs. WRITTEN BY: Edmund Beloin, Henry Garson. PRODUCED BY: Hal B. Wallis. DIRECTED BY: Norman Taurog. M.P.A.A. RATING: UR. RUNNING TIME: 104 minutes.

Elvis had been away from movie-making and serving in the U.S. Army for two years when it came time to make

G.I. Blues, a film that exploits the King's citizen service. Here, Elvis plays Tulsa McLean (great name, huh?), a young officer stationed in West Germany who dreams of performing at and owning his own night club.

In order to make that dream come true, Tulsa makes a bet that he will be able to bed (or rather spend the night alone with) the gorgeous Lili, a steamy, sultry, dancer played Juliet Prowse. Tulsa pursues this goal, but since he's played by a mainstream, de-fanged Elvis, experiences pangs of conscience and can't just go through with the mischievous wager.

Presley sings another bunch of instantly forgettable songs in *G.I. Blues*, including "Tonight Is So Right For Love," "What She's Really Like," "Frankfurt Special," "Wooden Heart," "G.I. Blues," "Pocket Full of Rainbows," "Big Boots," and "Didja Ever."

The only tune you'll recognize here is "Blue Suede Shoes."

DVD Available on DVD.

Gimme Shelter (1970)(DOC)

STARRING: Mick Jagger, Charlie Watts, Keith Richards, Mick Taylor, Bill Wyman, Marty Balin, Melvin Belli, Jerry Garcia, Ike Turner, Tina Turner.

FILM EDITORS: Joanne Burke, Robert Farren, Ellen Gifford. CINEMATOGRAPHY: Albert Maysles, David Maysles, Kent McKinney, George Lucas, Robert Primes, Peter Smokler. PRODUCED BY: Porter Bibb, Ronald Schneider. DIRECTED BY:

Albert Maysles, David Maysles, Charlotte Zwerin. M.P.A.A. RATING: R. RUNNING TIME: 91 minutes.

*"Everybody seems to be ready. Are you ready?"*With those memorable words begins this landmark Albert and David Maysles production, a concert film and documentary chronicling The Rolling Stones' free concert at Altamont, California in 1969. Shot by the Maysles, Peter Smokler (*This Is Spinal Tap*), Robert Primes, and future *Star Wars* creator George Lucas in the cinema verité style popular during the era, *Gimme Shelter* is much more than a series of musical performances on stage.

On the contrary, it escorts viewers behind-the-scenes, commencing with Mick Jagger, Charlie Watts, Keith Richards, Mick Taylor, and Bill Wyman watching their raw footage in the editing room, looking decidedly glum over the results. And they often have good reason to be so disturbed, for much of the film involves not just the preparations for a concert that would come to be attended by a whopping 300,000 people, but the terrible murder of an audience member (ostensibly by a Hell's Angel, who was providing security) shortly before a performance of the Stones' "Sympathy for the Devil," a tune they would not perform on stage again for six long years.

Like Pennebaker's Dylan bio-pic, *Don't Look Back*, *Gimme Shelter* charts the parameters of the uncomfortable relationship between rock music and big business, and grants viewers a sense of the logistics involved in putting on a show of this magnitude. The Stones, for instance, must be flown to the stage in a helicopter because there's no other way to make it through the crowd. In fact it takes a sky-bound helicopter to capture the full breadth of the undulating crowd in attendance, a breathtaking visual that lives up to the concert's billing as "the greatest party of 1969."

But getting to the charity concert is just one of many logistical hurdles. One involves the cranky owner of the Sears Point Race Track who doesn't want to foot the bill to rebuild his property after the destruction anticipated at the concert. Another problem includes finding a place to host the show in the first place, especially after the first venue, Golden Gate Park, bows out because of the estimated size of the crowd.

Stylistically, *Gimme Shelter* shares much in common with other rock 'n' roll documentaries of its era, featuring one-on-one interviews with fans discussing their favorite groups and songs, and incongruous (and unflattering) close-ups and zooms focusing on seemingly out-to-lunch band members during awkward, random moments. In this case, we're treated to a close-up of Keith Richards' less-than-straight teeth, for instance. And, as is *de rigueur* for the genre (and recreated in rock opera films including Todd Haynes' *Velvet Goldmine*), there is the requisite band *press conference* wherein the Stones discuss their work in what might be politely considered pretentious terms. Here, Jagger belabors a point about levels of "satisfaction" both sexually, philosophically, and financially.

Among those who make cameos in the film are famous attorney Melvin Belli and Tina Turner. The latter delivers a wild, sensual performance and looks like she's never more than a second away from performing fellatio on a microphone.

Rolling Stones Keith Richards and Mick Jagger contemplate "the lemmings of the sea" and the human tragedy that unfolded at their Altamont concert, in *Gimme Shelter* (1970).

Gimme Shelter remains famous not just for capturing the end of the "peace and love" 1960s era and revealing an unruly, violent crowd, but for Jagger's famous remark regarding the pack mentality of the crowd: *"It's like the lemmings of the sea…"*

Peter Smokler, later the DP on *This Is Spinal Tap*, was one of many cameraman filming the Altamonte concert, and still remembers the occasion vividly.

"We all thought we were going to do another *Woodstock*," he establishes. "We thought it was going to be a huge human document we would chronicle. The culture was still there, and, it was really cool that the time wasn't over yet. But when we got there it was just this big dusty bowl. It wasn't a pleasant circumstance, even if there wasn't rain and mud. It was hot and dry, and there were Hell's Angels everywhere and that's not always a fun mood to be around. They're a little scary."

To his chagrin, Smokler was also present when an audience member died from a heart attack. He was stationed near the helicopter, and while the injured man was still alive, urged action.

"We did go back to the helicopter and say, 'You know, you could fly this guy to a hospital and come right back before the concert is over.' And the Stones' manager said 'No one gets in this helicopter but The Rolling Stones.'"

"These are just memories I have of that incident…"

DVD *Gimme Shelter* is available on DVD.

Girl Happy (1965)(ELVIS)(MUS)

STARRING: Elvis Presley (Rusty Wells); Shelley Fabares (Valerie Frank); Harold J. Stone ("Big" Frank); Gary Crosby (Andy); Joby Blake (Wilbur); Nital Talbot (Sunny Daze); Mary Ann Mobley (Deena); Jackie Coogan (Sgt. Benson).

FILM EDITOR: Rita Roland. DIRECTOR OF PHOTOGRAPHY: Philip H. Lathrop. WRITTEN BY: Harvey Bullock, R.S. Allen. PRODUCED BY: Joe Pasternak. DIRECTED BY: Boris Sagal. M.P.A.A. RATING: UR. RUNNING TIME: 96 minutes.

"Elvis jumps with the campus crowd to make the beach ball bounce!" blared this movie's ads.

Another light-as-a-feather but inconsequential Elvis flick. This time, the King plays a Chicago-based singer who gets "recruited" by a mobster named "Big" Frank (Harold J. Stone) to watch after his college-age daughter Valerie (Shelley Fabares) while she's on Spring Break in Fort Lauderdale. It's an offer Elvis and his band can't refuse, and before long he's on the beach romancing the young lady himself. Believed to be inspired, in part, by the success of *Where the Boys Are* (1960), *Girl Happy* is fairly well-regarded in the Presley canon, yet still a far cry from the King's finest work.

Elvis sings a whopping twelve tunes here (which gives an indication of how slight the story really is). These include: "Do the Clam," "Girl Happy," "Cross My Heart and Hope to Die," "Do Not Disturb," "Spring Fever," "Wolf Call," "Puppet on a String," I've Got to Find My Baby," "The Meanest Girl in Town" and "Startin' Tonight."

DVD Available on DVD.

Girls! Girls! Girls! (1962)(MUS)(ELVIS)

STARRING: Elvis Presley (Ross Carpenter); Stella Stevens (Robin); Jeremy Slate (Johnson); Laurel Goodwin (Laurel Dodge); Benson Fong (Kin Young); Robert Strauss (Sam); Guy Lee (Chen); Frank Puglia (Papa Stavros); Lily Valenty (Mama Stavros).

FILM EDITOR: Stanley Johnson. DIRECTOR OF PHOTOGRAPHY: Loyal Griggs. MUSICAL NUMBERS STAGED BY: Charles O'Curran. MUSICAL SCORE: Joseph Lilley. STORY BY: Alan Weiss. WRITTEN BY: Edward Anhalt, Allan Weiss. PRODUCED BY: Hall B. Wallis. DIRECTED BY: Norman Taurog. M.P.A.A. Rating: PG. RUNNING TIME: 93 minutes.

This Elvis film, with its skeletal plot and ballyhoo title, brings out the worst impulses of the entertainer-turned-actor's career. Attempting at once to capitalize on both the exploitable sexual prowess of Presley and his mainstream wholesomeness, *Girls! Girls! Girls!* loses sight of what generally works in The King's pictures. Ross Carpenter (Elvis Presley) is a fishing captain who occasionally moonlights as a lounge singer. On the outs with his dour girlfriend Robin (Stella Stevens), Carpenter meets up with the lovely and level-headed Laurel Dodge (Laurel Goodwin), and after a series of unfulfilling encounters, seems poised to fall in love yet again. However, not all is well: dishonest businessman Wesley Johnson (Jeremy Slate) buys out Carpenter's ship, forcing our poor hero to work under duress for Johnson during the day and take up a permanent gig as a singer at night, all to the detriment of his blossoming love relationship.

Though all Elvis films have undeniably dated to a certain extent, *Girls! Girls! Girls!* is full enough of racial stereotypes and anti-feminist tropes to make even a socially moderate contemporary viewer gasp in horror. Compared with previous Elvis movies, the performances here feel like a stretch. Though the staging and delivery of "Return to Sender" produces the kind of ballad that would find a ready home in any early rock film, the rest of the feature is made up of fantastic, unbelievably trite material. While the title track masquerades as catchy pop and is appropriately placed at the beginning of the movie, its rousing reprise at the end invalidates a large amount of the narrative climax and is pretty antithetical to the film as a whole—it would be more at home in a Las Vegas variety review than at the end of a story that affirms the true love of a monogamous relationship. Elvis is at his honest best on screen when he recreates his own career and explores his rags-to-riches story (*Jailhouse Rock*, to name one). Grade C "entertainment" like *Girls! Girls! Girls!* rightly points to the early vestiges of his waning popularity.—Kevin Flanagan
DVD Available on DVD.

Girls Town (1959) (SNDTRK)(MUS)

STARRING: Mamie Van Doren (Silver); Mel Tormé (Fred); Ray Anthony (Dick); Maggy Hayes (Mother Superior); Paul Anka (Jim Parlow) Cathy Crosby (Singer); Gigi Perreau (Serafina); Elinor Donahue (Mary Lee); Gloria Talbot (Vida).

FILM EDITOR: Leon Barsha. DIRECTOR OF PHOTOGRAPHY: John L. Russell. WRITTEN BY: Robert Hay Andrews. PRODUCED BY: Albert Zugsmith. DIRECTED BY: Charles F. Haas. M.P.A.A. RATING: UR. RUNNING TIME: 90 minutes.

From the age of *High School Confidential* arrives this Mamie Van Doren vehicle. In *Girls Town*, a tough-talking and troubled young teen, Silver (Van Doren) gets enmeshed in a murder (though she's innocent) and the amply-proportioned but fresh talking teen ("*go bingle your bungle*") gets remanded into the care of the strict nuns at the halfway house known as "Girls Town."

There, a local rocker and good Catholic, Jimmy (played by Paul Anka) performs for the girls who have gone astray. Here, he sings "Lonely Boy" and "Ave Maria." Although his dreamy crooning helps some of the girls, Jimmy also picks up a celebrity stalker in the person of the confused Serafina (Gigi Perreau).

While Silver longs for cigarettes and freedom, Mel Tormé plays a threatening ruffian and juvenile delinquent (!) who has it out for her.

Girls Town was immortalized in the mid-1990s by the wisecracking gang on *Mystery Science Theatre 3000*, but even sans that snarky commentary, the movie remains fun, and viewers may find it impossible not to pay attention. DVD Not Available on DVD.

Give My Regards to Broad Street (1984)(REAL ROCKER)

STARRING: Paul McCartney (Paul); Bryan Brown (Steve); Ringo Starr (Ringo); Barbara Bach (Journalist); Linda McCartney (Linda); Tracey Ullman (Sandra); Ralph Richardson (Jim); George Martin (Producer).

FILM EDITOR: Peter Beston. DIRECTOR OF PHOTOGRAPHY: Ian McMillan. SCREENPLAY BY: Paul McCartney. MUSIC BY: Paul McCartney. PRODUCED BY: Andras Epaminendas. DIRECTED BY: Peter Webb. M.P.A.A. RATING: PG. RUNNING TIME: 108 minutes.

It's a bit depressing to witness one of the remarkable talents behind such rock-movie masterpieces as *A Hard Day's Night* (1964) and *Yellow Submarine* (1968) doing so poorly in a latter-day solo effort, yet that's precisely what happens to ex-Beatle Paul McCartney in the lackluster Eighties endcavor *Give My Regards to Broad Street*.

The film tries hard to be another "day in the life" effort like Lester's *A Hard Day's Night*, only up-to-date with modern flourishes like computers and rehearsals for music videos rather than a live TV-show broadcast, but a strange pall (Paul?) hangs over the film, as though no one had much enthusiasm for the project. The lightness and joyous absurdity of *A Hard Day's Night* is missing.

Give My Regards to Broad Street is the story of Paul McCartney experiencing a very bad day. He's just recorded a new album but the master tapes have disappeared, and now he has only a few hours to deliver them or his business will be taken over by the evil *record company*, Rathbone Industries. The last person who had the tapes was an ex-con that McCartney took pity on and hired, Harry Torrington. But now Harry's disappeared, and his girlfriend, played by Tracey Ullman, is concerned. Was Paul's judgment wrong? Is Harry really a bad apple?

While McCartney puzzles through the mystery and the clock ticks down to the impending deadline, he travels to the recording studio and records three tunes at a clip (including "Yesterday"). Then he goes to shoot a video for "Silly Love Songs" and dons a huge white pompadour with a black stripe, which makes him resemble a skunk. In this number, a Michael Jackson figure appears on stage and moonwalks in electric shoes.

Also on the soundtrack is the tune "No Values," which is cross-cut with footage of Torrington selling the valuable tapes to a grotesque Harry Knowles figure, but it's just a phantasm.

Give My Regards to Broad Street ends with the unusual conceit of featuring two lousy climaxes instead of just one. The first sees a desperate McCartney fortuitously stumbling upon the tapes at a train station, and rescuing Harry from a barn where he has locked himself in ("*thought it was a toilet*," he sheepishly admits). Then, this mess is all revealed as a fantasy of McCartney's, played out while he sits in traffic near London. The next thing you know, Patrick Duffy will turn up in McCartney's shower.

Ringo Starr, Linda McCartney, Ralph Richardson, and Barbara Bach (Mrs. Ringo Starr) cameo in this film, but everything feels so…flat. In part, this is because McCartney seems preternaturally calm, or even tranquilized, as though a star of his magnitude can't get nervous or anxious anymore.

"*Let's not all have tantrums,*" he says calmly at one point, sounding as though he's on Prozac. The ex-Beatle's performance in *Give My Regards to Broad Street* suggests that—to put it politely—he wasn't fully engaged in the material.

Los Angeles Times critic Patrick Goldstein put it well when he noted that *Give My Regards to Broad Street* is "undermined by more than just…flimsy backstage dreams. It's biggest mistake is casting McCartney—who with his open, inquisitive face would make a lovable vagabond or a charming rogue—as a listless cog in the pop-making machinery, gliding through life in a process of luxury cars and limos."[29]

The music underpinning *Give My Regards to Broad Street* represents a mix of the Beatles catalog and new McCartney efforts. The songs include "Yesterday," "Here, There, and Everywhere," "Wanderlust," "Ballroom Dancing," "Silly Love Songs," "Not Such a Bad Boy," "No Values," "So Bad," "For No One," "Eleanor Rigby," "The Long and Winding Road," and "No More Lonely Nights." DVD Available on DVD.

Glitter (2001)(FIC BAND)(BIO-PIC)

STARRING: Mariah Carey (Billie Frank); Max Beesley (Julian Dice); Da Brat (Louise); Tia Texada (Roxanne); Valerie Pettiford (Lillian); Ann Magnuson (Kelly).

FILM EDITOR: Jeff Freeman. DIRECTOR OF PHOTOGRAPHY: Geoffrey Simpson. STORY: Cheryl L. West. WRITTEN BY: Kate Lanier. PRODUCED BY: Laurence Mark. DIRECTED BY: Vondie Curtis Hall. M.P.A.A. RATING: PG-13. RUNNING TIME: 104 minutes.

Diva Mariah Carey suffered from a bout of mental and physical exhaustion near the release of this film in 2001, and it's no wonder: watching the movie is an exhausting experience. This is the fictional (though reportedly partially autobiographical) tale of Carey's *rags—to—riches* journey. As a child, her character, Billie, is abandoned (after a house fire) by a mother who can't care for her. As she grows up, she goes into the industry as a back-up singer for a music star. Eventually, Billie steps out into the spotlight herself, but the cost of fame may be her relationship with a manager/DJ played by Max Beesley.

Glitter received well-deserved savage reviews upon its release and is now synonymous with the word "bomb." Not "da bomb," mind you. On the soundtrack, Carey sings an overripe assortment of cloying pop rock tunes like "Loverboy," "Lead the Way," "If We," "Didn't Mean to Turn You On," "Don't Stop," "All My Life," "Want You," and "Never Too Far."

(DVD) Available on DVD.

Godspell (1973)(MUS)

STARRING: Victor Garber (Jesus); Katie Hanley (Katie); David Haskell (John/Judas); Merrell Jackson (Merrell); Joanne Jonas (Joanne); Robin Lamont (Robin); Gilmer McCormick (Gilmer); Jeffrey Mylett (Jeffrey); Jerry Sroka (Jerry); Lynne Thigpen (Lynne).

FILM EDITOR: Alan Heim. DIRECTOR OF PHOTOGRAPHY: Richard Heimann. CHOREOGRAPHY: Sammy Bayes. CREATIVE CONSULTANT: John-Michael Tebelak. WRITTEN BY: David Greene, John-Michael Tebelak. FROM THE MUSICAL CONCEIVED AND WRITTEN BY: John-Michael Tebelak. MUSIC AND LYRICS BY: Stephen Schwartz. PRODUCED BY: Edgar Lansbury. DIRECTED BY: David Greene. M.P.A.A. RATING: G. RUNNING TIME: 100 minutes.

If a Jesus Christ figure wearing a Superman shirt, suspenders, and clown shoes is your idea of fun, check out this musical based on the Gospel of St. Matthew.

Based on the popular and long-running theatrical production, David Greene's *Godspell* features some catchy folk-rock tunes, and concerns a modern day Christ (*Alias*'s Victor Garber with an afro) making time with a gang of mime-like disciples as they traverse authentic locations in New York City, including Central Park and the as-yet-unfinished Twin Towers.

Throughout, Jesus teaches his lessons (such as the fact that man can't serve God AND money, etc.). In the end, Judas (the late David Haskell) turns Jesus over for Crucifixion, an event which here is staged on a chain-link fence, not a cross.

Jesus Christ (Victor Garber) is a hippie clown in *Godspell* (1973). Here, he's tended to by Judas (David Haskell).

Godspell vacillates between being charming and kitschy, innocent and too-precious by half, but some of the tunes, including "By My Side" (by Peggy Gordon) will linger long in the mind after viewing. The scene atop the World Trade Center, with the New York skyline as a backdrop, is also awe-inspiring, especially post–September 11th.

It's interesting too, especially in the conservative age of the 21st century, that Jesus' disciples are basically portrayed as Flower Powered Hippies in this film, who paint their faces, eschew wealth and clearly don't vote Republican. Wonder what Pat Robertson would make of that?

(DVD) Available on DVD.

Graceland (GENRE CONVENTION) Elvis' home in Tennessee is the Mecca of rock 'n' roll movies. It's the blessed land where bands go on pilgrimages to center themselves after disappointment and lows (*This Is Spinal Tap*) and a shrine wherein to channel the greatness of the King and let it rub off on them (*U2: Rattle and Hum*). Jerry Lee Lewis (Dennis Quaid) also takes a Graceland drive-by in *Great Balls of Fire* (1989) and Colm Meaney discusses Graceland in *The Commitments* (1991).

Finding Graceland, a 1998 film, depicted a messianic, healing Elvis returning home to Graceland, the rock 'n' roll Jerusalem, on the anniversary of his death.

The Graduate (1967)(SNDTRK)

STARRING: Anne Bancroft (Mrs. Robinson); Dustin Hoffman (Benjamin Braddock); Katharine Ross (Elaine Robertson); William Daniels (Mr. Braddock); Murray Hamilton (Mr. Robertson).

FILM EDITOR: Sam O'Steen. DIRECTOR OF PHOTOGRAPHY: Robert Surtees. WRITTEN BY: Calder Willingham, Buck Henry. BASED ON THE NOVEL BY: Charles Webb. PRODUCED BY: Lawrence Turman. DIRECTED BY: Mike Nichols. M.P.A.A. RATING: R. RUNNING TIME: 105 minutes.

This classic sixties effort from director Mike Nichols introduced the world to actor Dustin Hoffman in a story about post-college malaise. Hoffman plays Benjamin Braddock, a graduate who engages in an illicit affair with that married shark, Mrs. Robinson (Anne Bancroft) and then determines he wants to marry her daughter, Elaine, played by Katharine Ross.

The Graduate captured the imagination of a generation in the late sixties, not just with its coming of age story, but with its stirring, melancholy soundtrack performed by Paul Simon & Art Garfunkel. The tunes on the memorable soundtrack include "The Sounds of Silence," "Mrs. Robinson," "April Come She Will," and "Scarborough Fair." (DVD) Available on DVD.

Graduation Day (1980)(HORR)

STARRING: Christopher George (Coach Michaels); Patch MacKenzie (Anne Ramstead); E.J. Peaker (Blondie); Michael Pataki (Principal Gugliani); Richard Balin (Roberts); E. Danny Murphy (Kevin).

FILM EDITOR: Martin Jay Sadoff. DIRECTOR OF PHOTOGRAPHY: Daniel Yarussi. MUSIC: Arthur Kempel. SCREENPLAY BY: Anne Marisse and Herb Freed, from a story by David Baughn. PRODUCED BY: David Baughn, Herb Freed. DIRECTED BY: Herb Freed. M.P.A.A. RATING: R. RUNNING TIME: 90 minutes.

In this cheapjack 1980s slasher film, someone is brutally murdering members of the track team at a local high school, and trying to pin the murders on Coach Michaels (Christopher George). The aggressively edited film stops in its horror movie tracks, however, to feature what is billed in the opening credits as "a special appearance" by the rock band called Felony. Ever heard of 'em?

Felony appears on stage during a school dance to sing a highly repetitive rock tune entitled "The Gangster Rock," written by Jeff and Joel Spry and Doug Burlison. This piece goes on interminably, and then is utilized on the soundtrack during a lengthy chase and murder scene in the park.

Those with eagle eyes will note that future *Wheel of Fortune* celebrity Vanna White plays one of the imperiled high school students.

(DVD) Not Available on DVD.

Graffiti Bridge (1990)
(REAL ROCKER)(FIC BAND)(MUS)

STARRING: Prince (The Kid); Ingrid Chavez (Aura); Morris Day, Jerome Benton, The Time.

FILM EDITOR: Rebecca Ross. DIRECTOR OF PHOTOGRAPHY: Bill Butler. WRITTEN BY: Prince. PRODUCED BY: Randy Phillips, Arnold Stiefel. DIRECTED BY: Prince. M.P.A.A. RATING: PG-13. RUNNING TIME: 95 minutes.

It's "The Kid" versus Morris Day and Jerome: Part II (The Armageddon…) in this dire, unofficial sequel to the classic film *Purple Rain* (1984). This time Prince directed the enterprise, and the film was shot entirely at Paisley Park Studios in Minneapolis over a period of six weeks. If anything, this one's even worse than the dreadful *Under the Cherry Moon*.

Graffiti Bridge finds The Kid (Prince) and Morris Day as rival owners of Minneapolis night clubs, still trying to one-up each other. In their ever-escalating game of brinkmanship, they agree to a song-writing contest and if Prince loses, he sacrifices his club. Fortunately for the Purple One, he finds inspiration under "Graffiti Bridge" with an angel named Aura played by Ingrid Chavez (a role passed over by Kim Basinger and Madonna). Unfortunately, Morris is interested in Aura too.

To get the good out of the way first, it's interesting that Prince always includes tailor-made nemeses in Morris Day and Jerome. What is Superman, after all, without Lex Luthor? But the relationship dynamic isn't that good; certainly not as much fun as *Purple Rain*. Additionally, the film boasts a cheap, thrown-together look and the sets are downright terrible (and strange too, as though they exist in a separate almost miniature universe). Some featured songs are musical operatic fashion (break-into-song) and other songs are supposed to be performances, so *Graffiti Bridge* is an especially weird hybrid.

Prince performs "New Power Generation," "The Question of You," "Elephants and Flowers," "We Can Funk," "Joy in Repetition," "Melody Cool," and "Thieves in the Temple" while The Time grooves with "Love Machine," "Release It," "Shake," "The Latest Fashion," and "Blondie." (DVD) Available on DVD.

Grease (1978)(MUS)(CAMEOS)

STARRING: John Travolta (Danny Zuko); Olivia Newton-John (Sandy); Stockard Channing (Rizzo); Jeff Conaway (Kenickie); Barry Pearl (Doody); Michael Tucci (Sonny); Kelly Ward (Putzie); Didi Conn (Frenchie); Eve Arden (Principal McGee); Frankie Avalon (Teen Angel); Joan Blondell (Vi); Sid Caesar (Coach).

FILM EDITOR: John F. Burnett. DIRECTOR OF PHOTOGRAPHY: Bill Butler. BASED ON THE MUSICAL BY: Jim Jacobs and Warren Casey. WRITTEN BY: Bronte Woodard. PRODUCED BY: Allan Carr, Robert Stigwood. DIRECTED BY: Randal Kleiser. M.P.A.A. RATING: PG. RUNNING TIME: 110 minutes.

Robert Stigwood, the man who produced *Saturday Night Fever* (1977), next turned his attention to an adaptation of a popular stage show. The result was the movie *Grease*. Like the earlier disco film, it starred John Travolta, but this

time he was cocky greaser Danny Zuko. The film added Olivia Newton-John to the mix as his star-crossed, high school lover, Sandy.

Travolta did great as the bad boy, and Newton-John proved sweet as a square, good girl. The two young lovers were kept apart, basically, by peer and class pressures, as strange as that sounds.

A retro treat, *Grease* became the top-earning musical of the decade, and featured a bevy of hits from the stage show, including "Summer Nights" and "Greased Lightning." Original songs were added to the mix too, including Olivia's ballad "Hopelessly Devoted to You," and the theme song "Grease" written by Barry Gibb and performed by Frankie Valli.

Among the other musical treats: Stockard Channing's mocking-Olivia song, "Look at Me, I'm Sandra Dee," and beach party movie star Frankie Avalon's cameo, in which (as a Teen Angel) the talent croons "Beauty School Drop Out" to Didi Conn's Frenchie. The movie version of *Grease* also features a lengthy scene at the high school prom and thus includes several performances by Sha Na Na of what one might call 1950s rock standards. These include: "Hound Dog," "Rock 'N' Roll is Here to Stay," and "Blue Moon." (DVD) Available on DVD.

Grease 2 (1982)(MUS)

STARRING: Maxwell Caulfield (Michael); Michelle Pfeiffer (Stephanie); Lorna Luft (Paulette); Maureen Teefy (Sharon); Alison Price (Rhonda); Adrian Zmed (Johnny); Peter Frechette (Louis); Christopher McDonald (Goose); Didi Conn (Frenchie); Eve Arden (Principal McGee); Tab Hunter (Mr. Stuart).

FILM EDITOR: John F. Burnett. DIRECTOR OF PHOTOGRAPHY: Frank Stanley. WRITTEN BY: Ken Finkelman. PRODUCED BY: Allan Carr, Robert Stigwood. DIRECTED BY: Patricia Birch. M.P.A.A. RATING: PG. RUNNING TIME: 115 minutes.

The much-maligned sequel, *Grease 2*, did do the world at least one favor. It introduced audiences to actress Michelle Pfeiffer, who would move on to bigger and better things. Ultimately, however, that introduction proved little consolation to disappointed fans of the original 1978 film, who found this lackluster musical a disappointment.

Damningly, *Grease 2* features neither John Travolta nor Olivia Newton-John. Instead, Patricia Birch's *Grease 2* picks up at Rydell High in 1961, just two years after the events of the original film, and dramatizes the story of new teen loves, Stephanie (Pfeiffer) and Michael (Maxwell Caulfield). The big twist this time is that it's the male who is the clean-cut kid and Stephanie the so-called "greaser." How's that for originality?

In a tenuous attempt to link the sequel to the popular original, Michael happens to be the English cousin of Newton-John's Australian character, Sandy. Though the ads optimistically promised that *"Grease is still the word,"* the film proved hard pressed to repeat the incredible business of its 1978 progenitor, which grossed more than $300 million worldwide. By contrast, *Grease 2* grossed about $6 million…not exactly "greased lightning."

Songs in the film include The Four Tops singing "Back to School Again," Ruby and the Romantics promising "Our Day Will Come," and Duane Eddy's "Rebel Walk." DVD Available on DVD.

Great Balls of Fire (1989)(BIO-PIC)

STARRING: Dennis Quaid (Jerry Lee Lewis); Winona Ryder (Myra Gale Lewis); Alec Baldwin (Jimmy Swaggart); Lisa Blount (Lois); Trey Wilson (Sam Phillips); John Doe (J.W Brown); Stephen Tobolowsky (Jud Phillips); Joe Bob Briggs (Dewey Phillips); Steve Allen (Himself).

FILM EDITORS: Lisa Day, Pembroke Herring, Bert Lovitt. DIRECTOR OF PHOTOGRAPHY: Affonso Beato. BASED ON THE BOOK BY: Myra Lewis, Murray Silver. WRITTEN BY: Jack Baran, Jim McBride. PRODUCED BY: Adam Fields. DIRECTED BY: Jim McBride. M.P.A.A. RATING: PG-13. RUNNING TIME: 107 minutes.

Dennis Quaid gives a gonzo, crazy-eyed, curly-haired performance in *Great Balls of Fire*, the involving biography of cocky rocker Jerry Lee Lewis and his meteoric rise to fame and just as lightning freefall. Yes, it's yet another rags-to-riches story, but this movie benefits from superb performances all around.

The film begins in Louisiana in 1944 as a young Jerry Lee sneaks into an African-American club and gets his first taste of proto-rock. It's something he'll never forget, and as he grows up, he uses his talents as a pianist to bring the same style of music into the American pop-culture main-stream. Does this appropriation make Jerry Lee a thief? The film never really addresses that point, unfortunately.

Despite the objections of his Christian cousin, Jimmy Swaggart (Alec Baldwin) who believes "*rock 'n' roll is the devil's music*," Jerry Lee Lewis takes Sam Phillips' offer to become a star ("*You take a white right hand and a black left hand and what've you got? rock 'n' roll*," Phillips tells him) and soon is sharing the spotlight with the likes of Johnny Cash and Elvis Presley.

Jerry Lee's biggest hit again comes from the African-American culture, a modified version of "Whole Lotta Shakin' Goin' On" (a tune which is banned in the South for sexually suggestive lyrics). But the controversy about this song is nothing compared to the controversy about Jerry Lee's marriage to a thirteen-year-old cousin (Myra).

This story breaks while Lewis is in England, and the uptight Brits revile the talent for his "child bride," rejecting the notion that this scamp could be the "next King of Rock."

The controversy follows Jerry Lee home, and his career trajectory heads south. His new tune, "High School Confidential" races to the bottom of the charts (**see:** *Billboard* **magazine**) and Jerry Lee is left to face a new reality: the fact that he is no longer the headliner he once was.

Great Balls of Fire is an energetic, exuberant film, one that reveals Lewis' Persian flaw: *hubris*. He considers himself the King of Rock and makes snarky comments about Elvis Presley ("*Oh, Elvis ain't so hot,*" he says at one point),

but Elvis' popularity is greater than his. Oddly, the film reflects Lewis' point of view that he would have become enthroned as the next king of rock, and features an Elvis lookalike in a cameo that suggests the King felt threatened by Lewis. Somehow, I'm not so sure about that one. Jerry Lee Lewis is undeniably great, but he never possessed Elvis' easy charm.

Lewis' hubris shows up in other ways. He marries a thirteen-year old child and expects no one to care. Then, when—during intercourse—she moves her body in a fashion he's uncomfortable with, he accuses her of having already lost her virginity to another man. It's just cruel and unnecessary. Lewis' final spiral through alcohol and drugs, before a last act reprieve, also reveals him to be a weak person. The movie acknowledges all these points, while still establishing him as a reigning power of rock music and sexually suggestive tunes.

On the latter front, one of director Jim McBride's more inventive shots reveals a dancer in the background framed inside Lewis' crotch and open legs (in the foreground). He's singing about shakin' (meaning sex) and the point is made visually: he's a "dangerous" guy.

All the piano and vocals in the film are performed by Jerry Lee Lewis, and the tunes include "Crazy Arms," "Whole Lotta Shakin' Goin' On," "Great Balls of Fire," and "High School Confidential."

(DVD) Available on DVD.

The Great Rock 'n' Roll Swindle (1980)(FIC)(DOC)(ANIM)

STARRING: Malcolm McLaren (The Embezzler); Steve Jones (The Crook); Paul Cook (The Tea-Maker); Sid Vicious (The Gimmick); Johnny Rotten (The Collaborator); Ronnie Biggs (The Exile); Liz Fraser (Woman in Cinema); Jess Conrad (Jess); Mary Millington (Mary); James Aubrey (Record Executive); Julian Holloway (Man); Johnny Shannon (Nazi); Helen of Troy (Helen); Tenpole Tudor (Tadpole); Faye Hart (Secretary); Alan Jones (Record Executive); Irene Handl (Cinema Usherette).

FILM EDITORS: Richard Bedford, Gordon Swire, Mike Maslin, Crispin Green, David Rae, Bernie Pokrzywa. CINEMATOGRAPHERS: Adama Barker Mill, Willie Patterson, Nick Knowland, John Metcalfe. 8MM PHOTOGRAPHY: Norman Moriceau, Ku Khanh. MUSIC: The Sex Pistols. PRODUCERS: Jeremy Thomas, Don Boyd. WRITTEN AND DIRECTED BY: Julien Temple. M.P.A.A. RATING: UR. RUNNING TIME: 100 minutes.

The movie that "*incriminates its audience*" is punk rock's flip-you-the-bird answer to the naïve Beatles' film milieu, a rash, stylish overturning of elements from *A Hard Day's Night* and even *Yellow Submarine*. Starring The Sex Pistols (though not Johnny Rotten, who is seen only in existing footage), *The Great Rock 'n' Roll Swindle* kicks off the 1980s in cynical and angry fashion and consists of a series of loosely connected vignettes (offered as a kind of rock industry Ten Commandments).

Some are animated segments, some are shot on 8mm film, others include archival documentary footage, and some "skits" were shot specifically for the film with coop-

erating (and surviving) Sex Pistols. In all cases, the helter-skelter presentation hangs together through its "ten lessons" concerning how to pull off the swindle of the title. The ostensible plot involves a detective played by Steve Jones attempting to track down the shady manager of the band, Malcolm McLaren, who provides a raspy voice-over throughout and hides under a creepy black fetish mask.

The Great Rock 'n' Roll Swindle's anarchic forms reflects its sense of chaotic content, and there's no sense of formal movie decorum here. What might be an innocuous pie-in-the-face joke in *A Hard Day's Night* becomes, with the ultra-violent Sid Vicious on hand, a virtual assault with a cake.

A harmless animated high-seas adventure *Yellow Submarine*-style becomes shark-infested waters with record companies (like Virgin) serving as swimming man-eaters, over the film's end credits. Some footage shot for the film is so grainy that clarity disintegrates and reality is deconstructed. When a random zoom does catch a relevant action, it's just as likely to be a shot of the drummer picking his nose as a band member accomplishing a particularly skilled riff.

There are ten very cynical lessons in the film. Some of these include "How to Manufacture Your Group," which establishes The Sex Pistols as a historical force at the 1780 Gordon Riots as a London mob hangs the group in Effigy…then burns the band.

The second lesson advises prospective rockers to "establish the name," and "prevent competition" by playing at unconventional venues such as strip clubs and prisons. "Forget about music," the narrator suggests "and concentrate" on creating "generation gaps." In other words: appeal to the youthful sense of rebellion and anti-authority hatred.

In fact, one such lesson suggests "Cultivate Hatred; It Is Your Greatest Asset." In this regard, The Sex Pistols not only created a cult following, but a coterie of critics tailor-made to hate them. "Most of these groups would be improved by sudden death," one stodgy commentator says in the film. The band is also referred to as "nauseating," "disgusting," and "a walking abortion."

The Great Rock 'n' Roll Swindle has been attacked as representing McLaren more than the band itself, and many have seen Temple's 2000 documentary *The Filth and the Fury* as an antidote. Yet, whether intentionally or not, this film perfectly captures the self-obsessed, nihilist world of late 1970s punk rock. A band that can't play well and can't be bothered to *learn* to play well, yet that somehow still had a powerful sound, goes on a mad spree through the world, noses bloodied, but never beaten.

They spit on their fans (literally), and in Sid Vicious' iconic rendering of Frank Sinatra's "My Way" (also featured in *Sid and Nancy*, 1986), blow away audience members in a bloody massacre. It's rock as protest; rock as rebellion; and rock, indeed, as swindle. But it speaks as cogently to its time as the Beatles did to theirs. Just that these times, clearly, are much darker, more pessimistic.

Accordingly, the film features Nazi imagery, some graphic nudity, a bit of blood, and anything else the makers can think of to offend audiences, but the self-reflexive film (which incorporates criticism of the band right into

its genetic make-up) indeed convinces one that The Sex Pistols, at least for a time, had the last laugh: earning fans who rave about their "deep" lyrics and songs, when, in fact, the band's main struggle has been not to play at all, but rather have gigs cancelled.

The Great Rock 'n' Roll Swindle ends, appropriately, with a gaggle of headlines about Sid Vicious' death. Maybe the swindle, the joke, was carried just a little too far in this case. "His way," his philosophy of life, didn't seem to bring Vicious much joy or happiness in the end.

On the soundtrack: "No Feelings," "God Save the Queen," "Anarchy in the U.K.," "Johnny Be Goode/Road Runner," "Silly Thing," and "C'mon Everybody." Oh, and Tenpole Tudor's unbelievable and whacked "Who Killed Bambi?"

DVD Available on DVD.

Guitar (or Guitar Collection)(GENRE CONVENTION) The guitar serves as the Excalibur of the rock movie. It is a sacred object; an instrument to be revered and appreciated. Wayne Campbell (Mike Myers) even takes periodic pilgrimages to view his "dream" guitar at a local music store in *Wayne's World*.

Meanwhile Nigel Tufnel takes director Marty DiBergi on a tour of his guitar collection in *This Is Spinal Tap*, finding one guitar so special, so unique that he entreats the director not to point at it or even look at it.

The guitar collection also appears in such films as *Rock*

and Roll Superhero (2003) and *Metallica: Some Kind of Monster* (2004).

In *The Who: The Kids Are Alright* (1979), John Entwistle's impressive guitar collection is seen decorating a landing and the entire wall next to a staircase. Hope he doesn't let his guitar-bashing bandmate Pete Townshend in to water the plants while he's away.

Bucking the trend of treating guitars reverently, the late Jimi Hendrix, appearing in *Monterey Pop* (1967), douses his instrument with lighter fluid then watches it burn up.

(is for *A Hard Day's Night*)

Hair (1979)(MUS)

STARRING: Treat Williams (Berger); John Savage (Claude); Beverly D'Angelo (Sheila); Annie Golden (Jeannie); Dorsey Wright (Hud); Don Dacus (Woof); Cheryl Barnes (Hud's Fiancée); Richard Bright (Fenton); Nicholas Ray (The General); Charlotte Rae (Lady in Pink); Miles Chapin (Steve); Fern Tailer (Sheila's Mother); Charles Denny (Sheila's Father); Nell Carter (Singer).

FILM EDITOR: Lynzee Klingman. DIRECTOR OF PHOTOGRAPHY: Miroslav Ondricek. MUSIC BY: Galt MacDermot. BASED ON THE MUSICAL PLAY, BOOK AND LYRICS BY: Gerome Ragni, James Rado. MUSIC: Galt MacDermot. CHOREOGRAPHY: Twyla Tharp. WRITTEN BY: Michael Weller. PRODUCED BY: Lester Persky, Michael Butler. DIRECTED BY: Milos Forman. M.P.A.A. Rating: PG. RUNNING TIME: 121 minutes.

Milos Forman directed this free-wheeling, exciting adaptation of the popular Broadway musical (music by Galt MacDermot, lyrics by Gerome Ragni and James Rado) at the end of the disco decade. Some important liberties have been taken with the source material, but nonetheless the film boasts momentum, zeal, and energy.

The story finds a Midwestern farmer's boy named Claude (John Savage) drafted to serve in the Vietnam War. But something funny happens on his way to the DMZ. In New York's Central Park, Claude encounters a counter-culture Loki figure named Berger (Treat Williams), one who immediately shatters all of his views about America in the 1960s. Perhaps more importantly, Claude falls in love with the aristocratic Sheila (Beverly D'Angelo). He spends time with a "gang" of Flower Powered young hippies and soon sees his whole life change. In the end, Berger makes the ultimate sacrifice for his new friend, one that allows Claude to remain with his lady love.

Hair takes viewers back to the conflicts of the *Vietnam War* era, the draft, and the requisite burning of draft cards. More importantly, hair itself serves as the ultimate rock symbol of the 1960s. It's difficult to conceive of this today, but in the late sixties, long hair on men represented an *anti—authority* statement, a fact which this film brings out. "*My hair like Jesus wore*," one lyric reads. "*Mary loved her son, why don't my Mom love me?*"

Indeed, Berger's (bad) father only cares that his son "*get a haircut.*" Thus long hair is a symbol of protest for the counterculture, not just the title of the film.

Hair's best sequence involves Berger and his gang crashing a high society dinner party. While the well-to-do dine and act "proper," the hippies infiltrate the gathering and go nuts…literally. Berger dances on the dinner table to "I Got Life" and the movie erupts into counter-culture pandemonium that reveals how hypocritical the upper crust—removed from the violence of war—has become.

Nell Carter also dazzles with the amusing (and bawdy) "Black Boys/White Boys" number, which enthuses at length about men of all shapes and colors. Even though the film's final gimmick, that Berger replaces Claude in the Army, doesn't make even a modicum of sense, it's difficult to deny the power of *Hair*'s emotional final scene…set at Berger's graveside while the soundtrack swells to the tune of "Let the Sun Shine In."

DVD Available on DVD.

Hairspray (1988)(MUS)(CAMEOS)

STARRING: Sonny Bono (Franklin von Tussle); Ruth Brown (Motormouth Maybelle); Divine (Velma von Tussle); Ricki Lake (Tracy); Jerry Stiller (Wilbur); Colleen Fitzpatrick (Amber).

FILM EDITOR: Janice Hampton. DIRECTOR OF PHOTOGRAPHY: David Insley. PRODUCED BY: Rachel Talalay. WRITTEN AND DIRECTED BY: John Waters. M.P.A.A. RATING: PG. RUNNING TIME: 92 minutes.

An amazing and humorous bull's-eye from Baltimore's low-budget movie king John Waters (and the director's first PG effort to boot). The camp-classic *Hairspray* proved so memorable an effort, in fact, it has transcended its original context as a 1988 film and in 2002 became a bona fide hit Broadway musical. On stage, this dynamic property has starred the likes of Harvey Fierstein and Michael McKean, though perhaps no performer, no matter how great, has truly filled the late drag star Divine's shoes.

Set in 1962 (*the age of American Innocence/Camelot*), *Hairspray* involves an overweight teenage girl, Tracy (Ricki Lake in her first screen role) who dreams of appearing on a local version of Dick Clark's *American Bandstand* TV show, here titled *The Corny Collins Show*. Despite her weight, Tracy dances better than all the girls on the program and wants to join the program's teen council. Unfortunately, she has a nemesis in perfect little Amber von Tussle (Colleen Fitzpatrick), and the film's climax includes their fierce competition for Miss Auto Show 1963 (**see: Dance Contest**).

What's both amazing and rewarding about *Hairspray* is that the film involves much more than Tracy's personal dilemma and home life (wherein Divine plays her mother). There's a subplot involving segregation and racism, beautifully lampooned during a sequence set in "the black part of town," and Waters slips in some trenchant points about body image too. Yet *Hairspray* is never preachy or less than funny. This is an example of a cult hit moving beyond a narrow audience and reaching wide audience appeal, but without sacrificing the elements that make it great.

Watch for humorous cameos from Waters (as a psychiatrist), Pia Zadora (as a beatnik), and The Cars' Ric Ocasek.

Hairspray's music confirms Waters' deep fund of knowledge about the era of early 1960s rock. Some of these groups and tunes are obscure, but all of their music is authentic to the time and place. On the soundtrack: Rachel Sweet ("Hairspray"), Ray Bryant Combs ("The Madison Time"), The Ikettes ("I'm Blue"), Jan Bradley ("Mama Didn't Lie"), Gene Pitney ("Town Without Pity"), Gene and the Wendells ("The Roach"), The Flares ("Foot Stompin'"), The Five Du-Tones ("Shake a Tail Feather" see: *The Blues Brothers; What's Love Got to Do With It*), Jerry Dallman ("The Bug"), and Toussaint McCall ("Nothing Takes the Place of You").

Critics reacted warmly to *Hairspray*, which isn't always the case for John Waters productions. David Denby in *New York* magazine heralded it as "something new in the annals of low camp. This movie…has great heart."[30] Likewise, David Sterritt at *The Christian Science Monitor* deemed the effort a "proudly silly picture" and enthused that it was "good to see an erstwhile sleazemaster like Waters invest his resources in a project that sincerely celebrates a small but memorable social advance."[31]

(DVD) Available on DVD.

A Hard Day's Night (1964)(MUS)

STARRING: George Harrison, John Lennon, Paul McCartney, Ringo Starr, Wilfrid Brambell (Grandfather); Norman Rossington (Norman); John Junkin (Shake); Victor Spinetti (TV Director); Anna Quayle (Millie).

FILM EDITOR: John Jympson. DIRECTOR OF PHOTOGRAPHY: Gilbert Taylor. WRITTEN BY: Alun Owen. FILM SOUNDTRACK: John Lennon, Paul McCartney. PRODUCED BY: Walter Shenson. DIRECTED BY: Richard Lester. M.P.A.A. RATING: G. RUNNING TIME: 90 minutes.

The rock movie wellspring.

This is a seminal rock film and one of the most important titles in rock history. This black-and-white effort represents The Beatles' big screen debut and remains a pioneer in the way modern rock is presented both on TV and in film. Director Richard Lester adopted many tenets of the French New Wave (black-and-white photography; existential absurdity regarding the human condition, and spontaneous-seeming sequences set in real locations) and in sixteen weeks of filming crafted a classic. It is tempting to view the film as a "mockumentary" (or mock documentary) since *A Hard Day's Night* features the Beatles going about their business to shoot a gig on a British TV show,

yet there's not a narrator present (à la *The Last Waltz*, 1978), and the Beatles don't sit down for one-on-one interview/confessionals with an awareness of the camera.

Instead, *A Hard Day's Night* is clearly a film that bends and breaks established movie decorum. It works both as an overall narrative (and indeed, its screenplay was nominated for an Academy Award for Alun Owen) and as a set of loosely connected vignettes (hence the frequent comparison to the new art form of music videos).

A Hard Day's Night finds The Beatles surviving what must have seemed a "normal" day for them at the height of Beatlemania: almost constantly under siege, whether running from a mob at a train station or facing dislike from *authority* figures (like one on a train who asks them to turn off their radio). Meanwhile "Paulie" McCartney must contend with his mischievous grandfather (Wilfrid Brambell) while the band rehearses for a performance on TV. Along the way, the film delights in absurd humor. Puns and gags, chases and races fly at the audience at lightning fast-speed in delightful fashion.

What may be most revolutionary about *A Hard Day's Night* is the manner in which Lester cuts each Beatles' tune to one particular scene, keeping the beat and song's rhythm intact and in essence making a music video. Also, there's a strong self-reflexive quality to the text. The movie audience watches The Beatles prepare for a live performance that studio and TV audiences will then themselves be watching, but which we are already seeing. During the rehearsal for "All My Lovin'," Lester cuts away from the Fab Four and to the monitors in the control

Behind the scenes of *A Hard Day's Night* (1964)—
a rock movie touchstone—it's the Beatles. John, Paul, Ringo, and George.

room, showing them in close-up and other angles, making us watch TV at the same time we watch a movie. In this sense, *A Hard Day's Night* is a film that understands film and television, and the importance of each in fostering the continuation of the Beatles phenomenon.

Also, *A Hard Day's Night* synthesizes the criticism against The Beatles (including the ludicrous claim that somehow they're "unclean") and fires it right back at the establishment, revealing the absurdity of such arguments.

A number of conventions of the rock-movie format are present in *A Hard Day's Night*, but are so fresh they hardly feel like clichés at this point. We meet The Beatles' *manager*, who seems to have a problem with John Lennon. We attend a *press conference* wherein reporters ask absurd questions ("How do you like your girlfriends to dress?" or "What do you call that hairstyle?"), we go *backstage* and witness the band letting its hair down by playing with make-up beards and prosthetic noses. We see *the Mob*, the screaming fans, go wild in close-up during a performance, and more. If today any of this seems hackneyed or old, it's only because so many films (*Spice World*, 1997, *I Wanna Hold Your Hand*, 1978, *The Great Rock 'n' Roll Swindle*, 1980) have attempted the same alchemy.

For my money, *A Hard Day's Night* also features the best Beatles soundtrack, as the group performs one classic tune after another. The titles include "I'll Cry Instead," "A Hard Day's Night," "I Should've Known Better," "Can't Buy Me Love," "If I Fell," "Tell Me Why," "I Wanna Be Your Man," "All My Lovin'" and "She Loves You."

(DVD) Available on DVD.

Hard to Hold (1984)(FIC-BAND)

STARRING: Rick Springfield (Jamie Roberts); Janet Eilber (Diane Lawson); Patti Hansen (Nicki); Albert Salmi (Johnny Lawson); Gregory Itzin (Owen); Peter Van Norden (Casserole); Bill Mumy (Keyboard); Mike Bard (Drums); Robert Popwell (Bass).

FILM EDITOR: Bob Wyman. DIRECTOR OF PHOTOGRAPHY: Richard H. Kline. MUSIC SCORE: Tom Scott. STORY: Tom Hedley, Richard Rothstein. SCREENPLAY BY: Tom Hadley. PRODUCED BY: D. Constantine Conte Productions. DIRECTED BY: Larry Peerce. M.P.A.A. RATING: PG. RUNNING TIME: 93 minutes.

In the year of *This Is Spinal Tap*, the truly wretched Rick Springfield vehicle *Hard to Hold* was also thrust into American theatres. Here, famous rocker Jamie Roberts (Springfield) romances a child counselor, Diane Lawson (Janet Eilber) and the resulting movie plays like a Mentos commercial, filled with strange miscues and behavioral gaffes that, based on the empirical evidence, are supposed to be funny.

Springfield, who bounds from scene to scene as if juiced on speed, attempts vainly to steal every scene he's in. In one memorable moment, he arranges for his lover to be serenaded by a Tony Bennett soundalike, but instead of letting the imitation-Bennett croon and hold center stage, Springfield gesticulates wildly and insanely, keeping attention squarely focused on him. Camera hog!

Hard to Hold is hard to stomach, and the film's script is baffling and nonsensical. For instance, Diane's father is an

Rick Springfield and Janet Eilber are hard to stomach in *Hard to Hold* (1984).

alcoholic, but she nonetheless wants him to meet Jamie so she arranges a date…*at a bar* of all places. Not surprisingly, the meeting goes badly, and alcohol is involved. Was this really a good idea? Why didn't they just go out for a coffee? Or a hamburger?

Hard to Hold also lingers on nude butt shots of Rick Springfield to satisfy the core demographic of *Tiger Beat* readers, but it is the film's aspiration to be a "serious" study of an "artist" that is most painful to witness. At a *recording session*, Jamie laughably laments that all the music is too "repetitious."

He shares an on-again/off-again relationship with his writer, Nicki, and tells her that he likes "up" messages even though things are bad in the world, not her persistent "negativity." Later, Jamie has an existential crisis when he realizes he has nothing "to say" in his music, an accurate perception of the bubble gum pop rock that the movie glides over quickly.

Finally, *Hard to Hold* ends in baffling style as Jamie goes on stage for a sold-out concert. He sings one song, "Love Somebody," and then abruptly leaves the concert and drives to the airport to catch up with Diane in time for a romantic finale. Just one song? Oh Jamie, how could you disappoint your fans that way? I hope the concertgoers got their money back…

Other songs in *Hard to Hold* include "Taxi Dancing," "Don't Walk Away," "Stand-Up," "Bop Till You Drop," and "Great Lost Art of Conversation," all performed by Rick Springfield.

DVD Available on DVD.

Deborah Harry (1945–   )(ROCK MOVIE HALL OF FAME) This sexy lead singer for the 1970s-era punk/new wave band Blondie has proven particularly versatile in her long career. She's been a rocker, a Playboy bunny, and—on occasion—a dramatic actress.

Harry saw perhaps her highest film profile come in the horror genre during the 1980s. She played the leading role of fetishist and masochist, the red-headed Nicki Brand, in David Cronenberg's kinky 1983 film, *Videodrome*, and then appeared in such horror anthologies as *Tales from the Darkside: The Movie* (1990) and *John Carpenter Presents: Body Bags* (1993).

Harry also had a cameo as Liam Neeson's sometimes-lover in the Justine Bateman vehicle *Satisfaction* (1988), and starred as Velma in John Waters' *Hairspray* the same year. Her other films include *Drop Dead Rock* (1995), *Cop Land* (1997), and *The Fluffer* (2001).

You'll also spy Harry in the 1980 misfire, *Roadie*, wherein she performs "Ring of Fire" and laments her long stint on *the road*.

Harum Scarum (1965)(ELVIS)(MUS)

STARRING: Elvis Presley (Johnny Tyronne); Mary Ann Mobley (Princess Shalimar); Fran Jeffries (Aishah); Michael Ansara (Prince Dragna); Jay Novello (Zacha); Philip Reed (King

Toranshah); Theo Marcuse (Sina); Billy Barty (Baba); Dick Harvey (Mokar); Jack Costanzo (Julna); Larry Chance (Captain Herat); Vicki Malkin (Sari).

FILM EDITOR: Ben Lewis. DIRECTOR OF PHOTOGRAPHY: Fred H. Jackman. WRITTEN BY: Gerald Drayson Adams. PRODUCED BY: Sam Katzman. DIRECTED BY: Gene Nelson. M.P.A.A. RATING: UR. RUNNING TIME: 85 minutes.

Who's sari now?

In this, the slightest and most ridiculous of the 1960s Elvis Presley vehicles, the King of Rock plays hunky matinee idol Johnny Tyronne (star of the new movie *Sands of the Desert!*), a likeable dullard who is soon abducted in the Middle East by the forces of Sina, Lord of the Assassins. As he soon discovers, this Hollywood star has been recruited by these age-old cultists to assassinate the King of a local kingdom that has been "*isolated from the world for 2,000 years.*"

Even though Johnny only uses his fighting hands (and black belt) for "self-defense," he is forced to attempt the murder, because the evil Aishah (Fran Jeffries) has threatened to kill three innocent slave girls and the little orphan girl, Sari (Vicki Malkin) if he fails.

On the run with an Arabian con-man and a mischief-prone dwarf (Billy Barty), Elvis finds time to sing "Kismet" to Mary Ann Mobley, who plays a princess masquerading as a slave girl.

Other than Michael Ansara (a Syrian), *Harum Scarum* doesn't appear to feature a single genuine Arab in its embarrassed-looking cast, and the plot line and dialogue are utterly ridiculous. Worse, Elvis himself doesn't project even the slightest sense of danger or threat at his dire predicament, even though his character has been whisked away to a world of brutal assassins who constantly threaten him with death. The King's disengagement with scripted material is never more obvious than here.

The whole Middle East milieu is portrayed in insulting fashion (is there any ethnic subgroup Michael Ansara has not played?) and in *Harum Scarum*'s finale Tyronne takes his experiences to Las Vegas to sing "Harem Holiday" to appreciative audiences. What a stinker! This is Elvis' nadir, and no way to win the War on Terror.

(DVD) Available on DVD.

Head (1968)(MUS)(CAMEOS)

STARRING: Peter Tork, David Jones, Micky Dolenz, Michael Nesmith, Annette Funicello (Minnie); Frank Zappa (The Critic); Terri Garr (Testy True); Victor Mature (The Big Victor), Dennis Hopper, Jack Nicholson.

FILM EDITOR: Mike Pozen. DIRECTOR OF PHOTOGRAPHY: Michel Hugo. WRITTEN AND PRODUCED BY: Bob Rafelson, Jack Nicholson. EXECUTIVE PRODUCER: Bert Schneider. DIRECTED BY: Bob Rafelson. M.P.A.A. RATING: G. RUNNING TIME: 85 minutes.

A crushing and pretentious disappointment for fans. This psychedelic vehicle for the once-popular TV act, *The Monkees*, is literally a stream-of-consciousness movie; a late 1960s head-trip apparently best viewed when stoned and utterly incomprehensible when sober. There's no linear narrative to enjoy here. Rather it's an eighty-five-

They give bad *Head* (1968). **It's the pre-fab Monkees**:

(l-to-r): Peter Tork, Mickey Dolenz, Davy Jones, and Michael Nesmith

minute collection of disconnected videos and images. Ask yourself: Who are these people? What are they doing? Why are they doing it? Why should I care? Just don't look for anything to make sense.

Head, which bombed in theatres following the cancelation of the TV series, is pure phantasmagoria as the Monkees—admittedly a "manufactured image"—conduct fast-motion antics, a riff on silent-screen perils, and end up back at the beginning of the film, jumping off a bridge into the water far below.

Along the way on this pointless trip, there are startling (and graphic) images of the Vietnam War and future President Ronald Reagan, but the movie makes no attempt to make these images relevant or meaningful. They don't even connect. To even compare this movie to *A Hard Day's Night* is probably sacrilege, but one senses that this was the intent; to make this a day in the life of The Monkees. Ostensibly they're making a movie.

The script was created by Jack Nicholson, but it's just a chunk of nonsense. A waitress in the film describes the rock group as *"God's gift to eight-year-olds"* but even that modest description is aiming high, given the movie's juvenile nature.

In reality, *Head* merely looks like an excuse for celebrities to party and get paid at the same time. In that spirit, the film is littered with *cameos* by the likes of Nicholson, Dennis Hopper, Annette Funicello, and Terri Garr. The movie's tunes—"Porpoise Song," "Can You Dig It," "As We Go Along," "Get Tuff," and "Circle Sky" are instantly forgettable, making this a long, long hour-and-a-half to get

through. Trust me, this isn't the best *Head* you'll ever get. (DVD) Available on DVD.

Heartbreak Hotel (1988)(ELVIS)(SNDTRK)

STARRING: (Elvis Presley) David Keith ; Tuesday Weld (Marie); Charlie Schlatter (Johnny Wolfe); Angela Gothals (Pam Wolfe); Jacque Lynn Colton (Rosie); Chris Mulkey (Steve).

FILM EDITOR: Raja Gosnell. DIRECTOR OF PHOTOGRAPHY: Stephen Dobson. WRITTEN BY: Christopher Columbus. PRODUCED BY: Debra Hill and Lynda Obst. DIRECTED BY: Christopher Columbus. M.P.A.A. RATING: PG-13. RUNNING TIME: 97 minutes.

This is a guilty pleasure and *"rock 'n' roll fantasy"* that fans of the King will adore, though mainstream critics hated and lampooned the schmaltzy film upon its release in 1988. This entertainment from the future crowd-pleasing director of *Home Alone* (1990), *Mrs. Doubtfire* (1993), and *Harry Potter and the Sorcerer's Stone* (2001) is a gentle comedy/fable about Presley becoming the ad-hoc "Papa" to a middle-class American family that desperately needs a father figure.

The action begins in Ohio in 1972 when a seventeen-year-old rock 'n' roller, Johnny (Charlie Schlatter), decides to kidnap Elvis as a gift for his mother (Tuesday Weld), an Elvis fan. Since the King's coming to Cleveland on tour, things work out just right and Johnny uses a fiendish decoy (a lookalike of Elvis' mother) to entrap the performer and bring him home.

Before long, the King is living in the family motel (the

Heartbreak Hotel), chipping in around the house, offering sage advice and guidance to Johnny's little sister (Angela Gothals), who is afraid to turn out the lights at night, and also mentoring Johnny for an upcoming talent show. The King himself receives a few important lessons in restoring his rock 'n' roll edge from the teenager before the sentimental ending.

David Keith plays Elvis Presley with a lot of heart, though nobody going's to be fooled by his performance, and the soundtrack includes Keith singing "Can't Help Falling in Love" and "That's All Right, Mama." The real Presley also turns up on the soundtrack with "Heartbreak Hotel" and "Baby, Let's Play House."

In all, this is a love letter to the King and his fans, a wish-fulfillment fantasy oddly typical of the 1980s (a decade when good father figures seemed missing, and fantasy figures like *E.T.* (1982) and even Elvis Presley substituted). Predictably, the critics were not kind to this syrupy concoction. "A real groaner,"[32] complained Michael Wilmington in *The Los Angeles Times*. Lynn Darling agreed, commenting in *Newsday* that *Heartbreak Hotel* "drifts into a pond of unadulterated treacle."[33]

(DVD) Available on DVD.

Hedwig and the Angry Inch (2001)
(MUS)

> STARRING: John Cameron Mitchell (Hedwig/Hansel); Andrea Martin (Phyllis Stein); Michael Pitt (Tommy Gnosis); Alberta Watson (Hansel's Mom); Rob Campbell (Krzysztof); Miriam Shor (Yitzhak).

FILM EDITOR: Andrew Marcus. DIRECTOR OF PHOTOGRAPHY: Frank G. De Marco. WRITTEN BY: John Cameron Mitchell. PRODUCED BY: Christine Vachon, Katie Roumel, Pamela Kofler. DIRECTED BY: John Cameron Mitchell. M.P.A.A. RATING: R. RUNNING TIME: 95 minutes.

During several rock performances at a restaurant chain called Bilgewater's, a cross-dressing "internationally ignored," would-be rock star named Hedwig recounts her life story. Born to a single mother in East Germany in 1961—as a boy named Hansel—Hedwig spent the seventies listening to American and British rock on the radio. Then, as a teenager, Hansel was romanced by an American soldier named Luthor, who offered to marry Hansel and take him back to the U.S.

However, to acquire a marriage license and emigrate to the West, Hansel had to leave something behind. To wit: he had to undergo a sex-change operation. Unfortunately, the surgery went wrong, leaving Hansel with only an "angry inch," where once there had been six. Thus was born Hedwig.

Hedwig becomes Luthor's wife in the U.S., but soon Luthor leaves her. Adding insult to injury, the Cold War ended and the Berlin Wall fell, rendering Hedwig's anatomical sacrifice unnecessary. Later, Hedwig formed a band, and before long, met an army brat named Tommy who wanted to learn everything about rock 'n' roll. When Hedwig falls in love with Tommy, he betrays her and steals her songs, becoming the rock star, Tommy Gnosis.

Now, Hedwig and her band, the Angry Inch, shadow Tommy's big American tour, as her husband Yitzhak con-

Stephen Trask and John Cameron Mitchell (Hedwig)

rock the crowd in *Hedwig and the Angry Inch* (2001).

templates another betrayal by joining a touring company of *Rent*. But Hedwig's world is turned upside down during a chance encounter with Tommy Gnosis in a limousine, and the moment leads her down the road of self-discovery.

This is the strange tale of *Hedwig and the Angry Inch*, a film that *Time* magazine called "this generation's *Tommy*. Only with better legs."[34] The material is adapted faithfully (with some modifications) from the popular stage show by creator John Cameron Mitchell, and the movie was filmed in Toronto and Ontario on a $6 million budget, with a scant twenty-eight days for shooting. This is what Mitchell said about the process of adapting his material from stage to screen:

"A lot of stage-to-film adaptations fall into the pitfall of thinking that everything that they say is sacred," Mitchell suggests. "Because they're just not. I had been saying the words, [in the play] for years, so I was bored with them and I was very excited to translate them into images. For example, we'd have a joke where Hedwig would wipe her face on a towel and say '*Oh, it's the Shroud of Hedwig,*' but in the film, you can tell the same joke without saying the words. You can just show the Shroud of Hedwig."

One of the unique aspects of *Hedwig and the Angry Inch* involves the manner in which director Mitchell seamlessly integrates the MTV, music-video style production number into the form of the movie musical. There are times during production numbers that Hedwig sings directly to the camera, and, a feeling of immediacy (and compassion) is generated. Mitchell, the director of 2006's controversial *Shortbus* suggests that music videos were

indeed part of his approach.

The production number "Wig in a Box," in particular, could be carved right out of the film and aired on MTV as a video clip. "They [videos] were certainly around me," Mitchell notes of the format. "And there was certainly this question throughout [about] when Hedwig could look at the camera, or—in other words—break the fourth wall. Was this [technique] going to ruin something emotional, or was it going to heighten something?"

However, "Wig in a Box," which serves as Hedwig's soliloquy about her life, represented one of the few spots where the director and his crew deemed the video conceit helpful. "In other words, it would have been inappropriate in some songs, like 'Angry Inch,'" Mitchell considers. "We had the convention that whenever Hedwig is performing in concert that she wouldn't [address the camera] because that would take you out of it a little bit, but for the ones that were a little more internal, it was possible."

"There were some [numbers] that were both internal and in concert like 'Midnight Radio' at the end. I suppose I could have looked at the camera, but it wasn't necessary," Mitchell says. "But that point of view [Hedwig's], was always important for us to think about."

Trask's magnificent score won some much-deserved kudos when *The Orange County Register*'s Ben Wener remarked that "the music of *Hedwig* is a revelation, marking the first time since *Hair* that the dreaded concept 'rock musical' has succeed so well."[35] *Hedwig* also serves as a didactic movie about the difficult process of self-actualization. Hedwig only begins to find happiness when she stops looking for satisfaction in exterior sources, in other people. The film's message (displayed in the ongoing motif of *Plato's Symposium*) is that internal happiness—joy in one's self-identity—is the first stage in finding happiness with others. Credit Mitchell for making one of the best, most significant and daring rock films in a generation.

On *Hedwig's* soundtrack: "Tear Me Down," "Origin of Love," "Angry Inch," "Wicked Little Town (Tommy Gnosis Version)", "Wig in a Box," "The Long Grift," "Hedwig's Lament," "Exquisite Corpse," "Midnight Radio," "Nailed," "Sugar Daddy," "Freaks," "Your Arms Tonight," "Wicked Little Town (Hedwig version)."

DVD Available on DVD.

Help! (1965)(MUS)

STARRING: The Beatles, Leo McKern (Clang); Eleanor Bron (Ahmed); Victor Spinetti (Professor); Roy Kinnear (Algernon); Patrick Cargill (Superintendent).

FILM EDITOR: John Victor-Smith, DIRECTOR OF PHOTOGRAPHY: David Watkin. WRITTEN BY: March Behm, Charles Wood. PRODUCED BY: Walter Shenson. DIRECTED BY: Richard Lester. M.P.A.A. RATING: UR. RUNNING TIME: 90 minutes.

"*Relax…*Help! *is just around the corner.*"

Everybody loves *A Hard Day's Night*. *Yellow Submarine* is difficult to dismiss as anything less than a masterpiece. However, if any Beatles film didn't feel the love, it's 1965's *Help!*, directed by Richard Lester. This is actually a James Bond-styled spoof (spy mania was at its peak at the time), wherein Ringo Starr is marked as a human sacrifice by a strange cult because of a special ring that has fallen into his possession. *Help!* features strange cultists led by Leo McKern (Clang), mad scientists, hapless policemen, dynamic locations, and—for the first time on film—the Fab Four in living color.

Arguing the film's "cons," *Help!* offers no coherent narrative besides that aforementioned outline. Lester seems to indulge his own film style at the expense of The Beatles, and the picture has aged badly since the pop culture has since moved on from such satire. Indeed, the Bond films have successfully satirized themselves for decades now.

However, to this author's eyes, *Help!* remains funny—if surreal—and notable if, for no other reason, that there are moments here which reveal nuances of each band member's personality. Expectations were high after *A Hard Day's Night*, and probably—in fairness—couldn't legitimately be met by any film. Besides, many movies in the mid-to-late 1960s featured no coherent narrative (see: *Head*) and yet *Help!* isn't merely phantasmagoria. It's *amusing* phantasmagoria and Ringo is very funny in the film. So "*stop worrying,*" as the ad lines and advised and just go along for the ride.

At the very least, *Help!* features some great tunes including the titular song, "The Night Before," "You've Got to Hide Your Love Away," "I Need You," and "Ticket to Ride."

DVD Available on DVD.

High Fidelity (2000)(SOUNDTRACK)(CAMEOS)

STARRING: John Cusack (Rob Gordon); Iben Hjejle (Laura); Todd Louiso (Dick); Jack Black (Barry); Lisa Bonet (Marie); Catherine Zeta-Jones (Charlie Nicholson); Joan Cusack (Liz); Tim Robbins (Ian); Lili Taylor (Sarah); Natasha Gregson Wagner (Caroline).

FILM EDITOR: Mick Audsley. DIRECTOR OF PHOTOGRAPHY: Seamus McGarvey. BASED ON THE BOOK BY: Nick Hornby. WRITTEN BY: D.V. De Vincentis, Steve Pink, John Cusack, Scott Rosenberg. PRODUCED BY: Tim Bevan, Rud Simmons. DIRECTED BY: Stephen Frears. M.P.A.A. RATING: R. RUNNING TIME: 113 minutes.

John Cusack stars in this comedy, *The Big Chill* for Generation X. This movie (based on the novel by Nick Hornby) concerns a slacker, Rob (John Cusack), who breaks up with his latest girlfriend and experiences an existential crisis.

In hopes of finding out why he's always alone, Rob counts down his top five break-ups (which include the likes of Catherine Zeta-Jones and Lili Taylor). Meanwhile, in his second-hand record shop, two dweebs (Jack Black, Todd Louiso) debate every bit of pop-culture minutiae under the sun.

On the soundtrack are over fifty songs, many played just briefly. Joan Jett and the Blackhearts' "Crimson and Clover," Katrina and the Waves' "Walking on Sunshine," Liz Phair's "Baby Not Going," Bruce Springsteen's "The River," Peter Frampton's "Baby I Love Your Way," and Queen's "We Are the Champions" are a few selections from the film.

Bruce Springsteen—the Boss himself—cameos. *High Fidelity*'s next incarnation was as a 2006 Broadway musical. (DVD) Available on DVD.

The Horror of Party Beach (1964) (HORR)

STARRING: John Scott (Hank); Alice Lynn (Elaine); Allan Laurel (Dr. Gavin); Eulabelle Moore (Eulabelle); Marilyn Clarke (Tina); The Del-Aires.

FILM EDITORS: Leonard De Munde, Richard L. Hilliard, David Simpson. DIRECTOR OF PHOTOGRAPHY: Richard Hilliard. WRITTEN BY: Richard Hilliard. PRODUCED AND DIRECTED BY: Del Tenney. M.P.A.A. RATING: UR. RUNNING TIME: 78 minutes.

A horror musical? Well, not exactly. Perhaps more accurately a horror beach movie...

The black-and-white *The Horror of Party Beach* commences when a passing ship dumps radioactive crud into the water near a beach populated by partying teens. From the ensuing muck arise several sea monsters that boast mouths that appear to consist wholly of gruesome-looking sausage links. Some intrepid teens (not Frankie and Annette, however) team up with a clever scientist to kill the monsters (who attack a teenage slumber party). This movie has an unpleasant racist strain to it, but that's not nearly so offensive as the terrible acting and ridiculous monster costumes.

The Del-Aires perform a half-dozen rock tunes including the immortal "The Zombie Stomp" and "Elaine."

(DVD) Available on DVD with *The Curse of the Living Corpse* as The Del Tenney Double Feature.

Horror Rock The horror genre and rock 'n' roll share much in common. They're both disdained by mainstream critics and both unreasonably feared by moral majorities (usually of the conservative Christian variety). Considering the fact that both art forms have persistently proven to be "dark horse" genres and extremely popular with teen audiences, it's no surprise that clever producers have been coupling horror movies and rock music for forty-five years.

Ever since Arch Hall Jr. and the Archers took time off from the plot to sing "Vicki" and other tunes in the low-budget *Eegah!* (1962), rock stars and rock music have been inseparably coupled with horror. Del Tenney's *The Horror of Party Beach* (1964) and its infamous tune "Zombie Stomp" is another early example of this joining.

Throughout the 1960s, faded horror stars like Vincent Price and Boris Karloff also appeared in beach party movies, (which would occasionally feature ghosts as well).

It was in the 1980s, however, that rock and horror truly became inseparable. In slasher films such as *New Year's Evil* (1980) and *Graduation Day* (1981), all action stopped for rock performances. The *Monster Club* (1981) is a British horror anthology set at a disco; *Howling II: Your Sister Is a Werewolf* (1985) features punk-rock werewolves; *Trick or Treat* (1986) reveals the truth behind Satanic lyrics in heavy metal; and *Slumber Party Massacre II* (1987) gave the world its first rock 'n' roll boogeyman; a killer who was armed with a guitar/power-drill combo.

Throughout the 1980s, rock legends appeared in horror films: Alice Cooper in *Monster Dog* (1985) and *Prince of Darkness* (1987), Gene Simmons and Ozzy Osbourne in *Trick or Treat* (1986) and David Bowie in *The Hunger* (1983). In a fun turnabout, an alien shape shifter took the form of a rock star in *Critters* (1985).

Rockers AC/DC composed the score of Stephen King's *Maximum Overdrive* (1986), and Anthrax and Buckethead contributed the hard-driving pulse behind *John Carpenter's Ghosts of Mars* (2001).

As late as 2005, rock stars including Jon Bon Jovi continue to appear in horrors such as *Cry_Wolf*.

The Hours and Times (1991)(BIO-PIC)

STARRING: David Angus (Brian Epstein); Ian Hart (John Lennon); Stephanie Pack (Marianne); Robin McDonald (Quinones).

WRITTEN, DIRECTED, EDITED, SHOT AND PRODUCED BY: Christopher Munch. M.P.A.A. RATING: UR. RUNNING TIME: 60 minutes.

A low budget, hour-long black-and-white drama that was shot in roughly a week, *The Hours and Times* concerns Beatles Manager Brian Epstein (David Angus) and John Lennon (Ian Hart: see *Backbeat*) on a three-day vacation together in Barcelona just before the worldwide phenomenon of Beatlemania.

The film suggests that there may have been a homosexual experience shared by the two men, but is interested not so much in sex, however, as in exploring the dynamics of the relationship. Epstein (a reserved, Jewish, upper-crust type) and Lennon (a lower-class fellow) were vastly different sorts, ice and fire, respectively, and we all know that opposites attract, right? The friendship presented here is fascinating and tantalizing, but there's a level of frustration with the material too. We'll never know the answers to the questions of "did they" or "didn't they" so why even bring it up? It's a tease. Worse, it's a pretentious tease.

The Hours and Times seems to occur in a little pocket universe of its director's fashioning, and at times resembles an overeager student filmmaker's attempt to imitate the French New Wave. The cinema verité approach can be illuminating in many films, but remember—all the conversations here are purely fictional.

(DVD) Not Available on DVD.

House (1985)(HORR)

STARRING: William Katt (Roger Cobb); George Wendt (Harold); Richard Moll (Ben); Key Lenz (Sandy); Michael Ensign (Chet).

FILM EDITOR: Michael N. Knue. DIRECTOR OF PHOTOGRAPHY: Mac Ahlberg. PRODUCED BY: Sean Cunningham. STORY BY: Fred Dekker. WRITTEN BY: Ethan Wiley. DIRECTED BY: Steven Miner. M.P.A.A. RATING: R. RUNNING TIME: 93 minutes.

What begins as a fairly traditional haunted house movie with novelist Roger Cobb (William Katt) facing his ghosts

from Vietnam both literal and metaphorical, at the fifty-minute point takes a hard right turn and begins to feature comical montages set to popular 1960s rock.

"You're No Good" by Clint Ballard, Jr. And "Dedicated to the One I Love," by Lowman Pauling and Ralph Bass dominate the soundtrack for a time as the film reaches for Baby Boomer nostalgia.

(DVD) Available on DVD.

How to Stuff a Wild Bikini (1965)
(MUS)(CAMEO)

STARRING: Annette Funicello (Dee Dee); Dwayne Hickman (Ricky); Brian Donlevy (B.D.); Harvey Lembeck (Eric Von Zipper); Beverly Adams (Cassandra); John Ashley (Johnny); Jody McCrea (Bonehead); Buster Keaton (Bwana).

FILM EDITOR: Fred Feitshans. DIRECTOR OF PHOTOGRAPHY: Floyd Crosby. WRITTEN BY: Leo Townsend, William Asher. PRODUCED BY: Samuel Z. Arkoff, Anthony Carras, James Nicholson. DIRECTED BY: William Asher. M.P.A.A. RATING: UR. RUNNING TIME: 93 minutes.

Something's gone badly astray in this slapdash Annette/Frankie beach party movie. For one thing, Annette Funicello was pregnant during the making of this entry and appears as though she'd rather be anywhere else. For another, the movie is mostly sans Frankie. Avalon appears only in an extended cameo (as does *Bewitched* star Elizabeth Montgomery). So really, what's the point?

The plot this time finds Frankie called away into the Naval Reserves but fretting that his girl, Dee Dee

(Funicello) won't prove faithful to her man. Frankie consults a witch doctor (Buster Keaton), who conjures a new girl, Cassandra (Beverly Adams) to take the boys' roaming eyes away from sweet Dee Dee. There's also a subplot involving Dee Dee's new suitor, the blander-than-bland Dwayne Hickman as Ricky.

How to Stuff a Wild Bikini is notable mainly for offering a performance of the once-popular group, The Kingsmen. Here, the band sings "Give Her Lovin'."

The good news (or bad news, depending on perspective): Eric Von Zipper is on hand to make a mess of things. Harvey Lembeck assays the role for the penultimate time, and sings "The Boy Next Door" and "I Am My Ideal."

This movie is nobody's ideal.

(DVD) Available on DVD.

Howling II: Your Sister Is a Werewolf (1985)(HORR)

STARRING: Christopher Lee (Steffan Crosscoe); Annie McEnroe (Jenny Templeton); Reb Brown (Ben); Sybil Danning (Stirba); Marsha A. Hunt (Mariana).

FILM EDITOR: Charles Bornstein. DIRECTOR OF PHOTOGRAPHY: Geoffrey Stephenson. EXECUTIVE PRODUCER: Graham Jennings. Based on the novel HOWLING II. SCREENPLAY BY: Robert Sarno and Gary Brandner. PRODUCED BY: Steven Lane. DIRECTED BY: Philippe Mora. M.P.A.A. RATING: R. RUNNING TIME: 91 minutes.

"It's not over yet," warned this film's original teaser trailer, promoting the B-movie sequel to Joe Dante's 1981 werewolf masterpiece, *The Howling*.

"It's the rocking, shocking new wave of horror," promised *Howling II*'s tag-line, and indeed, the film features several stereotypical 1980s "punk" werewolves.

The film, ludicrously subtitled *Your Sister Is a Werewolf* also includes the stage performance of a tune titled "Howling" by a new wave group called Babel, which consists of lead singer Stephen Parsons, Chris Pye on guitar, Simon Etchell on keyboard, and Steve Young on drums. The band performs their oddly catchy tune at an L.A. nightclub called Slammer. Star Christopher Lee is in attendance at the performance, playing an occult investigator hunting werewolves, and—in one ridiculous moment—the dignified former Dracula adorns punk sunglasses.

"I've got a hunger that's emotional," the song's lyrics suggest, *"a hunger that I can't control!"* Anyone watching the film will be able to recite the song chapter and verse (and in his or her sleep) because it is repeated no less than six times. On one occasion, footage of the act's performance at the Slammer is cross-cut with a werewolf orgy in the dark country, Transylvania.

And, over the end credits, the song recurs one last time, accompanying the *sixteen* quick-cuts of star Sybil Danning, as Stirba—*Queen Bitch of the Werewolves*—ripping off her top and revealing her oversized, melon breasts. The film also features a werewolf three-way, and the fur really flies. Talk about a blue moon.

Now *that's* rock 'n' roll...

(DVD) Available on DVD.

The Hunger (1983)(HORR)(REAL ROCKER)

STARRING: Catherine Deneuve (Miriam Blalock); David Bowie (John Blalock); Susan Sarandon (Dr. Sarah Roberts); Cliff De Young (Tom Haver); Beth Ehlers (Alice Cavender); Dan Hedaya (Lt. Allegrezza); Rufus Collings (Charlie Humphries); Suzanne Bertish (Phyllis); James Aubrey (Ron); Willem Dafoe, John Pankow (Men at Phone Booth); Shane Rimmer (Arthur); Ann Magnuson (Woman from Disco); Bauhaus (Disco Group).

FILM EDITOR: Pamela Power. DIRECTOR OF PHOTOGRAPHY: Stephen Goldblatt. WRITTEN BY: Ivan Davis, Michael Thomas. FROM THE NOVEL BY: Whitley Strieber. PRODUCED BY: Richard Shepherd. DIRECTED BY: Tony Scott. M.P.A.A. RATING: R. RUNNING TIME: 100 minutes.

This is Tony Scott's odd but atmospheric story of a vampire love-triangle. Catherine Denueve plays Miriam, an immortal creature who faces the passing of her lover, played by David Bowie, and selects a new one in the form of a doctor, Sarah (Susan Sarandon) (**see: *The Rocky Horror Picture Show***).

This meditation on aging and immortality is set in the modern culture of death: the punk rock scene of the early 1980s. There, life is disposable and many of the folks who attend the urban dance clubs are up for anything…which makes it a good hunting ground for the predatory undead. In this world of garish pink hair, Mohawks, anonymous sex, strobe lights, black leather and body piercing, it is easy for Miriam and John to find blood feasts. Also, *The Hunger* puts the final nail in the coffin of *roller boogie rock*, since one of John's victims is a roller skater.

Although critic John Simon, writing for *The National Review,* called *The Hunger* "…a vampire film permeated with a totally effete interior decorator sensibility,"[36] it's actually a perfect mirror for the early 1980s, when punk was becoming more mainstream, and making its way into fashion and movies.

In addition to the androgynous presence of David Bowie and the excavation of the punk-rock milieu, *The Hunger* features a commendable rock score. Iggy Pop performs "Funtime" (by Bowie and Pop) and "Nightclubbing." Bauhaus' appropriately-titled "Bela Lugosi's Dead" is also featured.

(DVD) Available on DVD.

I

(is for *It Happened at the World's Fair*)

I Wanna Hold Your Hand

(1978)(SNDTRK)

STARRING: Nancy Allen (Pam Mitchell); Bobby DiCicco (Tony Smerro); Marc McClure (Larry DuBois); Susan Kendall Newman (Janis Goldman); Theresa Saldana (Grace Corrigan); Wendie Jo Sperber (Rosie Petrofsky); Eddiee Deezen (Richard "Ringo" Klaus); Christian Juttner (Peter); Murray the K (Himself); Will Jordan (Ed Sullivan); Dick Miller (Officer); Claude Earl Jones (Al).

FILM EDITOR: Frank Morriss. DIRECTOR OF PHOTOGRAPHY: Donald M. Morgan. WRITTEN BY: Robert Zemeckis, Bob Gale. EXECUTIVE PRODUCER: Steven Spielberg. PRODUCED BY: Tamara Asseyev, Alex Rose. DIRECTED BY: Robert Zemeckis. M.P.A.A. RATING: R. RUNNING TIME: 104 minutes.

Robert Zemeckis' *I Wanna Hold Your Hand* is a frantic slapstick comedy centered on the idea of Beatles nostalgia, and as a work of film art shares much in common with George Lucas' *American Graffiti* (1974). Created a full decade after The Beatles popularity, around the same time as the stage show *Beatlemania*, the film focuses on a group of four friends (this time all girls) who share one magic day and night together, the day, in fact of The Beatles' performance on American television (**see:** *The Ed Sullivan Show*).

These four girls from Maplewood, New Jersey, are the fan, Rosie (Wendie Jo Sperber), the uptight Pam (Nancy Allen), who is destined to marry a dullard, the protester, Janis (Susan Kendall Newman) who wants to boycott The Beatles but ends firmly under their thrall, and the kindly Grace (Theresa Saldana) who believes her ticket to a career in photojournalism depends on her ability to snare photographs of the Beatles at their hotel.

Much of the film involves the foursome's hijinks as they try to get close to the Fab Four, though in the 1990s this brand of fan devotion was known as stalking. In one particularly memorable scene, Nancy Allen's Pam makes it to the promised land. She reaches the boys' vacant hotel room and proves that her love for The Beatles is particularly sexual in nature as she worships each and every object in the room with fetishistic delight, stroking guitars and so forth with orgiastic glee.

I Wanna Hold Your Hand also utilizes the device of the *radio ticket giveaway* (**see:** ***Rock 'n' Roll High School, Detroit Rock City***), the plot gimmick wherein desperate fans, unable to attend a concert, get one last shot.

In the film's most unfunny and borderline bad taste sequence, Grace pimps herself out as a hooker to get fifty dollars to pay for scalped tickets. She doesn't go all the way, but it's still pretty unsavory. The movie's structure is repetitive, to its own detriment, as viewers are treated to seemingly endless scenes of the girls evading hotel security. Much of *I Wanna Hold Your Hand*'s humor feels busy— meaning that people run around and scream a lot—rather than actually amusing, let alone funny, but attention to detail is strong, especially in the scenes involving a record store where Beatles albums fly off the shelf.

Grease's Eddie Deezen also shows up in *I Wanna Hold Your Hand*, playing the ultimate Beatle fanboy. His scenes are funnier than many in the film, but *I Wanna Hold Your Hand*'s strongest feature is its authentic soundtrack. Although Zemeckis utilizes tricky camera work to prevent the audience from actually seeing The Beatles play live (even though all the girls attend the concert), the film doesn't skimp on music. Featured here are some of The Beatles' best efforts including "I Wanna Hold Your Hand," "I Saw Her Standing There," "Love Me Do," "I Wanna Be Your Man," and "She Loves You."

(DVD) Available on DVD.

The Idolmaker (1980)(SNDTRK)

STARRING: Ray Sharkey (Vincent Vacarri); Tovah Feldshuh (Brenda); Peter Gallagher (Caesare); Paul Land (Tommy Dee); Joe Pantoliano (Gino Pilato); Olympia Dukakis (Mrs. Vacarri); Maureen McCormick (Ellen Fields); Richard Bright (Uncle Tony); Steven Apostlee Peck (Mr. Vacarri); Deney Terrio (Jerry Martin).

FILM EDITOR: Neil Travis. DIRECTOR OF PHOTOGRAPHY: Adam Holender. WRITTEN BY: Edward Di Lorenzo. MUSIC AND LYRICS BY: Jeff Barry. CHOREOGRAPHY BY: Deney Terrio. PRODUCED BY: Gene Kirkwood, Howard W. Koch, Jr. DIRECTED BY: Taylor Hackford. M.P.A.A. RATING: PG. RUNNING TIME: 119 minutes.

Taylor Hackford, who directed the award-winning *Ray* in 2004, earlier contributed a *rags-to-riches* rock movie to the genre in the form of this sentimental and deeply flawed (but nonetheless fascinating) effort entitled *The Idolmaker*.

This is the story of Vincent (Ray Sharkey) an aspiring songwriter and would-be talent manager (see: *Manager*) who navigates the local rock scene in 1959 New York. He seeks financial help establishing his career from his gangster father, and then bribes a local DJ to get his new act on the air. That act is Tommy Dee (Paul Land), an unrefined, Fabian-like figure. Vincent also romances Brenda (Tovah Feldshuh), the editor of *Teen Scene* magazine to get Tommy Dee on the cover, but soon finds he's genuinely in love with her.

Vinnie's story takes a turn when disloyal Tommy leaves him for a bigger and better deal (with an agent from a company called IAA), leaving the hard-driving manager to groom a replacement (one who, perhaps, represents Frankie Avalon). This character is Caesare (Peter Gallagher) a talentless wretch and waiter at Vinnie's brother's Italian restaurant. Caesare must be schooled in dance, vocals and decorum, and totally lacks confidence.

After months of preparation and obsessive focus, Vinnie creates his second superstar in Caesare, but keeps him sequestered after limited performances designed to tweak interest in the idol. Then, in a daring initiative, he sends Caesare down South, Memphis specifically. Otherwise known as Elvis territory. At first this looks to be a major Waterloo, but Vinnie conceives the brilliant notion of dedicating the show to the King, and Caesare becomes a full-fledged star. Unfortunately, he too leaves Vincent behind.

Now Vinnie must decide who he wants to be and what he wants to do with his life. He goes back to his dream of being a rock star. At the end of the film, he takes the stage of a small club himself and begins to sing his own compositions. His climactic song is "I Believe It Can Be Done," a paean to sticking to your guns. The message for those who missed it? *Never give up on your dreams.*

That sounds cheesy, and this is indeed a cheesy, overly-theatrical effort from the 1980s, but one with a terrific amount of heart. Some of the numbers and costumes today appear downright laughable, and the film is ham-handed and clunky stylistically. Still, the movie has a dedicated cult following, in part because some of the story seems based on reality (and the lives of 1960s teen idols), and partly because the story of a regular Joe struggling to make it never loses its appeal.

The Idolmaker features a rich soundtrack that evokes the era of the mid-1960s. The Sweet Inspirations and The London Fog sing "A Boy and a Girl," and Peter Gallagher acquits himself respectably with Caesare's signature tunes, which include "Baby," "However Dark the Night" and "It's Never Been Tonight Before."

Hackford obviously went on to bigger and better things, but one feels he must still harbor a soft spot for this early effort, with its big, sentimental heart and great performance from Ray Sharkey.

About the latter, Janet Maslin at *The New York Times* had this to say about the film: "It hinges on a central performance that is much better than the movie around it. Ray Sharkey, playing a rock Svengali in the days of Frankie and Bobby and Dion and Fabian, captures the drive and mono-mania of a man who shapes others' destinies rather than his own. In those days, it took looks to be a teen idol—or so the movie, with some cynicism, maintains."[37]

(DVD) Available on DVD.

Imagine: John Lennon (1988)(DOC)

STARRING: John Lennon, Yoko Ono, Paul McCartney, George Harrison, Ringo Starr, David Bowie, Brian Epstein, Elton John, George Martin.

FILM EDITOR: Bert Lovitt. DIRECTOR OF PHOTOGRAPHY: Néstor Almendros. WRITTEN BY: Sam Egan and Andrew Solt. PRODUCED BY: David L. Wolper, Andrew Solt. DIRECTED BY: Andrew Solt. M.P.A.A. RATING: R. RUNNING TIME: 103 minutes.

The makers of 1981's *This Is Elvis* turned their attention to the life and times of ex-Beatle John Lennon with this dedicated effort. It's a succinct crystallization of hundreds of hours of candid home movies and video footage (and recorded conversations) that presents, overall, an even-handed picture of a man who was a great artist, but in the end, ultimately a man.

The film includes interviews with John's aunt who raised him, Sean and Julian Lennon, and Yoko Ono too. The Beatles appear in archival footage but were not interviewed fresh for *Imagine*. The movie also gazes at the period in 1971 when Lennon and Yoko toiled on the album *Imagine* and looks at the famous 1969 "bed-in" incident, and Lennon's clash with cartoonist Al Capp. In certain touching instances (including one with a clearly nuts fan), Lennon reveals his tender and giving nature.

Some see *Imagine: John Lennon* as a response (Yoko Ono's?) to a negative biography of the artist that had been published the year before the film's release, but overall this film doesn't appear to boast any overt agenda except to illuminate the life of a great and talented man who—

like the rest of us—occasionally had bad days.

"At its best," suggested *The Los Angeles Times*, "it's a sensitive tribute; at its worst, it's a hero-worshiping whitewash."[38] Julian Petley at *Monthly Film Bulletin* also came to the same even-handed conclusion: "While not making a meal of the darker side of Lennon's life and personality, the film doesn't ignore them either…"[39]

(DVD) Available on DVD.

It Happened at the World's Fair

(1963)(ELVIS)(MUS)

> STARRING: Elvis Presley (Mike Edwards); Joan O'Brien (Diane); Gary Lockwood (Danny Burke); Vicki Tiu (Sue-Lin); H.M. Wynant (Vince Bradley); Edith Atwater (Mrs. Steuben); Guy Raymond (Barney Thatcher); Yvonne Craig (Dorothy); Kurt Russell (Kid who kicks Elvis in the ankle).
>
> FILM EDITOR: Fredric Stein Kemp. DIRECTOR OF PHOTOGRAPHY: Joseph Ruttenberg. WRITTEN BY: S. Rose, Seaman Jacobs. PRODUCED BY: Ted Richmond. DIRECTED BY: Norman Taurog. M.P.A.A. RATING: UR. RUNNING TIME: 105 minutes.

Ever wish you could tag along with Elvis at the 1962 World's Fair in Seattle? Here's your chance. About midway through *It Happened at the World's Fair*, all narrative momentum ceases and Presley, playing crop-duster Mike Edwards, escorts little Sue-Lin (Vicki Tiu) from attraction to attraction at the World's Fair. The film dutifully records him buying her cotton candy, popcorn, and egg rolls, and walking her to the Space Needle and the monorail. The odd thing about this detour is that it's actually the best part of the picture, like some weird reality show (win a day at the Fair with Elvis!).

Without the shackles of a ridiculous narrative, Elvis gets to be his charming self, and his charisma always work best with children, for some reason. Appropriately, little Sue-Lin is nothing short of adorable. Still, you know you're living in a totally different America when a caretaker (in this case, Uncle Walter) permits his five-year-old daughter to go off with two male hitchhikers (who he's just met that day!) for an outing at the World's Fair.

Along the way, Elvis falls in love with a nurse, Joan O'Brien, in a role that barely registers. He also belts out a few tunes including "One Broken Heart for Sale" and "Relax." The movie ends with Elvis and his love, Diane, marching ahead of a parade at the fair just after Mike has applied to become an astronaut for NASA. At this point, you may wonder if he's smart enough to be an astronaut, and then Elvis answers that question with a song called "Happy Endings" which indeed indicates (in its lyrics) that his character is not very smart.

This is another weird and unnecessary entry in the Elvis canon, but *It Happened at the World's Fair* nonetheless features that great little travelogue in the middle, when the King of Rock 'n' Roll feeds his little friend too much junk food and takes her to the nurse's station to have her stomach pumped. Oh, and there's a chase with some fast-motion footage at the end as Elvis rescues Sue-Lin from her dream car of *"the future"* (which resembles the Adam West Batmobile) and escapes the guards at the World's Fair.

Here's a fun historical footnote: A very young (and uncredited) Kurt Russell plays the little kid at the World's Fair whom Elvis pays to kick him in the shins. Ironically, Kurt Russell later played Elvis in a 1979 TV-movie. Also, in his flick, *3,000 Miles to Graceland* (2000), a little kid runs up to Russell and kicks him in the shins, just as Kurt did to the real King so many years earlier...
Ⓓ Available on DVD.

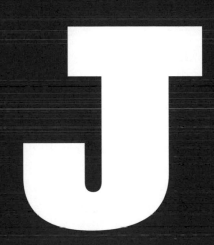

J

(is for *Jay & Silent Bob Strike Back*)

Mick Jagger (1943–)(ROCK MOVIE HALL OF FAME)

The lead singer for the immortal Rolling Stones began his film career in 1970 in Nicholas Roeg and Donald Cammell's daring and controversial *Performance*. He played the diabolical rock star (and manipulator extraordinaire), Turner in that film.

The same year saw the release of Jagger's Western, *Ned Kelly*, which featured the large-lipped icon in the titular role.

In 1992, Jagger played the soldier-villain doing Anthony Hopkins' evil bidding in the futuristic flop, *Freejack* (also starring Emilio Estevez). In 1997 he played the drag queen Greta in the film adaptation of the Broadway play *Bent*.

Of course, Jagger has also frequently appeared as himself on the silver screen, most notably in the documentary *Gimme Shelter* (1971). His vocals with The Rolling Stones can be heard in more films than could comfortably fit in this guide book. *Alfie* (2004), *Beyond the Sea* (2004), *S.W.A.T.* (2003), *Vanilla Sky* (1999), *The Royal Tennenbaums* (1999), and *Casino* (1995) are just a few recent examples.

The Stones' hit tune "Paint It Black" also served as the theme song to the TV series *Tour of Duty*, and also underpinned scenes in Stanley Kubrick's *Full Metal Jacket* (1987), making the song the official soundtrack of Vietnam.

Jailhouse Rock (1957)(ELVIS)(MUS)

STARRING: Elvis Presley (Vince Everett); Judy Tyler (Peggy Van Alden); Mickey Shaughnessy (Hunk Houghton); Jennifer Holden (Sherry Wilson); Dean Jones (Teddy Talbot); Ann Neyland (Laury Jackson).

FILM EDITOR: Ralph E. Winters. DIRECTOR OF PHOTOGRAPHY: Robert Bronner. PRODUCED BY: Pandro S. Berman. WRITTEN BY: Ned Young. DIRECTED BY: Richard Thorpe. M.P.A.A. RATING: UR. RUNNING TIME: 96 minutes.

The third Elvis film finally gives the man a wholly fitting role. Firebrand Vince Everett (Elvis Presley) kills an abusive man in a bar fight and is sent to jail as a result. While there, he learns music from Hunk Houghton, an old folk-circuit musician (Mickey Shaughnessy). Once out of prison, he tries his hand at a career in the new style of rock and blues, but doesn't get very far until he meets expert manager and eventual love interest Peggy Van Alden (Judy Tyler). The dizzying spiral to stardom forces Vince to re-evaluate his music, morals, and outlook, though as always, rock 'n' roll wins the day.

Love Me Tender (1956) and *Loving You* (1957) were but tastes of the iconic Elvis who was to emerge in *Jailhouse Rock*. Finally uniting echoes of Elvis' own career, the dangerous mystique of youth rock, and behind-the-scenes takes on rock culture into one package, *Jailhouse Rock* serves as a benchmark Elvis film. From more lulling ballads like "Young and Beautiful" to the rousing fame of "Jailhouse Rock," the film contains some fine tunes. The famous staging of "Jailhouse Rock" juxtaposes Elvis' "dan-

Elvis Presley, the King of Rock

(and Rock Movies too) struts in *Jailhouse Rock* (1957).

gerous" new moves against the old, outdated stylings of Hugh's cowboy folk. This historic film moment plays today as a campy relic of excess theatricality; one that was part and parcel of the 1950s rock production number. Played either for kitsch or for youthful enjoyment, *Jailhouse Rock* withstands many of the problems that plague Elvis' later films.

Central to *Jailhouse Rock* is the plot, common amongst rock films of the time, that the new youth music must supersede the old. Elvis and his refined, boppy blues, are shown as the only music that directly speaks to teens of the age, and through a comparison to Hunk's musty folk, emerges as the only financially viable option as well. All is not rosy, however: though far preferable to music of yesteryear in execution and in politics, the new rock does expose Elvis to the "dangers" of loose women, excessive money, and the predatory nature of the film and music businesses.

A sad postscript: *Jailhouse Rock's* lead actress, Tony Award-nominated Judy Tyler died in a car accident mere days after principal photography on the film. She died at the age of 23.—Kevin Flanagan.

Ⓓ Available on DVD.

James Bond In 1964, at the height of The Beatles' worldwide popularity, super spy James Bond, 007, fired a shot across the Fab Four's bow. In *Goldfinger*, Bond (played by Sean Connery) noted that drinking Dom Perignon '53

above 38 degrees Fahrenheit was like "*listening to the Beatles without earmuffs*."

Despite such public disdain for British rock, over the years the James Bond films produced by Albert Broccoli began to embrace rock 'n' roll. In fact, ex-Beatle Paul McCartney and Wings supplied the title song to the first Roger Moore Bond film, *Live and Let Die* in 1971.

Since then, rock—along with death itself—has been Bond's constant companion. Eighties super-group Duran Duran contributed the theme song for Moore's 1985 swan song, *A View to a Kill*, and 1987's *The Living Daylights* (starring Timothy Dalton) sponsored a title tune from A-Ha. The same debut featured two efforts from the Pretenders ("Where Has Everybody Gone" and "If There Was A Man").

Dalton's follow-up and swansong in the role, *Licence to Kill* (1989) featured Patti LaBelle singing Diane Warren's "If You Asked Me To."

The Pierce Brosnan era was ushered in to the strains of Bono and The Edge's composition *Goldeneye*, in 1995, a song sung by the Acid Queen herself, Tina Turner.

Sheryl Crow (*Tomorrow Never Dies*, 1997), and Garbage (*The World Is Not Enough*, 1999) have also sung Bond theme songs over the years. Most recently, material girl Madonna tried her hand at a Bond theme for *Die Another Day* (2002), but her techno-dance tune didn't find favor with some, including former Pinball Wizard Elton John, who criticized the composition as the worst Bond song ever.

Janis (1974)(DOC)

STARRING: Janis Joplin, Sam Andrews, Dick Cavett.

FILM EDITORS: Howard Alk, Seaton Findlay. CINEMATOGRAPHERS: James Desmond, Michael Wadleigh. PRODUCED BY: Howard Alk. WRITTEN BY: Howard Alk, Seaton Findlay. DIRECTED BY: Howard Alk. M.P.A.A. RATING: R. RUNNING TIME: 96 minutes.

The advertisements billed this documentary as *"The Way She Was…"*

Singer-songwriter Janis Joplin (1943–1970) is widely thought to be the inspiration for the hit film *The Rose* (1979) starring Bette Midler, but before that fictionalized cinematic enterprise there was this documentary from director Howard Alk which played briefly in theatres in 1975.

Janis is a compilation of archival footage that includes her appearances on *The Dick Cavett Show* just months before her death, performances at the Monterey Pop Festival in 1967 (with her group, Big Brother & the Holding Company), at Woodstock (in outtakes), in the recording studio working on her latest album, attending a ten-year high school reunion, and on tour in Europe.

This tragic native of Port Arthur, Texas was known to be a heavy drinker and heroin user (a balm to cover her insecurities and deep shyness, apparently), but *Janis* makes no mention of the talent's untimely death. Instead, it focuses primarily on Joplin's legendary performances and offers up a dozen of them.

Janis sings "Piece of My Heart," "Me and Bobby McGee," "Tell Mama," "Cry Baby," "Move Over, "Kozmic Blues," "The Good Days," "Summertime," "Ball & Chain" and more in the film, which plays as a testimonial to her talent and range, but which answers precious few questions about her personal troubles.

DVD Not Available on DVD.

The Jazz Singer (1980)
(FIC-BAND)(REAL ROCKER)

STARRING: Neil Diamond (Yussel Rabinovitch); Laurence Olivier (Cantor Rabinovitch); Lucie Arnaz (Molly); Paul Nicholas (Keith); Ernie Hudson (Heckler).

FILM EDITOR: Frank J. Urioste, Maury Winetrobe. DIRECTOR OF PHOTOGRAPHY: Isidore Mankofsky. BASED ON THE PLAY BY: Samson Raphaelson. WRITTEN BY: Stephen H. Foreman, Herman Baker. PRODUCED BY: Jerry Leider. DIRECTED BY: Richard Fleischer. M.P.A.A. RATING: PG. RUNNING TIME: 115 minutes.

A legendary Hollywood stinkeroo that opened the 1980s in putrid fashion (along with *Can't Stop the Music*). This is the second and by far the lesser remake of the 1927 original that ushered in the era of the talkie and had Al Jolson belting out "Mammy."

This re-imagination replaces the legendary Al Jolson with husky-voiced but charisma-challenged Neil Diamond (**see:** *The Last Waltz)*, and this performer is no actor. Furthermore, he comes across not as a likeable protagonist, but rather as a mean-spirited and selfish cad. Putting aside for the moment that there's no jazz in *The Jazz Singer*, though incongruously there is a scene with Diamond in blackface, the film fails primarily because Diamond plays a true louse who leaves his wife behind, then leaves his girlfriend/agent played by Lucie Arnaz, all for his own glory. Someone needed to tell him to turn on his "heart light."

The late Laurence Olivier is on hand too, as Diamond's draconian, conservative father; this great talent overacts badly, making his appearance in *Clash of the Titans* (1981) look good by comparison.

The Jazz Singer represents everything that a rock movie shouldn't be. It's maudlin, melodramatic, stupid, and oddly narcissistic. The film's ad-line suggests "*Sometimes you have to risk it all,*" but that only applies to the film's title character. *The Jazz Singer* gives Yussel (Diamond) a free pass to be cruel to others, all in the name of success and fame.

On the soundtrack: "America," "Love on the Rocks," "Summerlove," "Hello Again," "Songs of Life," and "Jerusalem."

(DVD) Available on a special 25th anniversary DVD edition!

Jay & Silent Bob Strike Back

(2001)(SNDTRK)(CAMEO)

STARRING: Ben Affleck (Holden/Himself); Jeff Anderson (Randal); George Carlin (Hitchhiker); Matt Damon (Himself); Eliza Dushku (Sissy); Shannon Elizabeth (Justice); Jason Lee (Brodie/Banky); Brian O'Halloran (Dante); Morris Day and the Time (Themselves); Jason Mewes (Jay); Kevin Smith (Silent Bob).

FILM EDITORS: Kevin Smith, Scott Mosier. DIRECTOR OF PHOTOGRAPHY: Jamie Anderson. WRITTEN BY: Kevin Smith. PRODUCED BY: Scott Mosier. DIRECTED BY: Kevin Smith. M.P.A.A. RATING: R. RUNNING TIME: 104 minutes.

Morris Day and the Time (see: *Purple Rain*) appear on stage to sing "Jungle Love" at the climax of this fifth View Askewniverse film from indie director and Jersey Boy Kevin Smith. Early in the film, stoners Jay (Jason Mewes) and Silent Bob (Smith) defend the tune "Jungle Love" from bratty twelve-year-olds at the Quick Stop who complain it's "gay" and Jay reports, to the contrary, that it was written by God *"and handed down to the greatest band in the world."*

Like *Purple Rain*, *Jay & Silent Bob Strike Back* ends on a freeze-frame. Here that moment comes after Morris Day and his band invite the New Jersey-ites on stage to dance alongside them.

(DVD) Available on DVD.

Jesus Christ Superstar (1973)(MUS)

STARRING: Ted Neeley (Jesus Christ); Carl Anderson (Judas); Yvonne Elliman (Mary Magdalene); Barry Dennen (Pontius Pilate); Bob Bingham (Caiaphas); Josh Mostel (King Herod).

FILM EDITOR: Antony Gibbs. DIRECTOR OF PHOTOGRAPHY: Douglas Slocombe. BASED ON THE MUSICAL BY: Tim Rice. WRITTEN BY: Norman Jewison, Melvyn Bragg. PRODUCED BY: Norman Jewison, Robert Stigwood. DIRECTED BY: Norman Jewison. M.P.A.A. RATING: G. RUNNING TIME: 108 minutes.

This is Norman Jewison's sterling adaptation of the Tim Rice stage musical, *Jesus Christ Superstar*. The show had run in London since 1969, and went to Broadway in 1971, but director Jewison makes the material his own, putting an incredible visual spin on it by shooting the film on location in Israel, often in the blazing heat, and gracing it with a modern sensibility.

Although the film occurs during the last week of Jesus' life, it blends eras in strange fashion. Jesus Christ is sometimes referred to as "J.C.," Roman soldiers wear contemporary-style military uniforms, and there's even a 20th century bus on display. Jesus is played by Ted Neeley, and Judas (Carl Anderson) is depicted as a black man. The songs all have Christian connotations including "The Last Supper," "Gethsemane," and "Crucifixion," but the vibe is pure pop-culture.

(DVD) Available on DVD.

Jimi Hendrix (1973)(DOC)

STARRING: Jimi Hendrix (archival footage); Eric Clapton, Mick Jagger, Little Richard, Lou Reed, Pete Townshend.

FILM EDITOR: Peter Colbert. PRODUCED AND DIRECTED BY: Joe Boyd, John Head, Gary Weiss. M.P.A.A. RATING: R. RUNNING TIME: 98 minutes.

Like *Janis*, this is a dedicated documentary about a lamented rock 'n' roller who died too young. Perhaps the greatest guitarist in rock history, the self-taught Jimi Hendrix (1942–1970) died under bizarre circumstances in London in 1970.

Made three years later, this documentary features talking-head interviews with the likes of Mick Jagger, Eric Clapton, Little Richard and Pete Townshend. Nothing too dramatic or controversial is said on camera, and the discussion focuses heavily on Hendrix's skills and influence, not personal matters. Again like *Janis*, there's also footage from *The Dick Cavett Show*.

Performance footage has been culled from a number of concerts and films, including the Monterey Pop Festival, Woodstock, Berkeley (**see: *Jimi Plays Berkeley***) and the Isle of Wight. Among the songs performed: "Hey Joe," "The Star-Spangled Banner" (**see: *Woodstock***), "Hear My Train a Comin'," "Machine Gun," "Purple Haze," and Dylan's "Like a Rolling Stone."

(DVD) Available on DVD.

Jimi Plays Berkeley (1971)(DOC)

STARRING: Jimi Hendrix, Billy Cox, Mitch Mitchell.

FILM EDITOR: Baird Bryant. CINEMATOGRAPHERS: Joan Churchill, Eric Saarinen. WRITTEN BY: Peter Pilafian. PRODUCED BY: Michael Jeffery, Peter Pilafian. DIRECTED BY: Peter Pilafian. M.P.A.A. RATING: UR. RUNNING TIME: 55 minutes.

On Memorial Day, 1970, just four short months before his death, Jimi Hendrix played a concert at the University of California at Berkeley, and it is that set that's recorded here. Hendrix played "Purple Haze, "Hear My Train a Comin'," "Lover Man," "Voodoo Chile," "Hey Baby," and Chuck Berry's "Johnny B. Goode." The footage in the film is sometimes interspersed with campus activities (including *Vietnam War* protests) and the film is considered some-thing of a classic today.

Peter Smokler was a young cameraman on the job during the concert, and had already shot footage on the Stones ill-fated documentary, *Gimme Shelter* (1970).

"I did all the stuff on the balcony," Smokler recalls. "A lot of it is kind of '*period photography.*' You know, say Jimi bends a note and I go a little out of focus and then back into focus."

"Then they got me down on the stage, and I was shooting just behind him. I was right in front of that Marshall amplifier just behind him. Sometimes you could see [cinematogrpher] Eric [Saarinen], there in the shot."

This brings up another memory. Particularly a lost opportunity.

"One time, he's [Saarinen], waiting for a film magazine, a film load, and he's not even looking at Jimi. And Jimi is plucking the guitar with his *teeth*, and Eric's looking away. It's pretty tragic because he's just waiting for film at that point."

(DVD) Available on DVD.

Johnny Suede (1991)(SNDTRK)

STARRING: Brad Pitt (Johnny Suede); Calvin Levels (Deke); Catherine Keener (Yvonne); Samuel L. Jackson (B. Bop); Nick Cave (Freak Storm).

FILM EDITOR: Geraldine Peroni. DIRECTOR OF PHOTOGRAPHY: Joe De Salvo. WRITTEN BY: Tom DiCillo. PRODUCED BY: Yoram

Mandel, Ruth Waldburger. DIRECTED BY: Tom DiCillo. M.P.A.A. RATING: R. RUNNING TIME: 97 minutes.

Brad Pitt in a pompadour! You won't be able to make heads nor tails of this quirky little film from the director of *Living in Oblivion* (1995). In it, Pitt plays a slow-witted fellow with big hair who adores Ricky Nelson and dreams of being a rock star. He lives in Brooklyn and one day blue suede shoes appear to make his off-kilter life complete.

Johnny dates the daughter of a record executive, but that relationship goes badly, and he switches to the more normal Yvonne, played by Catherine Keener. Samuel Jackson (before he was a star) is on hand as the band's bassist.

Other than that, your interpretation of this oddball material is as good as mine. The movie appears to occur in Brooklyn, but it's a pseudo-1950s Brooklyn, as if the world of *Streets of Fire* (1984) had been spun off into a cheap indie film.

Brad Pitt sings "Never Girl," "Midtown," and "Mamma's Girl," while Suede's competitor, Nick Cave, performs "Freak Mama's Boy."

(DVD) Not Available on DVD.

Josie and the Pussycats (2001)
(FIC BAND)

STARRING: Rachael Leigh Cook (Josie McCoy); Tara Reid (Melody Valentine); Rosario Dawson (Valerie Brown); Alan Cumming (Wyatt); Parker Posey (Fiona); Gabriel Mann (Alan).

FILM EDITOR: Peter Teschner. DIRECTOR OF PHOTOGRAPHY: Matthew Libatique. WRITTEN BY: Deborah Kaplan, Harry Elfont. BASED ON CHARACTERS CREATED BY: Richard H. Goldwater, Dan De Carlo, John L. Goldwater. PRODUCED BY: Tony De Rosa-Grund, Tracey E. Edmonds, Chuck Grimes, Marc Platt. DIRECTED BY: Harry Elfont, Deborah Kaplan. M.P.A.A. RATING: PG. RUNNING TIME: 95 minutes.

The old Archies comic book (and 1970s Saturday morning TV cartoon) gets its radical (and dreaded) face-lift for the 21st century and the age of corporate-promoted bubble gum rock in the eminently forgettable *Josie and The Pussycats*.

The film concerns the efforts of the evil record industry (**see: *Record Companies***) to pass subliminal messages through the releases of popular recording artists. The end result is that teens will be forced to spend money on commercial products, thus making business partners and the record company a bundle. When the boy band Du Jour is killed in a mysterious accident, girl band (think Spice Girls), the Los Angeles–based Josie and the Pussycats, gets recruited by evil Parker Posey and Alan Cumming to fill Du Jour's shoes.

Josie and the Pussycats exhibits a lot of nerve. It presents itself as a satire about mind control and product placement in the mass media, but succumbs to the very evils it rails against. As Susan Wlosczyzna wrote in *U.S.A. Today*: "Notice how none of the supposedly plot-driven product placements, everything from Target and Revlon to Steve Madden and Motorola, are misspelled. The promo ops sink to their lowest depths when Saturday morning TV's

cartoon answer to Chrissie Hynde, Josie (aptly kittenish Rachael Leigh Cook) and her would-be beau share a romantic interlude near an Aquarium's whale tank. A billboard for Evian water, presumably the H_2O of choice for belugas, looms large. The concept is so hypocritical, it's like Britney Spears calling Christina Aguilera underdressed and overexposed."[40]

Other critics found the anti-conformity message worth all the product plugs. "Even if you find the satire in *Josie and the Pussycats* self-serving," wrote David Edelstein at *Slate*, "you might still love the movie, buy the soundtrack, and surrender to the hype. That's what happened to me. I was hooked from the opening dead-on *NSYNC parody; convulsed by Alan Cumming's unflappably sleazy British band manager; then floored by the track 'Three Small Words'—delivered not as Archies-style bubble gum rock but with the driving power-pop backbeat of Juliana Hatfield or early Divinyls."[41]

The film's score includes "Three Small Words," "Pretend to Be Nice," "Spin Around," "You're a Star," and "Josie and the Pussycats [Theme]," all performed by the titular band, and Du Jour's "Du Jour Around the World."

Call me a cynic, but I'm not waiting with bated breath for the sequel: *Josie and the Pussycats in Outer Space*.
(DVD) Available on DVD.

(is for *Kurt & Courtney*)

Kid Galahad (1962)(ELVIS)(MUS)

STARRING: Elvis Presley (Walter); Gig Young (Willie Grogan); Lola Albright (Dolly); Joan Blackman (Rose); Charles Bronson (Lew); David Lewis (Otto Danzig); Liam Redmond (Father Higgins); Judson Pratt (Zimmerman).

FILM EDITOR: Stuart Gilmore. DIRECTOR OF PHOTOGRAPHY: Burnett Guffey. WRITTEN BY: William Fay. BASED ON THE STORY BY: Francis Wallace. PRODUCED BY: David Weisbert. DIRECTED BY: Phil Karsen. M.P.A.A. Rating: UR. RUNNING TIME: 95 minutes.

A musical remake of the Michael Curtiz 1937 drama starring Edward G. Robinson and Bette Davis, *Kid Galahad* stars Elvis Presley as an orphan soldier who trains to become a boxer at Grogan's Gaelic Gardens in upstate New York. Playing a kid with an incredible knockout punch (and a tough chin) who also happens to be an ace mechanic, Elvis sings six songs in the film and his character, Walter, romances Rose (Joan Blackman), the sister of Grogan (Gig Young), the camp owner with a gambling problem.

Raging Bull (1980) this ain't. Nor is it *Rocky* (1976) for that matter, but *Kid Galahad* is nonetheless a more engaging Presley vehicle than some because the King doesn't break character to sing quite so often, indulging in only half the usual number of songs.

Also, the characterizations are strong, and Elvis doesn't merely walk through his part as he does in some later efforts. Instead, he reveals a tender, sensitive side and Walter comes across as kind of sweet and gentle. Although the climactic fight against Sugar Boy Romero is bereft of suspense, *Kid Galahad* is a pleasant affair.

Kid Galahad opens with the song "King of the Whole Wide World" as Walter returns to his hometown of Cream Valley, and the King sings "This Is Living" with a bunch of boxing buddies. The other tunes are "Riding the Rainbow," "Home is Where The Heart Is," "I Got Lucky" and "A Whistling Tune."

(DVD) Available on DVD.

King Creole (1958)(ELVIS)(MUS)

STARRING: Elvis Presley (Danny Fisher); Carolyn Jones (Ronnie); Walter Matthau (Maxie Fields); Dolores Hart (Nellie); Dean Jagger (Mr. Fisher); Lilliane Montevecchi (Nina); Vic Morrow (Shark); Paul Stewart (Charlie Le Grand); Jan Shepard (Mimi Fisher); Brian Hutton (Sal); Jack Grinnage (Dummy); Dick Winslow (Eddie Burton); Raymond Bailey (Mr. Evans).

FILM EDITOR: Warren Low. DIRECTOR OF PHOTOGRAPHY: Russell Harlan. BASED ON THE NOVEL A STONE FOR DANNY FISHER BY: Harold Robbins. WRITTEN BY: Herbert Baker, Michael Vincent Gazzo. PRODUCED BY: Hal B. Wallis. DIRECTED BY: Michael Curtiz. M.P.A.A. RATING: UR. RUNNING TIME: 115 minutes.

King Creole is a superior effort in Elvis Presley's considerable stable of films. Buttressed by strong, nearly *film noir* quality photography, Harold Robbins' provocative source material, and fine work from director Michael Curtiz (*Casablanca*, 1942), this one is a winner, despite a downbeat but not unexpected ending.

Elvis plays young Danny Fisher, a high school student in New Orleans who, according to his principal boasts "*all the earmarks of being a hoodlum*." Technically, that's not true and Danny—famous at his school for two things: "*singing and flunking*"—has just had a bad spell of luck. He's been working himself to death at a variety of jobs, including as a bus boy in gangster Maxie Fields' (Walter Matthau) Bourbon Street bar because his father, a pharmacist, is unemployed.

Elvis spends the picture bouncing between kindly five-and-dime waitress Nellie (Dolores Hart) and a man-eating *femme fatale*, Ronnie, played by Carolyn Jones. He takes a job at the nearby King Creole club and becomes a singing sensation, but Fields' doesn't like having competition and with the help of a punk, Shark—played by *The Blackboard Jungle*'s resident thug, Vic Morrow—sets Danny up in a crime involving his own father. Danny will have no choice but to sing at Fields' club instead of King Creole, which belongs to a gentleman named Charlie (Paul Stewart).

Although there are plenty of songs for Elvis to sing in *King Creole*, they don't seem particularly jarring, nor do they slow down the action. Instead, they're a very enjoyable bunch. The film opens with Presley singing "Crawfish" to a neighbor (who may be a prostitute) while wearing a T-shirt. Later, he uses the song "Lover Doll" to distract attention away from Shark during a five-and-dime heist. Once he's ensconced at Charlie's club, he sings "King Creole" and a number of other tunes (including "Don't Ask Me Why") but closes the film with the moving tribute to the dead Ronnie, "As Long as I Have You."

It's fun watching *King Creole* and witnessing a young Walter Matthau play a thoroughly sinister, corrupt gang-

ster, especially if you're of the generation that's only familiar with him for his work in films like *Grumpy Old Men* (1992).

But still, it's Elvis who manages to hold the attention, and he crafts an interesting, complex character in Danny. The youngster is both responsible (working many jobs) and a scoundrel, at one point tricking Nellie into a motel room on the grounds that there's a "party" there. Carolyn Jones proves powerful as the film's "experienced" girl, a kept woman trapped in a gilded cage. In one moment, Matthau forces her to show off her legs, and her pain and embarrassment is palpable. The film's ending is predictable (and ties things up neatly for Nellie, who still has a thing for Danny) but also tragic, and the result is an Elvis Presley film that lingers in the memory long after a viewing. *King Creole* is right up there with *Kid Galahad* and *Follow That Dream* as one of the King's better cinematic endeavors.

King Creole is available on DVD in all of its black-and-white glory. If you decide to see just one Elvis film, it should be this one.

(DVD) Available on DVD.

Kurt & Courtney (1998)(DOC)

STARRING: Nick Broomfield, El Duce, Tom Grant, Hank Harrison, Courtney Love, Kurt Cobain (archival footage).

FILM EDITOR: Mark Atkins, Harley Escudier. DIRECTORS OF PHOTOGRAPHY: Joan Churchill, Alex Vender. EXECUTIVE PRODUCER: Nick Fraser. PRODUCED AND DIRECTED BY: Nick Broomfield. M.P.A.A. RATING: R. RUNNING TIME: 95 minutes.

This is Nick Broomfield's unofficial but fascinating documentary about the death of grunge rock idol Kurt Cobain. The lead singer for Nirvana and a pioneer in the Seattle music scene was found dead on April 8, 1994, a shotgun wound to his head. But was the twenty-seven-year-old's death a suicide as it was officially ruled? Or was it murder?

In sussing out the answer to such questions Broomfield delves into Cobain's background and history, revealing him as a sensitive soul who, at age two, sang Monkees and Beatles tunes for his Aunt Mary. There's footage of Kurt at a family Christmas party in 1987, and Broomfield introduces audiences to Cobain's first love, Tracy, who lived with him for three years. She reports how he was a skinny 120 pounds and wore layers of clothing to hide that fact. Nevertheless, he was often teased for being "effeminate."

As his celebrity grew, Cobain grew discomfited by the attention, the film reveals. "The reality of being famous is frightening," one of his friends declares. Cobain began to see his life as "phony," a Hollywood "mirage."

Meanwhile, Courtney Love is also profiled. And in somewhat less affectionate terms. The film notes that she and Cobain "bonded pharmaceutically" through drugs. They were married in 1992, and the film gets in some shots against Love, noting that Hole's first successful album was released the week of Cobain's suicide. Courtney's father, Hank Harrison (one-time Grateful Dead manager) is interviewed on-camera too. He's written a book called *Who Killed Kurt?* And he comments on a poem written in 1980 by his daughter, "Future Date," which he thinks reveals "a deranged thought process." He also provides a motive for Courtney to have murdered her husband: Cobain was apparently contemplating divorce and a change in his will, writing her out.

Courtney Love does appear in the film, though not willingly, so she can't make a case proving her innocence. Instead, it's strongly suggested that she is working behind-the-scenes to scuttle Broomfield's inquiry, getting MTV out of financing the picture. She also refuses to let Cobain's music be licensed for *Kurt & Courtney*, resulting in substitute grunge music being employed on the soundtrack instead (including "Potential Suicide" performed by Napalm Beach, and "Shake," written and performed by Theatre of Sheep). Broomfield also plays threatening phone answering machine messages left by Love for a writer, Victoria Clark, who had hoped to write a book about Nirvana.

The film ends ironically at an ACLU gathering wherein Courtney is a presenter of the "Torch of Freedom" Award, championing free speech. Nick Broomfield takes the stage and points out the hypocrisy of Love having anything to do with free speech, given her heavy-handed actions to prevent this movie from seeing the light of day.

Kurt & Courtney is ultimately a riveting documentary, but no solid answers are given about Cobain's demise. Many of the characters that do grant interviews to Broomfield are distinctly shady (including a hit-man named El Duce, who was reputedly offered $50,000 to kill the rock star). The case is never successfully made that Courtney Love is a murderer. That established, she does come off as a greedy, self-important exploiter.

DVD Available on DVD.

L

(is for *The Last Waltz*)

La Bamba (1987)(BIO-PIC)

STARRING: Lou Diamond Phillips (Ritchie Valens); Esai Morales (Bob Morales); Rosanna DeSoto (Connie Morales); Elizabeth Pena (Rosie Morales); Danielle von Zerneck (Donna); Joe Pantoliano (Bob); Rick Dees (Ted); Marshall Crenshaw (Buddy Holly).

FILM EDITOR: Don Brochu, Sheldon Kahn. WRITTEN BY: Luis Valdez. PRODUCED BY: Bill Borden, Taylor Hackford. DIRECTED BY: Luis Valdez. M.P.A.A. RATING: PG. RUNNING TIME: 108 minutes.

This film makes a nice bookend with *The Buddy Holly Story* (1978), since rocker Ritchie Valens (the subject of this bio-pic) died on February 3, 1959 in the same plane crash that stole the lives of the Big Bopper and Holly. Luis Valdez's popular 1987 film is constantly foreboding that ominous fate, referencing Valens' fear of airplanes from the first sequence (set in a playground).

The approach is a bit ponderous, not to mention cheesy and stereotypically Hollywood, but Valdez clearly didn't have much material to work with here. Valens only lived to be 17 years old, so the admittedly impressive talent didn't exactly have a rich life story to chronicle.

Instead, *La Bamba* is a better-than-average story that takes Valens (Lou Diamond Phillips in the role that made his career) from his home life as the son of Mexican-American migrant workers to his brush with fame (thanks to Alan Freed), which lasted not even a year. Along the way, the film depicts stress and resentment in Valens' relationship with his brother, played by Esai Morales, and charts a love affair with Donna (Danielle von Zerneck), who is white.

Otherwise, the film is rather mild, and not quite in the same league as *The Buddy Holly Story*. It engenders feelings of sadness that Valens' life was cut short, but not much else.

Ritchie Valens, we hardly knew you…

Los Lobos sings the Valens songs on the soundtrack (Phillips lip-synchs) and does a great job with these hummable tunes: "Rip It Up," "Oh Boy," "The Paddi Wack Song," "Come On, Let's Go," "La Bamba," and "Donna."

Critics responded to the film with unbridled enthusiasm, including David Sterritt. He explained that the film is a "sweet and funny account" of Valens' life, "charged with rock 'n' roll energy."[42] Michael Buckley at *Films in Review* commented that "Any time you have a good story, interesting characters, fine writing and direction, and superb performances—you've got a winner. And *La Bamba* is a winner."[43]

Ladies and Gentlemen, the Fabulous Stains (1981)(MUS)

STARRING: Diane Lane (Corinne Burns); Ray Winstone (Billy); Peter Donat (Harley); David Clamon (Dave); Laura Dern (Jessica); Cynthia Sikes (Alicia); Christine Lahti (Aunt Linda).

FILM EDITOR: Tom Benko. DIRECTOR OF PHOTOGRAPHY: Bruce Surtees. WRITTEN BY: Jonathan Demme, Rob Morton. PRODUCED BY: Joe Roth. DIRECTED BY: Lou Adler. M.P.A.A. RATING: R. RUNNING TIME: 87 minutes.

A portrait of the (not so) Fabulous Stains. Marin Kanter, Diane Lane,
and Laura Dern headline in *Ladies and Gentlemen: the Fabulous Stains* (1981).

A strange lost film that shares some ideas and ingredients with Allan Moyle's *Times Square* (1980). In both efforts, disenfranchised American teen girls adopt punk rock personas (there the Sleaze Sisters; here the Fabulous Stains) and flirt with rock fame.

In this case, a very young Diane Lane (see: *Streets of Fire*, 1984) plays Corinne Burns (stage name: Third Degree Burns), the leader of the Fabulous Stains. As an affectation, she has dyed her hair to make it resemble a skunk's black-and-white mane. The all-girl band opens for a couple of British punk bands (The Looters and The Tubes), and some ex-Sex Pistols (Paul Cook, Steve Jones) play roles in the film.

The Fabulous Stains was denied a mainstream theatrical release by Paramount back in 1982, but for a time in the 1980s was a fixture on late-night basic-cable television. Ironically, this movie seems to forecast how girl bands make, project, and sell their own pre-fab images, predicting the rise of Madonna and then Britney Spears.

(DVD) Not Available on DVD.

The Last Waltz (1978)(DOC)

STARRING: Robbie Robertson, Rick Danko, Richard Manuel, Levon Helm, Garth Hudson, Eric Clapton, Neil Diamond, Bob Dylan, Joni Mitchell, Neil Young, Ringo Starr, Dr. John, Van Morrison, Ronnie Hawkins, Ron Wood, Emmylou Harrison, The Staples.

FILM EDITORS: Yeu-Bun Lee, Jan Roblee. DIRECTOR OF PHOTOGRAPHY: Michael Chapman. ADDITIONAL DIRECTORS OF PHOTOGRAPHY: Laszlo Kovacs, Vilmos Zismond, Hiro Narita. PRODUCED BY: Robbie Robertson. DIRECTED BY: Martin Scorsese. M.P.A.A. RATING: PG. RUNNING TIME: 117 minutes.

On Thanksgiving Day, November 26, 1976, the long-lived group called The Band (formerly The Crackers, then the Honkies) held a concert at the Winterland in San Francisco, California and invited all their best friends to perform with them. This was a special event, the band's swan song together, and essentially a retirement bash after sixteen long years on the road.

Fortunately, director Martin Scorsese was also present at the event, armed with half-a-dozen 35mm cameras and some of the finest cinematographers in Hollywood to capture every detail. *The Last Waltz* is Scorsese's brilliantly-photographed concert film (and often termed the greatest rock documentary of all time). It's a film in which the director "*looks for rock heroes in the Olympian mode*"[44] and catches every detail of the performances by Eric Clapton, Neil Diamond, Bob Dylan, Joni Mitchell, Neil Young, Ringo Starr, and many, many more.

The Last Waltz is also packed with backstage conversations with The Band's members as they reflect on their dozen-plus year run, and discuss their reasons for retiring. They reminisce on their humble origins, coming down to America from Canada and living in poverty ("*At one point,*" they note, "*we had no food money*"). They remember a stop in Fort Worth, Texas where they played a burned out joint called the Skyline Lounge. There were three people in the audience (a one-armed go-go dancer and a couple of drunks) and only later did the members of The Band realize they were playing in Jack Ruby's old club.

In one instance, Scorsese's camera captures an impromptu jam to "Old Time Religion," and late in the game, Band member Rick Danko takes Scorsese to his clubhouse turned Master Control Music Room. "*It's like an office, I guess,*" Danko explains, "*but it used to be a bordello.*"

The interviews also cover such topics as groupies The Band met on the road ("I *love 'em! That's why I love the road!*") and—frankly—everybody appears strung-out and exhausted, bleary and hollow-eyed. Scorsese himself appears regularly onscreen as the interviewer and utilizes the unusual conceit of calling for "re-dos" from some of the participants to make the answers flow more smoothly.

"*Ask me that again,*" Band member Robbie Robertson insists at one point, hoping to reframe a particular answer. One shot (in that office that was once a bordello) reveals Scorsese rendered frozen, waiting to call action and begin walking down a corridor.

Why reveal all these "getting ready" moments before the actual interviews and specific shots? Perhaps to reveal the artificiality of The Band's answers to his queries, perhaps

just to imbue the film with a spontaneous, cinema-verité feeling, even though if the latter's truly the case, "actors" are not supposed to be directed, but behave naturally.

Martin Scorsese has often been named as the source for Rob Reiner's character, Marty DiBergi in *This Is Spinal Tap*, and Harry Shearer told me in *Best in Show: The Films of Christopher Guest and Company* that "the Scorsese model was there in *The Last Waltz*," and that "it was certainly something we were aware of, and we were certainly taking it into account."

Which brings this review to another point; all the music in the film is great, but there's something unintentionally funny about both The Band and Scorsese as narrator. Ridiculous questions get asked, and strange answers demonstrating *circular logic*, are tossed back. In the behind-the-scenes stuff, everyone just seems a bit addled, and Scorsese—for all his powerful intellect and curiosity as a filmmaker—doesn't ask probing questions that might expose more of The Bands' individual personalities and foibles.

Still, *The Last Waltz* is beautiful to watch, and it reaches an apex of visual poetry in its finale. As The Band plays on stage for the last time, their shadows—larger than life-loom over them against a black background, implicitly making the bond that this group is legend. Then, Scorsese's camera retracts, enacting a long slow pull-back until the group members are just tiny figures, their sixteen glorious years together on the road now behind them.

On the soundtrack, Neil Young performs "Helpless," Dr. John sings "Such a Night," Bob Dylan (wearing an obnox-

Van Morrison, Bob Dylan (in white cowboy hat) and Robbie Robertson celebrate the last days of The Band in Martin Scorsese's *The Last Waltz* (1978).

ious white cowboy hat) sticks around for two tunes, including "Forever Young," and Muddy Waters offers up "Ain't That a Man." The finale, "I Shall Be Released," is appropriately poignant.

In 2006 Scorsese filmed two concerts by the Rolling Stones at the intimate Beacon Theater in New York for a future film, prompting some fans to wonder if this tour might be the band's "Last Waltz."

The Last Waltz certainly ranks among the top ten "rock" titles any fan of the genre should see, and is currently available on a special remastered DVD.

(DVD) Available on DVD.

Let the Good Times Roll (1973)(DOC)

STARRING: Shirley Alston, Chuck Berry, Bill Haley and his Comets, Chubby Checker, Bo Diddley, Fats Domino, The Five Satins, Little Richard, The Shirelles.

FILM EDITOR: Jerry Schilling. CINEMATOGRAPHERS: David Myers, Robert C. Thomas. DIRECTED BY: Robert Abel and Sydney Levin. M.P.A.A. RATING: PG. RUNNING TIME: 100 minutes.

It's 1956 all over again, as some of the greatest rock 'n' rollers from that decade (and the 1960s too) play a concert at Madison Square Garden in New York City. The film makes extensive use of split-screen technology to balance acts like Chuck Berry, Chubby Checker, Fats Domino and the like against archival footage of the same talent in previous incarnations, as well as life in general in the 1950s (focusing on automobiles, educational shorts, and so forth).

The songs in the film include "Reelin' and Rockin'" by Chuck Berry, "Let's Twist Again" from Chubby Checker, "At the Hop" by Danny and the Juniors, "Blueberry Hill" from Fats Domino, The Five Satins doing "Earth Angel," Bill Haley and his Comets performing their standard "Rock Around the Clock," and Little Richard doing "Good Golly Miss Molly."

(DVD) Not Available on DVD.

Let It Be (1970)(DOC)

STARRING: The Beatles, George Martin, Linda McCartney, Yoko Ono, Billy Preston, Michael Lindsay-Hogg.

FILM EDITOR: Tony Lenny. DIRECTOR OF PHOTOGRAPHY: Tony Richmond. PRODUCED BY: Neil Aspinall, Mal Evans. DIRECTED BY: Michael Lindsay-Hogg. M.P.A.A. RATING: G. RUNNING TIME: 81 minutes.

All good things must come to an end. Even the Beatles. This rarely seen documentary charts the beginning of the end for the Fab Four.

Yoko Ono is on the scene by now, proving a glum and kind of grim presence throughout and harkening even worse days. George and Paul get sassy with each other in a *recording-studio session* over Harrison's guitar strumming, and there's not much pleasure or joy amongst the foursome, who must surely have been physically and mentally exhausted as they settled down to produce one more album. Lennon and Starr seem checked-out, George bitter, and Paul controlling—but undeniably pleased with himself.

Let It Be is famous primarily for its spontaneous studio rooftop performance (on January 30, 1969) that thrilled fans who happened by during their lunch hour. This was the last time the Beatles were together, and the show is like a little piece of Heaven for fans.

On the soundtrack: "Don't Let Me Down," "I've Got a Feeling," "The Long and Winding Road," "Shake, Rattle and Roll," "Get Back," and—of course—"Let it Be."

(DVD) Not yet released on DVD.

Let's Rock (1958)(SNDTRK)(MUS)

STARRING: Julius La Rosa (Tommy); Phyllis Newman (Kathy); Conrad Janis (Charles); Paul Anka (Himself); The Tyrones, The Royal Teens.

FILM EDITOR: S. Charles Rawson. DIRECTOR OF PHOTOGRAPHY: Jack Etra. WRITTEN BY: Hal Hackaday. PRODUCED AND DIRECTED BY: Harry Foster. M.P.A.A. Rating: UR. Running time: 79 minutes.

Danny and the Juniors perform the rousing "At the Hop" and The Royal Teens sing "Short Shorts" in the course of this obscure film about a crooner (Julius La Rosa) who is urged to consider a transition to rock music when his popularity fades. Paul Anka (singing "I'll Be Waiting For You") is among those trying to convince the old-fashioned talent to change his ways before it's too late. Rock is the future, babe.

(DVD) Not Available on DVD.

Let's Spend the Night Together (1983)(DOC)

STARRING: The Rolling Stones.

FILM EDITOR: Lisa Day. CINEMATOGRAPHERS: Caleb Deschanel, Gerald Feil. PRODUCED BY: Ronald L. Schwary. DIRECTED BY: Hal Ashby. M.P.A.A. RATING: PG. RUNNING TIME: 95 minutes.

Originally titled "Time Is On Our Side" this is a record of the Rolling Stones' 1981 American tour. It's a concert film with the exteriors lensed at Sun Devil Stadium in Tempe, Arizona. Reportedly, Keith Richards and Mick Jagger were at odds when they made the film, but this doesn't stop either talent from giving an energetic performance on stage.

Director Hal Ashby follows the *Woodstock* prototype by showcasing preparations for the show and also giving panoramic views of the vast audience. There's some backstage material too (shot at the Brendan Byrne Arena in New Jersey), and Jagger's main squeeze, Jerry Hall, cameos with a line of models during the performance of "Honky Tonk Woman."

The Stones perform two dozen of their best tunes including "Beast of Burden," "Jumpin' Jack Flash," "Let It Bleed," Let's Spend the Night Together," "Satisfaction," "Time Is on Our Side," and "You Can't Always Get What You Want."

(DVD) Though released theatrically in the States, the film hasn't been released on DVD, though VHS copies can still be found.

Light of Day (1987)(FIC BAND)

STARRING: Michael J. Fox (Joe Rasnick); Gena Rowlands (Jeanette); Joan Jett (Patti Rasnick); Michael McKean (Bo Montgomery); Jason Miller (Ben); Billy Sullivan (Benji); Michael Rooker (Oogie).

FILM EDITOR: Jacqueline Cambas, Rose Kuo, Jill Savitt. DIRECTOR OF PHOTOGRAPHY: John Bailey. WRITTEN BY: Paul Schrader. EXECUTIVE PRODUCER. Doug Claybourne. PRODUCED BY: Rob Cohen, Keith Barish. DIRECTED BY: Paul Schrader. M.P.A.A. RATING: PG-13. RUNNING TIME: 107 minutes.

Paul Schrader's *Light of Day* is a blue-collar rock film and an imaginative retelling of "The Prodigal Son" story, only this time with a wayward daughter, played by Joan Jett, reconnecting to her family in a time of grief and death. Michael J. Fox (wearing a mullet) also stars as Joe Rasnick, a sensitive rocker who headlines a rock band with his talented sister, Patti (Jett). Their group (which also includes *Spinal Tap*'s Michael McKean) play at small corner bars all over the Rust Belt, while contending with Patti's out-of-wedlock child, and recession-era factory closings.

Eventually, however, the irresponsible Patti leaves her son and the band behind to join a more successful band, The Hunzz. She wants to live by an idea, and that idea is rock 'n' roll, she notes. "*The beat is all there is.*"

When Patti returns just in time to reconcile with her dying mother (Gena Rowlands), Mom—a conservative, religious WASP—makes plain that Patti is the one who is most loved, and that all is forgiven. Joe, meanwhile, has always stayed true to his family, yet is somehow not cherished nearly as much.

Michael J. Fox and Joan Jett make convincing siblings in *Light of Day*, in part because they share the same haircut. More to the point, the actors share a nice chemistry; Jett is particularly strong playing a brooder and slightly aloof character.

Light of Day is also enlivened by a raft of hard-driving factory-town rock tunes that make a perfect time-capsule for the mid-1980s, including the titular "Light of Day" by Bruce Springsteen.

"This Means War" and "Rabbit's Got the Gun" come from Joan Jett and Kenny Laguna, and "Cleveland Rocks" appears on the soundtrack too. Fox shares a tender duet with Patti's child called "You've Got No Place to Go," and the film's ultimate message seems to be that even when times are bad, there's still rock 'n' roll.

Not everyone was convinced the Schrader film worked. At *The Washington Post* Rita Kempley called it "*Terms of Endearment*, on overtime. Only nobody, but nobody, cares about these women [Jett and Rowlands], both as shallow as sheet cake."[45]

Eagle-eyed watchers will note that during one scene, graffiti on the wall in a venue Green Room includes the title of Spinal Tap's infamous album, "Smell the Glove."

(DVD) Not available on DVD; though VHS copies are still available through secondary venues.

Lineage (or The History of the Band)

(GENRE CONVENTION) Rock bands seem to change members and names at the drop of a hat, and this equation is mirrored in many rock films.

In *The Last Waltz*, onscreen narrator Martin Scorsese learns the lineage of The Band. First they were The Crackers, then they become The Honkies, until they realized that the latter title sounded too "street."

In *This Is Spinal Tap*, the addled band-members describe for onscreen interviews with Marty DiBergi their heritage as The Creatures, The Lovely Lads, The Originals, then The New Originals, then The Thamesmen and then Spinal Tap.

In *That Thing You Do!*, the band goes from being The One-ders to The Wonders, but more significantly reveals its history, step-by-step. At first, the band was The Echoes, then The Corvettes, then The Band You Are About to Hear, then The Tempos, and then The Herdsman.

Love Me Tender (1956)(ELVIS)(MUS)

STARRING: Richard Egan (Vance Reno); Deborah Paget (Cathy Reno); Elvis Presley (Clint Reno); William Campbell (Brett Reno); Neville Brand (Mike Gavin).

FILM EDITOR: Hugh S. Fowler. DIRECTOR OF PHOTOGRAPHY: Leo Tover. WRITTEN BY: Maurice Geraghty, Robert Buckner.

PRODUCED BY: David Weisbart. DIRECTED BY: Robert D. Webb. M.P.A.A. RATING: UR. RUNNING TIME: 89 minutes.

A third-billed Elvis Presley makes his silver screen debut in this Civil War opus (the ads promised "*You'll Love Him Tender in the Story he was Born to Play!*"). Elvis plays a Confederate named Clint Reno who marries the beautiful Cathy, the woman one of his brothers (presumed dead) once loved. However, when older brother Vance (Richard Egan) shows up, alive and kickin' the drama really begins.

Debra Paget and Elvis Presley behind-the-scenes
on the set of the King's first movie, 1956's *Love Me Tender*.

Released in November 1956, and originally titled *The Reno Brothers* (until some clever marketer thought to exploit Elvis' song title), *Love Me Tender* was a major box-office hit, grossing nearly five times its cost of $1 million.

Surprisingly, especially when one contemplates the remainder of Elvis' screen canon, the King doesn't actually sing much in his debut, instead limiting himself to a mere four tunes: "Love Me Tender," "Let Me," "Poor Me," and "We're Gonna Move."

As for the King's acting chops: he's definitely got them. In *Love Me Tender*, he reveals rage, tenderness, and more, and isn't at all the zombie sleepwalker of later fare like *Harum Scarum*.

An interesting historical footnote: *Love Me Tender* has the distinction of being the only movie in which Elvis Presley's character dies onscreen.

(DVD) Available on DVD.

Loving You (1957)(MUS)

Starring: Elvis Presley (Deke Rivers); Lizabeth Scott (Glenda Markle); Wendell Corey (Walter); Dolores Hart (Susan); James Gleason (Carl).

Film Editor: Howard A. Smith. Director of Photography: Charles Lang. Written by: Herbert Baker, Hal Kanter, Mary Agnes Thompson. Produced by: Hal B. Wallis. Directed by: Hal Kanter. M.P.A.A. Rating: UR. Running time: 101 minutes.

It's a *rags-to-riches* story for Elvis Presley in his first color film. *Loving You* features elements that would accurately be described as "autobiographical" since the film concerns country boy Deke Rivers' ascent to fame and fortune as a rock star, as well as his troubles with a demanding, controlling manager. No, not the Colonel, but Lizabeth Scott's ambitious Glenda Markle.

Elvis bounces between romantic affiliation with Scott and the innocent, nice girl played by Dolores Hart. This would become a recurring battle in his later films (which almost always feature two women vying for his affection) so in a sense, one might see *Loving You* as the template for the movie "line."

Elvis sings "Mean Woman Blues," "(Let Me Be Your) Teddy Bear," "Loving You," "Hot Dog," "Party," and "Got a Lot o' Livin' to Do."

(DVD) Available on DVD.

M

(is for *Metallica: Some Kind of Monster*)

Madonna (1958–)(ROCK MOVIE HALL OF FAME)

The Material Girl rocketed to fame in the early 1980s and since then has produced fifteen solo albums, which combined have sold more than one 150 million copies. Back in the 1980s, however, Madonna inspired a particular sect of teenage girls to dress exactly in her distinctive style. This fan base became known forever after as "Madonna Wannabes."

Madonna's first big starring role came in Susan Seidelman's *Desperately Seeking Susan* (1984), a mistaken-identity comedy also starring Aidan Quinn and Rosanna Arquette. Although the film did well at the box office, its critical reaction was mixed.

Madonna then countenanced a double-header of financial and artistic cinematic failures, including *Shanghai Surprise* (1986), which she made with then-husband Sean Penn, and *Who's That Girl?* (1987).

The rocker-turned actress made something of a comeback in the 1990s with Warren Beatty's comic-book feature *Dick Tracy* (1990), for which she composed the hit "Vogue" with Shep Pettibone and starred as the sultry *femme fatale*, Breathless Mahoney.

Madonna's documentary film (lensed in black-and-white), *Truth or Dare*, impressed the critics, if for no other reason that it revealed her compulsive drive to succeed. Penny Marshall's 1992 baseball movie *A League of Their Own* featured Madonna in a supporting role (with stars Geena Davis, Tom Hanks, and Rosie O'Donnell), and drew both audience and reviewer praise. Another high point in her film career was her role in Alan Parker's adaptation of the Andrew Lloyd Webber musical, *Evita* (1996), in which Madonna drew raves for her performance as Argentina's Peron.

Unfortunately, Madonna's next move was a starring role (opposite Willem Dafoe) in the sexual thriller *Body of Evidence* (1993), another gross misstep, an attempt to play in Sharon Stone's *Basic Instinct* territory. Recently, she also received scathing reviews for her performance in second husband Guy Ritchie's remake of Lina Wertmuller's *Swept Away* (2002).

Madonna contributed a title song to the last Pierce Brosnan 007 film, *Die Another Day*, and also had a cameo in the picture as a fencing instructor. Her songs have been featured in a variety of films over the years, including 1991's *My Own Private Idaho* ("Cherish") 1994's *With Honors* ("I'll Remember") 2000's *Snatch* ("Lucky Star"), and 2005's *Ice Princess* ("Ray of Light").

In addition to her musical skills as a vocalist, composer, and performer, Madonna has also proven to be a best-selling author of children's books.

Magnolia (1999)(SNDTRK)(MUS)

STARRING: Julianne Moore (Linda); William H. Macy (Quiz Kid Donnie Smith); John C. Reilly (Jim Kurring); Tom Cruise (Frank T.J. Mackey); Philip Baker Hall (Jimmy Gator); Philip Seymour Hoffman (Phil Parma); Jason Robards (Earl Partridge); Melora

Walters (Claudia Gator); Ricky Jay (Narrator); Melinda Dillon (Rose Gator); Felicity Huffman (Cynthia).

FILM EDITOR: Dylan Tichenor. DIRECTOR OF PHOTOGRAPHY: Robert Elswit. ORIGINAL SONGS BY: Aimee Mann. PRODUCED BY: Paul Thomas Anderson and Joanne Sellar. WRITTEN AND DIRECTED BY: Paul Thomas Anderson. M.P.A.A. RATING: R. Running time: 188 minutes.

Paul Thomas Anderson, the wünderkind who had directed perhaps the best film of 1997 (and one of the best films of the 1990s), the extraordinary *Boogie Nights*, returns with a three-hour sophomore effort called *Magnolia*.

If his first film felt like an homage to the works of Martin Scorsese and Brian De Palma, this adopts a different tack, emerging as a Robert Altman-esque narrative consisting of interlocking vignettes and packed with dozens of characters (including ones played by Tom Cruise, Julianne Moore, the late Jason Robards, William Macy, and *Chicago*'s John C. Reilly). They all play troubled characters facing various personal crises in Los Angeles at the turn of the twenty-first century.

The film is by no means a traditional musical. However, at the two hour and twenty minute point of *Magnolia*, as the dramatic emotions roil and erupt, each of the *dramatis person-ae* suddenly pauses and begins to sing a tune entitled "Wise Up," along with performer Aimee Mann, the song's composer. It's a moment of sudden and expected cohesion that weaves the diverse characters and multitudinous stories together through music, and in the best tradition of the format, communicates their innermost feelings. Interestingly,

this sequence is no accident or twist of fate, no music video "inserted" awkwardly into the film's narrative.

On the contrary, Aimee Mann's compositions are the bedrock thematic gestalt of *Magnolia*, and in fact, represent Anderson's very impetus to create the film in the first place. He felt that Mann's songs fit in exactly with the theme he wanted to explore in a screenplay, particularly "emotional rescue."[46]

In addition to "Wise Up," *Magnolia* showcases eight of Mann's original and memorable compositions, including "Momentum," "Build That Wall," and "Save Me." "Wise Up" is the only song actually sung by the cast in *Magnolia* in old-fashioned "break into song"-style, and yet the sensitive, emotionally exhausting film finds meaning and resonance through Mann's compositions.

[DVD] Available on DVD.

The Manager (GENRE CONVENTION) Bands in

rock movies often boast a love/hate relationship with managers. In *This Is Spinal Tap*, the hapless Ian (Tony Hendra) oversees one promotional disaster after another on the band's U.S. tour, and is ultimately replaced on the job by David St. Hubbins' (Michael McKean) girlfriend, Jeanine Pettibone (June Chadwick).

In the documentary *The Filth and the Fury* (2000), The Sex Pistols refer to their manager, Malcolm McLaren as a "cunt" and blame him for their failure to appear at venues, or earn riches. Even worse, *The Great Rock 'n' Roll Swindle* is alleged to be McLaren's version of events, not the band's. See, he even stole the group's movie!

The relationship between rock bands and managers is a two-sided coin, however. Tom Hanks plays a kindly manager in *That Thing You Do!* (1996), one who takes The Wonders from nowhere to somewhere, at least before the group implodes. He's always on hand providing good business decisions and advice for the guys. He even plays matchmaker between Guy (Tom Everett Scott) and Faye (Liv Tyler).

Similarly, Jimmy (Chuck Patterson) in *The Five Heartbeats* turns out to be a real stand-up guy, getting the group signed and looking out for their interests. He's too good a manager, in fact, and the Big Red Record Company puts out a hit on him so they can continue to manipulate and exploit the band without his interference.

Eddie Izzard plays Brian Slade's manager, Jerry Devine, in *Velvet Goldmine* (1998), and he is neither good nor evil, merely amoral. All he cares about in the end is money. That description may also accurately refer to Albert Grossman, Bob Dylan's manager in the documentary *Don't Look Back* (1967). A scene in that film finds Grossman in the office of a British promoter, manipulating events behind the scenes to play two British TV stations against each other and boost Dylan's revenues.

Very few rock films have featured a manager as the central character, but one notable exception to that rule is Taylor Hackford's *The Idolmaker* (1981), starring Ray Sharkey. This film follows a manager attempting to groom two teen idols (named Tommy Dee and Ceasare) before

returning to his own love: singing and writing songs.

Other famous rock managers in film history include the sour-puss Billy Fish played by Rick Moranis in *Streets of Fire* (1984) and the very sarcastic Bullets (Paul Lynde) in *Beach Blanket Bingo* (1965). But if I had my druthers in choosing a manager, I'd select pre-adolescent Raoul, Elvis' manager in *Fun in Acapulco*. In a show-stopping scene, he really earns his 15 percent by pitting local hotel owners against each other in a bidding war for the King's singing services.

Meat Loaf (1949, or maybe 1951–)(ROCK MOVIE HALL OF FAME) This oversized talent made his big-screen debut in the midnight movie sensation of the mid-1970s, *The Rocky Horror Picture Show* (1975), and then went on (in 1977) to release *Bat Out of Hell*, one of the biggest selling rock albums of all time.

Born Marvin Lee Aday, this Texan has seen an up-and-down career at the movies, starring in such bombs as *Roadie* (1980) and cult hits including David Fincher's *Fight Club* (1999). In the latter, he starred as "Bob," part of Tyler Durden's terrorist cult…the ultimate in authority-bashing symbols.

Meat Loaf has also made cameo appearances in rock-oriented films including *Americathon*, *Wayne's World,* and *Spice World*. He recently appeared in the gone-so-fast-you-missed-it *Blood Rayne* (2005).

Metallica:
Some Kind of Monster (2004)(DOC)

STARRING: James Hetfield, Lars Ulrich, Kirk Hammett, Bob Rock, Eric Avery, Joe Berlinger, Jason Newsted.

FILM EDITORS: Doug Abel, M. Watanabe Milmore, David Zieff. CINEMATOGRAPHERS: Wolfgang Held, Robert Richman. PRODUCED AND DIRECTED BY: Joe Berlinger and Bruce Sinofsky. M.P.A.A. RATING: R. RUNNING TIME: 141 minutes.

"All next week is therapy…"

This Joe Berlinger/Bruce Sinofsky co-production is a superb 21st-century rock documentary, a fascinating and compelling peek behind-the-scenes at the so-called "unraveling of a band," in this case, the popular Metallica, the "biggest heavy metal band of all time."

Joe Berlinger's stunningly effective (and riveting) documentary opens with detailed background information about Metallica to help bring the uninitiated up to speed. Ninety million Metallica albums have been sold since 1981, the film reports, the band represented the top concert draw in North America during the 1990s, and in 2000 the group engendered the enmity of many fans by filing a lawsuit against the Internet file-sharing company Napster.

All this information comes quickly, and then—in the year 2001—the film's story proper commences. Jason Newstead has quit Metallica, and the group is in something of a shambles. On the film's "Day 1," (April 24, 2001), Metallica gathers and Berlinger and Sinofosky's cameras begin tracing the group's activities for a marathon span over a whopping 660 days.

"The monster," the band establishes, "lives."

Metallica rents out recording studio space in an empty barracks at the former military base, the Presidio, in San Francisco and the group's collective hope is to record a new album. But that task is easier said than done, and this chronicle bears harrowing witness to days in which various musicians experience "shit moods." It follows a critical period during which band member James Hetfield goes M.I.A. for a long spell, retreating to an "undisclosed location" (meaning rehab) to confront his issues with substance abuse.

Throughout the film, Metallica meets regularly with a therapist named Phil Towle, who attempts to solve some of the vexing traumas of each band member. Lars Ulrich, for instance, deals with an overly critical father. Hetfield is an arrogant adolescent who runs roughshod over the other band members. "You're just sitting there being a complete dick," he's told.

Towle attempts various methods by which to help Metallica through these trying times. At one point, the flailing band even attempts to develop a mission statement, a strangely establishment and corporate assignment for a rock 'n' roll band to undertake. At times, the movie's very existence itself is threatened, as band members complain about the ubiquitous cameras and wonder if they should just call a halt to the whole enterprise.

Metallica: Some Kind of Monster resurrects many rock movie clichés, including the *guitar collection* and the *press conference* (in which the band is laughably asked to briefly "sum up" a twenty-year career), but the film achieves frisson (and no doubt eternal fame) because of what it adds to the rock form, not what it repeats.

To wit, this is truly full-body-contact filmmaking. Unlike previous efforts such as *The Kids Are Alright* (1979) or *U2: Rattle and Hum* (1988), the plan here is not to maintain distance between percipient and perceived, but rather to foster a remarkable and unprecedented sense of intimacy.

This film doesn't throw up barriers to "knowing" Metallica, and, in fact, it tears them down. Through the rigorous and difficult process of therapy, it lays bare the group's conflicts and personal problems at the same time it reveals character flaws and foibles. Quite simply, there's never been a rock documentary so real.

There's no overt acting here (**see:** *Don't Look Back*) on the part of Metallica, and instead tough issues are breached head-on in frequently grueling, close-up terms. Taken as a whole, it's an incredible chronicle.

Ultimately, the vehicle of therapy in itself becomes a problem, as Towle inserts himself increasingly into the band's dynamic, and Metallica starts to wonder if there's a "conflict of interest" underpinning their healing. Phil is asked to leave in all kinds of roundabout ways, and he diabolically uses psychological jargon and psychobabble to stay in the loop; creating an additional burden for these musicians.

Rarely has a rock band permitted itself to so openly and closely be observed by its public. This is literally point-blank filmmaking, and *Metallica: Some Kind of Monster* is raw, powerful, and absolutely addictive. Berlinger and

Sinofsky's effort is impossible to turn away from, and it inspires empathy for its stars, who—when all is said done—emerge as beloved and "real" people, not remote icons.

Simply put, this is one of the ten greatest titles in the genre's history.

The soundtrack includes a combination of hard-driving Metallica tunes, old and new. These include: "Frantic," "Seek and Destroy," "Some Kind of Monster," "Dirty Window," "Tommy Boy," "My World," "Shoot Me Again," "Enter Sandman," "Purify," "Sad But True," "Sweet Amber," and "St. Anger."

⟨DVD⟩ Available on DVD.

Mister Rock and Roll (1957)(MUS)

STARRING: Alan Freed; Teddy Randazzo; Lois O'Brien (Carole Hendricks); Rocky Graziano; Jay Barney (Joe Prentiss); Frankie Lymon, Little Richard, Chuck Berry, Screamin' Jay Hawkins.

FILM EDITOR: Angelo Ross. DIRECTOR OF PHOTOGRAPHY: Maurice Hartzband. WRITTEN BY: James Blumgarten. PRODUCED BY: Howard B. Kreitsek, Ralph B. Serpe. DIRECTED BY: Charles S. Dubin. M.P.A.A. RATING: UR. RUNNING TIME: 86 minutes.

Don't Knock the Rock. *Again.* In the early days of rock history, genre films were understandably obsessed with validating and legitimizing the form, and this black-and-white example of the form is no different. Parents, repeat after me: Rock music does *not* cause juvenile delinquency. Got that?

Mister Rock and Roll Himself, disc jockey (and rock music booster) Alan Freed.

Mister Rock and Roll is the *"big story"* of the *"sensation that's swept the world!"* according to the film's advertising. It's told by *"the king of Rock 'n' Roll Himself."* No, not Elvis Presley, but rather DJ Alan Freed (see also: *American Hot Wax*). Here, the accent is on how Freed introduced the format to so many radio listeners and helped to popularize rock.

"Young people," the movie poster instructed *"Show your adults how terrific your music is! Take them to see this picture that explains all about the new exciting rhythm. They'll love it as much as you do!"*

That may have been a clever strategy to get more warm bodies into theatres, but the real "worth" of this movie to kids and parents alike was probably the performances of Little Richard (singing "Keep A Knockin'") and Chuck Berry (offering "Oh, Baby Doll").

(DVD) Not Available on DVD.

Mobbed! (GENRE CONVENTION) This is what occurs when rock stars interact with the screaming fans; and it happens all the time in rock movies. In *A Hard Day's Night* (1964), The Beatles resort to trickery (and hiding in a line of phone booths) when a mob of crazy fans chase them through a train station.

In *I Wanna Hold Your Hand* (1978) a mob likewise surrounds The Beatles' hotel room, and restricts their motions.

In *Don't Look Back* (1967) a crazy fan jumps on Bob Dylan's car and won't get off the hood...even while it's moving.

Screaming, out-of-control fans also appear in *The Doors* (1991), *The Idolmaker* (1981), *Rock Star* (2001) and many other genre pictures. Sometimes fans scream and faint, sometimes they throw things at the stage, and sometimes they wax enthusiastic about their favorite acts, but regardless of their behavior, they're an important part of the equation.

The Monster Club (1981)(HORR)

STARRING: Vincent Price (Erasmus); John Carradine (R. Chetwynd-Hayes); Barbara Kellerman (Angela); James Laurenson (Raven); Donald Pleasence (Pickering); Richard Johnson (Father); Britt Ekland (Mother); Stuart Whitman (Sam).

FILM EDITOR: Peter Tanner. DIRECTOR OF PHOTOGRAPHY: Peter Jessup. FROM THE NOVEL BY: R. Chetwynd-Hayes. SCREENPLAY BY: Edward and Valerie Abraham. PRODUCED BY: Milton Subotsky. DIRECTED BY: Roy Ward Baker. M.P.A.A. RATING: Unrated. RUNNING TIME: 104 minutes.

In the tradition of such 1970s British Amicus horrors such as *Tales from the Crypt* (1972) and *Vault of Horrors* (1973) comes this "fab" U.K. genre anthology starring Vincent Price and John Carradine. The film finds Price's starving vampire, Erasmus, bumming a little blood off of kindly old horror novelist Carradine, and then inviting the Good Samaritan to his favorite hang-out, the Monster Club. Once at the establishment, Erasmus tells his friend three ghoulish stories detailing monster genealogy and monster interaction with the human race.

Between the stories, however, Price and Carradine get funky to the strains of UB40 and such tunes as "Monster Club."

If you ever felt the burning desire to see horror legends Vincent Price and John Carradine dancing under a glitter ball like geriatric John Travoltas (only surrounded by monsters in cheesy masks rather than Brooklynites), this is the disco movie for you.

(DVD) Not Available on DVD.

Monster Dog (1985)(HORR)

STARRING: Alice Cooper (Vincent Raven); Victoria Vera (Sandra); Carlos Santurio (Frank); Pepita James (Angela); Emilio Linder (Jordan); Jose Sarsa (Marilou); Charley Bravo (Townie); B. Barta Barri (Old Man); Ricardo Palacios (Sheriff Morrison); Luisa Maluenda (Deputy).

FILM EDITOR: Antonio Jose Ochoa. DIRECTOR OF PHOTOGRAPHY: José García Galisteo. EXECUTIVE PRODUCERS: Helen Sarlui, Edward Sarlui. PRODUCED BY: Carlos Aured. WRITTEN AND DIRECTED BY: Clyde Anderson. M.P.A.A. RATING: NR. RUNNING TIME: 81 minutes.

Rock icon Alice Cooper plays "the hottest rock star in the world," Vincent Raven, in this cheapjack 1980s horror film. As *Monster Dog* commences, Raven returns to his ancestral home, a strange village, after a twenty-year absence in order to shoot a music video there. Once there, however, Raven must confront the legacy of his father, a man who turned into werewolf.

The best parts of the film involve Cooper taking center stage in a couple of mock music videos, including the catchy "Identity Chrises" [sic], the number which opens the film, and "See Me in the Mirror."

(DVD) Available on DVD.

Monterey Pop (1968)(DOC)

STARRING (IN ORDER OF APPEARANCE): Scott McKenzie, The Mamas and the Papas, Canned Heat, Simon & Garfunkel, Hugh Masekela, Jefferson Airplane, Grace Slick, Big Brother and the Holding Company, Janis Joplin, Eric Burdon and the Animals, The Who, Country Joe & the Fish, Otis Redding, Jimi Hendrix, Ravi Shankar.

FILM EDITOR: Nina Schulman. CINEMATOGRAPHERS: James Desmond, Barry Feinstein, Richard Leacock, Albert Maysles, Roger Murphy, D.A. Pennebaker, Nick Proferees, Bob Neuwirth, Tim Cunningham, Robert Leacock, John Maddox, Peter Pilifian, Robert Van Dyke. FESTIVAL PRODUCED BY: John Phillips, Lou Adler. DIRECTED BY: D.A. Pennebaker. M.P.A.A. RATING: UR. RUNNING TIME: 80 minutes.

The place to be from June 16 to June 18, 1967 (during the so-called Summer of Love) was the county fairgrounds in Monterey, California. It was there that a peaceful, large-scale rock festival, the first of its kind and the predecessor to Woodstock, was held. All proceeds for the concert went to charity and none of the big-name talents were paid (except sitar-player Ravi Shankar).

Over 200,000 well-behaved young people of all creeds attended the conference (roughly 50,000 a day) and D.A. Pennebaker, maestro of the Dylan documentary *Don't Look*

The late, great guitarist Jimi Hendrix.

Seen here in a moment from his performance in *Monterey Pop* (1968).

Back (1967), filmed it all. Although The Beach Boys were no shows and The Rolling Stones couldn't attend because of legal troubles, the acts who did appear on stage went on to become major stars of the rock genre. The Monterey International Pop Festival also carries the distinction of being America's introduction to Jimi Hendrix.

"The vibrations are just going to be flowing," one fan enthuses near the beginning of *Monterey Pop*, and the observation is an accurate one. Pennebaker's camera catches the construction of the stage and preparations for the show, all to the tune of "San Francisco (Be Sure to Wear Flowers in Your Hair)" by Scott McKenzie. From there, the cinema verité director cuts to views of a strong police presence. Apparently, there was fear that the Hell's Angels and Black Panthers would crash the festival, but in actuality, there was no violence.

Taking the stage first in the film, against a psychedelic backdrop no less, are the Mamas and the Papas, and they sing their mid-1960s hit "California Dreamin'." Simon & Garfunkel take the stage after Canned Heat, lit in a gorgeous apricot light (and filmed in loving close-up) as they perform "The 59TH Street Bridge song (Feelin' Groovy)."

Hugh Masekela is next as blobs of light play on a psychedelic backdrop. As *Monterey Pop* goes on, Pennebaker edits in specific footage of the festival routine with certain songs. During The Stones' "Paint It, Black," performed by Eric Burdon and the Animals, there are shots of attendees eating watermelon, corn on the cob and toasting marshmallows. Pennebaker's camera work grows more frenetic during The Who's performance of "My Generation,"

which ends—predictably—with Pete Townshend destroying his guitar (see: *Destruction of Property*). Country Joe & the Fish play a lengthy instrumental while folks sleep in the grass, and then Otis Redding drives the crowd wild. "We all love each other, don't we?" he asks, revving up the audience.

Then comes the phenomenon known as Jimi Hendrix. He plays "Wild Thing" (with a hair of "Strangers in the Night" in the mix). Before he's finished, Hendrix suggestively humps a speaker, and lights his guitar on fire onstage (again see: *Destruction of Property*).

Ravi Shankar closes the footage and his lengthy but impressive work with the sitar is cut to images of the crowd, which now includes painted cars and painted faces. There's even a love monkey on hand, literally: a monkey with the word "love" painted in red across his forehead.

All in all, this is quite an amazing document of that weekend nearly forty years ago, and in it's own way it may be as accomplished a film (if noticeably more brief) than the more well-known festival film, *Woodstock*.

(DVD) Available on DVD.

More American Graffiti

(1979)(SNDTRK)

STARRING: Paul Le Mat (John Milner); Ron Howard (Steve); Charlie Martin Smith (Terry the Tiger); Candy Clark (Debbie); Mackenzie Phillips (Carol); Cindy Williams (Laurie); Bo Hopkins (Joe); Harrison Ford (Falfa).

FILM EDITOR: Tina Hirsch. DIRECTOR OF PHOTOGRAPHY: Caleb Deschanel. WRITTEN BY: Bill Norton. EXECUTIVE PRODUCER: George Lucas. PRODUCER: Howard Kazajnan. DIRECTED BY: Bill Norton. M.P.A.A. RATING: PG. RUNNING TIME: 111 minutes.

This is the disappointing sequel to George Lucas' classic about early 1960s teen and cruising culture. *American Graffiti* gazed nostalgically at one night (in 1962) in the life of several ordinary American teens. It was a film about endings: of high school and of innocence both personal and national. The closing card of that film revealed the destinies of the individual characters, including, in one notable case, a tragic death. Considering that finale, a sequel was not only unnecessary, but probably ill-advised.

More American Graffiti offers a different kind of structure and takes on the turbulent 1960s full-bore. It looks at the returning characters over a series of progressive New Year's Eves (1964/65/66/67). John Milner (Paul Le Mat) races hot rods in 1964 and falls for a Swedish girl who doesn't speak English. Terry the Tiger (Charlie Martin Smith) goes AWOL in Vietnam in 1965. His girl, Debbie (Candy Clark) becomes a hippie in 1966 and hooks up with a band. And in 1967, married couple Laurie (Cindy Williams) and Steve (Ron Howard) get involved with

Laurie's "radical" brother, who is organizing a rally against the *Vietnam War* on a nearby campus. Confusingly, the film repeatedly cuts between years rather than featuring each story sequentially, meaning that one minute the audience is in 1964, the next in 1965, and so on. Since *American Graffiti*'s closing card revealed the fate of Milner (dying in a car accident, New Year's Day 1965) as well as Terry's fate (missing in action), the sequel merely grinds to a predetermined conclusion and loses all sense of inspiration or surprise.

The central problem with *More American Graffiti* is that it's difficult to feel nostalgia for the Vietnam War or Laurie and Steve's domestic problems. Also, the audience is always aware that Milner—the film's most likeable character—is going to die. That doesn't exactly make the film fun; more like a wake. The glory of the first *American Graffiti* was that it took place in one night that changed the life of all these characters, even though it was loosely structured. This film takes place over four nights across four years and is tightly structured, but reveals nothing new about the characters. One can see why Richard Dreyfuss decided not to participate in the project.

Rebellion against *authority*, a common rock-movie theme, is on hand here as Terry blows up a latrine in Vietnam, covering a Major and a U.S. politician in shit. Later, Steve assaults a police officer and steals a bus full of demonstrators.

The 1960s era is captured most powerfully, however, by the use of music. A football game in Vietnam is enlivened by Sam the Sham and the Pharoah's "Wooly Bully," and the police brutality at the 1967 anti-war rally explodes to The Doors' "Light My Fire." Debbie's coda is made more touching by Simon and Garfunkel's "The Sound of Silence," and the film also features a host of other memorable tunes, including Aretha Franklin singing "Respect," the Angels' "My Boyfriend's Back," The McCoys' "Hang on Sloopy" and Barry Sadler performing "Ballad of the Green Berets."

My recommendation? Buy the soundtrack but forget about the movie.

[DVD] Currently available on DVD.

Moulin Rouge (2001)(SNDTRK)

STARRING: Nicole Kidman (Satine); Ewan McGregor (Christian); John Leguizamo (Toulouse-Lautrec); Richard Roxburgh (The Duke); Jim Broadbent (Zidler); Garry McDonald (the Doctor); Jacek Koman (The Unconscious Argentinian); Kylie Minogue (Green Fairy).

FILM EDITOR: Jil Bilcock. DIRECTOR OF PHOTOGRAPHY: Donald M. McAlpine. WRITTEN BY: Baz Luhrmann, Craig Pearce. PRODUCED BY: Martin Brown, Baz Luhrmann, Fred Baron. DIRECTED BY: Baz Luhrmann. M.P.A.A. RATING: PG-13. RUNNING TIME: 127 minutes.

This stunning, Bollywood-esque musical from Baz Luhrmann is the Orphean tale of a Bohemian poet, Christian (Ewan McGregor), heading into the Underworld of the Moulin Rouge club to rescue his lady love, a doomed courtesan named Satine (Nicole Kidman). What makes *Moulin Rouge* a rock movie, however, is the

decision by director Luhrmann and writer Craig Pearce to feature contemporary rock and pop hits to serve as representations of Christian's period poetry.

Thus, the soundtrack is dominated by rock artists and rock tunes. Nicole Kidman sings "Sparkling Diamonds" (while swinging over the dance floor of the Moulin Rouge), and it's a fusion of "Diamonds Are a Girl's Best Friend" and Madonna's "Material Girl." Similarly, Madonna's "Like a Virgin" is resurrected for an amusing sequence involving Zidler (Jim Broadbent). Sting's "Roxanne" is transformed into "El Tango De Roxanne." David Bowie contributes "Nature Boy" and has penned "Diamond Dogs" for Beck.

Most impressive of all, perhaps, is the film's finest set piece, called "Elephant Love Medley," in which stars McGregor and Kidman sling snippets of love songs back and forth at one another in staccato succession. This staggering, warp-speed medley includes Paul McCartney and John Lennon's "All You Need Is Love," "I Was Made for Lovin' You" by Paul Stanley, Phil Collins' "One More Night," U2's "Pride (In the Name of Love)," Paul McCartney's "Silly Love Songs," "Heroes" by David Bowie and Brian Eno, and Elton John's "Your Song."

"Christian's got to do the ultimate thing," says writer Craig Pearce, explaining the presence and nature of this unusual medley. "It must be the ultimate expression of his Orphean gift so she, Satine, will fall in love with him. It's obvious what it must be: a medley of the greatest love tunes of all time. On top of an elephant. In the Moulin Rouge. In the middle of the night. What else could it be?"

The lovers' secret song in *Moulin Rouge* is one of the film's few original rock compositions, "Come What May" by David Baerwald. The film's biggest hit, however—especially with the MTV crowd—is Pink, Lil' Kim, Mya, Missy Elliot, and Christina Aguilera singing "Lady Marmalade."

DVD Available on DVD.

Muscle Beach Party

(1964)(MUS)(CAMEOS)

STARRING: Frankie Avalon (Frankie); Annette Funicello (Dee Dee); Luciana Paluzzi (Julie); John Ashley (Johnny); Don Rickles (Coach); Peter Turgeon (Theodore); Joel McCrea (Deadhead); Peter Lupus (Flex); Stevie Wonder.

FILM EDITOR: Fred R. Feitshans, Eve Newman. DIRECTOR OF PHOTOGRAPHY: Harold Wellman. WRITTEN BY: William Asher, Robert Dillon. PRODUCED BY: Samuel Z. Arkoff, Robert Dillon, James H. Nicholson. DIRECTED BY: William Asher. M.P.A.A. RATING: UR. RUNNING TIME: 94 minutes.

This sequel to the hit *Beach Party* (and the second film in the beach party movie franchise from American International Pictures) looks like Shakespeare compared to some of the efforts that would follow (*Ghost in the Invisible Bikini*, anyone?).

Here, original stars Annette Funicello and Frankie Avalon are in fine, youthful form as they find their blissful beach existence interrupted when an obnoxious coach (Rickles) brings his squad of muscular body builders (including a pre-*Mission Impossible* Peter Lupus) to take

over a stretch of sand.

At the same time, gorgeous Luciana Paluzzi, playing the wealthy Italian heiress Julie, arrives at the beach and makes waves. After a little romantic time with Flex (Lupus), the *Thunderball* (1964) Bond girl sets her eyes on Frankie, who—of course—is already spoken for...though he needs some reminding. Now Annette has to fight to keep her man!

Missing in action this time around is Harvey Lembeck's "Rats" leader, Eric Von Zipper.

Dick Dale and The Del Tones stop by to sing "Muscle Beach Party" and "My First Love," and "Little" Stevie Wonder performs "Clap Your Hands!" and "Happy Street." Frankie and Annette take turns with the film's musical leitmotif, "A Girl Needs a Boy."

DVD Available on DVD.

N

(is for *Neon Maniacs*)

Neon Maniacs (1986)(HORR)

STARRING: Allan Hayes (Steven); Leilani Sarelle (Natalie); Donna Locke (Paula); Victor Elliot Brandt (Devin); David Muir (Wylie); Marta Kober (Lorraine); P.R. Paul (Eugene); Jeff Tyler (Wally); Amber Austin (Lisa).

FILM EDITOR: Timothy Snell. DIRECTORS OF PHOTOGRAPHY: Oliver Wood, Joseph Mangine. MUSIC SCORE: Kendall Schmidt. MUSIC PRODUCERS: Murri Barber, Michael Gusick. WRITTEN BY: Mark Patrick Carducci. PRODUCERS: Steven Mackler, Christopher Arnold. DIRECTED BY: Joseph Mangine. M.P.A.A. RATING: R. RUNNING TIME: 90 minutes.

At a high school in California, a teen named Natalie (Leilani Sarelle) sees her friends murdered by a coterie of costumed mutants or madmen, the maniacs of this low-budget horror film's title. She is befriended by a boy named Steve, who heads his own rock band and helps her determine that water can kill the monsters.

At a high school dance and band competition, the kids suit up with water guns in the event of an attack, and Steve sings rock tunes including "Baby Lied" and "The Choice You Made," both by Rick Bowles, as well as "We Had Enough" by Split Sydney.

At one point in the competition, Rick also sings a number called "Let Me Ruin Your Evening," which is a good description of what could happen after watching this movie. The director, Joseph Mangine, spends an inordinate amount of time during his ostensible climax cutting back to the *battle of the bands* competition and rock numbers, rather dissipating the film's already meager suspense.

(DVD) Not Available on DVD.

New Year's Evil (1980)(HORR)

STARRING: Roz Kelly (Diane Sullivan); Kip Niven (Richard Sullivan); Chris Wallace (Lt. Clayton); Grant Creamer (Derek Sullivan); Louisa Moritz (Sally); Jed Mills (Ernie).

FILM EDITOR: Dick Brummer. DIRECTOR OF PHOTOGRAPHY: Edward Thomas. MUSIC: W. Michael Lewis, Laurin Rinder. STORY BY: Leonard Neubauer, Emmett Alston. DIRECTED BY: Emmett Alston. M.P.A.A. RATING: R. RUNNING TIME: 85 minutes.

Diane Sullivan (Roz Kelly), the host of "Hollywood Hotline," a rock 'n' roll celebration on New Year's Eve in L.A., is judging the best new wave song of the year when she receives a telephone call-in from a psychopath who calls himself Evil and informs her that his resolution is to commit murder.

In this early 1980s slasher film, the murders (one in each time-zone as it becomes midnight, New Year's Day) are cross-cut with several rock performances on stage before a dancing punk crowd.

Among the rock songs are those from the groups "Made in Japan" and also "Shadow." One of the songs is actually called "New Year's Evil," another, charmingly, "Suicide Ways."

(DVD) Not Available on DVD.

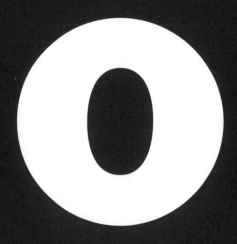

(is for *O Lucky Man!*)

O Lucky Man! (1973)(MUS)(REAL ROCKER)

STARRING: Malcolm McDowell (Mick Travis); Ralph Richardson (Sir Burgess/Monty); Rachel Roberts (Gloria); Arthur Lowe (Duff); Helen Mirren (Patricia).

FILM EDITOR: David Gladwell. DIRECTOR OF PHOTOGRAPHY: Miroslav Ondricek. WRITTEN BY: David Sherwin. PRODUCED BY: Lindsay Anderson, Michael Medwin. DIRECTED BY: Lindsay Anderson. M.P.A.A. RATING: R. RUNNING TIME. 183 minutes.

This Lindsay Anderson film (a follow-up to *If*, 1968) is a sprawling, three-hour satire-cum-fairy tale that commences with the legend *"once upon a time,"* and then proceeds to parody virtually all aspects of modern Western society, and in particular, British society (a theme he created in *If*).

O Lucky Man! stars Malcolm McDowell as Travis, a man who is the central figure in this modern-day odyssey. Hired as a salesman by the Imperial Coffee Company, Travis is tasked to run the northeast sector where the former salesman, Oswald, has mysteriously vanished. Travis performs this job ably for a time, partying with the locals when it pleases him, but then his life takes an odd turn when another sales assignment lands him in Scotland and he is (mistakenly) detained as a spy at a top-secret military facility.

After his brief incarceration (and torture) Travis survives what appears to be a nuclear blast, wanders out into a pastoral setting, and is nursed back to health via the bosom (literally) of a saint-like figure in a church. Travis hitchhikes back to London, but is waylaid at the Millar Research Facility, where doctors seek to experiment on him and transform him into a chimera. He escapes captivity again, and winds up in the van of a rock band. Travis remains with the group for a time, and romances a groovy groupie played by Helen Mirren.

When he learns that Helen Mirren's dad (Ralph Richardson) is the richest, most notorious businessman in the world, Travis ingratiates himself with the old man and becomes his assistant. He fully immerses himself in the corrupt corporate world. However, Travis is soon framed by the old man and made the fall guy for an international crime. He is sentenced to jail for five years of hard labor. When he is released, Travis is promptly mugged and attacked by the poor, some of whom he has sought to help through charity work. Beaten and bruised, Travis finally ends up at an audition for a movie, and wins a part in a film...*this* film!

As the preceding summary indicates, this is a wild and dynamic movie that travels many places and tries to achieve many things. It's a movie that, by critic Jay Cocks' assessment, "bursts with wit, rage, enterprise, stylistic audacity and social agitation."

Uniquely, the same troupe of actors, including Ralph Richardson, reappear over the course of the film essaying different roles, and part of the picture's interest is a result of seeing how these characters are reflections or contrasts of one another. Despite the huge shifts in locale, tone, and characterization, one constant throughout *O Lucky Man!* is indeed music.

In particular, composer Alan Price (formerly of the

rock band The Animals; see: *Don't Look Back*) appears
throughout the film, both within the narrative as a band
member, and outside the story confines, during real
recording sessions for his songs. The film thus occasionally "breaks," and reveals him singing tunes such as "Poor
People," or "Sell, Sell." All of his music comments in some
fashion, usually ironically, on the episode unspooling on
screen.

"It has an original score by Alan Price, and it's one of the
greatest scores ever written for a movie," enthuses Cocks.
"It's three hours long, and Anderson...not only integrated
the music, not only used it as counterpoint, and as a way
of getting into the scene and moving the story along, [but]
he integrated the performance of the music by the composer into the actual movie."

"This thing is stunning. Of course, it was a big flop,"
Cocks laments. "But you see this... it's got all kinds of
things going on in it. Just one of the greatest movies ever,
a true masterpiece."

(DVD) Not Available on DVD. VHS copies are still in rotation at some libraries,
universities, and on the secondary market.

P

(is for *Purple Rain*)

Pajama Party (1964)(MUS)

STARRING: Tommy Kirk (Go-Go); Annette Funicello (Connie); Elsa Lanchester (Wendy); Harvey Lembeck (Eric Von Zipper); Jesse White (J. Sinister Hulk); Jody McCrea (Big Lunk); Buster Keaton (Chief Rotten Eagle); Dorothy Lamour (Head Saleslady).

FILM EDITORS: Fred Feitshans, Eve Newman. DIRECTOR OF PHOTOGRAPHY: Floyd Crosby WRITTEN BY: Louis M. Heyward. PRODUCED BY: Samuel Z. Arkoff, Anthony Carras, James Nicholson. DIRECTED BY: Don Weis. M.P.A.A. RATING: UR. RUNNING TIME: 82 minutes.

Whoa! Did I just slip into an alternate universe? This 1964 film looks and sounds like a beach party movie, is produced by AIP, and stars Annette Funicello and Jody McCrea. But, Frankie Avalon is playing a Martian named Slocum not Frankie; Annette is now "Connie" not Dee Dee. Jody McCrea's playing the same doofy, good-natured character as always, but now he's not named Bonehead, but Big Lunk! What's going on? I mean, Harvey Lembeck is in the film too, assaying his old role of Eric Von Zipper (apparently an anchor in all quantum realities). So what the heck is going on?

While I ponder parallel universes, go ahead and avoid this daft beach movie, which finds a teenage Martian (played by Tommy Kirk) coming to Earth to make war, not love, but changing his mind when he gets a gander at Annette. Buster Keaton, in a career low, plays a stereotyped Native American Indian.

On the soundtrack: Tommy Kirk and Annette Funicello duet to "There Has to Be a Reason" (there does have to be, doesn't there?). Funicello also sings "Pajama Party" and "Stuffed Animal."

DVD Available on DVD.

Paradise, Hawaiian Style (1966)(MUS)

STARRING: Elvis Presley (Rick Richards); Suzanna Leigh (Julie Hudson); James Shigeta (Danny Kohana); Donna Butterworth (Jan Kohana); Marianna Hill (Lani Kaimana); Irene Tsu (Pua); John Doucette (Mr. Belden); Julie Parrish (Joanna); Jan Shepard (Betty Kohana).

FILM EDITOR: Warren Low. DIRECTOR OF PHOTOGRAPHY: W. Wallace Kelley. SCREENPLAY BY: Allan Weiss, Anthony Lawrence. STORY BY: Allan Weiss. PRODUCED BY: Hal B. Wallis. DIRECTED BY: Michael Moore. M.P.A.A. RATING: G. RUNNING TIME: 90 minutes.

This is another middling Elvis Presley vehicle; one from the late end of the Elvis cycle (and his last film shot in Hawaii). Here, the King of the Rock (growing noticeably chubbier in the cheeks) plays a carousing pilot named Rick Richards who has lost his job at the airlines after getting caught making it with a stewardess. He heads off to Hawaii and meets his friend, Danny (James Shigeta), pressuring him to start up a helicopter commuter business. Danny agrees and hires a girl Friday played by Suzanna Leigh, one who pretends to be married so Rick won't hit on her.

Soon there are troubles, however, when Danrick Airways is asked to shuttle dogs from one island to another, and Rick makes trouble at a local eatery, the

"Colonel's" (nudge, nudge) Plantation Steak House. All's well that ends well, however, when Rick gets himself and family man Danny out of trouble by singing several tunes at the Polynesian Greeting Festival, including "Drums of the Island."

Like many Elvis movies, *Paradise Hawaiian Style* finds the crooner interacting with a cute child, here Danny's daughter, in an apparent effort to blunt his dangerous side. The overlong finale finds Rick singing two other songs in addition to the reprise of "Drums of the Island," the slow and intimate "This Is My Heaven," and the rousing, up-tempo "Stop Where You Are." In the latter, the film pauses for a freeze frame whenever Elvis utters the lyric "Stop!," which gives the Jack Regas staging a little boost in an otherwise uninspiring film.

One early highlight, however, is Elvis's sexy duet with Marianna Hill, called "Scratch My Back (Then I'll Scratch Yours)." Hill and Presley have real sexual chemistry together, and the number is a little naughtier and bawdier than one might expect.

(DVD) Available on DVD.

Pat Garrett & Billy the Kid (1973)

(SNDTRK)(REAL ROCKER)

STARRING: James Coburn (Sheriff Pat Garrett); Kris Kristofferson (Billy the Kid); Bob Dylan (Alias); Richard Jaeckel (McKinney); Jason Robards (Governor); R.G. Armstrong (Deputy).

FILM EDITORS: David Berlatsky, Garth Craven, Richard Halsey, Roger Spottiswoode, Robert L. Wolfe, Tony de Zarraga. DIRECTOR OF PHOTOGRAPHY: John Coquillon. PRODUCED BY: Gordon Carroll. WRITTEN BY: Rudolph Wurlitze. DIRECTED BY: Sam Peckinpah. M.P.A.A. RATING: R. RUNNING TIME: 106 minutes.

Yep, this is the troubled Sam Peckinpah Western about the notorious criminal Billy the Kid and the lawman who stopped him. It's featured here solely because Bob Dylan appears in the film as one of Billy's sidekicks, named Alias, and because Dylan contributes songs to the soundtrack, including the hit "Knockin' on Heaven's Door."

(DVD) Now available in a modified DVD release rumored to be closer to Peckinpah's intended director's cut.

Performance (1970)

STARRING: James Fox (Chas); Mick Jagger (Turner); Anita Pallenberg (Pherber); Michele Breton (Lucy); Ann Sidney (Dana).

FILM EDITORS: Anthony Gibbs, Brian Smedley-Aston. DIRECTOR OF PHOTOGRAPHY: Nicolas Roeg. WRITTEN BY: Donald Cammell. PRODUCED BY: David Cammell, Sanford Lieberson. DIRECTED BY: Donald Cammell, Nicolas Roeg. M.P.A.A. RATING: R. RUNNING TIME: 105 minutes.

This landmark British effort was reviled by international critics upon its debut, but has steadily grown in reputation and esteem since its summer 1970 theatrical release. Filmed in 1966–1967 but held back for two years by a concerned Warner Bros. for re-edits, the X-rated *Performance* represents the early cinematic output of Nicolas Roeg, later responsible for the Bowie film *The Man Who Fell to Earth* (1976) and one of the great horror efforts of the 1970s, *Don't Look Now* (1973). Roeg co-directed with Donald Cammell, another brilliant but troubled artist who decades later took his own life.

Performance is a story presented in progressive, avant-garde style. The plot concerns a narcissistic gangster named Chas (James Fox) who, after a hit, ends up hiding up in the Notting Hill home of a faded rock star, Turner (Mick Jagger), who suffers from writer's block. Turner soon proves an aggressive, powerful figure with a woman lover on each arm (Anita Pallenberg and Michele Breton). He very quickly realizes that Chas is somebody he can manipulate and use to restore his luster. What follows is, in the words of many critics, a world-class "mind fuck" as Turner and Chas develop a strange codependent relationship that twists identities and ends in death for one of them.

"You with me?" Jagger's Turner pointedly asks at one point, and that query probably should have been the ad line for *Performance*, since it tends to sicken and confuse some viewers, tantalize and fascinate others. In some sense, the cinematic freedoms of the day convincingly echo the strange content of the film. It all fits together as a bizarre tapestry. J. Hoberman, reviewing the film for the *Village Voice*, wrote that *Performance* is "New wave with a vengeance" and that it "offers a non-stop farrago of strobe cuts, flash-forwards, percussive zooms, rack-focus shots, weird aural clues, and trippy interpolations." That's a good way of describing the film's psychedelic style, but yet doesn't really capture the depth of the odd material; which is weirdly psychological and ultimately disturbing.

Performance is also the notorious film in which—allegedly, Keith Richards' lover Anita Pallenberg and bandmate Mick Jagger engaged in sex on the set; the film which caused actor James Fox to abandon acting for over a decade (and seek solace in Christianity), and which famously offers one of the screen's early "music video"-style montages (to the Stones' "Memo from Turner").

Film reviewing is always a subjective game, despite critics who claim otherwise, and *Performance* is both a loved and hated venture, one that the viewer should ultimately experience for him or herself.

Performance is not available on DVD, though some old (pan-and-scan) VHS tapes remain in circulation. It was in that format, unfortunately, that I saw the film, but even in this compromised venue, one thing remains certain: *Performance* represents Mick Jagger's finest and most memorable screen role.

(DVD) Not available.

Phantom of the Paradise (1974)(MUS)

STARRING: George Memmoli (Philbin); Gerrit Graham (Beef); Jessica Harper (Phoenix); Paul Williams (Swan); William Finley (Phantom).

FILM EDITOR: Paul Hirsch. DIRECTOR OF PHOTOGRAPHY: Larry Pizer. WRITTEN BY: Brian De Palma. PRODUCED BY: Edward R. Pressman. DIRECTED BY: Brian De Palma. M.P.A.A. RATING: PG. RUNNING TIME: 92 minutes.

This is an early entry in the midnight movies sweepstakes, but one that somehow hasn't achieved the luster and infamy of its compatriot from 1975, *The Rocky Horror Picture Show*. Directed in crazed but stylish fashion (replete

He'll haunt your nightmares! It's the *Phantom of the Paradise*! (1974).

with his signature split-screens) by Brian De Palma, *Phantom of the Paradise* is an over-the-top, glam-rock-opera that blends the horror tales of *Phantom of the Opera* and *Faust* with pop rock.

Phantom of the Paradise concerns a brilliant musician named Leach (William Finley), the composer of a brand new rock cantata on the subject of *Faust*, but this talent is betrayed by Paul Williams' duplicitous Swan, a Death Records executive (see: *Record Company*) and the proprietor of the new Paradise theatre/nightclub. Swan attempts to have Leach killed (by crushing him in a record press) but Leach returns to haunt him as the masked, metal-toothed Phantom, and falls in love with a young singer, Phoenix (Jessica Harper). A bizarre high-point of the film is Gerrit Graham's performance as the flamboyant rock star, Beef.

Paul Williams contributed the rock score to this over-the-top, camp oddity and has a ball playing the evil record producer. His score includes "Faust" (performed by Finley), "Old Souls" (performed by Harper), "Goodbye, Eddie, Goodbye" (performed by the *fictional band* The Juicy Fruits). Paul Williams also sings "The Hell of It."

The New York Times termed *Phantom of the Paradise* an "elaborate disaster" while simultaneously praising its "comic orchestrations that trace the evolution of rock from the duck-tailed surfing nineteen-fifties and sixties to the seventies and the triumphant emergence of androgyny."[47]

The movie also happens to be a hell of a lot of fun. (DVD) Available on DVD.

Pink Floyd: The Wall (1982)(MUS)(ANIM)

STARRING: Bob Geldof (Pink); Christine Hargreaves (Mother); James Laurenson (Father); Eleanor David (Wife); Kevin McKeon (Young Pink); Bob Hoskins (Manager); David Bingham (Little Pink); Jenny Wright (American Groupie); Alex McAvoy (Teacher); Ellis Dale (English Doctor).

FILM EDITOR: Gerry Hambling. DIRECTOR OF PHOTOGRAPHY: Peter Biziou. SCREENPLAY BY: Roger Waters. FILM MUSIC: Roger Waters, David Gilmour, James Guthrie. MUSIC WRITTEN BY: Roger Waters. EXECUTIVE PRODUCER: Stephen O'Rourke. PRODUCED BY: Alan Marshall. DIRECTED BY: Alan Parker. M.P.A.A. RATING: R. RUNNING TIME: 99 minutes.

Another one of the genre greats; a film packed wall-to-wall with unforgettable and at times deeply disturbing imagery. This Alan Parker/Pink Floyd collaboration forecasts the development of the music video and MTV-style editing in the 1980s, and also takes the rock odyssey format pioneered by *Tommy* (1975) one step further. Interestingly, *Tommy* and *Pink Floyd: The Wall* both share one earth-shattering event that changes forever the life of the film's protagonist: the death of a father during World War II. Here, that death is but the first "brick" in the emotional wall that young Pink (Bob Geldof) builds as a barrier between his fragile inner self and the outer world.

Later, bad school experiences also cause Pink to withdraw from contact with others. His schoolmaster mocks his poetry and ridicules him before his classmates. To the tune of "Another Brick in the Wall" the film depicts the cookie-cutter nature of public school as little gray children march lockstep in a hopeless world. They are mass-processed in a factory assembly line, transformed into faceless mutants and ground out like sausage. This sequence is a show-stopper, and one of the greatest *anti-authority* images in rock history.

Told mostly without benefit of conventional dialogue, *Pink Floyd: The Wall* continues to tell Pink's story as he reaches maturity and becomes a rock star. He inhabits the wreckage of a hotel room he has trashed (see: *Destruction of Property*) and adds another "brick in the wall" when he learns of his wife's infidelity. Eventually, Pink is so turned off, so separated from humanity, that he becomes an Adolf Hitler figure (replete with Swastika-like arm band), one who commands a cult of other disenfranchised people. This is the film's ultimate (and valuable) message: that someone hurt by life will eventually strike back and hurt others. The irony is that the first hurt, the death of Pink's father, was caused in a sense by Adolf Hitler, and now that very death has spawned a new Hitler.

The Wall is a sad but stirring movie about what is required to tear down a wall that has taken over a lifetime to construct. The movie is exceptionally powerful in rendering Pink's point of view. At one point he sees himself as a worm-ridden corpse. In the vignette about his unfaithful wife, animation involving a flower-as-devouring-vagina appears, and there's the eternally disturbing image of Bob Geldof in a pool where the water has turned to blood.

"*Pink Floyd: The Wall* has become a cult movie," Sir Alan Parker told me during an interview for my book *Singing a New Tune*. "It was very different from my other films. All the music was recorded—they'd [Pink Floyd] sold 11 million albums already. In a way, it's an experiment in cinematic language. The parameters were never set, and creatively, that can be a wonderful freedom. The whole film was like the image of Bob Geldof lying amongst the debris of his trashed room: the pieces put back together to create a weird and wonderful work of art.

"To be honest, we made it up as we went along. Day by day and shot by shot. I don't mean that in a disparaging way, because it was a very creative environment, and more than a touch anarchic, considering the dollar bills being burned. The challenge was to tell a story with just music and images."

That's merely one challenge that this emotional, raw and memorable film rises to meet. *Pink Floyd: The Wall* survives as a cult film, a trailblazer, and as a dark and deeply troublesome reminder that hatred and war only beget more hatred and war.

Of course, all works of art that are ahead of their time tend to be dismissed by critics at the time of their unveiling, and that was the case for *The Wall*, which met with savage reviews. "It is in every respect a lie," argued Gerry Marta at *Films in Review*; "To pin any blame for the hero's desperate state of mental health on the Second World War or war movies or on the British education system rather than his overuse of drugs and booze is fallacious."[48].

David Denby had more grounded concerns, noting that this film set "a new record in rock pretentiousness, which isn't easy."[49]

DVD Available on DVD.

The Postman (1997)(CAMEO)

STARRING: Kevin Costner (The Postman); Will Patton (Bethlehem); Larenz Tate (Ford); Olivia Williams (Abby); James Russo (Idaho); Tom Petty (Bridge City Mayor).

FILM EDITOR: Peter Boyle. DIRECTOR OF PHOTOGRAPHY: Stephen Windon. BASED ON THE BOOK BY: David Brin. SCREENPLAY BY: Eric Roth, Brian Helgeland. PRODUCED BY: Jim Wilson, Steve Tisch and Kevin Costner. DIRECTED BY: Kevin Costner. M.P.A.A. RATING: R. RUNNING TIME: 178 minutes.

In Kevin Costner's lumbering, three-hour post-apocalyptic vision of America (no, not *Waterworld*, 1995) in the year 2013, a number of rock music allusions are highlighted.

When Costner's character, pretending to be a U.S. Postman, brings news of a reconstituted United States to a remote village in the Pacific Northwest, he fabricates a new Commander-in-Chief, one named "Richard Starkey." As Beatles fans are well-aware, Richard Starkey is the real moniker of drummer Ringo Starr. The fictitious President's slogan in the film is the Beatles-related mantra (from "Getting Better"): "It's getting better all the time."

Also, rocker Tom Petty, headliner for the band Tom Petty and the Heartbreakers, cameos in *The Postman* in the small role of the mayor of "Bridge City." Kevin Costner's character asks the rocker if he's famous, and Petty—looking wistful and a little dazed—replies *"I was once. Sort of. Kind of. Not anymore."*

DVD Available on DVD.

Press Conference (GENRE CONVENTION)

Another crucial element of the standard rock band film. Ever since The Fab Four came to New York in August 1964 and succumbed to a press gaggle to reveal their thoughts, it's been an accepted convention in genre films for rockers to say outrageous (and often nonsensical) things at press conferences. A *Hard Day's Night* (1964) offers an early (and funny) view of the press conference as the Beatles are inundated with strange questions from journalists. One writer asks if Ringo is a "mod" or a "rocker" and he famously answers that he's a "mocker."

In *U2: Rattle and Hum* (1988), a press conference is broached, and the band is asked about American influence on its music. In Oliver Stones' *The Doors* (1991), Jim Morrison lies about his parents' death during a hostile press conference.

In *Velvet Goldmine*, Brian Slade and Curt Wild have reporters ask about their sexuality in a press conference in what James Lyons, the editor of that film, terms "the white and gold" scene. The scene was nearly deleted by Miramax, who didn't understand the importance of the press conference in rock lore.

"There's a white set, and all the different characters are in white and gold [and there are] very arty references," says Lyons. "They are all being asked questions by the reporters, and they answer in different aphorisms that we collected from, [Oscar] Wilde and art history, which we loved." Miramax objected, however, because the conference didn't move the story along.

As late as 2001's *Rock Star*, the press conference continues to be an important turning point in rock films. In that movie, Izzy joins Steel Dragon and impresses skeptical reporters with his vocal stylings.

More press conferences can be found. At the beginning of *The Concert for Bangladesh* (1971) featuring George Harrison; one in *Gimme Shelter* (1971) with Mick Jagger debating levels of satisfaction, and of course, *Don't Look Back* (1967) where Bob Dylan grows combative with a *Time* magazine journalist.

Prey for Rock & Roll (2003)

(SNDTRK)(FIC BAND)

STARRING: Gina Gershon (Jacki); Lori Petty (Faith); Drea de Matteo (Tracy); Marc Blucas (Animal); Shelly Cole (Sally); Ivan Martin (Nick); Eddie Driscoll (Chuck).

FILM EDITOR: Allyson C. Johnson. DIRECTOR OF PHOTOGRAPHY: Antonio Calvache. SCREENPLAY BY: Cheri Lovedog. BASED ON THE PLAY BY: Cheri Lovedog. ORIGINAL SONGS: Cheri Lovedog. EXECUTIVE PRODUCERS: John Bonanno, Adam Weiner, Gregg Lazarescu. PRODUCERS: Donovan Mannato, Gina Resnick, Gina Gershon. DIRECTED BY: Alex Steyermark. M.P.A.A. RATING: R. RUNNING TIME: 96 minutes.

"*All my life, all I wanted to be is a rock 'n' roll star,*" Gina Gershon's character, Jacki, states in the opening narration of this 2003 film about the fictional rock band called "Clamdandy," an adaptation of the play by Cheri Lovedog. Jacki, who is just two days shy of forty when the film opens, and her band mates are dedicated lesbians, except for Tracy (Drea De Matteo), whose boyfriend is the abusive Nick. When Animal (Marc Blucas), Sally's (Shelly Cole) hunky brother is released from prison a twenty-seven-year-old virgin, however, Jacki starts to reconsider her sexual orientation. At the same time, she questions her dreams of being a rock star. On the latter front, she faces the reality that Clamdandy is grossly underpaid (at their last gig, each band member took in only $13.50) and worse, the outfit isn't likely to get a good record deal anytime soon.

Prey for Rock & Roll is an unrepentant, hard-rock chick flick, but a darn good one. It features some angry lesbian rock, beautiful women, and meditates with charm on the notion of what happens when you're forty years old and still haven't made your dreams come true. In this age of celebrity and *American Idol*, few productions bother to consider that question. Is there an age when it's appropriate to stop trying? When it's time to settle down? Get a "real" job? In pondering these ideas, *Prey for Rock & Roll* carves out a nice little niche for itself.

Daily Variety's Ronnie Schreib appreciated the film too. He noted that *Prey for Rock & Roll* is "propelled by a smashing performance from Gina Gershon," and that it emerges as "an engaging upbeat saga" which "feels authentic from first frame to last."[50]

Not that the film doesn't feature a few missteps. It veers from rock drama to revenge picture when Tracy's boyfriend Nick rapes Sally and leaves her bleeding on the floor of her apartment. Jacki and the others get sweet revenge, but this seems like awfully heavy-handed material to feature in essentially a subplot. Still, this rock film effectively hits all the genre convention notes.

In a supreme act of *anti-authority* hatred, Jacki urinates on an inadequate contract from an exploitive agent. There's also the *break-up*, the moment when the band finally calls it quits. Perhaps more interesting than any of this is the hot lesbian sex scene between Jacki (Gershon) and her African-American girlfriend in the film's opening fifteen minutes. *Prey for Rock & Roll* also gives the genre one of its truly great lines: *"What is this?"* a character demands, *"a rock 'n' roll intervention?"*

Prey for Rock & Roll's soundtrack includes "My Favorite Sin," "Prey for Rock & Roll," "The Ugly," "Every Six Minutes," and "Punk Rock & Roll" by Cheri Lovedog, and performed by Gina Gershon and the women of Clamdandy.

(DVD) Available on DVD.

Prince (1958–   )(ROCK-MOVIE HALL OF FAME) This diminutive but prodigious rock talent is one of the genre's true originals. Prince made his impressive big screen acting debut in the semi-autobiographical hit film from 1984, Albert Magnoli's *Purple Rain*.

Since that blockbuster (which was the tenth-highest-grossing film of the year) however, Prince has found it difficult to repeat his silver screen success.

Prince has directed himself in two stink bombs: *Under the Cherry Moon* (1986), a black-and-white endeavor which found him playing a charming gigolo named Christopher Tracy; and *Graffiti Bridge* (1990), the unofficial sequel to *Purple Rain*. The latter film was shot in Prince's Minneapolis-based studio, Paisley Park.

Prince's other big screen appearance occurs in *Sign 'o' the Times*, his 1987 concert film, which also features appearances by Sheena Easton, Sheila E., and "Cat." Prince is never less than amazing in this effort as he dances, sings, plays the drums and guitar, and generally struts his stuff.

In addition to his onscreen work, Prince has composed a number of songs specifically for individual films. In 1989, he crafted a memorable soundtrack for the Tim Burton mega-hit *Batman*, including such tunes as "Batdance," "The Future," "Vicki Waiting," "Electric Chair," "Partyman," "Trust," and "Scandalous."

Spike Lee's *Girl 6* (1996) also boasts a Prince-related soundtrack, though many tunes there had been featured previously (in *Under the Cherry Moon* and in *Sign 'o' the Times*). Among the compositions: "She Spoke 2 Me," "House Quake," "How Come U Don't Call Anymore," "Don't Talk 2 Strangers," and "Erotic City."

Psych-Out (1968)(FIC BAND)(SNDTRK)

STARRING: Susan Strasberg (Jenny Davis); Dean Stockwell (Dave); Jack Nicholson (Stoney); Bruce Dern (Steve); Adam Roarke (Ben); Max Julien (Elwood); Gary Marshall (Plainclothesman).

FILM EDITOR: Renn Reynolds. DIRECTOR OF PHOTOGRAPHY: Laszlo Kovacs. WRITTEN BY: Betty Tusher, Betty Ulius, E. Hunter Willett. PRODUCED BY: Dick Clark, Norman T. Herman. DIRECTED BY: Richard Rush. M.P.A.A. RATING: UR. RUNNING TIME: 101 minutes.

Ad line: "Taste a moment of madness... listen to the sound of purple..."

Deaf girl Jenny Davis (Susan Strasberg) runs away to San Francisco as the result of a cryptic message mailed by her spaced-out brother Steve (known as "The Seeker," played to whacked perfection by Bruce Dern). She first falls in with Stoney (Jack Nicholson) and his bandmates, practitioners of the Haight-Ashbury philosophy of doing-one's-own-thing. Through a haze of psychedelic drugs, trippy camera work, and a fitting Strawberry Alarm Clock soundtrack (which includes the tunes "Incense and Peppermints," "Rainy Day Mushroom Pillow," "The World's on Fire" and "The Pretty Song from Psych-Out"), the movie chronicles both Jenny's search for her brother and Stoney's disaffected battle with the possibility of his band going commercial while maintaining the hippie dream. *Psych-Out* is a film that predominately celebrates the emerging Hippie culture, doing so at the height of its pseudo-legitimacy, yet ultimately stands as a warning against the excesses that come with the lifestyle.

Though full of interesting visual ideas, including some discernable French New Wave influence (the film's opening montage, general disregard for narrative causality, and disquieting camera work), the movie is clearly a quickly made, low-budget exploitationer. Riffing off the earlier cycle of Beat and Biker youth culture movies, *Psych-Out* seems to merely apply the old stories and tropes to the latest vogue. The exciting possibilities of youth shine through, with the Haight depicted as a paradise-oasis, removed of the "straight" world.

However, more formally interesting and radical films such as Anthony Stern's *San Francisco* (1968, a dizzying documentary short scored with a spacey version of Pink Floyd's "Interstellar Overdrive") and Michelangelo Antonioni's *Zabriskie Point* (1970) more accurately capture the enthusiasm of the zeitgeist. Director Richard Rush is able to solicit decent performances from the actors and does justice to the material, yet in the final analysis only succeeds in forging an uneven vision of a naïve utopia.—Kevin Flanagan.

DVD Available on DVD on a double feature with *The Trip.*

Pump Up the Volume (1990)(SNDTRK)

STARRING: Christian Slater (Mark Hunter); Andy Romano (Murdock); Keith Stuart Thayer (Luis); Cheryl Pollak (Paige); Jeff Chamberlain (Mr. Woodward); Samantha Mathis (Nora).

FILM EDITORS: Larry Bock, Janice Hampton. DIRECTOR OF PHOTOGRAPHY: Walt Lloyd. WRITTEN BY: Allan Moyle. PRODUCED BY: Rupert Harvey, Sandy Stern. DIRECTED BY: Allan Moyle. M.P.A.A. RATING: R. RUNNING TIME: 105 minutes.

Christian Slater (fresh from playing a James Dean-like suicide junkie in *Heathers*) rages against the machine in this teen-rebellion, *authority*-bashing Allan Moyle (*Times Square*) flick. Slater portrays Mark Hunter, a shy high school student by day, shock-jock "Happy Harry Hard-On" by night. Hunter's family has recently moved to Arizona from New York, and Mark has found the transition difficult. His nighttime pirate radio show echoes his teen angst with its syllabus which includes a call to arms for his angsty brethren, scores of alternative rock songs, and the occasional (faked) on-air masturbation.

Mark finds his real on-air voice, however, when he truly has issues to rage against, including a corrupt principal at Hubert Humphrey High, and society's "blame the messenger" approach to handling moral crises after a listener to his show commits suicide.

In exploring these issues, *Pump Up the Volume* takes direct aim at the corporate mainstream media, which blames movies, video games, and even subversive radio programs for the failures of parents and the establishment to raise well-adjusted healthy kids. *Pump Up the Volume* is buttressed by Slater's electric, dead-on teen rebel performance, and remains far and away the best of Moyles' three rock efforts.

Buoyed by its soundtrack, the film includes Concrete Blonde's "Everybody Knows," Liquid Jesus performing "Stand," Above the Law's aptly named "Freedom of Speech," Soundgarden's "Heretic," Stan Ridgeway offering "Talk Hard," and The Beastie Boys charting "The Scenario." DVD Available on DVD.

The Punk Rock Movie (1978)(DOC)

STARRING: Billy Idol, The Sex Pistols, The Clash, The Slits, Subway Sect, Johnny Thunders and the Heartbreakers, Siouxsie and the Banshees, Eater, Slaughter and the Dogs.

DIRECTOR OF PHOTOGRAPHY: Don Letts. PRODUCED BY: Peter Clifton. DIRECTED BY: Don Letts. M.P.A.A. RATING: PG. RUNNING TIME: 90 minutes.

Look out for this rock 'n' roll rarity if you can find it. The so-called *The Punk Rock Movie* is actually more like a home movie, but who cares, it's still an historical chronicle of the dawn of punk. Don Letts super-8mm film of the London punk rock scene is bluntly shot, with some footage taken at the Roxy Club in London. Among the performances recorded here is Sid Vicious' first show with the Sex Pistols in the spring of 1977.

The soundtrack includes The Sex Pistols doing "God Save The Queen," Slaughter and the Dogs performing "Cranked Up Really High," The Clash's "White Riot," and more. DVD This one is a rarity and available only as a lousy-quality EP VHS tape.

Anarchy in the U.K. The Sex Pistols take the stage. The band appears in such films as *The Punk Rock Movie* (1978) and *The Filth and the Fury* (2000).

Purple Rain (1984)

(BIO-PIC)(FIC BAND)(SNDTRK)

STARRING: Prince (The Kid); Apollonia Kotero (Apollonia); Morris Day (Morris); Olga Karlatos (Mother); Clarence Williams III (Father); Jerome Benton (Jerome); Billy Sparks (Billy Sparks); Wendy (Wendy); Lisa Coleman (Lisa); Bobby Z (Bobby Z); Matt Fink (Matt Fink); Brown Mark (Brown Mark).

FILM EDITOR: Albert Magnoli. DIRECTOR OF PHOTOGRAPHY: Donald E. Thorn. ORIGINAL SONGS COMPOSED AND CONDUCTED BY: Prince. WRITTEN BY: Albert Magnoli, William Blinn. PRODUCED BY: Robert Cavallo, Joseph Ruffalo, Steve Fargnoli. DIRECTED BY: Albert Magnoli. M.P.A.A. RATING: R. RUNNING TIME: 84 minutes.

Purple Rain is the landmark 1984 rock film that introduced a wide American audience to the diminutive powerhouse named Prince. The film's story involves a potent, flamboyant young rocker called "The Kid" (Prince) and his myriad problems with family (particularly his abusive, musically frustrated father).

The Kid is also on the ropes over his difficulties with competitors, Morris (Day) and Jerome (Benton) and his complicated relationship with his new aspiring-singer girlfriend (Apollonia). Also, The Kid feels pressured to perform a song written by his band mates, an act which he stubbornly resists. All these stresses are almost too much to bear, but one night The Kid takes the stage at the First Avenue Club and belts that special song, "Purple Rain," changing everything.

Ironically, *Purple Rain* almost didn't get made according to director Albert Magnoli. He was editing another movie for a friend in late 1983 when a script for a Prince vehicle (by William Blinn) landed on his desk. One of Prince's managers, Robert Cavallo, asked for his opinion about it.

Magnoli, to his chagrin, realized that Cavallo had spent $100,000 on a bad screenplay. "It really didn't work. I was distressed and depressed," he admits. Still, following a hunch, Magnoli met with Cavallo for lunch, and almost on a whim came up with a new story on the spot, one that felt more authentic.

"I hesitated for about two seconds and then launched into a storyline that just came out of nowhere. I'm not really sure where it came from," he notes. "It was the bare bones of *Purple Rain*. I even had the father writing music and hiding it. The family angle was in there, because I've always been oriented toward the family angle. So I knew the father was angry and embittered and putting that energy into his kid, and Prince was combating it. I pretty much had the three acts."

Cavallo responded favorably, but now it was time to sell the new idea to Prince, and Magnoli wanted to conduct more research first. He very quickly got a hold of all the videos and film footage he could find of Prince. What he saw impressed but also vexed him.

"As I watched all the footage that was available, I got more and more depressed because I realized trying to bring Prince to a public—and I always knew I wanted to cross over from an urban base to a wider one —[was going to be difficult]. I said 'Oh my God,' because I'm watching Prince in a bikini and high-heeled shoes dancing naked in front of a crowd of black people in Minneapolis."

Still Magnoli flew to Minneapolis to meet Prince and pitch his story idea. He was met at the airport by another Prince representative.

"At the time, Prince had three managers. It was one management company, but there were three individuals who were essentially managing Prince's career. One was Bob Cavallo. The second guy was Steve Fargnoli. And the third gentleman's name was Joseph Ruffalo."

Farnoli, whom Magnoli jokingly calls "the second part of a three part series," approached him with grave seriousness. "The first words out of his mouth are *"'Understand that I don't give a damn about the story you told Bob [Cavallo]. We're doing the story that's already written.' And I said, 'Uh huh.'"*

Next, it was off to meet Prince at a hotel lobby at midnight. There, Magnoli met Chick, Prince's bodyguard ("a very tall, Viking-looking person," by his memory).

"I separated myself from the two guys and found a chair in the lobby off to the side," Magnoli continues. "To my right were the elevator doors. To my left, across the lobby, was the front door of the building where Steve and Chick were positioned. Then the doors opened at the crack of twelve midnight sharp, and out walks Prince by himself."

"Because he didn't know who I was, he didn't see me. He saw Chick and Steve at the end of the hall, and walked to them, which allowed me to do a right to left pan with Prince, unencumbered of him knowing I was looking at him. As a result, I ended up filling in the whole story based on him walking across the lobby. Because what I saw was

extreme vulnerability, in spite of all the bluster and the costume and the music. This was a vulnerable young man…I saw all the heart and soul, I saw all the emotional stuff, I saw the tragedy of his upbringing. I just saw stuff and I felt stuff, so that filled in the three act story."

Together, the foursome went to a diner to talk business. "I was looking at Prince, and I could tell that he didn't like being looked at. He's very shy," Magnoli explains. "Everybody ordered food, and as soon as the waitress left, Prince looked at me and said, *'Okay, how did you like my script?'* I realized a few things there. One, he said *my* script, which meant that he had personally invested himself in whatever it was that William Blinn had written. Two, that he hadn't been told anything that I felt about it."

"The words that came out of my mouth were the following. *'Well, I think it sucked.'"*

Magnoli pauses for effect. "At that moment, Steve dropped his head, Chick leaned closer to me, and Prince looked startled. Then I could see him thinking, and what he was thinking was, *'I wasn't told this before this meeting was to take place. Why wasn't I told?'* Then he looked towards Steve, because obviously Steve had told him nothing. That look to Steve took about three seconds, but it was very telling to me, because now I saw how the operation works. He had been kept in the dark about this."

"So then Prince looked back to me and said, *'Why does it suck?'* And I said, *'You know what, it's not important why, but here's what we can do about it. Let me tell you the story.'* So now with even more passion, because I have more information now that I'm looking at this kid, I told this story."

"There was five seconds of silence. Then he looked at Steve and said, 'Why don't you take Chick and go home?' Then he looked at me and said, 'Why don't you come with me? I just want to take Al for a ride.'"

"We got in his car, he got behind the wheel [it was a BMW], I got into the passenger's seat and he took off fast," Magnoli remembers. "The next thing I knew, we were driving in pitch-black darkness. Not a light in sight. I had no idea where we were. It looked like we were driving into a black tube. A day later, I realized we were in horizon-to-horizon farmland, but there were no lights. So I was thinking, '*He didn't like the story and now I'm dead*'..."

But it turns out, Prince had no such violent action in mind. Instead, he was surprised and baffled that Magnoli—a man he had never met—had just shared with him (in that diner), the essence of his true life-story. A bond was forged and suddenly, *Purple Rain* had its director.

Pre-production on the film commenced in mid-September 1983, with shooting to begin during the Minneapolis winter, in November.

"I only had eight days of research because I needed to start writing right away," Magnoli notes. "Basically I spent the first eight days talking to Prince, Morris Day, Jerome Benton, and Vanity extensively, and going to clubs. I literally stayed up for eight weeks, and maybe got two hours sleep a night, because I would work with the musicians whenever they woke up. Musicians don't wake up till around one [in the afternoon]. So at one o'clock I'd be on their doorstop and ask them a ton of questions, and then I'd go from one to the other for the entire day."

Prince, it turns out, was very good taking direction. "It [the relationship], worked great," Magnoli explains. "The interesting thing is that I never felt he couldn't take directions, because he's a musician. And based on my whole experience in that scene as a kid, it's an extremely disciplined world. If you're going to be successful you have to be disciplined. And I already knew inherently that Prince was a clean liver. He didn't smoke and he didn't drink. He had an enormous work ethic and commitment to the work, and made sure that the people around him felt the same way or he got rid of them. So even if their prior history in the business was one of a haphazard approach to the whole thing, when they got involved with his organization, they basically realized, '*Okay, this is boot camp.*'"

"There was a wonderful camaraderie and wonderful work ethic in place when I already got there," Magnoli continues. "So bringing the film business to them was just another kind of discipline. To be honest with you, the biggest hurdle was simply making them aware of the fact that we started shooting at 7:00 a.m. That was the biggest thing they couldn't get. '*You start shooting when?*' These kids were going to bed at 7:00 a.m. not getting up."

Purple Rain was shot in forty-five days, with ten days devoted to shooting the musical performances. "We did it film school style," Magnoli stresses. "We did it raw, rugged, and ragged. We were making essentially a low-budget film for its time, with a very big reach, hopefully, because I wanted a crossover film."

When the film premiered, *Purple Rain* indeed opened big. "It did $7.6 million the first weekend; it knocked

Ghostbusters out of the first-place position," Magnoli says. "It rose fast and furious from that point. It was a hit right off."

Purple Rain became the tenth highest grossing film of 1984 (the year of not just *Ghostbusters*, but *Indiana Jones and the Temple of Doom*, *Gremlins*, *Star Trek III* and several other blockbusters).

Many of the songs featured in *Purple Rain* also became hits, particularly "When Doves Cry," featured in a music video–style montage, during which there's a sex scene with Prince and Apollonia in a barn, shots of The Kid brooding on his (purple) bike, and so forth.

Another memorable moment in the film finds Prince singing "Darling Nikki," a naughty little ditty that gives Prince the opportunity to writhe and simulate sex on stage (and atop a speaker). The film's opening number, "Let's Go Crazy" is also a raucous set-piece, intercutting Prince's performance with an enthusiastic audience.

(DVD) Available on DVD.

(is for *Quadrophenia*)

Quadrophenia (1979)(REAL ROCKER)(SNDTRK)

STARRING: Phil Daniels (Jimmy); Leslie Ash (Steph); Philip Davis (Chalky); Mark Wingutt (Dave); Sting (Ace Face); Raymond Winstone (Kevin); Timothy Spall (Projectionist).

FILM EDITORS: Sean Barton, Mike Taylor. DIRECTOR OF PHOTOGRAPHY: Brian Tufano. WRITTEN BY: Dave Humphries, Franc Roddam, Pete Townshend. PRODUCED BY: Roy Baird, Bill Curbishley, Roger Daltrey, John Entwistle, Keith Moon, David Gideon Thomson, Pete Townshend. DIRECTED BY: Franc Roddam. M.P.A.A. RATING: R. RUNNING TIME: 120 minutes.

Taking The Who's celebrated concept album of the same name and setting it as the aural stage for a teenage melodrama, Franc Roddam's *Quadrophenia* is a thoughtful, accessible tale of youthful alienation. Jimmy Cooper (Phil Daniels) plays a to-the-hilt Mod struggling with the realities of coming of age in working class Britain. Obsessed with fashion, his moped, modified American blues music, and women, he drinks, fights, and doses himself into a tragic oblivion. An episodic narrative eventually points Jimmy, his love Steph (Leslie Ash), and his mates to Brighton, where the Mods clash with their sworn enemies the Rockers. Sting cameos as Ace, the most enviable of the youth, who is eventually reduced to working as a bellboy. Pete Townshend largely envisioned the album as an ode to the days when The Who were an iconic part of the Mod scene.

Worlds away from the intricate, total structure of Ken Russell's *Tommy*, this Who album, put to film, forgoes artistic bravura in favor of ready understanding. Everything in Jimmy's life points to rebellion, from his inability to keep a job to his rows with his parents. One hardly recognizes how youthful and angry the music of the original album is until it is put to the screen, with "Love Reign O'er Me" situated as the perfect coda. In addition to music from the album, there are period songs ranging from James Brown's "Night Train" to The Supremes' "Baby Love," not to mention early anthems from The Who. In one sense, Franc Roddam's conception is a lot like *American Graffiti*, albeit with different cultural and stylistic influences. *Quadrophenia* is an essential companion-document to *Tommy*, and is among the essential films of British angst.—Kevin Flanagan

(DVD) Available on a special edition DVD.

Sting is the leader of the pack in Franc Roddam's
impressive collaboration with The Who, *Quadrophenia* (1979).

(is for *Rock 'n' Roll High School*)

Radio Concert Ticket Contest/ Giveaway (GENRE CONVENTION) Another rock-movie convention. Here, a group of kids who hope to get to an important concert call in to a radio contest to win tickets. Sometimes the kids win, sometimes they lose. The Radio Giveaway appears in several films including *Rock 'n' Roll High School* (1979), *I Wanna Hold Your Hand* (1978) and *Detroit Rock City* (1999).

Rags-to-riches (GENRE CONVENTION) This is the easily traceable arc of every good rock star and rock movie bio-pic.

Inevitably, these films begin with future icons as troubled young children living in unfortunate home situations and under the thumb of bad parents (*Walk the Line*, 2005, *What's Love Got to Do With It*, 1993) then striking out to make it on their own.

Sometimes, along the way, there's a deep trauma (*The Rose*, 1979) or a setback (like Jim Morrison at film school in *The Doors*, 1991) but then—after much trial and tribulation—success is broached, as is stardom. All goes well for a while as the talent in question enjoys the wealth and celebrity of rock stardom. However, then booze and drugs enter the picture (*The Five Heartbeats*, 1991, *Boogie Nights*, 1997, *The Rose*, 1979, *54*, 1998, *What's Love Got to Do With*

It). Sometimes a sexual scandal occurs too (*Great Balls of Fire*, 1989).

Anyway, album sales start to slide, crowds get smaller, and the death spiral officially begins. At this point, groups break up (*This Is Spinal Tap*, 1984, *That Thing You Do!*, 1996) and the rags-to-riches story ends with either a second chance for redemption and a comeback (*Boogie Nights*, *What's Love Got to Do With It*) or oppositely, untimely death and its ensuing mythmaking (*The Doors*, *The Rose*).

Rainbow Bridge (1972)(DOC)(CAMEO)

STARRING: Jimi Hendrix, Pat Hartley, Bob Amacker, Baron Binger, Jimmy Cameron, Yella Cameron, Barry De Prendergast, Paul Gebaur, Chuck Wein.

FILM EDITOR: John F. Schreyer. DIRECTOR OF PHOTOGRAPHY: Vilis Lapenieks. WRITTEN BY: Charlie Bacis. PRODUCED BY: Barry De Prendergast. DIRECTED BY: Chuck Wein. M.P.A.A. RATING: R. RUNNING TIME: 125 minutes.

Certainly more (or perhaps in ways, decidedly less) than the Jimi Hendrix concert film it is often billed as, Chuck Wein's *Rainbow Bridge* is an unironic attempt at utopian thinking at the twilight of countercultural credibility. The movie, which is pseudo-improvised toward questionable ends, follows Pat Hartley, a New Yorker sent to Hawaii to report on the happenings of the Rainbow Bridge meditation commune. A series of very heady encounters with various dropouts (faux-mystics, surfers, former apologists for "straight" life) crescendos with a visit and concert by

Jimi Hendrix. This ultraviolet burst of drugs, yoga, nature, speculation on UFOs, and music never quite creates the big bang it self importantly claims to channel.

There is a very quaint, naïve innocence about *Rainbow Bridge*, as its subjects seem to all implicitly feel that the "way out" is possible through a reorganized mixture of some of the oppressive things that molded mainstream society in the first place (religion, definitive truths, constant arguing). Some of the film's hallucinogenic sequences betray a mildly interesting visual sensibility, but the clumsy stylelessness of other moments, in particular the Hendrix concert sequence, stop the buck there. The Jimi Hendrix Experience plays a hurried set, presenting middle-of-the-road renditions of "Foxy Lady," "Voodoo Chile," and "Purple Haze." Jimi also does some interview rap sessions, providing a candid forecast of his inevitable death.

Never quite clicking in the ways of other countercultural masterpieces (*Zabriskie Point*, *La Vallée*, *Easy Rider*), *Rainbow Bridge* ends up feeling like little more than a group therapy session for hippie mass neuroses.—Kevin Flanagan.

(DVD) Available on DVD.

Ray (2004)(BIO-PIC)

STARRING: Jamie Foxx (Ray Charles); Kerry Washington (Della Rea Robinson); Regina King (Margie); Clifton Powell (Jeff Brown); Harry Lennix (Joe Adams); Bokeem Woodbine (Fathead Newman); Larenz Tate (Quincy Jones); Terrence Dashon Howard (Gossie).

FILM EDITOR: Paul Hirsch. DIRECTOR OF PHOTOGRAPHY: Pawel Edelman. WRITTEN BY: James L. White. STORY BY: Taylor Hackford, James L. White. DIRECTED BY: Taylor Hackford. M.P.A.A. RATING: PG-13. RUNNING TIME: 152 minutes.

Directed by Taylor Hackford (*see: The Idolmaker*), this biography of a legendary rock and soul icon was filmed in New Orleans (doubling as Atlanta) and made under the title *Unchain My Heart: The Ray Charles Story*. It starred Jamie Foxx as the legendary Ray, an assignment the actor earned after meeting Ray and his family and establishing his chops at the piano alongside the blind artist.[51]

Once shooting had begun, Foxx endured twelve-to-fourteen hours a day in special contact lenses to mimic Ray's handicap,[52] but his amazing performance ultimately went far beyond physical mimicry. "I wanted to touch some part of his spirit. That's all," the actor described. "There were a lot of little touches which I tried to layer—his musicality, his warmth, his sense of balance, his posture…"[53]

The result of Foxx's efforts was a heartfelt performance and eventually an Academy Award for Best Actor.

Ray itself generally received mixed reviews, mostly for appearing to be such a safe and traditional "bio-pic," though the critics unanimously singled out Foxx's contribution. "His portrayal is an exalting tribute to a flawed, fascinating musical icon,"[54] wrote Philip Wuntch for *The Dallas Morning News*. Audiences agreed, and the film earned a staggering $20.1 million on its opening weekend, Halloween 2004, and overall (by early 2005) more than $70 million against its $40 million budget.

(DVD) Available on DVD.

Record Company (GENRE CONVENTION) *Pure evil.*

In rock genre movies, record companies are both saviors and villains. The former, because they sign up obscure acts like The Wonders or The Five Heartbeats, the latter because they stifle creative freedom, make bad promotional decisions, and care only about profits. In many a rock film, evil record companies have even been equated with the Devil or "selling your soul," (B.D. Records in *Sgt. Pepper's Lonely Hearts Club Band*, 1978).

Another example is Paul Williams' Death Records in the Faustian De Palma film *Phantom of the Paradise* (1974).

In *This Is Spinal Tap* (1984), Ian Hogg's Polymer Records caves to pressure from American department stores and refuses to release "Smell the Glove" with its intended cover. In *Give My Regards to Broad Street* (1984), a Paul McCartney vehicle, evil Rathbone Industries hopes to take ownership of the star's business when master tapes for his latest album are stolen.

In *The Five Heartbeats* (1991), Big Red Records resorts to murder to keep the group in its thrall. In *The Filth and the Fury* (2000), The Sex Pistols reveal their thoughts about record companies when they perform the tune "EMI." Likewise in Frank Zappa's bizarre *Baby Snakes* (1979), a fan holds up a sign reading "*Warner Bros. sucks*" in support of Zappa's creativity.

Yet another movie with an evil record company (trying to brainwash America's impressionable youth) is the 2000 film *Josie and the Pussycats*. A word to the wise: if you get a record deal, read the fine print and be careful!

Recording Studio Session (GENRE CONVENTION)

Where all the tensions and resentments between members of rock bands always bubble over in rock movies. In *This Is Spinal Tap* (1984), David St. Hubbins (Michael McKean) can't get his guitar licks right, and Nigel Tufnel angrily tells him it's the destructive influence of girlfriend Jeanine Pettibone. "*It's your wife! It's your fuckin' wife!*," he insists.

In *Boogie Nights* (1997), Dirk Diggler attempts to jump-start a career in rock music at a recording studio with his composer Reed Rothschild, but these artists are vexed when the sound engineer doesn't record their rehearsal. Later, they can't afford to get their tapes and get into a scuffle with the owner of the studio.

In *The Doors* (1991), one recording sessions turns ugly when Jim Morrison (Val Kilmer) accuses his bandmates of selling out after witnessing a car commercial scored to the tune of "Light My Fire." He throws and destroys a TV set in anger (see: *Times Square*). Another recording session in the film finds Morrison vocalizing intently while wife Pam (Meg Ryan)—down on her knees—performs fellatio on him.

Rock Star (2001) also includes a recording studio sequence, this one involving Izzy (Mark Wahlberg) and his first failed then successful attempt to sing a Steel Dragons hit.

The Return of the Living Dead

(1985)(SNDTRK)(HORR)

STARRING: Clu Gulager (Burt); James Karen (Frank); Don Calfa (Ernie); Thom Matthews (Freddy); Miguel Nunez (Spider); Brian Peck (Scuz); John Philbin (Chuck); Linnea Quigley (Trash); Beverly Randolph (Tina); Jewel Shepard (Casey); Mark Venturini (Suicide).

FILM EDITOR: Robert Gordon. DIRECTOR OF PHOTOGRAPHY: Jules Brenner. STORY: Rudi Ricci, John Russo, Russell Streiner. SCREENPLAY BY: Dan O'Bannon. PRODUCED BY: Tom Fox. DIRECTED BY: Dan O'Bannon. M.P.A.A. RATING: R. RUNNING TIME: 91 minutes.

Director Dan O'Bannon made this parody of George A. Romero's famous living dead series and infused the zombie saga with a new and welcome thematic element: a punk aesthetic.

To wit, several of the teen victims in the film, including the one played by Linnea Quigley, play punk rockers with names like "Trash," "Scum," and "Suicide." *The Return of the Living Dead* features a nihilistic ending too; one that perfectly exemplifies *"the no future"* aesthetic of punk rock, particularly a "friendly fire" nuclear bombing from the government. In keeping with this punk theme, the soundtrack is seeded with a variety of fantastic (and sometimes very funny) rock tunes.

On the soundtrack, The Cramps perform "The Surfing Dead," a tune which accompanies a siege on a crematorium, TSOL has "Nothing for You," and Grave offers "Partytime," an effort which reflects the film's punk adline: *"Back from the Grave and Ready to Party."* Other punk tunes include SSQ's "Trash's Theme" and the delightfully-evocative "Tonight (We'll Make Love Until We Die)." DVD Available on DVD.

The Road (GENRE CONVENTION) The rock 'n'roll

wilderness. Robbie Robertson described it best in *The Last Waltz* when he noted of the road (after sixteen years navigating it): *"You can press your luck. The road has taken a lot of the great ones; Hank Williams, Buddy Holly, Otis Redding, Janis, Jimi Hendrix, Elvis…it's a goddamn impossible way of life."*

In *Roadie* (1980), Deborah Harry, looking a bit glazed, off-handedly remarks that she's been on the road for a long time.

Roadie (1980)(SNDTRK)(REAL ROCKER)(CAMEOS)

STARRING: Meat Loaf (Travis W. Redfish); Khaki Hunter (Lola); Art Carney (Corpus C. Redfish); Rhonda Bates (Alice); Joe Spano (Ace); Alice Cooper.

FILM EDITOR: Tom Wallis. DIRECTOR OF PHOTOGRAPHY: David Myers. WRITTEN BY: Big Boy Medlin, Michael Ventura. PRODUCED BY: Zalman King, Carolyn Pfeiffer, John E. Pommer. DIRECTED BY: Alan Rudolph. M.P.A.A. RATING: PG. RUNNING TIME: 106 minutes.

Rock movie icon Deborah Harry appears in the Meat Loaf comedy, *Roadie* (1980).

In rock movie history, there have been films about those who promote rock groups (*American Hot Wax*), groupies (*Almost Famous*), managers (*The Idolmaker*) and so on, so why not a movie about the folks who actually get the equipment to the stage? Thus you have Alan Rudolph's cult film *Roadie* (1980), which boasts the ad-line: *"Bands Make It Rock, But Roadies Make It Roll."*

This is the legendary (bad) movie that reportedly scared Rob Reiner and the other creators of *This Is Spinal Tap* off from the idea of centering their prospective rock film on roadies. Critic Janet Maslin called it "turgid, humorless and loud," while also suggesting that "It's possible that *Roadie* is one of those late night specialty items, a movie that requires the right audience and the right mood to seem clever. It's also possible that no late-night hour would be late enough."[55]

This effort (shot around Austin, Texas) stars Meat Loaf as Travis W. Redfish, a truck driver in Texas with a knack for electronics and a heart of gold. Our head-butting, occasionally "brain-locked" and oversized hero falls in love with an under-age groupie named Lola (Khaki Hunter) and becomes a roadie…the vocation where his talents can finally be used appropriately. At home is inventor Dad (Art Carney) ready with sage advice, and on the road Redfish meets with the likes of Alice Cooper.

Several rock acts appear in the film, including Roy Orbison and Hank Williams Jr., who have a barroom duet of "The Eyes of Texas." Blondie's Deborah Harry is also around, looking dazed and confused.

On the soundtrack, Eddie Rabbitt's "Drivin' My Life Away," Pat Benatar's "You Better Run," Styx with "Crystal Ball" and Blondie doing a cover of June Carter Cash's "Ring of Fire."

(DVD) Available on DVD.

Rock Around the Clock (1956)

STARRING: Bill Haley and his Comets, The Platters, Alan Freed, Johnny Johnston (Steve Hollis); Alix Talton (Corinne); Lisa Gaye (Lisa); John Archer (Mike).

FILM EDITORS: Saul A. Goodkind, Jack Ogilvie. DIRECTOR OF PHOTOGRAPHY: Benjamin H. Kline. PRODUCED BY: Sam Katzman. WRITTEN BY: James B. Gordon, Robert E. Kent. M.P.A.A. RATING: UR. RUNNING TIME: 77 minutes.

"See and hear this international rock session!" this movie's poster urged, and audiences complied.

Although *Blackboard Jungle* is often referred to as the first rock film, it's only claim to fame in that regard is the main theme song: Bill Haley and his Comets performing "Rock Around the Clock." Otherwise, there's no mention of rock music in that production.

By contrast, this film, titled after that song *and* starring Haley (as himself) may be the first actual film *about* rock 'n' roll. But perhaps that's a distinction without a difference.

Rock Around the Clock is the story of a big-band promoter, Steve Hollis (Johnny Johnston) who "discovers" Bill Haley and his Comets in a small town and then sets about making them famous. Along the way there's a contrived love story involving Steve and a woman named Lisa

(Gaye), but in essence this is a semi-fictionalized account of rock's formative period.

A smash at the box office, this low-budgeter from exploitation filmmaker Sam Katzman reportedly caused riots in certain theatres in the U.S. and in England. That may be apocryphal, but here's one thing that's no lie: this film boasts a great collection of 1950s-era tunes. Bill Haley and his Comets contribute "Rock Around the Clock, "See You Later, Alligator," and "Rock-a-Beatin'-Boogie'" while The Platters sing "The Great Pretender" and "Only You (And You Alone)."

(DVD) Not Available on DVD.

Rock 'n' Roll High School

(1979)(SNDTRK)(CAMEO)

STARRING: P.J. Soles (Riff Randall); Vincent Van Patten (Tom Roberts); Clint Howard (Eaglebauer); Dey Young (Kate Rambeau); Mary Woronov (Mrs. Togar); Paul Bartel (Mr. McGree); Dick Miller (Police Chief); Don Steele (Screamin' Steve); The Ramones.

FILM EDITORS: Larry Bock, Gail Werbin, Kent Beyda. DIRECTOR OF PHOTOGRAPHY: Dean Cundey. SCREENPLAY: Richard Whitley, Russ Dvonch, Joseph McBride. EXECUTIVE PRODUCER: Roger Corman. PRODUCED BY: Michael Finnell. DIRECTED BY: Allan Arkush. RATED PG. RUNNING TIME: 95 minutes.

In this low-budget rock gem from director Allan Arkush, the draconian and imposing Mrs. Togar (Mary Woronov) becomes the new principal at Vince Lombardi High School, imposing a buttoned-down, tyrannical regime.

Meanwhile, football captain Tom Roberts (Vincent Van Patten) wants to date the school's hottest girl, Riff Randall (P.J. Soles), but she has eyes only for her favorite rock group, "*the hottest band this side of the Iron Curtain*," The Ramones.

The famous rockers are scheduled to give a concert on Thursday at "The Rockatorium," and Riff wants to attend so she can pass on the song she's composed expressly for the Ramones, "Rock 'n' Roll High School."

To accomplish this critical task, Riff and her best friend Kate (Dey Young) must overcome Gestapo-like hall monitors, survive gym class, and outwit Togar. Meanwhile, Tom gets lessons in dating from the school's guru, Eaglebauer (Clint Howard), who maintains a busy office in the rest room. Before the day is done, Togar and the students clash, and The Ramones help the beleaguered, oppressed kids destroy the symbol of their oppressors: high school!

Allan Arkush describes how he first became involved with this project: "When I first came out to Los Angeles, I started working for Roger Corman and I wanted to direct a movie. And the only way you could was to present Roger with an idea he might like based on a genre he was doing. But among the ones [movies] that I wrote was one called *Heavy Metal Kids*, which was based on an idea I had and a song by Todd Rundgren. It had some rebellion in it, and it was based on a daydream that I had in high school in which the bands that I liked would come to the high school and play. And in those days the bands were the Stones and the Yardbirds."

"Roger wasn't that excited about it and wanted to change it to [a setting in a] girl's gym," Arkush remembers. "He wanted to have nude gymnastics. We did a script for that and it was terrible. It was just a mess."

"Then I went and did some more work on him for *Death Sport*," Arkush continues. "*Saturday Night Fever* (1977), *Grease* (1978), and *Thank God It's Friday* (1978), were making money, so he said, '*Why don't you work on that music idea?*'"

"Roger Corman had no understanding of what that movie was about," film editor Kent Beyda adds. "He wanted to call it *Disco High*. He wanted to focus on whatever the latest trend was that was popular with kids. Punk rock wasn't very commercial at that point."

With plans in place and a script written, now it was time to plug in a popular group, a rock band for young Riff Randall to be enthusiastic about.

"It was originally for Todd Rundgren," Arkush reveals. "[But] he was interested in a more serious movie, not a comedy. He actually understood all the references. He's a very smart man. He connected it to the British picture by Lindsay Anderson, *If*. That was exactly one of the inspirations. As was a French movie called *Zero for Conduct*, which is a silent movie about some kids that rebel in a grammar school."

"Then we started thinking about who else we liked," Arkush explains. "Cheap Trick we liked because they were cartoony, so we found their management and talked to them. They wouldn't let us use *Live at the Rubicon* as our soundtrack album. Then we had a meeting at Warner Brothers where many bands were discussed. They suggest-ed Devo, which was a very new band at the time. They also suggested Van Halen. Then they said The Ramones, and I started laughing because I loved The Ramones."

Beyda remembers being "delighted" over the selection, because the group was "very cutting edge at that point."

And not, necessarily, as Arkush learned later, easy to direct. In particular, he remembers the great scene in which Riff fantasizes a bedroom visit by the band, and The Ramones miraculously appear to sing to her.

"That was the first scene we shot with them [The Ramones], and that might have been the second or third day of shooting. That scene was kind of easy, because it was just a matter of getting Joey clear on the lip-synching. He took to it. The dialogue scenes were much more difficult, because they couldn't do the dialogue with any sort of reading that made sense dramatically. The people who I thought were going to be good actors in the band tended to be more uptight, and the ones who were less so had more spontaneity. John was always the spokesman for the band. Dee Dee at the time was kind of messed up, so he didn't say much. But getting him to say '*Pizza, let's dig in*,' took him about twenty-five takes. They were very, very long days.

Also, we tried to keep them [The Ramones] amused. We had no real schedule. They would get there and we might not get to them for three, four or five hours."

Regarding the remainder of the film's casting, Arkush reveals he had always intended for Mamie Van Doren [see: *Girls Town*], to be Coach Steroid, but that "Roger didn't want to pay her salary."

Dee Dee, Johnny, Marky, and Joey Ramone ambush the camera in the anarchic Allan Arkush masterpiece, *Rock 'n' Roll High School* (1979).

As for Mary Woronov, she was also a surprise choice. "Mary we met through Paul Bartel. When Paul did *Death Race 2000*, that's when we saw Mary for the first time. Then we got to know her socially through Paul. Once I knew she had been part of The Velvet Underground scene and all that, that made a big impression. She's in [Arkush's previous film] *Hollywood Boulevard*. There's a scene where she plays a villain and walks around killing people at night."

"That night we sat around all night lighting, shooting, and talking with Mary about her days with The Velvet Underground and the New York Warhol scene, and that's when I became friends with her. So when it came time for the idea of Mrs. Togar, it was because we thought she'd be funny as a sort of prison warden, in the Barbara Steele mold. In the new DVD she mentions a lot about the hairdo and it's true. Once she had the hair and the costume, she became that person, but she's nothing like Mrs. Togar."

One interesting detail about the shooting of the film is that Arkush didn't get to shoot the famous gymnasium musical number. "That had been laid out with a choreographer, and that's the day I got really sick and had to be taken to the hospital. So Joe Dante actually directed that with Dean Cundey as DP. Joe came in as a favor, and though it was laid out, it was really more a creation of Dean and Joe."

And his inspiration for naming the school after Lombardi? "It was an anti-authority thing. That's why it's called Vince Lombardi High School. I don't have anything in particular against Vince Lombardi, but the ethos of winning at all costs and authority was what I was going after.

"Once the film was completed shooting, a process that allowed for a great deal of improvisation, Kent Beyda and a gaggle of others began the editing process," he explains. "It was a very unique and freewheeling atmosphere, editing that movie. A lot of people would sit down and do editing on it. There were two official editors on it, Gale Werbin and Larry Bock. Allan did some editing. Joe Dante did some editing. Paul Bartel did some editing. I did some editing with an assistant. It was a real communal effort, because it was a very tight schedule and that was the atmosphere. The cutting rooms were in this dumpy office building and it was a hangout for people who were interested in movies. Other people would come by and talk movies, and it was really like a film school in a lot of ways.

"Our first screening of the movie was at this screening room on Sunset Boulevard called the 8 o'clock Screening Room and it was on a Monday morning I think," Beyda relates. "My fellow assistant and I had come in that morning to get the film ready to go to the screening. We started running some of the reels of the concert performance, because there was so much footage shot that no one had time to go through it all, and we found this take where the camera was slowing down. P. J. Soles and Dey Young were in the crowd cheering on The Ramones and they were waving their arms around, and as the camera started to slow down, they were circling faster and faster and it became like a blur. And we were like '*This has to be in the movie!*' So we cut it into the sequence, making us late for the screening. We got yelled at by the producer. But then when we were running the movie and people saw it, they were like '*Wow, this is cool.*' It was that kind of atmosphere. Allan, the director, is very, very musical and musically oriented. He knows how to cover concert footage, so there were a lot of good choices [in editing]."

After all the hard work, it was frustrating for Beyda to see the film neglected by the distributor. "The head of distribution at New World also didn't understand the movie, and decided to open it in Lubbock, Texas or something. It should have opened in New York, but they didn't want to spend the money to open it in New York, so they just opened it regionally here and there. They never gave much of a push to the movie, so we knew it was kind of doomed."

Still, *Rock 'n' Roll High School* found an appreciative young audience (especially at midnight showings), and the film's cult status grew. In fact, it was featured in the film reference book called *Cult Movies*, which praises the film's "high-spirited young cast," and the Ramones, noting that they're "amusing" and "fun to watch when performing."[57]

This anarchic, anything-goes comedy is surely one of the high-water marks for the rock genre, a film whose free spirit and overwhelming joy (and silliness) reflects the wildness one feels while listening to bands like The Ramones.

(DVD) This movie is currently available on DVD, as is the less successful sequel, *Rock 'N' Roll High School Forever*.

Rock & Roll Superhero (2003)(DOC)

STARRING: Watt White, Jay Salley, Asaf, Zak.

FILM EDITORS: Miranda and Peter Devin. DIRECTOR OF PHOTOGRAPHY: Peter Devin. PRODUCED AND DIRECTED BY: Peter Devin. M.P.A.A. RATING: UR. RUNNING TIME: 89 minutes.

This the story of Watt White, an almost-thirty rock-and-roller from Connecticut who dreams of making it big. Although he's released several CDs of his own fashioning (including *Watt You Want*, 1993, and *Winter Blues*, 1995) he's never really been discovered or made it big. As the film opens, Watt has fired most of his band and is working on the idea that he thinks will make him famous: fashioning his new band as superheroes, in the outrageous mold of KISS.

While trapped in his "menial" day job at Athlete's Foot (a shoe store), Watt and his Nordic-looking buddy, bassist Jay Salley audition female vocalists, but can't find one they like. Then they hire two Israelis, a drummer named Asaf and a guitarist named Zak. As the band practices, Watt drops the idea of rock superheroes at Asaf's urging, since his music doesn't fit the KISS template.

This documentary film follows Watt, Jay, Zak, and Asaf from spring of 1999 to December 31, 1999, to gigs in New York City in 2000, to an industry showcase in July 2000. Nothing but nothing gets Watt or his band signed by industry insiders, but the film nonetheless plays as an inspiring look at a fellow who doesn't give up.

Of course, the movie tacitly makes the point that Watt is also his own worst enemy. He betrays friends, fires bandmates, switches concepts and so forth at the drop of a hat rather than focusing on improving his own musical skills. Still, Watt boasts an admirable dedication to making it big, and even though he never achieves fame, this project suggests there's something indomitable in his spirit. After all, rock'n'roll is about never giving up, never giving in. (DVD) Available on DVD.

Rock and Rule (1983)(ANIM)(MUS)

STARRING (the voices) of: Don Francks (Mok); Susan Roman (Angel); Paul Le Mat (Omar); Catherine O'Hara (Edith); Iggy Pop (Monster from Another Dimension); Deborah Harry (Angel's Singing Voice); Lou Reed (Mok's Singing Voice).

FILM EDITOR: G. Scott La Barge. CINEMATOGRAPHER: Lenora Hume. WRITTEN BY: John Halfpenny, Patrick Loubert, Peter Sauder. PRODUCED BY: Michael Hirsch, Patrick Loubert. DIRECTED BY: Clive A. Smith. M.P.A.A. RATING: PG. RUNNING TIME: 90 minutes.

Originally titled *Drats*, this animated import from Canada saw only spotty release in American theatres, but nonetheless garnered a small and devoted fan following.

Rock and Rule—a hand-drawn epic—is set in a bizarre post-apocalyptic future in the city Ohm, and involves a diabolical rock star named Mok (voiced when talking by Don Francks; when singing by Lou Reed) who plots and schemes to resurrect a monstrous demon from another dimension (singing voice: Iggy Pop).

To do so however, Mok requires punk rocker Angel (speaking voice, Susan Roman, singing voice—Deborah Harry) to give voice to a particular invocation song. Mok

kidnaps Angel, much to the dismay of her band-mate, who has feelings for her, Omar (Paul Le Mat).

This very strange cartoon from the early 1980s straddles the line between sophomoric and bawdy, juvenile and sexy, but boasts a remarkable array of talents on the soundtrack. Harry sings "Angel's Song" and "Invocation Song." Cheap Trick contributes "Born to Raise Hell" and "Ohm Sweet Ohm," while Lou Reed offers "My Name is Mok" and "Triumph." Earth, Wind and Fire are present too, with "Dance, Dance, Dance."

Writing for the *Village Voice*, film reviewer J. Hoberman found much to praise in this effort, which he reviewed simultaneously with the Disney effort, *Black Cauldron* (1985):

"The rotoscoped humanoids are surprisingly limber, the character animation is often quite forceful. What's more, the cartoon is interspersed with some fairly bold graphics—the smoggy aerials of Ohmtown, backgrounds that anticipate the decrepit deco futurism of David Lynch's *Dune*, a free use of video screens and computer designs. The zappy cartoon colors (violet, aquamarine, fuschia) have a Warner Brothers zing; the iconography is borrowed from sources as varied as hot rod decals, the *echt*—65 *San Francisco Oracle* and Japanese transformer toys. The scene where Mok takes a walk in his garden, dazzling Angel with assorted changes while singing a Lou Reed song, is sufficiently sustained to evoke the more psychedelic, pure animation passages of *Dumbo*, *Fantasia* or *Alice in Wonderland*."[56]

(DVD) Available on a two-disc collectors DVD.

Rock Star (2001)(FIC BAND)(SNDTRK)

STARRING: Mark Wahlberg (Chris Cole/Izzy); Jennifer Aniston (Emily Poule); Jason Flemyng (Bobby Beers); Timothy Olyphant (Rob Malcolm); Timothy Spall (Max); Dominic West (Kirk Cuddy); Matthew Glave (Joe Jr.); Beth Grant (Nicole).

FILM EDITOR: Trudy Ship. DIRECTOR OF PHOTOGRAPHY: Veli Steiger. WRITTEN BY: John Stockwell. EXECUTIVE PRODUCERS: Steven Reuther, George Clooney, Mike Ockrent. PRODUCED BY: Robert Lawrence, Toby Jaffe. DIRECTED BY: Stephen Hack. M.P.A.A. RATING: R. RUNNING TIME: 106 minutes.

A twenty-first-century rock fable about the hair band days of the mid-1980s. *Rock Star* is also the story of a talented young man named Chris Cole (Mark Wahlberg) who leads his own tribute band for the popular heavy metal group Steel Dragons. His band is growing tired of being a tribute band, however, and throws Chris out. His girlfriend, Emily (Jennifer Aniston) encourages Chris to follow his own voice, but he doesn't have confidence in his own skills yet. When Steel Dragons comes knocking, wanting Chris to take over for the "retiring" lead singer, it's an opportunity too good to pass up.

For a time, all is well for Chris and Emily. Cole is introduced to the world as "Izzy" at a *press conference*, and he survives a disastrous and bloody first performance (see: *Stagecraft 101*). But before long, the groupies and pervasive drugs get to Chris, and he and Emily split. Only when Chris recognizes himself in a young fan at a concert does he realize he has outgrown Steel Dragons and his mentors.

He brings the talented fan on stage to replace him and walks away, never to be seen again.

In the climax, however, we learn that Chris traveled to Seattle to follow Emily, and that, once there, he began to explore his own music, becoming a pioneer in the "grunge" scene of the early 1990s.

Predictable and schmaltzy at times, *Rock Star* nonetheless makes a good point about how many new rock artists begin. It's a dirty little secret (with movies too), but most artists start out as fans and then imitate someone they admire, a group or a singer, or even a movie director. Then, as confidence grows, that talent starts to evidence a belief in his or her own "voice" and a new, perhaps even better, star emerges. *Rock Star* is one of the few rock films to acknowledge this process of adulation, acceptance, and surpassing. Interestingly, the movie also suggests in its own fashion that all rock musicians are essentially the same animal, since the break-up of the Steel Dragons tribute band and the break-up of Steel Dragons eerily echo one another (see: the *Break-Up*). *Rock Star* also reveals how members of that exclusive club see themselves: "*He's a rock star now,*" the group's manager tells Emily, "*regular rules don't apply.*"

Just like *Almost Famous* the year before, *Rock Star* didn't perform very well at the box office, perhaps because audiences felt they had seen it all before. Yet the film is never less-than-entertaining, and it offers enough fresh insights not to feel like a total retread of earlier triumphs. And, as always, it's great to see 1980s heavy metal hair bands back on stage, rocking the house where they belong. In one scene, Wahlberg expresses every male adolescent's rock fantasy by dousing his audience with water from a hose held at his crotch.

The tunes in *Rock Star* sound authentically 1980s, and include the power anthem "Stand up," "Livin' the Life" and the appropriately-titled "Long Live Rock'N'Roll." Non-original rock tunes include Boy George's "Karma Chameleon," and The Beach Boys' standard "California Girls."

ⅅⅤⅅ Available on DVD.

Rock, Rock, Rock (1956)(REAL ROCKER)

STARRING: Tuesday Weld (Dori); Teddy Randazzo (Tommy); Alan Freed, Frankie Lymon, Chuck Berry, The Johnny Burnette Trio, The Moon Glows, The Flamingos, Jimmy Cavallo, The House Rockers, Frankie Virtue and the Virtues, Bert Conway (Mr. Barker).

FILM EDITOR: Robert Brockman, Blandine Hafela. DIRECTOR OF PHOTOGRAPHY: Morris Hartzband. STORY: Phyllis Coe. WRITTEN BY: Milton Subtotsky. PRODUCED BY: Max Rosenberg, Milton Subotsky. DIRECTED BY: Will Price. M.P.A.A RATING: UR. RUNNING TIME: 85 minutes.

A very young Tuesday Weld (see: *Heartbreak Hotel*, 1988) makes her screen debut in this nearly forgotten relic about a high school girl, Dori, worrying over getting a dress for the prom and fighting back her rival, Gloria, for the affections of a boy named Tommy (Teddy Randazzo).

Things pick up significantly in the last half of the film as DJ Alan Freed arrives and brings along a gaggle of acts to

Dori's prom, including Chuck Berry, who duck-walks and sings "You Can't Catch Me." Connie Francis dubs over a lip-synching Weld, and Frankie Lymon sings "I'm Not a Juvenile Delinquent."

ⅅⅤⅅ Not Available on DVD.

The Rocky Horror Picture Show

(1975)(MUS)(REAL ROCKER)

STARRING: Tim Curry (Dr. Frank-N-Furter); Susan Sarandon (Janet Weiss); Barry Bostwick (Brad Majors); Richard O'Brien (Riff Raff); Patricia Quinn (Magenta); Peter Hinwood (Rocky Horror); Meat Loaf (Eddie); Charles Gray (Criminologist).

FILM EDITOR: Graeme Clifford. DIRECTOR OF PHOTOGRAPHY: Peter Suschitzky. WRITTEN BY: Richard O'Brien, James Sharman. PRODUCED BY: Lou Adler, John Goldstone, Michael White. DIRECTED BY: Jim Sharman. M.P.A.A. RATING: R. RUNNING TIME: 100 minutes.

"Don't dream it. Be it!" the greatest midnight/cult movie of all time advises. Thousands upon thousands of dedicated aficionados have taken up the suggestion.

The Rocky Horror Picture Show is a dedicated rock musical from the age of *Phantom of the Paradise* (1974) and *Tommy* (1975), and a production highly resistant to any objective school of film criticism. How can you quibble with a film that cost $1 million but has grossed $140 million; that rose phoenix-like from the ashes of its own original theatrical failure and became the quintessential audience-participation picture?

The Rocky Horror Picture Show succeeds, perhaps, because

ANNUAL TRANSYLVANIAN CONVENTION

The cast of *The Rocky Horror Picture Show* (1975) does the time warp. Again.

it's a clever reflection of the way America changed in the late 1960s and early 1970s. This is a film, after all, in which two very traditional, 1950s Americans (who might have been what Nixon had in mind when he named a "Silent Majority") get unexpectedly exposed to a "counterculture" that is figuratively and literally alien to them. The film is an eye-opener for its protagonists (Brad and Janet) in terms of what's out there, especially in terms of sexuality. Nixon even makes an (audio) cameo of sorts in the film…

Most people remember the plot of *The Rocky Horror Picture Show*, but here's a brief synopsis anyway. Brad Majors (Barrry Bostwick) and Janet Weiss (Susan Sarandon) are a buttoned-down American couple on a trip to visit their old professor who, because of rain and a flat tire, end up at the out-of-the-way castle of a mad-scientist/cross-dresser/transsexual from Transylvania named Dr. Frank-N-Furter (Tim Curry in a knockout performance).

The Doc's been building his own Frankenstein Monster of sorts, a would-be sex slave, the hunky Rocky Horror. Frank-N-Furter takes the unwitting guests on a sexual adventure that finds Bostwick and Sarandon (playing a virgin) ultimately losing their inhibitions and basically joining the equivalent of a musical orgy.

Based on the London stage show by Richard O'Brien, *The Rocky Horror Picture Show* makes up in sex appeal, performance and soundtrack what it so clearly lacks in production values. Is it a horror film? A sex film? A musical? All of the above? Who knows, but any movie that features Meat Loaf driving around an interior set on a motorcycle

and a strutting Tim Curry garbed in black fishnet stockings is something special.

The rock tunes in the film are unforgettable and that's a major part of the film's appeal. The performances include ones by O'Brien ("Science Fiction Double Feature"), Bostwick ("Dammit Janet"), Meat Loaf ("Hot Patootie"), Sarandon ("Touch-a, Touch-a, Touch Me") and, of course, Curry ("Sweet Transvestite," "I'm Going Home"). The real show-stopper and the one I can't get out of my head no matter how much I try, however, is "The Time Warp." (DVD) Available on DVD.

Roller Boogie Rock (GENRE CONVENTION)

For a terrifying spell in the late 1970s and early 1980s, roller skates eclipsed the disco dance as the craze *du jour*. For the first time since the 1950s, roller rinks became the national rage again, and a number of rock films featured young actors on skates or were set in rinks.

Roller Boogie (1979) starring Linda Blair was essentially a more youth-oriented version of *Saturday Night Fever* (with no sex), and Steve Guttenberg roller-skated his way through the streets of Manhattan in the opening frames of the Village People vehicle *Can't Stop the Music* (1980). Olivia Newton-John's *Xanadu* (1980) climaxed in a brand new club that featured a skating rink. Finally, 1983's *The Hunger* literally and metaphorically ended the roller rock era by having icon David Bowie—as a vampire—murder a disco dancer on skates. Thank Heavens!

In 1997, *Boogie Nights* briefly called attention back to the fad with a primary character named "Roller Girl" played by Heather Graham. She doesn't take her skates off, even during sex. Appropriately, Roller Girl's theme song was Melanie's "Brand New Key."

Roller Boogie (1979)(SNDTRK)

STARRING: Linda Blair (Theresa Barkley); Jim Bray (Bobby James); Beverly Garland (Lillian Barkley); Roger Perry (Mr. Barkley); Jimmy Van Patten (Hoppy); Kimberly Beck (Lana); Sean McClory (Jammer Delaney); Mark Goddard (Mr. Thatcher); Albert Insinnia (Gordo); Stoney Jackson (Phones); M.G. Kelly (DJ); Chris Nelson (Franklin Potter); Nina Axelrod (Bobby's Friend).

FILM EDITOR: Howard Kunin. DIRECTOR OF PHOTOGRAPHY: Dean Cundey. MUSICAL NUMBERS STAGED BY: David Winters. ORIGINAL SONGS: Bob Esty, Michele Eller, Michael Brooks. SCREENPLAY BY: Barry Schneider. FROM A STORY BY: Irwin Yablans. EXECUTIVE PRODUCER: Irwin Yablans. PRODUCER: Bruce Cohn Curtis. DIRECTED BY: Mark L. Lester. M.P.A.A. RATING: PG. RUNNING TIME: 104 minutes.

As noted in the previous entry, for one blazing moment during the late 1970s and early 1980s, rock 'n' roll, disco, and roller skates combined to form a white-hot national fad. Hence this Linda Blair romance, which was marketed with the tagline "*together, they're love on wheels.*"

Roller Boogie, a film which informs us that skating is actually a *sport*, finds Beverly Hills society girl Theresa Barkley (Linda Blair) falling for "*the best skater on the Boardwalk,*" Bobby James (Jim Bray), during one long, hot summer at Venice Beach. He trains her to become a better skater at Jammer's Roller Rink, but the venue is threatened by an evil land developer, Mr. Thatcher (Mark Goddard). He wants to turn the kids' hangout into a shopping mall because the rink only "*stands in the way of progress.*" Meanwhile, Theresa must contend with her snooty father, who doesn't want her roller skating anymore, and—under Bobby's tutelage—win an upcoming skate contest.

Everything turns out okay in the end in this intensely silly movie that plays like a 1980s variation (in hot pants) of the Frankie and Annette beach movies of the sixties. The film is highlighted by the requisite disrespect for authority (namely parents), and climaxes with Bobby's tender last number, where someone mysteriously works a spotlight from behind the scenes. Slow-motion photography is featured to show this sensitive skater in all his athletic glory.

The songs on the soundtrack include "The Roller Boogie" and "Summer Love" by Bob Esty, "Top Jammer" performed by The Cheeks, and "Boogie Wonderland" performed by Earth, Wind & Fire.

(DVD) Available on DVD.

The Rose (1979)(FIC BAND)(BIO-PIC)

STARRING: Bette Midler (Mary Rose Foster); Alan Bates (Campbell); Frederic Forrest (Huston Dyer); Harry Dean Stanton (Billy Ray); Barry Primus (Dennis); David Keith (Mal).

FILM EDITOR: C. Timothy O'Meara, Robert Wolfe. DIRECTOR OF PHOTOGRAPHY: Vilmos Zsigmond. WRITTEN BY: Bo Goldman. STORY: Bill Kerby. PRODUCED BY: Tony Ray, Aaron Russo, Marvin Worth. DIRECTED BY: Mark Rydell. M.P.A.A. RATING: R. RUNNING TIME: 125 minutes.

Bette Midler won a Golden Globe and was nominated for an Academy Award for "Best Actress" for her scorching, incredible performance in *The Rose*. Midler's on center stage in virtually every scene during this film, and she carries that responsibility brilliantly. Not with ease, mind you, because it never looks easy, but with talent, energy, and heart to spare.

This is a fictionalized version of the Janis Joplin story (**see:** *Janis*) but it's no rip-off. Instead, Midler makes the character of Mary "The Rose" Foster her own creation, a woman who grew up in Florida and has found hard-fought fame, but not without first succumbing to demons like alcoholism. Also, as the film reveals at a critical juncture, she has a traumatic personal (and sexual) history at the root of her melancholy and despair.

The Rose takes place in the *Vietnam War* era, in 1969, as the over-worked, fatigued Rose hopes to take a year-long rest from the business to recharge her batteries. Unfortunately, her evil *manager*, played by Alan Bates, wants Rose to keep working because she's at the pinnacle of pop culture fame.

The Rose alternates between concert performances (wherein Midler is dazzling) and intense, behind-the-scenes drama (where she also shines). Part of the plot involves Rose's ill-fated meeting with a country star played by Harry Dean Stanton. This occasion goes badly and Rose runs off with a limo driver, played by Frederic Forrest, who soon becomes a lover.

In all likelihood, you've watched this rock story before, but you haven't seen anything if you haven't seen Midler play the role of a rocker in distress. I like Sally Field (*I really like her...*), and she gave a good performance in *Norma Rae* (1979), but watching this film today, you have to wonder if Midler wasn't robbed on Oscar night in 1980. She's just staggeringly credible here, equally at home with the music and the dramatic scenes. Really, how many other actresses could have pulled off so complex a part this well?

Midler sings the Golden Globe Award–winning tune "The Rose," as well as "When a Man Loves a Woman," "Midnight in Memphis," the exquisitely-titled "Sold My Soul to Rock 'n' Roll," "Fire Down Below," and others. (DVD) Available on DVD.

Roustabout (1964)(MUS)

STARRING: Elvis Presley (Charlie Rogers); Barbara Stanwyck (Maggie); Joan Freeman (Cathy); Leif Erickson (Joe); Sue Anne Langdon (Madam Mijanou); Pat Buttram (Harry Carver).

FILM EDITOR: Warren Low. DIRECTOR OF PHOTOGRAPHY: Lucien Ballard. MUSIC SCORE: Joseph Lilley. STORY BY: Allan Weiss. WRITTEN BY: Anthony Lawrence, Allan Weiss. PRODUCED: Hal B. Wallis. DIRECTED BY: John Rich. M.P.A.A. RATING: UR. RUNNING TIME: 101 minutes.

"Rambling. Roving. Restless. Reckless."—That's how the advertisements described Elvis in *Roustabout*, a slightly

more edgy vehicle for the King of Rock 'n' roll. Here he plays an orphan named Charlie Rogers who goes from town to town on his Japanese motorcycle singing at small venues (like Mother's Tea House) and picking fights with local fraternity boys (and decimating them with his black belt karate skills).

One day, Charlie is run off a rural road by a drunk carny named Joe (Leif Erickson) and the carnival manager, Maggie (Barbara Stanwyck) offers to fix his motorcycle for free and give him a job as a roustabout on the grounds; a roustabout being one who erects and dismantles tents, cares for the grounds, and handles animals and equipment. Charlie agrees, in part because he hopes to romance Joe's daughter, Cathy (Joan Freeman). Soon, however, Charlie is a huge draw at the faltering carnival because of his singing skills, and a competing carnival run by Harry Carver (Pat Buttram) tries to steal him away.

In *Roustabout*, Elvis regularly dresses in black leather, tries to make time with a leggy fortune teller (Sue Ann Langdon) and talks about his preference to make love outdoors. He braves the carnival's "Wall of Death" on his motorcycle and generally seems much less wholesome than in many of his previous screen appearances.

Again, however, the movie is a fairly mechanical, predictable romance enlivened only by Elvis's performance of several songs (accompanied vocally by The Jordanaires and staged by Earl Benton). "Poison Ivy League" is the number Elvis uses to put the snobby fraternity boys in their place, and "Big Love, Big Heartache" is the featured love song.

The *Roustabout* album went to number one on *Billboard*'s chart, and the movie is one of Elvis's better films, if only because some of the King's sexual charisma translates well to his character.

(DVD) Available on DVD.

(is for *The School of Rock*)

Satisfaction (1988)

(FIC BAND)(SNDTRK)(CAMEO)

STARRING: Justine Bateman (Jennie); Liam Neeson (Martin Falcon); Trini Alvarado (Mooch); Scott Coffey (Nickie); Britta Phillips (Billy); Julia Roberts (Daryl); Debbie Harry (Tina); Chris Nash (Frankie); Michael De Lorenzo (Bunny).

FILM EDITOR: Joel Goodman. DIRECTOR OF PHOTOGRAPHY: Thomas Del Ruth. WRITTEN BY: Charles Purpura. EXECUTIVE PRODUCERS: Robert Alden, Armyan Bernstein. PRODUCERS: Aaron Spelling, Alan Greisman. DIRECTED BY: Joan Freeman. M.P.A.A. RATING: PG-13. RUNNING TIME: 92 minutes.

A coming of age story set during summertime, *Satisfaction* stars TV's *Family Ties* star Justine Bateman as Jennie Lee, the lead singer of a cover band also featuring Trini Alvarado (see: *Times Square*, 1980) and a young Julia Roberts. They win a summer-long gig at a club called Falcon's, named for famous lyricist and writer Martin Falcon (Liam Neeson), a "self-indulgent ass" who falls for Jennie.

Each band member in this Aaron Spelling production is handed a pat emotional crisis to overcome during the film. Alvarado's tomboy, Mooch falls for the only boy in the band, the naïve Nickie (Scott Coffey). Roberts' starry-eyed Daryl ponders marrying an abusive greaser named Frankie from back home. Finally, Jennie must decide if she wants to move in with Martin, go to college, or tour Europe as a rock star.

Deborah Harry of Blondie cameos as a rival for Neeson's affections, and all the while the band performs cover tunes like "Mr. Big Stuff" and "Come on, Everybody." At the climax, the band plays some original tunes such as "Lies" and Falcon's supposed masterpiece "Talk to Me," both by Beau Charles and Michele Colombier.

Satisfaction is a lightweight but highly predictable and rather dull effort that boasts little genuine rock attitude. Instead, the tepid screenplay insists on spotlighting "wacky hijinks" like Neeson and Bateman falling out of a rowboat at sea; a fast-motion volleyball game in the sand; and worst of all, a truly horrifying scene in which Daryl and Frankie make love (off-camera) all day in a stolen van. *Satisfaction*'s idea of humor is to focus on the van shaking up and down constantly, while outside the other band members go about a day's worth of business: heading to the beach, getting lunch, going back to the beach, etc. Julia Roberts must look back at this one and cringe.

"Watching *Satisfaction*…sometimes feels like being dropped into a time-warping Vegematic" wrote Michael Wilmington at the *Los Angeles Times*. "This is a movie supposedly about an '80s rock band—where the songs date from the '60s, the language and sexual attitudes suggest the '70s and the plot is pure '50s."[58]

DVD Available on DVD.

She can't get none. Justine Bateman stars in *Satisfaction* (1988).

Saturday Night Fever (1977)(SNDTRK)

STARRING: John Travolta (Tony Manero); Karen Lynn Gorney (Stephanie); Barry Miller (Bobby); Joseph Cali (Joey); Donna Pescow (Annette); Julie Bovasso (Flo Manero).

FILM EDITOR: David Rawlins. DIRECTOR OF PHOTOGRAPHY: Ralf D. Bode. BASED ON A STORY BY: Nik Cohn. WRITTEN BY: Norman Wexler. PRODUCED BY: Robert Stigwood. DIRECTED BY: John Badham. M.P.A.A. RATING: R. RUNNING TIME: 118 minutes.

Forget *Star Wars*. The year 1977 was also the season of another blockbuster: *Saturday Night Fever*, a production based on Nik Cohn's *New York* magazine article (later reported to be mostly fiction) entitled "Tribal Rites of the New Saturday Night."

In short order, this movie from director John Badham became a blockbuster and the soundtrack album by the Bee Gees sold more than twenty million copies. The film remains a touchstone of pop culture; no other production better says Seventies than this one.

Saturday Night Fever commences with a young Brooklynite, Tony Manero (John Travolta), going about his regular Friday work schedule. He toils all day at a paint store, and the film opens with views of Travolta—*looking cocky and confident*—strutting the streets of New York in smooth close-up to the strains of "Stayin' Alive."

After this introduction, Badham shines fetishistic illumination on Travolta's "suit up" ritual before the weekend's activities (to the tune "Night Fever"). Comb in one hand, blow dryer in the other, Tony perfects his hair while gazing lovingly into the mirror. Then, as if securing a talis-

man, he puts on his gold necklaces and heads out to 2001 Odyssey, a local club.

And heaven help anyone if they mess up his hair!

Tony's first time on the disco floor is also filmed memorably by Badham, who adopts the first-person-subjective shot as the camera moves confidently through a mass of gyrating dancers. This perspective lands the audience right in the middle of the action, and it is not only intense, it's actually immersing.

Shortly, Tony dances to "You Should Be Dancin'" and it's an amazing display that establishes him as the god of disco. Travolta is mesmerizing in this number, and this moment, more than any other, may be what sold the country on the disco craze.

"*You're the King out there*," Manero is told, and it's an accurate perception. One female patron at the club practically worships him, asking if he's "*as good in bed*" as he is on the floor.

In realistic, authentic fashion (with finely observed performances), Badham effectively introduces the world to this particular disco scene. Tony's story is an important one too, because it's about striving to be the best and finding a way—*any way*—to escape the confines of a world that seems limited or dull. For Tony, that world is Brooklyn, where his family and friends live.

Manero and a partner (Karen Lynn Gorney) eventually participate in a *dance contest* at the discotheque (with the prize being $500) but by the time the couple wins, Manero has already moved on. He's hungry for more, and his tiny taste of celebrity in that Brooklyn disco is no

Sweat hog John Travolta (left) rehearses with choreographer Deney Terrio—future *Dance Fever* host—on the set of *Saturday Night Fever* (1977).

longer enough. He's destined for bigger and better things, and that's something his friends—who kinda hold him back—can't understand.

It's hip and cool these days for some to mock disco, especially those outrageous fashions (platform shoes and big lapels, anyone?) but *Saturday Night Fever* so effortlessly and gloriously captures a moment in American history that it feels like 1977 all over again whenever you watch it.

The soundtrack also includes "More Than a Woman," and "How Deep Is Your Love" by the Bee Gees. Other disco era hits include "Disco Inferno," and "Boogie Shoes."

An inferior sequel, *Staying Alive*, followed in 1983. (DVD) Available on DVD.

The School of Rock (2003)(FIC)(SNDTRK)

STARRING: Jack Black (Dewey Finn); Joan Cusack (Rosalie Mullins); Mike White (Ned Schneddely); Sarah Silverman (Patty); Lee Wilkoff (Mr. Green); Adam Pascal (Theo); Suzzanne Douglass (Tomeka's Mom); Miranda Cosgrove (Summer); Kevin Clark (Freddy); Joey Gaydos Jr. (Zack); Robert Tsai (Lawrence); Aleisha Allen (Alicia); Caitlin Hale (Marta); Maryam Hassan (Tameka).

FILM EDITOR: Sandra Adair. DIRECTOR OF PHOTOGRAPHY: Rogier Stoffers. WRITTEN BY: Mike White. EXECUTIVE PRODUCED BY: Steve Nicolaides, Scott Aversano, Jeremy Conway. DIRECTED BY: Richard Linklater. M.P.A.A. RATING: PG-13. RUNNING TIME: 108 minutes.

This wise and witty Richard Linklater film may be the best comedy *about* rock 'n' roll yet produced by Hollywood.

The music in the film isn't that earth shattering, but the ideas contained in the screenplay capture perfectly the essence of the genre as comedian and rocker (Tenacious D) Jack Black schools audiences in the history and glory of the form.

School of Rock begins as Dewey Finn (Black), a hopeless wannabe rocker, is ejected from his band (for performing unwarranted stage dives) just as preparations are being made to win the all important *Battle of the Bands*. Strapped for cash, Dewey masquerades as his roommate, Ned (Mike White) and takes a job as a substitute teacher at a ritzy preparatory school called Horace Green.

On the job, Dewey immediately declares recess, but then, upon witnessing the remarkable skills of his students in music class, decides to transform the children into his own rock band. He still wants to win the battle of the bands (and the $20,000 prize), and for him, his avenue may be those talented moppets.

"*You could be the ugliest sad sack on the planet, but if you're in a rock band, you're the coolest guy in the world,*" Dewey tells his students, who very quickly come around to his way of thinking. Dewey then proceeds to lecture about rock history and influences (including artists such as Christina Aguilera, Liza Minnelli, and Puff Daddy).

He teaches the kids that "*rock is about the passion*" and explains that the key to writing a good rock ballad is tapping into what pisses you off. He also splits up his class into groups. Lawrence takes over the keyboard (and plays *The Doors*), Zack becomes the guitar player, over the objections of his (bad) father (representing *Authority*), who says that it's a waste of time. Other students become roadies and the band's security detail. One girl, Summer, a brown-noser, even takes over as the band's *manager*.

At the end of the day, Dewey's new band "The School of Rock" narrowly loses the battle of the bands to a group called "No Vacancy," but it's almost immaterial, since Dewey Finn has found his own self-worth in teaching rock, and the children have "stuck it to the man." This is a delightful and funny movie, and to those who rock hard in it, I salute you.

On the soundtrack: "Touch Me" by The Doors, "Substitute" by The Who, and "Math is a Wonderful Thing" by Jack Black and Mike White.

ⅅⅤⅅ Available on DVD.

Selena (1997)(BIO-PIC)

STARRING: Jennifer Lopez (Selena); Jackie Guerra (Suzette); Constance Marie (Marcela); Alexandra Meneses (Sara); Edward James Olmos (Abraham).

FILM EDITOR: Nancy Richardson. DIRECTOR OF PHOTOGRAPHY: Edward Lachman. WRITTEN BY: Gregory Nava. PRODUCED BY: Robert Katz. DIRECTED BY: Gregory Nava. M.P.A.A. RATING: PG. RUNNING TIME: 127 minutes.

The tragic tale of a murdered pop star gives Jennifer Lopez one of her earliest and most dramatic screen roles. *Selena* dutifully follows the rags-to-riches path to stardom tracked of a young Mexican tejano star (who died tragically at the age of 23).

Selena's relationship with her father, played by Edward James Olmos, is tenderly vetted here, as is the young woman's secret marriage to the band guitarist. Selena's professional path from obscurity to a concert at the Houston Astrodome is also charted. Finally, the film edges up to that fateful day when the president of Selena's fan club murdered her. The pop star's demise is handled tastefully and without sensationalism, and this film serves as both a memorial and tribute to the talents of a young woman for whom the sky could have—and should have—been the limit.

On the soundtrack, Selena sings "Dreaming of You," "I Could Fall in Love" and "I Will Survive/Funky Town."

ⅅⅤⅅ Available on DVD.

Sgt. Pepper's Lonely Hearts Club Band (1978)

(MUS)(FIC BAND)(SNDTRK)(CAMEOS)

STARRING: Peter Frampton (Billy Shears); Barry Gibb (Mark Henderson); Robin Gibb (David Henderson); Maurice Gibb (Bob); Frankie Howerd (Mean Mr. Mustard); Paul Nicholas (Douglas); Donald Pleasence (B.D. Brockhurst); Sandra Farina (Strawberry Fields); Steve Martin (Dr. Maxwell Edison); George Burns (Mr. Kite); Aerosmith (Future Villain); Alice Cooper (Father Sun); Billy Preston (Sgt. Pepper); Aretha Franklin, Earth, Wind and Fire, Stargard, Wolfman Jack, Robert Palmer, Sha Na Na.

FILM EDITOR: Christopher Holmes. DIRECTOR OF PHOTOGRAPHY: Owen Roizman. CHOREOGRAPHY: Patricia

Birch. MUSIC AND LYRICS BY: John Lennon, Paul McCartney, George Harrison. EXECUTIVE PRODUCER: Dee Anthony. PRODUCED BY: Robert Stigwood. WRITTEN BY: Henry Edwards. DIRECTED BY: Michael Schultz. M.P.A.A. RATING: PG. RUNNING TIME: 114 minutes.

Sgt. Pepper's Lonely Hearts Club Band, from Heartland U.S.A. is invited to Hollywood to make a deal with Big Deal Records, but one of the band members, Billy (Peter Frampton) is upset about separating from his girlfriend, Strawberry Fields (Sandra Farina). Heartland is also the home of the original Sgt. Pepper and his magical instruments and weather vane, and those instruments are coveted by Mean Mr. Mustard (Frankie Howerd).

While the band is away in Los Angeles, being tempted by record executive B.D. Brockhurst (Donald Pleasence), Mustard hatches a plan to steal the magical coronet, drums and other instruments. Strawberry Fields warns the band of the plot, but the nefarious Mustard succeeds. Now it's up to Sgt. Pepper's Lonely Hearts Club Band to retrieve the instruments from a series of villains including evil doctor Maxwell Edison (Steve Martin), cult figure Father Sun (Alice Cooper) and Future Villain (Aerosmith).

Sgt. Pepper's Lonely Hearts Club Band is a film dramatized with title cards superimposed over the imagery (resembling silent movie cards), and there's precious little spoken dialogue, only songs. Although George Burns serves as the narrator of the tale, the leads—the Bee Gees and Peter Frampton—actually speak little beyond the song lyrics, which consist entirely of the Beatles' repertoire

from the famous concept album and others. Thus, as Frampton and Strawberry Fields awake to idyllic peace in a rural barn, they sing "Here Comes the Sun." When Frampton's character, believing Fields to be dead, is about to commit suicide by jumping from a second-story ledge, Sgt. Pepper comes to life (as Billy Preston), zaps Frampton back onto the ledge with a blue laser bolt and sings "Get Back!"

Although this isn't a popular view, the Bee Gees actually do a credible (if not inspired) job with the Beatles tunes here, but it is Aerosmith that steals the show with their rendition of "Come Together." Still, one wishes this film had been made back in 1965 with the Fab Four playing the central roles, sans the hideous Spandex fashions of the disco era. Instead, viewers will have to settle for an uncredited cameo in the closing scene by Paul McCartney and George Harrison.

It's not quite the same thing, is it? The Bee Gees do sing just fine, but personality-wise, the group lacks charm and at times individuality. The Beatles (on film, at least) always seemed to have a light way about themselves. Not so with these designated successors.

(DVD) Available on DVD.

Shag: The Movie (1989)(SNDTRK)

STARRING: Phoebe Cates (Carson); Scott Coffey (Chip); Bridget Fonda (Malaina); Annabeth Gish (Pudge/Caroline); Page Hannah (Luanne); Robert Rusler (Buzz); Tyrone Power Jr. (Harley); Jeff Yagher (Jimmy Valentine); Paul Lieber (The Manager); Carrie Hamilton (Nadine); Donald Craig (Senator Clatterback).

FILM EDITOR: Laurence Mery-Clark. DIRECTOR OF PHOTOGRAPHY: Pete MacDonald. STORY BY: Lanier Laney, Terry Sweeney. WRITTEN BY: Robin Swicord, Lanier Laney, Terry Sweeney. PRODUCED BY: Julia Chasman, Stephen Wodley. DIRECTED BY: Zelda Barron. M.P.A.A. RATING: PG. RUNNING TIME: 98 minutes.

In the summer of 1963 (see: *Camelot*), four Southern girls tell their parents they're going away for a weekend of "historical appreciation" at Fort Sumter but instead head to Myrtle Beach to meet boys. There, the Pavilion is holding a Shag *dance contest* as well as a beauty pageant for Miss Sun Queen.

Shag: The Movie is essentially a period version of the 1988 misfire *Satisfaction* (1988), only here the girls are Southerners and don't play in a rock band. But the character conflicts, including a wedding engagement that goes sour, are virtually the same. Enhancing the similarities, Scott Coffey appears in both films as a likeable joe with a crush on one of the stars.

Still, *Shag: The Movie* is a more enjoyable and better-produced film than *Satisfaction*, in part because it doesn't share the Justine Bateman vehicle's sense of pomposity and pretension. *Shag: The Movie* is frequently funny, and often sweet too. The performances are strong, and Bridget Fonda does an incredible dance in a bikini, draping a Confederate flag around her body and between her legs to the tune of "Dixie." Jeff Yagher also registers strongly as an Elvis-wannabe named Jimmy Valentine, a clueless clothes horse and rock idol who can bust a move but who has been sequestered away from real teens by his protective *manager* (a Colonel Parker figure, perhaps).

Shag: The Movie also shares qualities in common with George Lucas's *American Graffiti*: it's set in the early 1960s as America's "Age of Innocence" gives way to trauma. This film occurs in the summer before the Kennedy assassination, and there are only hints of the dangers of Vietnam (Coffey's character plans to attend Annapolis). This is also pre-Beatles America and so that means American rock is still developing unimpeded by foreign influence. The Voltage Brothers play Big Dan and the Sand Dollars, the African-American stage act that rocks the pavilion to tunes such as "Sixty-Minute Man" and "What Kind of Fool Do You Think I Am?" The soundtrack also features performances of "Since I Don't Have You" by The Skyliners, "Alley Oop" by the Hollywood Argyles, "Under the Boardwalk" by The Drifters, and "The Shag."

DVD Available on DVD.

Shake, Rattle & Rock (1956)

STARRING: Touch Connors (Gary Nelson); Lisa Gaye (June); Sterling Holloway (Axe).

FILM EDITORS: Rupert S. Eisen, Charles Gross. DIRECTOR OF PHOTOGRAPHY: Frederick E. West. WRITTEN BY: Lou Rusoff. PRODUCED BY: Alex Gordon, James H. Nicholson. DIRECTED BY: Edward L. Cahn. M.P.A.A RATING: UR. RUNNING TIME: 72 minutes.

Yet another rock movie from the dawn of time, apparently. On this go round, DJ Gary Nelson (a very young Mike Connors, here branded "Touch") sees his TV show and livelihood threatened when moralizing local parents threaten to ban rock music from their humble burg on the grounds that it promotes juvenile delinquency. Connors responds by putting rock music on trial, and it's the young versus the old, the hip versus the squares in a very battle for the very survival of rock 'n' roll.

Fats Domino stops by to sing "Ain't That a Shame" and Big Joe Turner submits "Lipstick, Powder and Pain." ⑩ Available on DVD.

Shout! (1991)(SNDTRK)

STARRING: John Travolta (Jack); James Walters (Jesse); Heather Graham (Sara); Richard Jordan (Eugene); Linda Fiorentino (Molly); Scott Coffey (Bradley); Gwyneth Paltrow (Rebecca).

FILM EDITOR: Seth Flaum. DIRECTOR OF PHOTOGRAPHY: Robert Brinkman. WRITTEN BY: Joe Gayton. PRODUCED BY:

Robert Simonds. DIRECTED BY: Jeffrey Hornaday. M.P.A.A. RATING: PG-13. RUNNING TIME: 89 minutes.

John Travolta stars as Jack, a free-wheeling teacher at a boy's school in 1955 Texas. He quickly introduces his new students to the burgeoning art of rock 'n' roll music (an early school of rock, perhaps?) and faces off against Jordan's school director, who would rather knock the rock than accept it.

"Rock and Romance Explodes in a Texas Town!" the ads promised, and *Shout!* also features a familiar stock character: *the disc jockey*, here called Midnight Rider.

Eagle-eyed viewers will recognize a young Heather Graham and Gwyneth Paltrow in supporting roles here. This isn't one of Travolta's better pictures (though considering *Staying Alive*, 1983, it's not the worst either), but it's interesting primarily for its time period, the age of Elvis Presley, Chuck Berry and the like. The birth of rock. ⑩ Available on DVD.

Sid and Nancy (1986)(BIO-PIC)

STARRING: Gary Oldman (Sid Vicious); Chloe Webb (Nancy Spungeon); David Hayman (Malcolm); Debby Bishop (Phoebe); Andrew Schofield (John); Xander Berkeley (Bowery Snax); Perry Benson (Paul); Tony Condon (Steve); Sy Richardson (Methadone Counselor).

FILM EDITOR: David Martin. DIRECTOR OF PHOTOGRAPHY: Roger Deakins. WRITTEN BY: Alex Cox and Abbe Wool. PRODUCED BY: Eric Fellner. DIRECTED BY: Alex Cox. M.P.A.A. RATING: R. RUNNING TIME: 111 minutes.

This is a searing and disturbing bio-pic that gazes at the pathological relationship between ex–Sex Pistol Sid Vicious and his groupie girlfriend, Nancy Spungen (a woman alleged to be a prostitute, and a paranoid schizophrenic, among other things). This film, which doesn't balk from the ugliness and despair of some of the punk lifestyle, opens with the first meeting of Vicious (Gary Oldman) and Spungeon (Chloe Webb) in London and then follows the duo right through their depressing death spiral in America.

A groupie with a temper, Nancy introduces Vicious to heroin, the drug that eventually killed him (in 1979), and Vicious repays this kindness by murdering his girl (at her urging), stabbing her to death in their sleazy Hotel Chelsea room. But well before that final act, it's clear there's something seriously wrong here. For instance, Vicious' idea of courting Nancy involves smashing his head several times into a brick well for no apparent reason, and that kind of scene sets the stage for their inevitable fall, which involves a lot of screaming, pain, and self-abuse.

Cox's film is a good one, and though many critics and fans of The Sex Pistols have accused it of romanticizing the story of Vicious and Spungeon, it's certainly not romantic by any traditional definition of that word. *Sid and Nancy* concerns people who don't respect their own bodies, don't respect each other, and don't even really respect music. They steal, they do drugs, they vomit, they fuck, they spit, and they hurt each other.

In that regard, the film adheres to the punk value of self destruction. What the film also captures is the notion that this view of life as being worthless pretty much precludes any sense of joy or happiness. It's a "*nihilistic generation*" the film reminds the audience, and Cox—after a fashion—does attempt to make some aspect of the ugliness beautiful, or at least palatable. There's one scene, for instance, wherein Sid and Nancy share a kiss next to a dumpster in an alley, while trash falls all around them like confetti during a parade. If it is romance, it's romance via the gutter.

In another moment, George Romero's *Night of the Living Dead* is shown playing on the TV in the Chelsea, and the implication is that Nancy and Sid have joined the zombie ranks as they plunge into a sewer of despair and drugs.

Very little motivation is given for Sid Vicious' apparent hatred of life and self, but the film attempts to make Nancy understandable to some small degree. "*At least you were something,*" she confides in Sid. "*I've never been anything…*"

Sid and Nancy also recreates the moment in *The Great Rock 'n' Roll Swindle* (1980), when Sid Vicious audaciously performs Frank Sinatra's "My Way" in his own unique and unconventional fashion. Oldman seems truly to be channeling Vicious' anarchic spirit at this point and throughout the film, but one thing that the documentary footage transmits that his performance does not is Vicious' youth. This guy was *a kid*, and if that doesn't make his death tragic, it certainly makes his life tragic.

On the soundtrack "My Way," "No Feelings," and "I Wanna Be Your Dog."

🄳🅅🄳 Available on DVD.

Sign 'o' the Times (1987)(DOC)

STARRING: Prince, Sheila E., Sheena Easton, Dr. Fink, Miko Weaver, Atlanta Bliss, Boni Boyer, Cat.

FILM EDITOR: Steve Purcell. DIRECTOR OF PHOTOGRAPHY: Peter Sinclair. ORIGINAL SONGS BY: Prince. PRODUCED BY: Steven Fargnoli, Robert Cavallo, Joseph Ruffalo. M.P.A.A. RATING: PG-13. RUNNING TIME: 85 minutes.

This is the much-lauded Prince concert film that the Purple One made during his European tour following the success of *Purple Rain*. An atmospheric show bolstered by many impressive special effects (including glowing electric spheres, a suffusing blue light, and a mist that falls gently to the stage), Prince and a few friends (including Sheila E. and Sheena Easton) deliver high energy performances, replete with Prince's amazing dance style. A swooping camera catches all the action, and at times, Prince retreats to the background to man the drums. Sheila E. wears a white two-piece outfit that reveals every nook and cranny of her sexy body, and looks terrific.

Albert Magnoli, who directed *Purple Rain*, recalls the "times" of the documentary, and how it came about. "I was in Los Angeles developing another project, and Warner Bros. was looking for me to do another project with Prince, another musical. They were thinking they would do *Purple Rain 2*, and I said, '*I have something much better than that.*'

"Prince at that time was in Europe on tour with *Sign 'o' The Times*. So I said to Warner Bros. and [Prince manager] Robert Cavallo, '*Send me to Europe, let me talk to Prince, let me sit down with him, hear this concert and get some ideas.*' This was 1986. I saw Prince, we hugged, and he asked me if I was going to stay around, and I said '*for a few days.*' I was going to try to figure what we were going to do next. He said '*Great.*'

"When I saw the concert, I already knew what we were going to do next," Magnoli notes. "I wanted to do a musical called *The Dawn*. This was something we had talked about earlier, but listening to that concert, I just got inspired and said '*Okay.*' When Prince got off the stage, I said '*We're doing The Dawn next.*'"

Unbeknownst to Magnoli, this idea of a new movie musical thrilled Prince so much he wanted to start immediately. "Cavallo called me and said '*Prince is so excited he doesn't want to tour anymore.*' I said, '*He should stay on tour, because it's going to take me at least six or seven months to get this organized.*' Well, Prince closed down the tour and came back to Minneapolis, but the managers were attempting to salvage all the money that was hemorrhaging by canceling a tour, so they came up with *Sign 'o' the Times*, the documentary)."

"They started shooting and Cavallo said '*Come and help us.*' I went there and got the film shot and edited, and then went back to developing *The Dawn* film. Then I got another phone call, which was a phone call where Prince was asking me to take over his management. As relationships go, they go into their autumn and winter. And this was [management] going into it's autumn and winter. I said to Prince, '*I don't want to do this, I just want to get you back on solid footing and then we'll go onto The Dawn.*'"

Unfortunately, the musical effort, *The Dawn* never got made, and Prince made *Under the Cherry Moon* instead. Still, the documentary *Sign 'o' the Times* was a piece between *Purple Rain* and *Cherry Moon*. Even without knowing the context of the concert, it remains easy to enjoy. There's some magnificent camera work (thanks to the use of a Louma crane), and the little acted-out vignettes between songs are appropriately surreal and fun.

On the soundtrack: "Sign 'o' the Times," "Play in the Sunshine," "Little Red Corvette," "Housequake," "Slow Love," "Hot Thing." "You Got the Look," "If I Was Your Girlfriend," and "The Cross."

The film is not available on DVD in the United States, but it's a regular fixture on HBO, so check those TV listings.

Gene Simmons (1949–   )(ROCK MOVIE HALL OF FAME)

This co-founder of KISS is one of the giants of rock and is known far and wide for his oversized tongue, which he likes to flash during concert and in film appearances. Simmons has played a movie villain in such action flicks as *Never Too Young to Die* (1986) and *Wanted: Dead or Alive* (1987). He played Tom Selleck's nemesis in the 1984 science fiction thriller, *Runaway*, and had a cameo in the Charles Martin Smith horror flick *Trick or Treat* (1986) as a radio station DJ who planned to broadcast the final album of a dead rock icon named Sammi Curr. Simmons also served as a producer of the 1999 film *Detroit Rock City* (1999), which heavily featured KISS tunes, and culminates

at a KISS concert. Memorably, that film features a Gene Simmons tongue-cam.

The Singing Detective (2003)(MUS)

STARRING: Robert Downey Jr. (Dan Dark); Robin Wright Penn (Nicola/Nina/Blonde); Mel Gibson (Dr. Gibbon); Jeremy Northam (Bark Binney); Katie Holmes (Nurse Mills); Adrien Brody (First Hood); Jon Polito (Second Hood); Carla Gugino (Betty Dark/Hooker); Saul Rubinek (Skin Specialist); Alfre Woodard (Chief of Staff).

FILM EDITOR: Jeff Wishengrad. DIRECTOR OF PHOTOGRAPHY: Tom Richmond. WRITTEN BY: Dennis Potter. BASED ON THE TV SERIES BY: Dennis Potter. PRODUCED BY: Mel Gibson, Steven Haft, Bruce Davey. DIRECTED BY: Keith Gordon. M.P.A.A. RATING: R. RUNNING TIME: 104 minutes.

Suffering from disfiguring psoriatic arthritis, pulp novelist Dan Dark (Robert Downey, Jr.) spends his days convalescing in a bright hospital ward. Resentful, Dark often retreats to an alternate and much more palatable reality, namely that of his first novel's lead character, a singing gumshoe working the case of a murdered woman. Dark fantasizes himself (and his nurses) performing 1950s numbers like "At the Hop," and "Mr. Sandman," but also imagines that his loving and concerned wife (Robin Wright Penn) is disloyal, embroiled in a torrid affair with an agent named Mark Binney (Jeremy Northam), who (in Dark's fevered imagination) is trying to steal a valued screenplay of his novel, *The Singing Detective*.

As a quirky therapist, Dr. Gibbon (Mel Gibson), helps

Dark sort out his issues and family history (particularly relating to his mysterious mother), Dark begins to unravel his memories and fantasies, and return to reality as it is, not as he fears it.

This is the 2003 adaptation of the popular 1970s TV miniseries by Dennis Potter. The original BBC program concerned the 1940s, but Potter himself (shortly before his death) updated the material to include the 1950s, and thus, rock 'n' roll. Director Keith Gordon explains:

"First of all, Potter was always—among other things—a social satirist. He was always interested in skewering and examining the culture of the society he was writing about. England in the 1940s was a very specific moment. The end of the war was also the end of England as a global power, and there was certainly a loss of identity that came with that. This was a nation losing its power, and his character was a man who had lost his power in life. These were the things he was doing by examining that era [in the miniseries]."

"I don't know that America in the 1940s has the same resonance. Whereas America in the 1950s had something else that he [Potter] was examining, that weird schizophrenia of what he calls in the script '*the sexuality of proto-rock 'n' roll*'—this kind of outwardly free and wild thing," notes Gordon. "Yet at the same time, it was still a very repressive society where women were either whores or virgins. There was the blacklist going on and McCarthyism. It was a very different time, but it was a much more rich time with which to deal with the irony of the themes he was interested in."

Even though Potter left behind a blueprint for Gordon to follow, it was not necessarily an easy thing to acquire the right music for the piece. "We made this film for about $7 million, and that meant that we couldn't do what Hollywood normally does, which is throw hundreds of thousands of dollars per song at publishers and musicians," Gordon explains.

"Our whole music budget was a couple of hundred thousand dollars, so we had to go out and make remarkable deals. We had a wonderful guy who did get the rights for us [music supervisor], Ken Weiss. He had to go out and do all the negotiating. It wasn't hard for me, but I'm sure he had a lot of moments where it was a nightmare.

"The one song that Potter had in his script that we couldn't get was Fat Domino's 'Blueberry Hill.' That was the one song where the estate, or the publishers...they just weren't interested in cutting a deal," Gordon remembers. "They still wanted whatever it was, $180,000. So we replaced it with the Conway Twitty song, 'It's Only Make Believe.' I felt it had a similar emotional vibe. Both songs came from the same era, and there was something about the feel of it that felt right to me."

The Singing Detective succeeds as a "uniquely dark and bizarre fantasy-reality" not just because of its "wild eruptions into musical numbers,"[59] but because the rock score serves as a comment on the lead character's need for escape, and counterbalance to his feelings of entrapment. Also, in typical Potteresque style, the music reveals the influences of pop culture on a particular soul. As an unconventional musical experiment, and one in which form determinedly reflects content, the film represents an unqualified success, even if most critics chose to make invidious comparisons to the Michael Gambon BBC production.

(DVD) Available on DVD.

Slaves to the Underground (1996)

(FIC-BAND)(SNDTRK)

STARRING: Molly Goss (Shelly); Marisa Ryan (Suzy); Jason Bortz: (Jimmy); Bob Neuwirth (Big Phil); Claudia Rossi (Brenda); Natacha LaFerriere (Zoe); James Garcia (Brian); Peter Szumlas (Dale).

FILM EDITOR: Eric Vizens. DIRECTOR OF PHOTOGRAPHY: Zoran Hochstatter. ORIGINAL MUSIC: Mike Martt. EXECUTIVE PRODUCERS: Joel Soisson, Judy Friend. WRITTEN BY: Bill Cody. PRODUCED BY: Kristine Peterson, Bill Cody, Raquel Caballes Maxwell. DIRECTED BY: Kristine Peterson. M.P.A.A. RATING: R. RUNNING TIME: 93 minutes.

This is a just-barely-professional "indie" production from the halcyon days of indies (and Burns, Smith and Tarantino) in the mid-1990s. *Slaves to the Underground* is the "grunge" era story of the "No Exits," an all-girl band jobbing in the alternative scene in Seattle. A slacker named Jimmy (Jason Bortz) learns that an ex-girlfriend, Shelly (Molly Goss), now a lesbian, was raped by a buddy. He re-connects with her and becomes part of a love triangle including Shelly and her musician girlfriend, Suzy (Marisa Ryan).

In the end, it's a rite-of-passage or coming-of-age story as Shelly learns she can be "whole" and complete without committing to either a man or a woman. The film ends with her performing on stage, staying in touch with Jimmy (who has miraculously been gifted a comic-book store by a retiring friend) while Suzy heads off to Washington D.C. to do more for "the cause."

Remaining true to the heritage of rock movies, plenty of *authority* symbols are bashed in the film, particularly those of the Newt Gingrich/Contract with America age, when Republicans took back both houses of Congress. To wit, the young women of No Exits tear into Joe Bunch, a conservative talk-show host (and Rush Limbaugh surrogate) for his views on women and date rape. They use their feminine wiles to hijack his show and burn all of his tapes.

At another point, No Exits—apparently objecting to porn—attacks a shop's collection. Along the way, Jim refuses to get a job at a real company because "*Bill Gates is Satan.*"

In terms of style, *Slaves to the Underground* bears the uncomfortable trademarks of a really cheap 1990s indie film. Actors break character and address the camera as though they're presenting a real world confession, describing terms like "proto slacker" and dissecting the meaning of the film *The Graduate* (1968). The film is not particularly technically accomplished either, and there is awkward cutting, non-professional grade performances, and it isn't uncommon to detect unintended jump cuts between shots.

In other words, *Slaves to the Underground* is 1990s hip; 2006 hackneyed. Today's audiences will quickly tire of the lead character, Shelly, who unfairly ping-pongs back between Jim and Suzy and ends up hurting a lot of feelings in the process. In the end, it's all supposed to represent the latest variation of the teenage journey, but these teens are selfish and self-obsessed, and transmit not as kids growing up, but as self-indulgent brats.

The score includes: several No Exits songs written by Betty Carmellini and Jenni McElrath. Molly Goss, the actress who plays Suzy, performs these numbers, including "Ego," "Little Mind," and "Sometimes the Truth."
(DVD) Available on DVD.

Slumber Party Massacre 2

(1987)(HORR)

STARRING: Crystal Bernard (Courtney Bates); Kimberly McArthur (Amy); Juliette Cummins (Sheila); Patrick Lowe (Matt); Heidi Kozak (Sally); Atanas Ilitch (The Driller Killer).

FILM EDITOR: William Flicker. DIRECTOR OF PHOTOGRAPHY: Thomas L. Callaway. MUSIC BY: Richard Cox. PRODUCED BY: Deborah Brock, Don Daniel. WRITTEN AND DIRECTED BY: Deborah Brock. M.P.A.A. RATING: R. RUNNING TIME: 75 minutes.

This sequel to 1982's slasher sleeper *Slumber Party Massacre* concerns a young survivor of the first cinematic massacre, Courtney (Crystal Bernard) and her perpetual nightmares about another such happenstance. A member of an all-girl rock band, Courtney imagines a bogeyman played by Atanas Ilitch, a singing, leather-jacket-clad Elvis wannabe who is armed with an electric guitar-turned-power drill.

At a sparsely furnished condominium in Desert Springs for *"the ultimate slumber party weekend,"* Courtney and her band rehearse (and listen to rock tunes like "Tokyo Convertible") while the killer materializes in the flesh and begins murdering Courtney's friends.

This film is especially relevant as a rock movie because the Driller Killer makes joking rock music references whenever he murders his victims. "This is dedicated to the one I love," he cackles, drilling a character named Jeff from the back seat of a car. "Come on baby, light my fire," he chortles as Courtney attempts to burn him with a torch. An especially funny *bon mot* arrives when the killer's guitar/drill malfunctions and he complains, "I can't get no satisfaction."

Among the songs featured in *Slumber Party Massacre 2*: "If Only" performed by Wednesday Week from the album *What We Had*, written by Kristy and Kay Callan; "Don't Let Go" written by Michael Monagan; "Hell's Café" written by Gregory Lee Schilling and performed by Hell's Café; "Let's Buzz" written by John Logan, and "Can't Stop [Lovin' You]," written by Sterling E. Smith.
(DVD) Available on DVD.

The Song Remains the Same

(1976)(DOC)

STARRING: Led Zeppelin.

FILM EDITOR: Humphrey Dixon. DIRECTOR OF PHOTOGRAPHY: Ernest Day. PRODUCED BY: Peter Grant. DIRECTED BY: Peter Clifton, Joe Massot. M.P.A.A. RATING: PG. RUNNING TIME: 137 minutes.

This is the filmed record of Led Zeppelin's 1973 "Houses of the Holy" tour, specifically the concert at Madison Square Garden in New York. The film's ad line promised a concert *"and beyond,"* and follows through, since many scenes involve bizarre, psychedelic dream sequences/hallucinations (including one involving medieval knights and another involving gangsters). Each band member gets his own trip, and this is a weird relic from the Bicentennial.

Songs on the soundtrack include: "Rock and Roll," "The Song Remains the Same," "Dazed and Confused," and "No Quarter."

ⒹⓋⒹ Not Available on DVD.

Speedway (1968)(ELVIS)(MUS)

STARRING: Elvis Presley (Steve Grayson); Bill Bixby (Kenny); Nancy Sinatra (Susan Jacks); Gale Gordon (Mr. Hepworth); William Schallert (Abel); Victoria Meyerink (Ellie); Ross Hagen (Paul); Carl Ballantine (Birdie).

FILM EDITOR: Richard Farrell. DIRECTOR OF PHOTOGRAPHY: Joseph Ruttenberg. WRITTEN BY: Phillip Shuken. PRODUCED BY: Douglas Laurence. DIRECTED BY: Norman Taurog. M.P.A.A. RATING: PG. RUNNING TIME: 95 minutes.

This Elvis picture, set in Charlotte, North Carolina at the motor speedway and in the world of NASCAR racing, finds the King playing racer Steve Grayson. He lives in a "trailer trap" (bachelor pad) with his womanizing best friend and accountant, Kenny (Bill Bixby) and has miraculously won his last twenty races, though he spends all of his money on charity cases, like the homeless Esterlake

family and a waitress hoping to get married in a proper wedding.

Steve's lucky winning streak piques the interest of undercover IRS agent Susan Jacks, played by Nancy Sinatra. It turns out that Kenny has been playing fast and loose with Steve's money and lost almost all of his savings on "the horses." Now Steve owes Uncle Sam $145,000 in penalties and back taxes, and his wages are garnished.

If Steve can just win one big race, however, he'll still be able to help those in need.

Speedway is a slightly more sexy Elvis film than some. Most of the up-tempo numbers are performed in a wild club called "The Hang Out," and this venue, replete with dining booths that look like car interiors, provides ample opportunity for the King and Ms. Sinatra to strut their stuff. Nancy Sinatra belts out "Your Groovy Self" (by Lee Hazelwood) and practically steals the show.

For once, Elvis doesn't have two females to choose from, and as is typical of his work (including *Fun in Acapulco*), scenes feature him crooning to children. Here he dances around a tree outside The Hang Out with little Ellie (Victoria Meyerink) and serenades her with "Your Time Hasn't Come Yet, Baby."

The strangest (but oddly rousing) number in the film is a set piece at the IRS office, replete with dancers in business suits. There, Elvis sings of Uncle Sam, "He's Your Uncle Not Your Dad" by Ben Weisman and Sid Wayne. There's much racing footage in *Speedway* too, awkwardly intercut with rear projection and process work to make it look as though Presley is behind the wheel during several lengthy races. Real racers such as Richard Petty, Tiny Lund and Cale Yarborough also make cameos.

Speedway ends on an unusually happy note, with Presley and Sinatra singing at The Hang Out, even though Steve only finished third in his big race and still owes the government $137,000. D'oh!

DVD Available on DVD.

Spice World (1997)

(SNDTRK)(CAMEOS)(REAL ROCKERS)

STARRING: Victoria Adams (Victoria); Melanie Brown (Melanie B); Emma Bunton (Emma); Melanie Chisholm (Melanie C); Geraldine Halliwell (Geri); Dean Anderson (Jack); Richard Briers (Bishop); Alan Cumming (Piers), Roger Moore (The Chief); Richard E. Grant (Clifford); George Wendt (Martin Barnfield).

FILM EDITOR: Andrew MacArthur. DIRECTOR OF PHOTOGRAPHY: Clive Tickner. WRITTEN BY: Kim Fuller. PRODUCED BY: Uri Fruchtmann, Mark L. Rosen, Barnaby Thompson. DIRECTED BY: Bob Spiers. M.P.A.A. RATING: PG. RUNNING TIME: 93 minutes.

"*When you're feeling sad and low,*" suggests a signature Spice Girl tune, "*spice up your life!*" Sadly, this film, *Spice World*, fails to offer much spice or entertainment. It's a vehicle for the British group that was an international sensation in the mid-to-late 1990s but which soon faded to obscurity. Back in the day, the group's first single "Wannabe" became the "biggest selling debut single ever"[60] and hit the number one slot in over thirty countries. The Spice Girls' first CD sold more than fifty million copies in the year of its release.[61]

The Spice Girls consisted of five female performers: Baby, Ginger, Scary, Sporty, and Posh Spice, and the popularity of this team made a film vehicle inevitable. With a script fashioned by scribe Kim Fuller (who gave the world *From Justin to Kelly* in 2002), the film serves as an insubstantial homage to the classic Beatles' film *A Hard Day's Night* with its raucous blend of music, fantasy and reality.

The film concerns the Spice Girls—who play themselves—as the group endlessly circles London in their oversized, fully-equipped bus, which, like the TARDIS time machine on the BBC's *Doctor Who*, is apparently dimensionally transcendent: larger on the inside than out. The girls are in the employ of a mysterious benefactor, played by former *James Bond* Roger Moore, and soon clash with a nasty tabloid editor out to destroy their reputations. Throughout the film, they also hear incessant movie pitches from an American producer played by George Wendt. An over-the-top Alan Cumming (see: *Josie and the Pussycats*) is in the movie too, playing a hapless filmmaker who is shooting a documentary about the girls that aspires to "*crash through the show business wall.*"

Any way you tart it up, *Spice World* is a charmless, stitched-together film that connects a number of light fantasy moments so as to provide the group opportunity to perform several of their cookie-cutter musical hits. In one fantasy, the girls imagine they're pregnant. In another, they encounter extraterrestrials in the forest taking a pee. No danger though: the aliens just want their autographs.

Another video-esque music sequence reveals the Spice Girls at an elaborate photo shoot, and they dress up as iconic characters such as Wonder Woman, Marilyn Monroe, Olivia Newton-John in *Grease*, and Honey Ryder from *Dr. No* (1962).

Considering that this movie is supposed to concern girl power, it's strange that the Spice Girls are powered by a male chief (Moore) and managed by a man (Richard E. Grant). Mostly, the Spice Girls just come across as whiners and the only scene that might have evidenced some charm—featuring the group in its early "hungry days"—is instead a desperate grasp for legitimacy; laughably suggesting the Spice Girls are all about music and not merely a commercial product packaged for premium pop culture consumption.

Spice World is filled with rock cameos from the likes of Bob Geldof, Meat Loaf, and Elton John. Among the Spice Girls tunes performed for the soundtrack: "Wannabe," "Stop," "Spice Up Your Life," "Never Give Too Much," "Saturday Night Divas," "Say You'll Be There," "2 Become 1," "Mama," and "Viva Forever."

(DVD) Available on DVD.

Spinout (1966)(ELVIS)(MUS)

STARRING: (Elvis Presley (Mike McCoy); Shelley Fabares (Cynthia Foxhugh); Diane McBain (Diana); Dodie Marshall (Susan); Deborah Walley (Lisa); Jack Mullaney (Curley); Will Hutchens (Lt. Richards).

FILM EDITOR: Rita Roland. DIRECTOR OF PHOTOGRAPHY: Daniel L. Fapp. WRITTEN BY: Theodore J. Flicker, George Kirgo. PRODUCED BY: Joe Pasternak. DIRECTED BY: Norman Taurog. M.P.A.A. RATING: UR. RUNNING TIME: 90 minutes.

Elvis Presley is Mike McCoy, a band leader, race car driver and all-around stud. In this outing, the King has his hands full as he is forced to select from a surfeit of available and willing babes (three women, this time!). He plays multiple choice, and—surprise—there's a happy ending. But will he choose the drummer (Deborah Walley), the author (Diane McBain), or wealthy Cynthia (Shelley Fabares)? The suspense won't exactly kill you.

Originally titled *Never Say No*, *Spinout* (not to be confused with Elvis' other racing venture, *Speedway*) was heralded by author Harry Medved as one of the fifty worst films of all time and termed a "tiring exercise for the unhappy"[62] King. That about sums it up.

Spinout is saddled with a ton of unremarkable songs for Elvis including "Stop, Look and Listen," "Adam and Evil," "All That I Am," "Beach Shack," "Spinout," "Smorgasbord," "I'll Be Back," and "I'll Remember You."

(DVD) Available on DVD.

Stagecraft 101 (GENRE CONVENTION) Wherein something goes horribly wrong during a live stage performance.

In *This Is Spinal Tap*, one can pick any variety of embarrassing moments involving stage mechanics. Derek becomes hermetically sealed in a translucent embryo during the band's live performance of "Rock and Roll Creation." While jamming to "Hellhole," Nigel falls down and can't get up until aided by the band's roadie, Moke.

Perhaps the funniest stagecraft disaster in *This Is Spinal Tap* involves a stage prop that isn't designed right: the underwhelming Trilithon Horseshoe from Stonehenge. Intended to be eighteen feet in stature, the final prop stands at a meager eighteen inches, making even the dancing dwarves in the production number tower over it.

Another famous mishap in music history includes Bob Dylan's malfunctioning microphone in D.A. Pennebaker's landmark documentary *Don't Look Back*. But that film may be more famous for the scene in which Dylan gets lost in the twisting corridors back stage (a joke reflected in *This Is Spinal Tap*).

Likewise in *Rock Star* (2001), up-and-coming rocker Izzy (Mark Wahlberg) makes his debut in the heavy metal rock band Steel Dragons by falling down a tall staircase onstage and bloodying his forehead. The fans love it, however.

In *The Commitments* (1991), a performance goes badly wrong when a singer hits the guitar player with a falling microphone stand and short circuits the instrument, causing the band-member to be electrocuted. Yikes! Who knew rock stars could be so clumsy?

Stand By Me (1986)(SNDTRK)

STARRING: Wil Wheaton (Gordie); River Phoenix (Chris); Corey Feldman (Teddy); Jerry O'Connell (Vern); Kiefer Sutherland (Ace); Richard Dreyfuss (Writer).

FILM EDITOR: Robert Leighton. DIRECTOR OF PHOTOGRAPHY: Thomas Del Ruth. BASED ON THE NOVELLA BY: Stephen King. WRITTEN BY: Raynold Gideon, Bruce A. Evans. PRODUCED BY: Bruce A. Evans, Raynold Gideon, Andrew Scheinman. DIRECTED BY: Rob Reiner. M.P.A.A. RATING: R. RUNNING TIME: 89 minutes.

Rob Reiner, the auteur behind the camera on *This Is Spinal Tap* later directed this nostalgic adaptation of the Stephen King novella called *The Body*.

Stand By Me is set in the 1960s as a group of pre-teens boys (including Wil Wheaton, the late River Phoenix, Corey Feldman, and Jerry O'Connell) wander out into the woods (and over railroad tracks) in search of a corpse. Kiefer Sutherland plays their nemesis, a bully named Ace. A deeply nostalgic film, *Stand By Me* captures the time period well courtesy of a great soundtrack from the era.

The tunes in the film include "Everyday" performed by Buddy Holly, "Let the Good Times Roll" performed by Shirley and Lee," "Come Go with Me" by the Del Vikings,

"Yakety Yak" by the Coasters, "Great Balls of Fire" by Jerry Lee Lewis," and of course, "Stand By Me" performed by Ben E. King.

(DVD) Available on DVD.

Stay Away Joe (1968)(ELVIS)(MUS)

STARRING: Elvis Presley (Joe Lightcloud); Burgess Meredith (Charlie Lightcloud); Joan Blondell (Glenda Callahan); Thomas Gomez (Grandpa); Henry Jones (Slager); L.Q. Jones (Bronc).

FILM EDITOR: George W. Brooks. DIRECTOR OF PHOTOGRAPHY: Fred J. Koenekamp. WRITTEN BY: Michael A. Hoey. BASED ON THE NOVEL BY: Dan Cushman. PRODUCED BY: Douglas Laurence. DIRECTED BY: Peter Tewksbury. M.P.A.A. RATING: PG. RUNNING TIME: 102 minutes.

Stay away from this effort, one of the King's bottom of the barrel movies. Here Elvis portrays a rodeo-riding Native American (!) named Joe Lightcloud. The movie concerns his return to the reservation. There, he meets his pop, played by Burgess Meredith and they plan to raise cattle.

In the meantime, there's a lot of beer drinking, in what amounts to a fairly stereotyped portrayal of the American Indian.

Before *Stay Away Joe* is done, Elvis sings the title song, "Lovely Mamie," "Dominick," and "All I Needed Was the Rain."

(DVD) Available on DVD.

Staying Alive (1983)(SNDTRK)

STARRING: John Travolta (Tony Manero); Cynthia Rhodes (Jackie); Finola Hughes (Laura Revell); Steve Inwood (Jesse); Julie Bovasso (Mrs. Manero); Charles Ward (Butler); Joyce Hyser (Linda); Kurtwood Smith (Choreographer); Frank Stallone (Carl).

FILM EDITORS: Don Zimmerman, Mark Warner. DIRECTOR OF PHOTOGRAPHY: Nick McLean. FEATURING SONGS BY: The Bee Gees. BASED UPON CHARACTERS CREATED BY: Nik Cohn. WRITTEN BY: Sylvester Stallone, Norman Wexler. PRODUCED BY: Robert Stigwood, Sylvester Stallone. DIRECTED BY: Sylvester Stallone. M.P.A.A. RATING: PG. RUNNING TIME: 96 minutes.

In Sly Stallone's misconceived sequel to *Saturday Night Fever*, Tony Manero (John Travolta) has fled Brooklyn for Manhattan in his journey to become a successful Broadway dancer. Although he dates the lovely dancer Jackie (Cynthia Rhodes), Tony soon finds himself simultaneously romancing the haughty ingenue, Laura (Finola Hughes), who sees him as a plaything. While Tony questions himself, he wins a role in Laura's new Broadway play, "Satan's Alley," and makes a bid to become the male lead. But first he must decide what kind of person he wishes to be: a nice guy or a star.

Staying Alive culminates with a hysterically funny fifteen-minute production of "Satan's Alley," which involves many lithe dancers in torn, revealing clothes, writhing about as though trapped in Hell. Travolta prances, animal-like between glowing laser lights and tumbling dancers before ascending a platform to Heaven. Yep, it's that kind of movie. Although the Bee Gees have returned to provide a clutch of new tunes, including "The Woman in You," "I Love You Too Much," "Breakout," "Someone Belonging to Someone," and "Life Goes On," not a single tune captures the punch of their 1977 disco album, and the tune that ends the film: *Stayin' Alive*.

The message of *Staying Alive* is uniquely rock 'n' roll, however. Tony realizes that it is better to be an asshole reigning in Hell (literally, Satan's Alley) rather than a nice guy who doesn't make it as a star. Accordingly, the final moments of the film find Travolta choosing neither the likable Jackie (whom he has twice stood up for a date in the middle of the night) nor the selfish Laura. Instead, he decides that he loves himself best and goes out on the street to "strut," thus giving occasion for that reprise of the famous Bee Gees Tune, "Stayin' Alive." Oddly, this sequence is punctuated by a series of close-up shots of Travolta's ass and crotch. The actor has never been in better shape than in this film, but I mean, really...

Staying Alive also suffers from a bad case of nepotism, since director Sylvester Stallone (seen in a cameo bumping into Travolta) casts his brother Frank Stallone in a supporting role and worse—has Frank provide a number of tunes on the soundtrack including "Moody Girl" and "Far From Over."

For much of its Running time, *Staying Alive* feels far from over. The film should be seen, however, if nothing else than for the camp highlight of "Satan's Alley," a cheesy Broadway show that goes way over the top.

To assert that *Staying Alive* received bad reviews is an understatement. Critic David Denby, for instance, wrote the following in *New York* magazine: "This is no ordinary terrible movie; it's a vision of the end. Not the end of the world, which will probably be much quieter than *Staying Alive*, but the end of movies...As you watch it, the idea of what a movie is—an idea that has lasted more than half-a-century—crumbles before your eyes."[63]

(DVD) Available on DVD.

Still Crazy (1998)(FIC BAND)

STARRING: Stephen Rea (Tony Costello); Billy Connolly (Hughie); Jimmy Nail (Les Wickes); Timothy Spall (David "Beano" Baggot); Bill Nighy (Ray Simms); Juliet Aubrey (Karen); Bruce Robinson (Brian).

FILM EDITOR: Peter Boyle. DIRECTOR OF PHOTOGRAPHY: Ashley Rowe. WRITTEN BY: Dick Clement, Ian Le Frenais. PRODUCED BY: Steve Clark-Hall, Amanda Marmot. DIRECTED BY: Brian Gibson. M.P.A.A. RATING: R. RUNNING TIME: 95 minutes.

What happens when the writers of *The Commitments* (1991) and the director of the Tina Turner bio-pic *What's Love Got to Do With It* (1993) get together? Well, you get this touching, earnest, and gently humorous comedy about aging rockers, which takes its name from the Paul Simon song "Still Crazy After All These Years."

This is the story of a band called Strange Fruits (or sometimes, for shorthand, just The Fruits). They were a phenom in the 1970s, but the band broke up in a blaze of glory when, during their final show, lightning struck the stage. Now, it's the 1990s, and the lead singer of the band is dead and much mourned by the band's former manager/secretary, girl Friday, Karen (Juliet Aubrey). The surviving members of the band have scattered and are going about their lives in menial jobs, as roofing contractors and the like. But it's time to get the band back together for a Dutch Club reunion tour, even as keyboarder Tony Costello (Stephen Rea) struggles with the notion of turning...gasp...fifty.

Timothy Spall, playing the band's flatulent drummer "Beano," almost walks away with the show, but the whole ensemble is effective here, in part because this rock film charts a different course than most in the genre. It's not so much *This Is Spinal Tap* as it is a nostalgic acknowledgment that time has passed and that many of the greatest rockers in the world are now entering their golden years. And to think, this film was made almost ten years ago. Today, the great rock stars of the 1960s are actually surpassing sixty.

Rock stars have shown audiences how to defy authority, how to destroy property, how to spiral out of control, how to make comebacks, and now—in films like *Still Crazy*—one has to wonder if they'll show their fans how to age with grace. Can there be such a thing as a senior citizen rock star?

On the soundtrack, the Strange Fruits perform a number of their tunes, including "The Flame Still Burns," "All Over the World," "Dirty Town," and "Scream Freedom."
(DVD) Available on DVD.

Sting (1951–   )(ROCK MOVIE HALL OF FAME) Born Gordon Matthew Sumner in the UK, the charismatic Sting was part of the group The Police until 1985, whereupon he embarked on a successful solo music career that continues to this day. Over the decades, Sting has also become an accomplished actor, debuting in Fran Roddam's rock odyssey *Quadrophenia* (1979) and then following that up with 1982's *Brimstone and Treacle*. Sting's choice of roles has tended toward the offbeat, and he played Feyd, a sociopath and Harkonnen warrior (who seems modeled on Sid Vicious) in David Lynch's *Dune* (1984).

The next year, he played Baron Frankenstein opposite *Flashdance*'s Jennifer Beals, in the revisionist Frankenstein movie, *The Bride* (1985).

An athletic and physically-fit sex symbol, Sting has also proved a sex object for partners Meryl Streep and Kathleen Turner in such fare as *Plenty* (1985) and *Julia and Julia* (1987), respectively. Other performances include his turns in the modern film-noir, *Stormy Monday* (1988), and *Lock, Stock and Two Smoking Barrels* (1998), the latter directed by Madonna's husband, Guy Ritchie.

Sting was nominated for an Oscar in 2004 for his original composition for *Cold Mountain*, "You Will Be My Ain' True Love," and his vocals can be heard in such diverse films as *48 Hours* (1982), *The Wedding Singer* (1998), and *The X-Files* (1998).

In 2001, Baz Luhrmann re-interpreted Sting's rock standard "Roxanne" for a smoldering tango dance sequence in *Moulin Rouge*. *Bring on the Night* (1985) is Sting's "rockumentary" (and features the birth of his son).

Stop Making Sense (1984)(DOC)

STARRING: Talking Heads.

FILM EDITOR: Lisa Day. DIRECTOR OF PHOTOGRAPHY: Jordan Cronenweth. WRITTEN BY: Jonathan Demme, the Talking Heads. PRODUCED BY: Gary Goetzman. DIRECTED BY: Jonathan Demme. M.P.A.A. RATING: PG. RUNNING TIME: 102 minutes.

This is Jonathan Demme's rock documentary on the Talking Heads, who, back in 1984—as the film was shot—had just seen the success of their latest album, *Speaking in Tongues*. *Stop Making Sense* is really an old-school concert film rather than a *Don't Look Back* or *Last Waltz*–type exposé, because Demme slights the confessional one-on-one interviews and other behind-the-scenes material to focus squarely on performance.

Stop Making Sense is a document culled from two live performances (held on succeeding nights) at Hollywood's Pantages Theatre. The tour was known as the "big suit" tour due to lead singer David Byrne's outfit. The Talking Heads performs nearly twenty songs (some accented by a multimedia slide presentation), and Demme restricts his attention to the band itself, rarely cutting away to the audience.

Byrne opens with "Psycho Killer," and then the band performs several more tunes including the hit single "Burning Down the House," "Life During Wartime," and "Once in a Lifetime."

(DVD) Available on DVD.

Strange Days (1995)(FIC BAND)

STARRING: Ralph Fiennes (Lenny Nero); Angela Bassett (Lornette "Mace" Mason); Juliette Lewis (Faith Justin); Tom Sizemore (Max Peltier); Michael Wincott (Philo Gant); Vincent D'Onofrio (Burton Steckler); Glenn Plummer (Jeriko One); Brigitte Bako (Iris).

FILM EDITOR: Howard Smith. DIRECTOR OF PHOTOGRAPHY: Matthew F. Leonetti. WRITTEN BY: James Cameron and Jay Cocks. PRODUCED BY: James Cameron and Steven-Charles Jaffe. DIRECTED BY: Kathryn Bigelow. M.P.A.A. RATING: R. RUNNING TIME: 145 minutes.

This is Kathryn Bigelow's millennial tale focusing on the eve of December 30, 1999. Nero (Ralph Fiennes), a down on his luck trader in a new technology that allows viewers to experience the memory of others, finds that one of his tapes holds the secret key to the murder of a famous and outspoken African-American rapper, Jeriko One (Glenn Plummer).

The tape implicates the Los Angeles Police Department and with the help of a limo driver, the beautiful Mace (Angela Bassett), Nero attempts to get it into the right hands. At the same time, however, Nero grieves and whines over his messy break-up with Faith Justin (Juliette Lewis) a sexy up-and-coming rock star dating the paranoid but influential *manager*, Philo Gant (Michael Wincott).

Strange Days, penned by Jay Cocks and James Cameron, features a number of stage performances by Juliette Lewis. These moments all occur in a wild nightclub. Lewis sings "Hardly Wait" and the soundtrack includes "Strange Days" performed by Prong, and "Get Your Gunn" performed by Marilyn Manson.

(DVD) Available on DVD.

Streets of Fire (1984)(SNDTRK)(FIC BAND)

STARRING: Michael Paré (Tom Cody); Diane Lane (Ellen Aim); Rick Moranis (Billy Fish); Willem Dafoe (Raven); Bill Paxton (Clyde); Amy Madigan (McCoy); Deborah Van Valkenburgh (Reva); Richard Lawson (Ed); Rick Rossovich (Officer Conley); Lee Ving (Green).

FILM EDITORS: Freeman Davies, Michael Ripps. DIRECTOR OF PHOTOGRAPHY: Andrew Laszlo. SPECIAL MUSICAL MATERIAL WRITTEN BY: Jimmy Iovine. WRITTEN BY: Walter Hill, Larry Gross. PRODUCED BY: Lawrence Gordon, Joel Silver. DIRECTED BY: Walter Hill. M.P.A.A. RATING: PG-13. RUNNING TIME: 93 minutes.

"A Rock 'n' Roll Fable" set in "Another Time, Another Place," Walter Hill's epic *Streets of Fire* takes place in a world of unending night, Studebakers, rain-soaked streets, neon signs, black leather jackets and rock music. It's a world where perhaps the 1950s never ended and the motorcycle culture grew into a real menace. Here, Raven's (Willem Dafoe) gang, "The Bombers" have taken control of part of the city, the Battery, and regularly make incursions into the civilized part of town to make trouble. On one night, they attack a concert and kidnap rock star Ellen Aim (Diane Lane).

A Western-style loner, Tom Cody comes to town to rescue his old girlfriend, Ellen, and teams with a lesbian gunslinger, McCoy. Also along for the ride is Billy Fish (Rick Moranis), Ellen's *manager*, but Cody only succeeds in sparking what could be full-scale street warfare when he saves Ellen from the grip of the nefarious Bombers.

In 1979, Hill directed another bizarre "street" fantasy about gangs called *The Warriors*; *Streets of Fire* is a bold genre film that looks terrific and exists in an enigmatic alternate world that we don't quite recognize as ours. Although *Streets of Fire* peters out after an exciting rescue action set piece in the Battery, it is still one of the most beautifully filmed and unique fantasies of the 1980s. Michael Paré, late of *Eddie and the Cruisers*, is perfect as the mysterious, strong-but-silent hero, Cody and Amy Madigan as McCoy makes a good loyal sidekick. In terms of music, the film features several concert performances, including Fire Inc.'s "Nowhere Fast," and the climactic "Tonight Is What It Means to Be Young."

Eagle-eyed viewers will also recognize a young Robert Townsend in the film, playing one of the "Sorels," an all-black rock group that serves as Fish's "new discovery" at the film's end. This group performs the hit "I Can Dream About You" (by Dan Hartman and performed by Winston Ford), and later Townsend would star in and direct his own movie about a black rock group in the 1960s and

1970s, *The Five Heartbeats* (1991).

As for *Streets of Fire*, any film that boasts the line of dialogue "Long live rock 'n' roll!" can't be all bad.
(DVD) Available on DVD.

Sympathy for the Devil (1968)(DOC)

STARRING: The Rolling Stones, Anita Pallenberg, Marianne Faithful.

FILM EDITORS: Agnes Guillermot, Kenneth F. Rowles.
CINEMATOGRAPHERS: Colin Corby, Tony Richmond. WRITTEN
BY: Jean-Luc Godard. PRODUCED BY: Eleni Collard, Michael
Pearson, Iain Quarrier. DIRECTED BY: Jean-Luc Godard.
M.P.A.A. RATING: R. RUNNING TIME: 100 minutes.

Hmmm. This is a real curiosity from the Age of Aquarius. It's Jean-Luc Godard's rock documentary-cum-political statement. Part of the film involves the studio-bound Rolling Stones rehearsing their song, "Sympathy for the Devil," while the remainder is a bizarre (staged?) series of political statements and readings.

The Stones' tune is featured at all stages of development, before appearing in its totality over the end credits.

Apparently, it wasn't Godard's intention to include the complete song at that spot, and the legendary director was upset that the choice was made by the film's producer.
(DVD) Available on DVD.

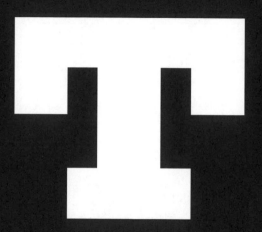

(is for *This Is Spinal Tap*)

Thank God It's Friday (1978)(MUS)

STARRING: Phil Adams (Tarzan); Hilary Beam (Shirley); Judith Browne (Badmouth); Marianne Burche (Salesgirl); Jeff Goldblum (Tony Di Marco); Andrea Howard (Sue).

FILM EDITOR: Richard Halsey. DIRECTOR OF PHOTOGRAPHY: James Crabe. WRITTEN BY: Barry Armyan Bernstein. PRODUCED BY: Rob Cohen. DIRECTED BY: Robert Klane. M.P.A.A. RATING: PG. RUNNING TIME: 89 minutes.

This is a slapdash effort rushed into theatres to capitalize on the popularity of disco and the success of *Saturday Night Fever* (1977). The film concerns a typical day (a Friday) in the nightlife of a very busy disco, and multiple stories unfold simultaneously.

In one, a married couple celebrates their fifth anniversary, only to encounter a creepy club owner, Tony (a leering Jeff Goldblum). One subplot involves an aspiring dancer hoping to make it big, and another, two teen girls entering a *dance contest*.

On the soundtrack, Donna Summer performs the Academy Award winner for Best Song: "Last Dance." The Commodores also show up to sing "Brick House," "Easy," and "Too Hot ta Trot."

(DVD) Available on DVD.

That Thing You Do! (1996)

(FIC BAND)(SNDTRK)(CAMEOS)

STARRING: Tom Everett Scott (Guy Patterson); Liv Tyler (Faye); Jonathan Schaech (Jimmy); Steve Zahn (Lenny); Ethan Embry (The Bass Player); Tom Hanks (White); Charlize Theron (Tina Powers); Obba Babatundé (Lamarr); Giovanni Ribisi (Chad); Chris Ellis (Phil Horace); Alex Rocco (Sol); Bill Cobbs (Del).

FILM EDITOR: Richard Chew. DIRECTOR OF PHOTOGRAPHY: Tak Fujimoto. PRODUCED BY: Gary Goetzman, Jonathan Demme, Edward Saxon. WRITTEN AND DIRECTED BY: Tom Hanks. M.P.A.A. RATING: PG. RUNNING TIME: 108 minutes.

Tom Hanks' directorial debut is an affectionate story of a rock 'n' roll "One-Hit Wonder" from the Beatles era, a fictional four-boy band called, appropriately enough, "The Wonders."

The story commences in Lake Erie in 1964 as the lead character, Guy Patterson (Tom Everett Scott)—a drummer who works long hours in his father's appliance store—sits in with a local band because the regular drummer (Giovanni Ribisi) has broken his arm. That band is The Wonders, and on the night of its first performance, the jazz-loving Guy turns the slow-tempo original tune "That Thing You Do!" into a driving, upbeat song that garners an instant positive reaction. Before long, the group has been picked up by a local manager, "That Thing You Do!" is playing on the radio, and the band is headlining gigs at shows in Pittsburgh, all to great enthusiasm.

Soon, a manager named White (Hanks) comes in and offers to record the band on its Playtone label, where it can join the *other stars of the Playtone Galaxy*." The ascent to fame (see: *Billboard* magazine) sweeps The Wonders ("*the new teen sensation!*") all the way to *The Hollywood Television Showcase* and beyond, but just after this triumph, the group starts to fall apart.

The Wonders' bass player (Ethan Embry, a.k.a. Ethan Randall) is scheduled to go to Vietnam, and leaves the band for Disneyland on the night of the big show. The egotistical lead singer Jimmy (Jonathan Schaech) treats his beautiful and sweet girl, Faye (Liv Tyler) shabbily and then refuses to record the songs that White demands. Lenny (Steve Zahn) starts gambling in Las Vegas and ultimately remains there. Finally, Guy turns to Faye for succor, and gets to record a session with his idol, Del Paxton (Bill Cobbs). Along the way, Guy comes to realize that "*bands come and go*," but that he has been part of something special.

By focusing on the idea of the one-hit wonder, Hanks has crafted a unique movie of the "fictional band" variety. What's even more interesting is that instead of featuring an array of tunes, Hanks chooses instead to repeat "That Thing You Do!" (by Adam Schlesinger) over and over. After all, that's the group's one hit. The catchy tune is repeated over a half-dozen times in the film and each time the staging is different and the characters in the band are at a different point in their rags-to-riches-back-to-rags story. The audience hears the song in a restaurant by the airport (where planes fly overhead), during its first appearance on the radio (a scene of utter exuberance), then at the big show in Ohio, and then triumphantly on the TV program, hosted by Hanks' *Bosom Buddies* co-star, Peter Scolari.

In terms of its screenplay, *That Thing You Do!* follows the well-charted trajectory of many rock films. There's the

meteoric ascent to fame, the final band *break-up*, the botched *recording session* and more. Also, the film is particularly good with its history, remembering that the mid-1960s was also the era of the *Beach Party movies*. Accordingly, The Wonders (embarrassed to be dressed like sailors) perform a tune at a "Shrimp Shack" on camera for the movie *Weekend at Party Pier* starring Rick and Anita (thinly-veiled replacements for Frankie and Annette).

"*It's a very common tale*," says manager White, "*One-hit wonders*." Yet Hanks has forged an upbeat, amusing, and affectionate rock film in *That Thing You Do!*, and that's a most uncommon tale.

(DVD) Available on DVD.

This Is Elvis (1981)(DOC)(BIO PIC)

STARRING: David Scott (Elvis at 18); Paul Boensch III (Elvis at 10); Johnny Harry (Elvis at 42); Laurence Koller (Vernon Presley); Rhonda Lyn (Priscilla Presley); Debbie Edge (Gladys Presley).

FILM EDITORS: Bud Friedgen, Glenn Far. DIRECTOR OF PHOTOGRAPHY: Gil Hubbs. WRITTEN, PRODUCED, AND DIRECTED BY: Malcolm Leo and Andrew Solt. M.P.A.A. RATING: PG. RUNNING TIME: 101 minutes.

This is the controversial 1981 theatrical production that mixes dramatic recreations (with actors portraying Elvis at various stages of his life) with archival documentary footage (including authentic home movies) of Presley. The film endeavors to tell the whole life story of Elvis, and the filmmakers were granted permission from the King's estate to shoot in Graceland. The film's technical advisor is Elvis' manager, Colonel Tom Parker, and *This Is Elvis* also includes interviews with members of the "Memphis Mafia," meaning his bodyguards.

This Is Elvis creates fictionalized scenes from Elvis' youth utilizing child actors (to not very dramatic effect), marshals clips from Elvis' film career (including scenes from *Love Me Tender* and *Jailhouse Rock*), features home movies of Elvis in the Army (1958–1960), and includes footage from a Frank Sinatra TV special welcoming him back to civilian life. The movie is also narrated by an Elvis sound-alike (a cheesy touch) and depicts events right up to the night of his tragic death (another fictionalized recreation).

The saddest and most intriguing portions of *This Is Elvis* reveal footage of the rock star during his later years. He looks miserable (and perpetually drugged), and has grown puffy and uncomfortably sweaty. Watching this footage, you'll get an idea of what his torturous last days must have been like, including a horrifying sequence in which the King forgets some of the lyrics to his songs.

In *This is Elvis*, Presley sings "My Way" and "Are You Lonesome Tonight?" Both prove crushingly depressing, given the entertainer's last days on this mortal coil.

(DVD) Not currently available on DVD; only available in VHS format on secondary market.

This Is Spinal Tap (1984)

(FIC BAND)(SNDTRK)(MUS)

STARRING: Christopher Guest (Nigel Tufnel); Michael McKean (David St. Hubbins); Harry Shearer (Derek Smalls); Rob Reiner (Marty DiBergi); Ed Begley Jr. (John "Stumpy" Pepys); Paul Benedict (Hotel Clerk); June Chadwick (Jeanine Pettibone); Billy Crystal (Morty the Mime); Fran Drescher (Bobbi Flekman); Tony Hendra (Ian Faith); Howard Hesseman (Duke Fame); Anjelica Huston (Polly Deutsch); David Kaff (Viv Savage); Bruno Kirby (Tommy Pischedda); Patrick MacNee (Sir Denis Eton-Hogg); R.J. Parnell (Mick Shrimpton); Paul Shaffer (Artie Fufkin); Paul Shortino (Duke Fame); Fred Willard (Lt. Hookstratten).

FILM EDITORS: Kent Beyda, Kim Secrist. DIRECTOR OF PHOTOGRAPHY: Peter Smokler. SCREENPLAY BY: Christopher Guest, Michael McKean, Harry Shearer, Rob Reiner. PRODUCER: Karen Murphy. DIRECTED BY: Rob Reiner. M.P.A.A. RATING: R. RUNNING TIME: 82 minutes.

This Is Spinal Tap remains this author's candidate for the best rock film of all time. It is indeed a "rockumentary," that notorious subgenre of rock documentary which includes titles such as *Don't Look Back* (1967), *Monterey Pop* (1967), and *Gimme Shelter* (1970). The only pertinent difference is that this production is actually a "mock" roc doc. Got that? It's a film concerning a fictional band, Spinal Tap and its daily travails, as well as its history. The entire film is played straight, and yet remains hysterically (and often tragically) funny.

To recap the premise, Spinal Tap (formerly the Thamesmen and the New Originals) is a heavy metal band fumbling its way through a North American tour in 1982. The tour was designed to promote the band's new album, *Smell the Glove*, but the album hasn't been released yet due to problems over sexist cover art imagery. As one of the band members points out, it's difficult to promote something that doesn't exist, but guitarist Nigel Tufnel (Christopher Guest), lead singer David St. Hubbins (Michael McKean) and bassist Derek Smalls (Harry Shearer) give it a whirl anyway.

Meanwhile, director Marty DiBergi (Rob Reiner) (see: *The Last Waltz*) records all of the band's foul-ups, bleeps, and blunders for his concert film. As the band stumbles from Chapel Hill, North Carolina. to Cleveland, Ohio to the West Coast, it is joined by David's bossy girlfriend, Jeanine (June Chadwick) (**see: The Yoko Factor**).

A brief break-up of Tap occurs when Nigel quits over Jeanine's management of the band, but the artist ultimately returns (with former *manager*, Ian [Tony Hendra] in tow) for a victory lap encore in Japan, where the Spinal Tap single "Sex Farm" has inexplicably rocketed up the charts.

It sounds like a simple premise, but *This Is Spinal Tap* is an ingenious enterprise, and one that has contributed many catchphrases into the American pop culture lexicon (including the remark "there's a fine line between stupid and clever," and Nigel's description of his amp that it "*goes up to 11.*") It was also a very difficult film to produce; nobody in Hollywood wanted to touch it, and the project collapsed several times before Norman Lear's Avco-Embassy bit the bullet and decided to ante-up financial backing.

A very non-traditional comedy, *This Is Spinal Tap* began production in the spring of 1982, with cinematographer

Peter Smokler (*Gimme Shelter*, *Jimi Plays Berkeley*) behind the camera and Rob Reiner at the helm. A departure from standard filmmaking, *Spinal Tap* is a film wherein virtually *all* the dialogue is improvised, save for DiBergi's introduction at the film's beginning. The shooting script (or treatment) for the project was approximately ten pages long, and functioned only as an overall outline. For each sequence fresh, spontaneous-sounding and realistic dialogue had to be forged by the actors. What was more daunting is that it had to appear genuinely funny, but not planned or rehearsed.

Actress Gloria Gifford, who plays the airport official who discovers the tinfoil-wrapped cucumber in Smalls' pants during a security inspection, still remembers how strange it was to shoot a film based on the art of improvisation.

"We were at the airport, and Rob said '*Okay, well, uh this is the scene*,' and he described it." The director then said to her, "*There's just one line you have to say. And the rest is improv.*' So we did it, and maybe we did two takes. And he said '*Fine, cut.*'"

And that was a wrap.

"I was driving home at 10:30 in the morning thinking, '*Did I just do a movie?*'" Gifford recollects. "Because I've never been in a movie in my life that you arrived at then came home for in an hour and-a-half. It was *that* fast, because it was improvised."

Cinematographer Smokler recalls that shooting many of the film's now-trademark scenes represented a challenge for him. For instance, the long tracking shot involving the

Currently residing in the "where are they now?" file...it's Spinal Tap!

Up front, (left to right): David St. Hubbins (Michael McKean), guitarist Nigel Tufnel (Christopher Guest),

and bassist Derek Smalls (Harry Shearer) strike a pose in *This is Spinal Tap* (1984).

band lost backstage at the Xanadu was a bear from a logistical standpoint.

"There was no dialogue in the script, so that tracking scene was tough because it was very confined…so you had to sort of calculate the areas where they [the cast] could possibly go, and then light those areas."

"The thing about the way the film was shot, you never really knew where they [the actors] were going to go, or what they were going to do… [Originally] it was a much, much longer sequence."

"Almost every take was totally different than every other take, dialogue-wise and blocking wise," Smokler explains, and so his training in the documentary framework really came in handy.

"That's what they were looking for, someone who could really make that work. If you see a shot in the film that's coming into focus, for instance, it wasn't planned. It was that I was zooming in to get focus on a new person, and that's the way you do a documentary. Essentially, it *was* a real documentary."

Since *This Is Spinal Tap* was fashioned as a real documentary, an incredible amount of footage was recorded, fifty hours in all. A laborious editing process (by some accounts six months, by some accounts eight) followed. Kent Beyda, who had served as an assistant editor with Joe Dante and others on Allan Arkush's cult classic *Rock 'n' Roll High School* (1979) joined the project after Kim Secrist, supervising editor Robert Leighton and Rob Reiner waded into the cutting process.

"I came on [*Spinal Tap*] after they'd finished shooting,

actually, because they realized they had so much material to deal with, and they needed some help," Beyda comments. "My first job was cutting the number for 'Hellhole.' I sat down to cut it on Monday afternoon, and that evening I told everybody I was ready to show it, and they said, '*What?*' And they said, '*You have a cut on it?!*' because it had taken them a week to cut the musical numbers. So they were flabbergasted I had done it so quickly, and we looked at it, and it was good…and it just kind of evolved from there.

"We looked at our first cut about a month later, which was like six or six-and-a-half hours," Beyda remembers. "We sat down at this dumpy screening room in Hollywood and we ordered Chinese food and just watched the whole thing for hours. It was quite something. It was an epic. It was fantastic. It was a really good movie. It was full of all kinds of currents and eddies and subplots and characters…all of which got dropped in the final eighty-five minute version.

"After we had finished the movie, we had some test screenings and they didn't go well," Beyda reports. "So Rob brought me back with an assistant, and we sat down for about a week and re-cut the movie from top to bottom, and we put in a couple of songs that had been taken out. We re-shuffled it a bit and refocused it based on the audience reactions from the test screening."

The last minute tweaking didn't really help, however, since the film opened and virtually disappeared. Critics were boisterous in their admiration for *Spinal Tap* but audiences stayed away until the release of the picture on VHS.

Today, Reiner's film is acknowledged as a classic, as the gold standard of the mockumentary form.

"I think it's one of the most brilliant movies I've ever seen," notes Gifford. "When I see it, I laugh at every single actor and every single situation," she adds. "I don't even have a favorite one, because they're all funny to me. Whenever people talk about the funniest movie of all time, *This Is Spinal Tap* is always in the top five."

Indeed, in 2003 *Rolling Stone* dubbed *This Is Spinal Tap* the number one rock 'n' roll movie of all time. In 1992, *Entertainment Weekly* ranked the film as the third funniest film in cinema history. It placed behind *Airplane!* (1980) and *Some Like It Hot* (1959) and nosed ahead of Woody Allen's Academy Award winner *Annie Hall* (1977). In 2002, The National Film Registry in the Library of Congress officially added *This Is Spinal Tap* to its rolls, honoring the production as one of the select titles in a hundred years of movies (alongside such luminaries as *From Here to Eternity*, 1953, and *In The Heat of the Night*, 1967) to boast a critical triple-threat: aesthetic, cultural, and historical significance.

This Is Spinal Tap is so beloved a film because it accurately observes the rock scene, and doesn't go for easy laughs. Instead, its observational humor is born from smarts, from an intelligence and curiosity about the amusing aspects of the rock world. It accurately mocks a number of rock movie conventions, including *Stagecraft 101* (the accident on stage), *the Yoko Factor* (a woman gets between boys in a band), the inevitable *break-up*, and more. There's an evil *record company*, a botched *recording session*, an

incompetent *manager*, a *"well-versed in the classics moment"* (in which Nigel solos with a violin and composes a symphony on the piano) and even a visit to Rock Mecca, *Graceland*. All these elements allude to the rock movie paradigm and ratchet the humor right up to 11.

In terms of its accurate, unflinching look at the rock scene, *Spinal Tap* never hits a false note. Indeed, many rockers see themselves in the characters and situations the film portrays. "We do love that," Harry Shearer once told me, "the musicians who have said *'Man, I can't watch* Spinal Tap, *it's too much like my life.'* That's the highest compliment of all. It beats all the Oscar nominations we never got."

"We're really proud of *Spinal Tap*," Shearer added, "because we basically had to will that film into being and into release every step of the way. There was absolutely no encouragement and no understanding, with the exception of Norman Lear who said 'Okay,' fled the scene and left the company [Avco-Embassy]. So we were just pushing that rug uphill all the time and I think we're entitled to feel a little vindicated that we were right and all those assholes were wrong."

(DVD) Available on DVD.

Times Square (1980)(SNDTRK)

STARRING: Tim Curry (Johnny LaGuardia); Trini Alvarado (Pamela Pearl); Robin Johnson (Nicky Marotta); Peter Coffield (David Pearl); Herbert Beighof (Dr. Huber); David Margulies (Dr. Zymansky); Anna Maria Hosford (Rosie Washington); J.C. Quinn (Simon).

FILM EDITOR: Tom Priestley. DIRECTOR OF PHOTOGRAPHY: James Contner. SCREENPLAY BY: Jacob Brockman. STORY BY: Alan Moyle, Leanne Unger. PRODUCED BY: Robert Stigwood, Jacob Brackman. DIRECTED BY: Alan Moyle. M.P.A.A. RATING: PG. RUNNING TIME: 111 minutes.

Johnny La Guardia (Tim Curry) is a rock 'n' roll DJ on WJAD Radio New York, broadcasting every night, all night. One of his most faithful listeners is young Pamela Pearl (Trini Alvarado), daughter of city commissioner David Pearl (Peter Coffield), a self-important "liberal" who's made it his mission to reclaim and restore Manhattan's Great White Way, turning the X-rated Times Square back into a place for families.

When she's tested for epilepsy in a hospital, Pamela meets an adventurous girl named Nicky, and they flee onto the streets together. While David seeks to get his daughter back and evade a political nightmare, Pamela and Nicky—now runaways—become street rebels who flout rules and only communicate with La Guardia. Pamela dances at the Cleopatra club, and the girls form a punk rock band called "The Sleaze Sisters." Together, they engage in a campaign to throw TV sets from the roofs of high buildings. Before long, this teenage rebellion hooks an entire generation and The Sleaze Sisters perform from a rooftop to their adoring fans.

"*Let it be passionate or not at all*," one character notes in *Times Square*, and this is a 1980s movie about resisting *authority* to the max. The girls won't take their medicine ("*Don't take your pills*," one advises, or "*you lose your fight. And your fight's all you got.*") Despite such admirable ideas,

Times Square doesn't confront one of its most important tenets: that Nicky and Pam are actually still being exploited, only not by parents, but by La Guardia, who is using their campaign of terror to raise ratings…not because he innately believes in their cause. Also, there are hints in the film that Nicky may be a lesbian in love with Pamela, but nothing is ever made of that plot point.

At times, *Times Square* also feels woefully disjointed. The girls' hair length changes radically, sometimes between shots, and it seems as though a great deal of material was cut during the editing process. The story leaps around in spots, and refers to events the audience hasn't been privy to. Still, if you're thirteen and pissed off, *Times Square* might just prove your anthem. The film's primary strength is its authentic location work. The film exists at "street level" in New York, and every frame bustles with life and energy, even when the script doesn't work. Thirteen-year old punks might sound like a joke, but more likely they provide evidence of a mainstreaming of the form.

Times Square's rock score is also memorable. "I Wanna Be Sedated" by the Ramones, "Dangerous Type" by The Cars, and "Walk on the Wild Side" by Lou Reed make a strong impact. As do the tunes performed by star Robin Johnson, "Damn Dog," and "Your Daughter Is One."

(DVD) Not Available on DVD.

Tommy (1975)

(SNDTRK)(MUS)(REAL ROCKER)(CAMEOS)

STARRING: Roger Daltrey (Tommy); Ann-Margret (Nora); Oliver Reed (Frank); Elton John (The Pinball Wizard); Eric Clapton (The Preacher); John Entwistle (Himself); Keith Moon (Uncle Ernie); Paul Nicholas (Cousin Kevin); Jack Nicholson (The Specialist); Robert Powell (Captain Walker); Pete Townshend (Himself); Tina Turner (Acid Queen).

FILM EDITOR: Stuart Baird. DIRECTORS OF PHOTOGRAPHY: Dick Bush, Ronnie Taylor. MUSICAL DIRECTOR: Pete Townshend. BASED ON THE ROCK OPERA BY: Pete Townshend. ADDITIONAL MATERIAL BY: John Entwistle and Keith Moon. PRODUCED BY: Robert Stigwood, Ken Russell. DIRECTED BY: Ken Russell. M.P.A.A. RATING: PG. RUNNING TIME: 111 minutes.

"*Your senses will never be the same*," the adverts for this excessive, 1970s era Ken Russell/Who rock opera promised. They didn't lie. *Tommy* is a rich treat for all your senses, assuming you have a fair amount of stamina. It's one glorious, bizarre, and exhausting scene after the other, a cavalcade of orgiastic rock music and trippy imagery.

This movie is the journey of one unfortunate soul named Tommy (played by The Who's Roger Daltrey from the 26-minute-point on). He's born after the tragic death of his father in World War II (see: *Pink Floyd: The Wall*), and his mother (Ann-Margret) struggles to make ends meet working in an industrial factory, at least until she marries Frank (Oliver Reed), a fellow (and soon *bad father*) who works at Bernie's Holiday Camp.

One night, little Tommy spies Frank and Mum Nora (Ann-Margret) doing something untoward in the bedroom, and consequently loses his senses: both sight and hearing. Director Russell displays this traumatizing handicap graphically in one scene as Tommy wears a black box over his head, effectively keeping his head framed inside a world of its own.

Desperate to save her son, Nora pushes Tommy headlong into the world of religion, represented here by movie star Marilyn Monroe as an iconic Mary figure, but even her power to heal can't save the boy. "*How can he be saved*," Nora sings, when "*he doesn't know who Jesus is*," or "*what praying is?*" Good questions.

As Tommy grows into a man, his experiences deepen. Frank takes him to a hooker, the Acid Queen, a sizzling, gyrating Tina Turner, to mend his broken heart. Later, Tommy is left alone in the care of his Uncle Ernie (The Who's Keith Moon), who molests the young man.

Finally, Tommy finds something he's good at. At the film's fifty-one minute point, pinball is introduced and Tommy beats the reigning champ, the Pinball Wizard (played by a flamboyant Elton John in platform shoes and oversized sunglasses). Tommy is thus worshiped as the reigning pinball idol, and his family grows filthy rich.

In one thoroughly decadent sequence, a now-alcoholic Nora—Ann-Margret wearing seductive white chainmail—writhes orgiastically on the floor of an all-white, immaculate bedroom. She moans and twists in apparent sexual frenzy, alternating between champagne-drinking hedonism and self-loathing over Tommy's exploitation. Then, just when the scene can't possibly get any better,

Tommy, can you hear me? The pinball champion of the world (Roger Daltrey) is carried on the shoulders of his adoring fans in Ken Russell's dazzling tour-de-force, *Tommy* (1975).

the commercial images on her television come to life with a spurting vengeance.

After a laundry commercial, soap suds are voided from the boob tube. Immediately, Nora rinses herself in the cleansing, soapy mix, but then suddenly baked beans (from a Rex Baked Beans TV commercial) dump out of the tube and douse her in the rusty red mix.

Finally, following a chocolate commercial, Nora slithers sexily around in a thick chocolatey mix. This show-stopping scene culminates with Ann-Margret humping a long hot-dog-shaped pillow, and that alone is worth the price of a rental.

After taking Tommy to a specialist (Jack Nicholson in a *cameo*), the key to his unusual handicap is discovered. After shattering a mirror, Tommy regains his perception and uses his newfound fame to become a religious figure, one who sells Tommy merchandise. "*Come back to our house and be one of us,*" the messiah, a new Jesus Christ, implores. In the end however, the cult turns violent. Frank is stabbed and Mom beaten to death. Only Tommy survives. Barefoot, young Tommy scales a mountain summit and faces the sun as the movie ends.

This audacious, dazzling rock film never stops, ceases or lets up. It's been called an indictment of organized religion, but it also takes savage shots at big business, the need to commercialize everything, even God. The film also comments on celebrity culture, and how unfulfilled people elevate their favorite movie stars (or rock groups?) to the status of godhood (**see: *Finding Graceland***).

Tommy is packed with strange symbols. There are phallic snakes (an image Russell would play with more in his 1988 film, *Lair of the White Worm*), but "balls" seem to be the central image. Early in the picture, Ann-Margret works in a factory assembly line scooping up metal ball-bearings which resemble pinballs. Later, Christmas balls also appear, forecasting Tommy's skill with pinball.

What does it all mean? Another good question, and certainly critics are divided on the issue of overall meaning. What remains crystal-clear is that Ken Russell's *Tommy* is a perfect fusion of rock music with magnificent and awesome imagery. The film is a proto music-video, and had enormous influence on the genre. Vincent Canby wrote in *The New York Times* that "*Tommy* is composed of excesses. Bad jokes or heavy-handed satire are redeemed by everyone—director, production designer, orchestrators, actors—going too far, which is, after all, what the original *Tommy* is all about: a world inhabited by people too jaded to react to anything but overdose."[64]

That's a good point, but certainly the film is also about the universal nature of society's "Kool-Aid drinkers;" the lost souls who—in the endless search for meaning—leap head first into capitalism, or conservatism, or Christianity, or pop culture worship...often never seeing how empty their lives really are.

(DVD) Available on DVD.

Top Secret! (1984)(MUS)

STARRING: Val Kilmer (Nick Rivers); Lucy Gutteridge (Hilary Flammond); Peter Cushing (Bookstore Proprietor); Jeremy

Kemp (Streck); Christopher Villiers (Nigel); Jim Carter (Deja Vu); Omar Sharif (Agent Cedric).

FILM EDITORS: Francois Bonnot, Bernard Gribble. DIRECTOR OF PHOTOGRAPHY: Christopher Challis. WRITTEN BY: Jim Abrahams, David Zucker, Jerry Zucker, Marilyn Burke. PRODUCED BY: John Davidson, Hunt Lowry. DIRECTED BY: Jim Abrahams, David Zucker, Jerry Zucker. M.P.A.A. RATING: PG. RUNNING TIME: 90 minutes.

An underrated comedy jewel from the team who gave the world *Airplane!* (1980) and *The Naked Gun* (1988), *Top Secret* is a brilliantly-crafted parody of the Elvis Presley movie canon. The fast-paced picture tells the tale of a hip-swinging American rock star, Val Kilmer (Jim Morrison in *The Doors*) as the blandly named Nick Rivers. He goes on tour in Eastern Europe to sing and dance but runs afoul of evil East German Nazis (?) and helps the French resistance (including a fighter named Deja Vu). Rivers never breaks a sweat or even seems truly aware of danger, and the film is a hoot, taking glorious swipes at inane Presley "adventure" films like *Harum Scarum*.

In addition to his skills with comedy, Kilmer proves well ahead of *The Doors* that he's a more-than-passable singer. In *Top Secret!*, he performs a bevy of tunes, including the Beach Boys inspired tune "Skeet Surfin,'" Little Richard's "Tutti Frutti," and *Top Secret*'s accurately titled anthem, "How Silly Can You Get."

(DVD) Available on DVD.

Trick or Treat (1986)(HORR)

STARRING: Marc Price (Eddie "Rag Man"); Tony Fields (Sammi Curr); Lisa Orgolini (Leslie Graham); Doug Savant (Tim); Elaine Joyce (Angie Weinbauer); Gene Simmons (Nuke); Ozzy Osbourne (Reverend Gilstrom); Charles Martin Smith (School Principal).

FILM EDITOR: Jane Schwartz Jaffe. DIRECTOR OF PHOTOGRAPHY: Robert Elswit. ORIGINAL MUSIC COMPOSED AND PERFORMED BY: Fastway. STORY BY: Rhet Topham. WRITTEN BY: Michael S. Murphey, Joel Soisson, Rhet Topham. PRODUCED BY: Michael S. Murphey, Joel Soisson. DIRECTED BY: Charles Martin Smith. M.P.A.A. RATING: R. RUNNING TIME: 93 minutes.

"Rag Man" (Marc Price) is a bullied teenager shattered to learn that his heavy metal rock icon, Sammi Curr (Tony Fields) has died in a hotel fire. He begins hearing Satanic messages from Curr's final album when he plays it backwards. The messages spur him to vengeance against those kids at school who have tormented him. But soon Curr's "death" rock is too ugly even for "Rag Man" and he attempts to renounce the bogeyman's power before a concert at school where Curr promises to kill further students.

Trick or Treat is a darkly satirical 1980s horror movie that looks at the trend of "Death" metal music in the mid-1980s. Parents of adolescents feared that Satanic messages were being "back casted" in albums, and the issue came to a head in December of 1985 when two teenage boys attempted suicide after allegedly listening to a Judas Priest album and hearing the subliminal message *"Do it."*

Considering this backdrop, it didn't take Hollywood long to produce a movie in which a demon or devil truly *was* communicating through rock. In this ripped-from-the-headlines, low-budget horror effort, a boy who believes that *"rock's chosen warriors will rule the apocalypse"* and who decorates his room with posters of Anthrax and Ozzy Osbourne, gets more than he bargained for when he plays backwards the final album of the late, great Sammi Curr, an antisocial, controversial musician known for suggestive lyrics and theatrical stunts.

Ozzy Osbourne plays a TV evangelist, Reverend Gilstrom, who rails against "rock pornography." He amusingly declares that rockers are "out and out sick people." KISS's Gene Simmons is also on hand, playing a friendly local radio DJ who passes on Curr's last album to "Rag Man."

Charles Martin Smith's film features tunes such as Fastway's "Don't Stop the Fight," "Get Tough," "Trick or Treat," and "Hold Onto the Night" and ends on a funny note as Osbourne's man of the cloth warns TV viewers that music like this (and no doubt films too) "...could kick you off into becoming an absolute pervert." ⓥ Available on DVD.

(Madonna) Truth or Dare

(1991)(DOC)

STARRING: Madonna, Warren Beatty, Kevin Costner, Sandra Bernhard, Luis Camacho, Christopher Ciccone, Martin Ciccone, Sharon Gault.

FILM EDITOR: Barry Alexander Brown. CINEMATOGRAPHERS: Chistopher Lanzenberg, Robert Leacock, Doug Nichol, Daniel Pearl, Toby Phillips, Marc Reshovsky. PRODUCED BY: Tim Clawson, Lisa Hollingshead, Madonna, Jay Roewe. DIRECTED BY: Alek Keshishian. M.P.A.A. RATING: R. RUNNING TIME: 114 minutes.

"Like You've Never Seen Her Before!" the ads promised, and boy they were true to their word. We hadn't seen Madonna like this before; only Bob Dylan in *Don't Look Back*.

That 1960s Pennebaker documentary is actually the closest antecedent to this documentary film, because one gleans clearly that Madonna—whether onstage performing or backstage fooling around—is never really "off." Her whole life is a show.

Madonna's boyfriend of the day, superstar Warren Beatty, makes essentially the same point during one scene in *Truth or Dare*: Madonna doesn't want to live off-camera. Everything she does is for posterity; for image enhancement.

This Alex Keshishian documentary follows the Material Girl on every leg of her 1990 Blond Ambition tour. She plays Japan, visits her father in Michigan, and heads to Canada, where her outrageous onstage antics (particularly

She's just...neat, isn't she? Madonna stars in the tantalizing documentary *Truth or Dare* (1991).

simulated masturbation) result in authorities complaining about public indecency. In a prayer circle before one show, Madonna responds to the charge by calling Toronto a fascist state. In Italy, there's more controversy and Madonna doesn't get to play there.

Causing a commotion wherever she travels, Madonna spends plenty of time primping in front of a mirror in *Truth or Dare*, and one notable occasion depicts her preferred technique for performing fellatio (which is demonstrated on a bottle).

Another moment in the film finds Kevin Costner (see: *The Postman*) visiting Madonna backstage and calling her concert performance "*neat.*" After he's gone, Madonna simulates vomiting (sticking her finger down her throat), as protest over his white bread terminology.

Madonna seems a mercurial presence in *Truth or Dare*, giggling at inappropriate times, providing uber-support to her underlings at some junctures, and vamping it up as much as she possibly can. The backstage scenes are presented in black-and-white to make the effort appear cinema verité, but there's nothing truthful or direct here. Madonna controls everything and the audience sees only what she cares for them to see.

On the soundtrack: "Express Yourself," "Oh Father," "Like a Virgin," "Promise to Try," "Holiday," "Live to Tell," "Vogue," and "Causing a Commotion."

(DVD) Available on VHS.

24 Hour Party People (2002)

(BIO-PIC)(CAMEOS)(SNDTRK)

STARRING: Steve Coogan (Tony Wilson); Lennie James (Alan Erasmus); Shirley Henderson (Lindsay); Martin Hancock (Howard Devoto); Chris Coghill (Bez); Mark Windows (Johnny Rotten); John Simm (Bernard Sumner); Andy Serkis (Martin Hannett); Raymond Waring (Vini Reilly); Sean Harris (Ian Curtis); Kate Magowan (Yvette Wilson); Christopher Eccleston (Boethius).

FILM EDITORS: Trevor Waite, Michael Winterbottom. CINEMATOGRAPHER: Robby Muller. PRODUCED BY: Andrew Eaton. DIRECTED BY: Michael Winterbottom. M.P.A.A. RATING: R. RUNNING TIME: 117 minutes.

This is Michael Winterbottom's raucous, entertaining, and highly fictionalized biography of Tony Wilson, the guru of the Manchester, England (a.k.a. "Madchester") music scene from the mid-1970s through the 1990s.

A TV journalist for Granada TV, a manager of several (failed) nightclubs, a game show host, the creator of a record label and an all-around *bon vivant*, Wilson is portrayed in *24 Hour Party People* in mostly affectionate terms by sly Steve Coogan. Wilson comes across as a charismatic, well-read, more-than-slightly absurd personality who frequently shatters the fourth wall and directs his witticisms to the camera and hence the audience itself.

In Wilson's own words, *24 Hour Party People* is an "Icarus" story; meaning that at least symbolically, it's a tale of a man who dares to fly too close to the sun; attempting to achieve greatness and ultimately going down in flames.

After a comedic interlude involving Wilson's attempt to fly a hang glider, a scene which includes a montage of crashes—including a botched landing on a barbed-wire fence—the film settles down to focus on the music scene of the disco decade. Wilson attends an early Sex Pistols performance in Manchester during the fall of 1976. There are just forty-two people in the audience (and there were only twelve at the Last Supper, Wilson points out), and the film cuts to authentic stock footage of the Pistols and Johnny Rotten on stage as Wilson concludes that he is witnessing the future of rock music.

Also in the audience sharing this moment of inspiration are several talents who will play important roles pioneering the next post-punk stage of the genre; including the core of the group Joy Division.

Wilson becomes consumed with New Wave music and brings it to Manchester via his latest endeavor, a new night club named the Factory. The venue books the likes of Iggy Pop, The Jam, Vini Reilly, and Siouxsie and the Banshees, and the movie re-creates the first performances at the Factory by Joy Division and its troubled lead singer Ian Curtis, utilizing shaky camera work and occasional cuts to black-and-white photography to provide immediacy and a "you are there" aura.

24 Hour Party People covers a tremendous amount of narrative territory, gazing at everything from the suicide of Curtis and the formation of New Order, to Wilson's double waterloo: the opening of a boondoggle nightclub called the Hacienda (credited as the location where the Rave movement began) and a famous label called Factory Records.

Wilson's failed relationship with his girlfriend Lindsay is also charted to amusing effect. At one point, she discovers Wilson in the back of a van getting a blow job from a hooker; only to revenge herself by engaging in sex with another man in a Factory bathroom stall. Wilson interrupts the coitus, notes the infidelity and then comments testily "I only got a blow job...that looks like full penetration."

In total, *24 Hour Party People* proves an eclectic mix of moods and techniques. Its diverse imagery incorporates everything from dive bomber pigeons on a Manchester rooftop and a close encounter with a UFO to Wilson's comedic vision of God; a supreme being who—not surprisingly—looks like Tony himself. Along the way, Wilson also frequently offers his unique brand of wisdom directly to the camera. "Nobody beats gravity," he notes about the ups and down of the Hacienda's history. "The history of music is like a double helix," he describes at another point, and so on. Sometimes characters even stop to tell the audience that things didn't *really* happen the way they are depicted here; and that given the choice to record the legend or record the truth, the former has been selected.

24 Hour Party People received extremely positive reviews from many mainstream film critics for its ingenious blend of fact, fiction and comedy. Unfortunately, the movie dilutes its own power through a diffident script and its diffuse sense of focus. It also suffers from thematic inconsistency. "This is not a film about me," Wilson tells the audience at one point. "I'm not Prince Hamlet nor was meant to be," he argues. "I'm a minor character in my own story.

This is a film about the music and the people who made the music."

It's an interesting monologue, yet it rings 100% false since Wilson clearly remains the celestial body that all others—the Happy Mondays, New Order, etc.—orbit throughout the film. What drives the members of New Order? What's the group's music really about? Why is it important historically? What was new about it? What does it represent? If *24 Hour Party People* were truly about the music and the musicians, these questions would be addressed, and they're not. Such issues are not even granted lip service.

What does the film focus on? Objections by the protagonist to the contrary, it gazes at his turbulent rise and fall…but not the reasons behind them. Still, the Icarus analogy is far more apt than Wilson's contradictory assertion that he's not the center of the drama. Wilson's a great dreamer, but a lousy businessman, and his steadfast belief in artistic freedom seems to come at the exclusion of self-preservation and at times, common sense; that's the crux of the film more than the music or the musical talents. But what makes Wilson such a loser? Why does he always self-destruct and make such bad decisions? Can a person be a patron of the arts *and* a bad businessman? Again, the movie doesn't say. It's content to chronicle the ups and downs of Wilson's career, but not gaze intently or closely at Wilson's character and self-destructive impulses.

What audiences are left with at the end of the day is a dazzling film in terms of visuals, style and performance, but one with inconsistent narrative purpose.

On the soundtrack: The Happy Mondays ("24 Hour Party People," "Tart Tart," "Wrote for Luck," "Kinky Afro," Sunshine and Love"), Joy Division ("Digital," "Love Will Tear Us Apart," "Transmission," "Atmosphere,"); New Order ("Here to Stay," "Blue Monday,"); The Sex Pistols ("Anarchy in the U.K."); Iggy Pop ("The Passenger"); and Siouxsie and the Banshees ("Make Up to Break Up"). Durutti Column also performs Vini Reilly's "Dream of a Child."

DVD Available on DVD.

Tina Turner (1939–   )(ROCK MOVIE HALL OF FAME) One of the rock screen's sexiest and most long-lived icons, Tina Turner has been in the music business for nearly half-a-century. A native of Tennessee, Turner boasts a full-throated voice and the finest set of legs ever to hit a stage. Turner performed in the documentary *Gimme Shelter* (1970), and then dazzled audiences as The Acid Queen in Ken Russell's tour de force, *Tommy* (1975).

Years after doing a cameo for the Bee Gees vehicle, *Sgt. Pepper's Lonely Hearts Club Band* (1978), Turner made real impact as the villainous despot of Barter Town, Auntie Entity, in the George Miller future thriller, *Mad Max: Beyond Thunderdome* (1985). On that film, she contributed two songs to the soundtrack, the hit "We Don't Need Another Hero" and "One of the Living."

Tina's life story, *What's Love Got to Do With It*, an adaptation of her successful autobiography, *I, Tina*, premiered to great acclaim in 1993, and the actress portraying Turner, Angela Bassett, won a Golden Globe, an Image Award and was nominated for an Oscar for her performance.

In 1995, Tina Turner ushered in the Pierce Brosnan era of James Bond with her rendition of the Bono and The Edge title track for *Goldeneye*. Turner also appears (in archival footage) as inspiration in the 2003 rock film starring Gina Gershon, *Prey for Rock & Roll*.

Two Minutes Fifty Seconds (ROCK CONVENTION) The length of a rock song. By tradition. (According to The Who in *The Kids Are Alright*).

(is for *U2: Rattle and Hum*

Under the Cherry Moon (1986)

(REAL ROCKER)(SNDTRK)

STARRING: Prince (Christopher Tracy); Jerome Benton (Tricky); Steven Berkoff (Isaac Sharon); Emmanuelle Sallett (Katy); Alexandra Stewart (Mrs. Sharon); Kristin Scott Thomas (Mary Sharon); Francesca Annis (Mrs. Wellington).

FILM EDITOR: Eva Gardos. DIRECTOR OF PHOTOGRAPHY: Michael Ballhaus. MUSIC: Prince and the Revolution. SCREENPLAY BY: Becky Johnston. PRODUCED BY: Robert Cavallo, Joseph Ruffalo, Steven Fargnoli. DIRECTED BY: Prince. M.P.A.A. RATING: PG-13. RUNNING TIME: 98 minutes.

Prince's sophomore slump. *Under the Cherry Moon* is a pretentious black-and-white effort that's intended to feel as light as a feather, much like a high-society Fred Astaire musical from the 1930s. Unfortunately it doesn't boast either the simplicity or the charm of efforts like *Top Hat* (1935). For all his incredible talents and gifts, Prince isn't nearly as likable a guy as Fred Astaire, and the result is that this movie, which finds the androgynous Prince playing a gigolo, feels uncomfortably like one massive ego trip. One won't be surprised to learn that Prince helmed the picture after replacing original director (now billed as "creative consultant") Mary Lambert.

Under the Cherry Moon finds Christopher Tracy (Prince) living in a timeless black-and-white world of pomp and elegance, where the most he has to complain about is pits in his grapes. He lives off his wealthy clientele, including the Lady in White, Mrs. Wellington (Francesca Annis), but he's set his sights on a spoiled rich girl and a heir to a fortune, Mary Sharon (Kristin Scott Thomas in her big screen debut).

Audiences are supposed to realize that Christopher and Mary are in love with each other because they constantly trade insults and feign moral indignation over bad behavior. "*I must have that disease. What's the name of it?*" Tracy asks. "*It's called stupid,*" Mary replies.

This sort of thing goes on for ninety-eight excruciating minutes before the movie ends on an unintentionally funny note as poor Christopher is gunned down (in the back, no less) by Dad's (Steven Berkoff) goons, and his tragic love with Mary is destroyed. Oh, the humanity! The tragedy of androgynous gigolos!

Amazingly, *Under the Cherry Moon* doesn't even boast the good sense to end on this campy note. Instead, it flashes forward to find Tracy's ex-partner, Tricky (Jerome Benton) running an apartment complex in Florida. He's visited by Mary, and neither is aware that an angelic Tracy lives yet in the Kingdom of Heaven, singing from his perch in the clouds above.

Under the Cherry Moon must be one of the most laughable vanity pieces to come from the rock genre in years, but at least the soundtrack is pleasant, though not as memorable as *Purple Rain* (1984). Among the Prince and the Revolution compositions: "Christopher Tracy's Parade," "Sometimes It Snows in April," "Kiss," and "New Position." DVD Available on DVD.

Prince is just a gigolo, wherever he goes, in the melodrama *Under the Cherry Moon* (1986).

U2: Rattle and Hum (1988)(DOC)

STARRING: Bono, The Edge, Adam Clayton, Larry Mullen, Phil Joanou, Dennis Bell, Adam Gussow, Jack Hale, Jim Horn.

FILM EDITOR: Phil Joanou. DIRECTOR OF PHOTOGRAPHY (color): Jordan Cronenweth. DIRECTOR OF PHOTOGRAPHY (black and white): Robert Brinkman. PRODUCED BY: Michael Hamlyn. DIRECTED BY: Phil Joanou. M.P.A.A. RATING: PG-13. RUNNING TIME: 98 minutes.

In this late-Eighties documentary, U2 takes a "*musical journey*" that chronicles the band's travails as it "*goes through certain stages*." Some of these stages include a trip to Harlem where Bono and the group sings "Still Haven't Found What I'm Looking For" with an African-American gospel choir, and a session at Sun Studios, where they record five songs in five hours and team with B.B. King. U2 also stops at *Graceland* and ruminates on Elvis and his motorcycles, and band members feel uneasy that the King's grave is nearby.

Later, U2 performs in a concert at San Francisco, then Texas. As the film climaxes, Bono contemplates the wisdom of featuring "Sunday, Bloody Sunday" at all because by the time of the movie's release, he fears, the original context may not be understood. Bono then explains that very context on stage, lecturing the audience about famine, Irish immigrants, and the wild acts of terrorism occurring in his country.

Filmed in pretentious black-and-white, which later gives way to spectacular color at a show in Tempe, Arizona, *U2: Rattle and Hum* doesn't reveal its cards very often. It's an opaque "band" film that doesn't show much of Bono or U2's personal side or inner workings, and this is very much to its detriment. *Rattle and Hum* plays more like promotion than a legitimate behind-the-scenes enterprise. Indeed, at times it seems the band (and the filmmakers) actually throw up a screen between the stars and the audience. In one scene that appears to include fairly important dialogue, the audience isn't privy to the conversation…music is recorded over the band's comments instead. Perhaps fearful of *Spinal Tap*–style revelations, *U2:Rattle and Hum* focuses less on the people and more on their music. It's a concert film more than a traditional documentary, and that makes the film less appealing. Unlike *Metallica: Some Kind of Monster*, which draws viewers in by exposing every personality in the band, there's no feeling of learning here.

Regardless, the music in the film stirs the emotions, and some of the cinematography is spectacular. On the soundtrack are such U2 hits as "With or Without You" and "Pride."

(DVD) Available on DVD.

(is for *Velvet Goldmine*)

Velvet Goldmine (1998)(FIC BAND)

STARRING: Ewan McGregor (Curt Wild); Jonathan Rhys-Meyers (Brian Slade); Toni Collette (Mandy Slade); Christian Bale (Arthur Stuart); Eddie Izzard (Jerry Devine); Emily Woof (Shannon); Michael Feast (Cecil).

FILM EDITOR: James Lyons. DIRECTOR OF PHOTOGRAPHY: Maryse Alberti. WRITTEN BY: Todd Haynes. PRODUCED BY: Christine Vachon. DIRECTED BY: Todd Haynes. M.P.A.A. RATING: R. RUNNING TIME: 122 minutes.

Glam or glitter rock was a phenomenon of the early 1970s, sponsored by such icons as David Bowie, Iggy Pop, Lou Reed, and Marc Bolan of T.Rex. It was a British movement in pop culture that arrived "between Woodstock and disco,"[65] wherein the traditional lines of sexuality were blurred, along with male and female fashions.

The fascinating, ambitious Todd Haynes film *Velvet Goldmine* weaves its tale of glam rock beginning in Dublin in 1854, as an alien spacecraft leaves behind a baby who is destined to be the world's first "pop idol," the poet Oscar Wilde. A green medal worn by young Wilde then passes down to another young boy several generations later: Jack Fairy. Fairy matures to become one of the originators of glam rock.

In the 1970s, another up-and-comer on the music scene steals the unusual emerald pin from Fairy and becomes famous himself as the glam rocker Brian Slade (Jonathan Rhys-Meyers), together with his extraterrestrial, onstage alter ego, Maxwell Demon (think David Bowie and Ziggy). With the help of his wife, Mandy (Toni Collette),

Slade becomes a worldwide phenomenon, and inspires fans with music, his bold sexuality, and flamboyant costumes. He even very publicly takes a male lover—American rocker Curt Wild (Ewan McGregor). But then, one day, Brian Slade stages his own public assassination, only to have it outed as a hoax. His record sales plummet, he becomes enmeshed in a cocaine scandal, and the age of glam rock comes to an abrupt end.

Ten years later, in the Orwellian world of the conservative 1980s dominated by President Reynolds, a young journalist named Arthur (Christian Bale) who once idolized Brian Slade, is assigned by his editor to pen a story about "what really" happened to the glam rock pop star after his fall from grace. Arthur commences an investigation and a series of interviews, including one with Slade's wife Mandy, to learn whatever became of his former role model. The answers prove elusive, until, with the help of Wild, Arthur uncovers Brian Slade's re-invention.

Shot in early 1997 on a budget of approximately $7 million, *Velvet Goldmine* utilizes the Citizen Kane structure (**see: *Eddie and the Cruisers***) to keep its main character, Slade, commendably opaque. His motivations are never truly understood. Bale's reporter constantly searches for the truth in the film but doesn't find it. Even when he believes he knows what became of Slade (a disappointing transformation into a 1980s pop rocker), he still doesn't understand the reasons behind the change.

Though Miramax wasn't sure how to market *Velvet Goldmine* (and disappointingly attempted to sell it as a murder mystery), the film has nonetheless become a cult hit, especially for the young generation.

"I was inspired to make a film for exactly that age, because I loved those movies that came out of the late sixties, like *Performance* (1970) and Kubrick's films," says director Todd Haynes. "And so many films came out of drug culture, and radical culture that were aimed at young people and kind of trippy, and a little bit hard to pin down, and full of layers that you could analyze with your friends, and see over and over again, and play the music, and really enter into these unknown worlds that shouldn't be completely visible on the first viewing.

"It should have layers and passages and secret trapdoors that lead you through them," Haynes suggests. "That was what I wanted *Velvet Goldmine* to be, and for a certain group of people, that's exactly what it is, and that's so cool. They just don't make movies like that anymore."

"*Velvet Goldmine* should be read as a fantasy," advises *New Statesman* critic Jonathan Romney, "and like the best fantasies, it's fabulously superficial at first sight before revealing hidden depths and resonances."[66] Romney's suggestion represents a good way of gazing at this remarkable and multifaceted gem, which, as Haynes suggests, opens up more and more on repeat viewing.

On the soundtrack Rhys-Meyers contributes vocals for "Sebastian" and "The Ballad of Maxwell Demon," while McGregor (who would sing again in *Moulin Rouge*, 2001), voices "Gimme Danger." Brian Eno performs "Needle in the Camel's Eye," Freda Payne sings "Band of Gold," and T.Rex contributes "Cosmic Dancer."

DVD Available on DVD.

Vietnam War (GENRE CONVENTION) This 1960s "police action" serves as the backdrop for many rock movies, including *Alice's Restaurant* (1968), *More American Graffiti* (1979) and *Hair* (1979). Some of the images in the trippy Monkees film *Head* (1968) also revolve around the conflict. The war was unpopular with the young Americans of the day, in no small part because of the Draft. Therefore, in the *authority-defying* rock movie genre, the Vietnam War was an irresistible target and *cause célèbre*.

"It might have been 1965," comments director Allan Arkush. "I was reading the Sunday paper and there was a full-page ad taken out in it protesting the Vietnam War.

"I remember looking at it and reading the names in the ad, and these were all people whose music was in my collections, or people I'd heard of. Peter, Paul and Mary, Bob Dylan, Joan Baez," he relates. "I remember looking at that ad and being confused why people had such a strong opinion about it. I was only seventeen, but seeing all those names in that ad made me stop and think because here were people I respected, singers I respected. Now I was learning to think about their opinions, which at that point seemed to be different than mine. That was a moment that really caught me; that said *'There's a message here.'* I realized when Bob Dylan was singing 'The Times Are A-Changin' he was not just singing those words, he *meant* those words."

Viva Las Vegas (1964)(ELVIS)(MUS)

STARRING: Elvis Presley (Lucky Jackson); Ann-Margret (Rusty Martin); Cesare Danova (Count Elmo Mancini); William Demarest (Mr. Martin); Nicky Blair (Shorty).

FILM EDITOR: John McSweeney. DIRECTOR OF PHOTOGRAPHY: Joseph Biroc. WRITTEN BY: Sally Benson. PRODUCED BY: Jack Cummings, George Sidney. DIRECTED BY: George Sidney. M.P.A.A. RATING: UR. RUNNING TIME: 85 minutes.

Aptly named Lucky Jackson (Elvis Presley), a working man with a hankering for women and racing, arrives in Las Vegas eager to excel with both. Befriending but later competing with racer Count Elmo Mancini (Cesare Danova), he attempts to both purchase the engine that will solidify his car's success and keep pool girl Rusty Martin (Ann-Margret) as his. Jackson ostensibly works as a waiter, but he really excels at song and dance. Martin and Jackson's chemistry is put to the test at an employee talent show, but the latter's rendition of "Viva Las Vegas" pegs him as the audience favorite. With love, money, and a chance at the Las Vegas Grand Prix in tow, Jackson puts all of his stock in one big chance at glory.

Though *Viva Las Vegas* manages to keep Presley's popular persona of "naïve-boy-does-good" intact, it is clear by this stage in his career that his iconic function as a musician has changed. No longer a rebellious rocker in the mold of *Jailhouse Rock* (1957), Presley has instead assumed the guise of the consummate entertainer. With songs as diverse as Astaire/Rogers send-up "The Lady Loves Me" (a duet with Ann-Margret) to the rollicking "What'd I Say"

(written by Ray Charles), it seems Presley seeks more to be a mainstream darling than a symbol of youthful revolt.

A financially successful picture with colorful glamor, *Viva Las Vegas* is a film that showcases a mentality that the city of Las Vegas proper would later adopt wholeheartedly. Presley singing "Viva Las Vegas" is forever ingrained in pop-cultural memory. Despite George Sidney's pedestrian direction, the film persists as a curiosity piece which provides glimpses of what Las Vegas looked like just before our current era of gigantic/themed resorts. *Viva Las Vegas* represents one apex of Elvis' film career. The social, cultural, and political upheavals of the later 1960s, however, would soon show his screen antics to be woefully out of step with the times.—Kevin Flanagan

(DVD) Available on DVD.

(is for *Woodstock*)

Walk the Line (2005)(BIO-PIC)

STARRING: Joaquin Phoenix (Johnny Cash); Reese Witherspoon (June Carter); Ginnifer Goodwin (Vivian); Robert Patrick (Mr. Cash); Dallas Roberts (Sam Phillips); Dan John Miller (Luther); Larry Bagby (Marshall); Tyler Hilton (Elvis Presley); Waylon Malloy Payne (Jerry Lee Lewis); Shooter Jennings (Waylon Jennings); Jonathan Rice (Roy Orbison).

FILM EDITOR: Michael McCusker. DIRECTOR OF PHOTOGRAPHY: Phedon Papamichael. BASED ON Man in Black AND Cash: An Autobiography, WRITTEN BY: Johnny Cash. WRITTEN BY: Gill Dennis, James Mangold. PRODUCERS: James Keach, Cathy Konrad. DIRECTED BY: James Mangold. M.P.A.A. RATING: R. RUNNING TIME: 136 minutes.

Walk the Line is the Academy Award–winning story of the late Rock and Roll Hall of Famer, Johnny Cash, forever known as the "Man in Black." The film begins with familial tragedy in 1944, when Johnny loses his older brother in a terrible (and bloody) accident. Sadly, his father (Robert Patrick) blames Johnny for the accident, even though he is not responsible.

Johnny marries Vivian (Ginnifer Goodwin) after a stint in the military, and after failing in his career as a salesman in Memphis, auditions for Sam Phillips, the same man who brought the world Elvis Presley and Jerry Lee Lewis. At first, Johnny does poorly, but Phillips advises him that the music "has to do with believing in yourself," and Johnny succeeds and records his first record (in six hours, no less): "Cry, Cry, Cry."

Cash's life changes when he meets the exuberant, charming June Carter (Oscar winner Reese Witherspoon) in Texarkana. He begins to fall in love with her and their friendship lasts for many years, even as his marriage to Vivian falls apart (**see: First Marriage**). Cash, it's clear, loves June not only because she sings with him, but because she *plays* with him, as a scene of the two talents fishing together demonstrates so tangibly.

Still, all is not well, and Cash begins a dangerous career spiral. In 1957, he begins taking amphetamines (according to the movie, thanks to Elvis Presley) and eventually collapses on stage in Las Vegas, the victim of an overdose. June Carter stands by his side but won't marry him. Cash even goes to jail for a time on drug possession charges before he can turn his life around.

Walk the Line climaxes on a triumphant beat as June and Johnny marry, John puts his house in order, and he records his famous album *At Folsom Prison*—literally at the prison.

Although *Ray* (2004) also made a tremendous splash a year earlier, *Walk the Line* is one of the best bio-pics to come down the pike in many a year. It is one of the best films of 2005 in part because it forges such a clear case about Johnny Cash's insecurities. His father always made him feel responsible for his brother's death (**see: Bad Father**), and so Johnny just never felt he was as good as his sibling. It's amazing to witness the ways a person can punish himself when he believes he's worthless; how he can live down to the expectations of others, even when he boasts remarkable talent.

James Mangold directs such an entertaining and involving picture that even at 136 minutes, this film feels short. Joaquin Phoenix and Reese Witherspoon share a brilliant playful chemistry, and the love story between Cash and Carter transmits powerfully, buoyed by funny, playful banter. It's also fascinating to see how *Walk the Line* depicts other rockers. Jerry Lee Lewis is in the film, worrying that they're all going to Hell for playing the Devil's music, and Elvis Presley appears as a kind of dangerous influence.

Amazingly, the cast performs its own vocals in the film—that's not actually Cash singing, but Phoenix! Phoenix performs "I Walk the Line," "Ring of Fire," "Cry, Cry, Cry," and "Folsom Prison Blues." Witherspoon performs "Juke Box Blues."

(DVD) Available on DVD.

Wayne's World (1992)(SNDTRK)(CAMEOS)

STARRING: Mike Myers (Wayne Campbell); Dana Carvey (Garth); Tia Carrere (Cassandra); Brian-Doyle-Murray (Vanderhoff); Lara Flynn Boyle (Stacy); Rob Lowe (Benjamin Kaye); Alice Cooper (himself); Chris Farley (Security Guard); Ed O'Neill (Mikita).

FILM EDITOR: Malcolm Campbell. DIRECTOR OF PHOTOGRAPHY: Theo van de Sande. BASED ON CHARACTERS CREATED BY: Mike Myers. WRITTEN BY: Mike Myers, Bonnie and Terry Turner. PRODUCED BY: Lorne Michaels. DIRECTED BY: Penelope Spheeris. M.P.A.A. RATING: PG-13. RUNNING TIME: 95 minutes.

"*You'll Laugh. You'll Cry. You'll Hurl,*" the advertisements for *Wayne's World* promised, and enthusiastic audiences responded by making this 1992 comedy the highest-grossing film based on a *Saturday Night Live* skit ever. Directed by Penelope Spheeris, the blockbuster film generated a sequel and earned more than $120 million at the box office.

Wayne's World follows the misadventures of Wayne Campbell (Mike Myers) and his buddy Garth Algar (Dana Carvey), two slackers who star in their own cable access show, *Wayne's World*. On the program (shot in Wayne's basement), these two long-haired kids debate rock music, degrees of supermodel hotness, and also spontaneously break into strange interludes involving the camera, like EXTREME CLOSE-UP! When they aren't producing the show, they cruise the streets of Aurora, Illinois to the tune of Queen's "Bohemian Rhapsody."

One night, a slick TV executive, Benjamin Kane (Rob Lowe) catches the amateur show and decides it would be perfect for his network. Even more so because he has a corporate sponsor in mind, Noah Vanderhoff (Brian Doyle-Murray) of "Noah's Arcade." Wayne and Garth take $5,000 each to continue producing the show for Kane, while Wayne romances Cassandra (Tia Carrere), the leader of a band that Wayne sees as a "real babe" (meaning that every time he looks at her, she's surrounded by gauzy stage lights, and the soundtrack plays Gary Wright's "Dream Weaver"). *Schwing!*

Kane has his eye on Cassandra too, and attempts to get Wayne out of the way by sending him to an Alice Cooper concert in Milwaukee, a location that spawns an homage to *Laverne and Shirley*, particularly its opening montage. When the guys meet Alice Cooper (who sings "Feed My Frankenstein" in concert) they learn he's a history expert who knows everything about Milwaukee, and they determine they're "not worthy" to be in his presence.

In the end, Wayne must reclaim his show from the corporate takeover and win the hand of Cassandra (by making her a rock music idol). Meanwhile, Garth finds his confidence with a dream lady (played by Donna Dixon), and Lowe's Benjamin Kane is the victim of a particularly invasive cavity search. However, if the movie really wanted to be daring, there would have been some joke about Lowe's sexcapades at the 1988 Democratic Convention. Instead, that obvious source of humor is left untapped.

Anarchic, bold, and revolutionary in 1992, with its fourth-wall-shattering narration and multiple endings (including the Scooby Doo climax), in retrospect *Wayne's World* looks little more than silly and inconsequential. About half the jokes don't hit the target, while the other half are quite funny (particularly a bit about product placement in movies). Carrere sings a great deal in the film, and looks terrific during the music video set-piece that sees a snake coiled around her semi-nude body, but she isn't much in the vocal department.

(DVD) Available on DVD.

Wayne's World 2 (1993)(SNDTRK)(CAMEOS)

STARRING: Mike Myers (Wayne Campbell); Dana Carvey (Garth Algar); Chris Farley (Milton); Tia Carrere (Cassandra); Christopher Walken (Bobbie Cahn); Aerosmith.

FILM EDITOR: Malcolm Campbell. DIRECTOR OF PHOTOGRAPHY: Francis Kenny. WRITTEN BY: Mike Myers, Bonnie Turner, Terry Turner. PRODUCED BY: Lorne Michaels. DIRECTED BY: Stephen Surjik. M.P.A.A. RATING: PG-13. RUNNING TIME: 95 minutes.

The ghost of Jim Morrison (and his Indian spirit guide) visit Aurora, Illinois' Wayne Campbell, host of the public access cable show *Wayne's World* (now broadcasting out of a doll factory warehouse!) and instructs the callow youth to organize a rock concert. "*If you book them, they will come,*" Morrison suggests (thus simultaneously satirizing *The Doors* and *Field of Dreams*). Wayne embarks on assembling Waynestock, but needs the help of the world's greatest roadie to do it; necessitating a trip to London.

Also, Garth (Dana Carvey) falls in love with a *femme fatale* (Kim Basinger) and Wayne's girlfriend, Cassandra (Tia Carrere) wants Wayne (Mike Myers) to meet her father, a martial arts expert from Hong Kong. At the same time, a sinister record promoter (Christopher Walken) tries to lure Cassandra away from Wayne to a new life in Los Angeles.

This amusing if unnecessary sequel to *Wayne's World* is loaded with *cameos* (Charlton Heston!) as well as some funny skits (including a hilarious one involving The Village People and their hit "Y.M.C.A."). The soundtrack resurrects "Dream Weaver" (which also featured in the original) and finds opportunity for the super rockers of Aerosmith to strut their stuff. On the soundtrack, they perform "Dude (Looks Like a Lady)" and "Shut Up and Dance." (DVD) Available on DVD.

Well-Versed in the Classics (GENRE CONVENTION) When rock was born, the form was considered evil. No two ways about it. People in positions of authority called it "jungle music" and disdained it as immoral "noise." Over the years, up-to-and-including iterations such as punk rock, the genre's artistry was rarely acknowledged. Considering this perpetual degradation and disapproval, it's no surprise that rockers sometimes boast an inferiority complex the size of Derek Smalls' cucumber. Accordingly, there's a focus in many rock films on a validation of the form of rock 'n' roll itself, as well as its practitioners. It's as though being a rock star simply isn't good enough by itself. No, one must actually be a *classically trained* musician too.

Such training apparently grants the band or act a shot at greatness for the ages. In other words, this is a plea to the musical establishment and musical elitists to—*pretty please*—consider rock 'n' roll a legitimate avenue of artistic expression.

In *Spinal Tap*, Marty DiBergi records a session wherein Nigel plays a lovely and haunting portion of a newly-composed "musical trilogy" at the piano (called "Love Pump")

thereby establishing his credentials as a "serious" artist. Nigel also utilizes a violin in one performance, and discusses his appreciation of Bach and Mozart, synthesizing this love into the unholy thing he calls "Mach."

These moments feel like an echo of *The Last Waltz* in which—during "Old Time Religion"—a violin also inevitably gets trotted out. Also, Gaelic is spoken during a performance in the concert, another pretentious touch. The makers of the film might as well shout, "See, rockers are really, really smart!"

Likewise, in *The Buddy Holly Story*, a classical violinist (why is the violin *always* involved?) points out to Buddy the similarities between Beethoven and the rocker's body of work.

What's Love Got to Do With It

(1993)(BIO-PIC)

STARRING: Angela Bassett (Tina Turner); Laurence Fishburne (Ike Turner); Vanessa Bell Calloway (Jackie); Jennifer Lewis (Zelma Bullock); Chi McBride (Fross); Phyllis Yvonne Stickney (Alline); Khandi Alexander (Darlene); Pamala Tyson (Leanne); Penny Johnson (Lorraine).

FILM EDITOR: Stuart Pappe. DIRECTOR OF PHOTOGRAPHY: Jamie Anderson. WRITTEN BY: Kate Lanier. BASED ON I, Tina BY: Tina Turner and Kurt Loder. PRODUCED BY: Doug Chapin and Barry Krost. DIRECTED BY: Brian Gibson. M.P.A.A. RATING: R. RUNNING TIME: 118 minutes.

This is the emotional, at times harrowing bio-pic of throaty (and leggy) rock sensation Tina Turner, adapted from her book with Kurt Loder, *I, Tina*.

What's Love Got to Do With It commences with young Tina/Anna Mae Bullock countenancing the sudden departure of her mother from Nutbush, Tennessee. In 1958, Tina follows her mother to St. Louis and meets up with the charismatic and controlling musician Ike Turner at the Club Royale, only to become his new protégé and lead singer. Ike grooms the immensely talented Tina for fame, but a dark side soon emerges when he chooses business over her health.

Unfortunately, the pain keeps coming as Ike proves to be a ritual abuser. Because she remembers how it felt to be abandoned as a child, Tina remains with Ike and her children for nearly twenty years, until a friend named Jackie introduces her to Buddhism and she finds the strength to strike off on her own. The film ends in triumphant fashion, in mid-performance, as Bassett is replaced by the real Tina Turner, who sings the title track.

In a film punctuated by cogent, raw and honest performances, the insidiousness of Ike Turner's abuse is made plain. In fact, he first seduces Tina on the very night his current girlfriend, Lorraine (Penny Johnson) shoots herself. He makes Tina promise not to leave him, and that is the crisis of Tina's life. How much does she owe this benefactor? And when does that debt expire? *What's Love Got to Do With It* charts some answers to those interrogatives as, over time, Tina attempts to leave behind Ike, who has punched her with his closed fist and in one egregious circumstance, raped her.

What's even sadder, perhaps, is that Tina's mother is also a betrayer and user, foiling her daughter's attempt to escape Ike because Ike has purchased her a house and set her up in the wealthy lifestyle she prefers. But that's part of Ike Turner's dark psyche as portrayed in the film: he knows precisely what approach to use on people; he seems to understand and exploit characteristics in an uncanny fashion (like Tina's need to be loved and fear of abandonment; and her mother's avarice and greed).

The rock music in *What's Love Got to Do With It* is the viewer's guide to passing epochs. The late 1950s and early 1960s bring Ike's composition "A Fool in Love." The era of the British Invasion is heralded by Tina's appearance on an *American Bandstand*–type dance program to sing "Shake a Tail Feather." A musical montage to the tune of John C. Fogerty's "Proud Mary" diagrams the years from 1971 to 1974, when a frightened and sad—but professionally successful—Tina resorts to an overdose and a suicide attempt. Tina sings "Disco Inferno" in a Las Vegas lounge (with transvestites in the audience) when attempting to make a comeback in 1980, and finally returns triumphantly to the big stage (after a final backstage confrontation with Ike) for the valedictory "What's Love Got to Do With It."

As deeply affecting today as it was in 1993 upon its release, *What's Love Got to Do With It* is a gripping biography of rock's reigning queen, but it transcends the genre in its depiction of domestic abuse, victimization, and self-actualization. Angela Bassett's performance is one of the greats of the genre, and Laurence Fishburne skillfully makes Ike a frightening but ultimately tragic figure, one undercut by his own insecurities. A monster, indeed, but one with so much potential. It's amazing that Tina Turner escaped his grasp, but this film makes clear that the process of escape was violent, terrifying, and anything but glamorous.

DVD Available on DVD.

Where Are They Now? (GENRE CONVEN-

TION) In the rock movie, "Where Are They Now?" Is the equivalent to "Hell" or "Purgatory."

It's the place where rock bands end up after a break-up, or when popularity fades. It's the place a rock group never wants to end up in. In movies such as *Eddie and the Cruisers* and *Velvet Goldmine*, reporters go in search of rock icons who have disappeared, who have fallen out of the public eye. In *This Is Spinal Tap*, a radio station plays a Thamesman tune ("Cups & Cakes") and then the DJ announces that they are currently residing in the "Where Are They Now?" file.

It is a *Rolling Stone* cover article pointedly entitled "Where Are They Now?" that prompts the memories of a former band member in Robert Townsend's *The Five Heartbeats*.

Or as this convention is described in *Metallica: Some Kind of Monster* (2004): *"How quickly we become yesterday's news..."*

The Who: The Kids Are Alright

(1979)(DOC)(CAMEOS)

STARRING: Pete Townshend, Roger Daltrey, Keith Moon, John Entwistle, Ringo Starr, Tommy Smothers, Jimmy O'Neill, Keith Richard, Steve Martin, Rick Danko.

FILM EDITOR: Ed Rothkowitz. DIRECTORS OF PHOTOGRAPHY: Peter Nevard, Norman Warwick, Tony Richmond. WRITTEN BY: Jeff Stein. EXECUTIVE PRODUCER: Sydney Rose. PRODUCERS: Bill Curbishley, Tony Klinger. DIRECTED BY: Jeff Stein. M.P.A.A. RATING: PG. RUNNING TIME: 109 minutes.

This is an involving if superficial documentary about the career of The Who, spotlighting various concert and venue appearances by the group. There are some brief interview clips, but mostly this compilation focuses on performances, not behind-the-scenes revelations.

The Who appear on *The Smothers Brothers Comedy Hour* (where they sing "My Generation"), and perform at Woodstock ("*I hated it*," declares Pete Townshend on the subject).

The Kids Are Alright also gazes at the manner in which the group responds to pretentious critics (usually in monosyllabic grunts like "*yeah*"), and much fuss is made over the late Keith Moon's apparently irrepressible penchant to *destroy property*, particularly hotel rooms (an act seen here in a montage). Smashing guitars also seems to be in vogue too, and newspaper headlines refer to The Who as "*the richest vandals in the world*." In fact, the film focuses on a voucher showing the cost of Pete Townshend's destroyed

A view of Roger Daltrey on stage.

From the documentary *The Who: The Kids Are Alright* (1979).

guitars. Oppositely, the film also features a tour of John Entwistle's home, where he keeps an impressive *guitar collection*.

Ex-Beatle and drummer Ringo Starr also appears in the film for a time and interviews Keith Moon, who notes that he's "*just been sittin' in*" with The Who "*for fifteen years.*" The legendary Moon comes across here as a silly, sweet guy.

The Kids Are Alright is enlivened by a great soundtrack that includes "Tommy Can You Hear Me," "Pinball Wizard," "Pictures of Lily," "Can't Explain," "Young Man Blues," and "Who Are You." In all the film serves as an extraordinary introduction to the group for beginners, even if longtime fans will want to know more "dirt" on the group and its talented and distinctive artists.

ⓓⓥⓓ Available on DVD.

Wild Guitar (1962)(FIC BAND)

STARRING: Arch Hall Jr. (Bud Eagle); Nancy Czar (Vickie); William Watters (Mike); Cash Flagg (Steak).

FILM EDITOR: Anthony Lanza. DIRECTOR OF PHOTOGRAPHY: Joe Mascelli. WRITTEN BY: Nicholas Merriwether, Robert O'Wahlin. DIRECTED BY: Ray Dennis Steckler. M.P.A.A. RATING: UR. RUNNING TIME: 92 minutes.

The creative brain trust that brought the world *Eegah!* (1962) returns with this rock 'n' roll follow-up, which utilizes the same actors, some of the same sets, and even has unpleasant-looking Arch Hall Jr. (playing aspiring rocker Bud Eagle) sing one of the same songs, the lamentable "Vickie." At least here, the song makes sense, since

Nancy Czar plays a character named Vickie; unlike the object of Hall's serenade in *Eegah!* (who was named Roxie).

Wild Guitar concerns Bud Eagle's arrival in Los Angeles—guitar in hand—as he hooks up with Vickie, who happens to be a dancer on a local rock 'n' roll show that very night. Through an improbable series of events, Bud ends up singing on the TV show instead of the featured act, and instantly becomes a rock star!

Unfortunately, record company owner/agent Mike (played by William Watters; actually Arch Hall Sr.) becomes Bud's manager and attempts to control the young artist's career trajectory. Helping in that regard is an evil sidekick named Steak, played by the film's director (Cash Flagg...really Ray Dennis Steckler).

ⓓⓥⓓ Available on DVD.

Wild in the Country (1961)(ELVIS)(MUS)

STARRING: Elvis Presley (Glenn Tyler); Hope Lange (Irene Sperry); Weld (Noreen); Millie Perkins (Betty Lee); John Ireland (Phil Macy); Gary Lockwood (Cliff Macy).

FILM EDITOR: Dorothy Spencer. DIRECTOR OF PHOTOGRAPHY: William C. Mellor. WRITTEN BY: Clifford Odets. BASED ON A NOVEL BY: J.P. Salamanca. DIRECTED BY: Philip Dunne. M.P.A.A. RATING: UR. RUNNING TIME: 114 minutes.

Here's an oddity in the King's canon, a soap opera melodrama that resembles *Peyton Place* (1957) more closely than *Viva Las Vegas* or *It Happened at the World's Fair*. Elvis keeps his crooning to a strict minimum, performing only three tunes ("Wild in the Country," "I Slipped, I Stumbled, I Fell," and "Husky Dusky Day") focusing instead on delivering a fine, touching performance as an "ignorant country boy," one of Presley's standout efforts.

Wild in the Country finds Elvis playing Glenn Tyler, a "bad boy" given to bouts of fighting and carousing. As the film opens, he's put on parole after a recent infraction (beating up his brother) and remanded into the custody of his uncle. Before long, Glenn is dividing his time between three women, "easy" divorcee Noreen (Tuesday Weld), the wholesome reverend's daughter, Betty Lee (Millie Perkins) and, most significantly, Irene Sperry (Hope Lange), his social worker.

Many scenes in the film involve Irene and Glenn sharing therapy sessions and growing close as personal secrets are divulged. Glenn has had a difficult life because he lost his mother when he was nine, and ever since, he's been nursing anger issues. "*Hate's like a snake biting its own tail,*" he tells the lovely Irene. Importantly, she's a little broken inside too, because she "married for love" a young, impulsive man who ended up killing himself. While Irene and Glenn grow increasingly close, she also pushes him to attend college because she's uncovered a latent literary bent in the troubled young man.

Wild in the Country reaches its emotional pinnacle as Irene and Glenn share a motel room together following a thunderstorm, where they begin in quiet, compelling fashion to explore their romantic feelings for one another. This turn of events, however, leads to a townwide scandal, an attempted suicide attempt, and Glenn on trial at an inquest after he accidentally kills an obnoxious local boy with a bad heart (Gary Lockwood).

Everything works itself out for a predictable happy ending, but the characters are still drawn in more human, realistic terms than many Elvis films, probably due to the fact that the screenplay is by the acclaimed playwright Clifford Odets. It's a relief to report there are no cute kids for Elvis to sing to (a rarity in his oeuvre), no racist overtones (**see: *Girls! Girls! Girls!***) and the songs do arise gracefully from the story rather more than in other efforts. Despite all these fine qualities, *Wild in the Country* was one of the few Elvis films not to be successful at the box office.

(DVD) Available on DVD.

Wild in the Streets (1968)

(FIC BAND)(SNDTRK)

STARRING: Shelly Winters (Daphne Flatow); Christopher Jones (Max); Diane Varsi (Sally Le Roy); Hal Holbrook (Senator Fergus); Richard Pryor (Stanley); Millie Perkins (Mary).

FILM EDITORS: Fred Feitshans, Eve Newman. DIRECTOR OF PHOTOGRAPHY: Richard Moore. WRITTEN BY: Robert Thom. PRODUCED BY: Samuel Z. Arkoff, James Nicholson. DIRECTED BY: Barry Shear. M.P.A.A. RATING: R. RUNNING TIME: 90 minutes.

No, this isn't a sequel to Elvis's *Wild in the Country*.

Instead, it's a political parable (and cult movie) about Max Frost (Christopher Jones), a rock star who enters the political arena and initiates sweeping changes in the American political system.

Frost reduces the voting age to adolescence (fourteen), becomes the President of the United States and institutes a wide-ranging seemingly counterculture agenda. "*If you're thirty, you're through*," the ad-lines suggested, and the candidate follows through on his promises. All the over-thirty crowd in America is delivered to concentration camps, where it is rendered useless and toothless by force-fed LSD.

Many rock films including *Pink Floyd: The Wall* (1982) include a dark and troubling theme about fascism; and about the rock (or media) star's unique ability to hold absolute sway over a committed, nearly fanatical audience. *Wild in the Streets* meditates on this notion as well, revealing how easily misled people can be by a wolf in sheep's clothing. It's like leading the lemmings to the sea, to coin a phrase.

Wild in the Street's soundtrack is punctuated with rock tunes including "Free Lovin'" and "Fourteen or Fight" by The 13th Power, and Jerry Howard's titular tune.

ⒹⓋⒹ Available on DVD on a double feature with Gas-s-s-s.

Woodstock (1970)(DOC)

STARRING: Richie Havens, Joan Baez, The Who, Sha Na Na, Joe Cocker, Country Joe & the Fish, Arlo Guthrie, Crosby, Stills and Nash, John Sebastian, Santana, Sly and the Family Stone, Canned Head, Jefferson Airplane, Janis Joplin, and Jimi Hendrix.

FILM EDITOR: T. Schoonmaker. CINEMATOGRAPHERS: Michael Wadleigh, David Myers, Richard Pearce, Don Lenzer, Al Wertheimer. PRODUCED BY: Bob Maurice. DIRECTED BY: Michael Wadleigh. M.P.A.A. RATING: R. RUNNING TIME: 184 minutes.

This Academy Award–winning feature (for best documentary and best editing) is inarguably one of the ten greatest films ever made, regardless of genre. It's an incredible document of a specific time and a place (in this case Bethel, New York), on a specific weekend when 1.5 million kids (the size of a city!) showed up for what ultimately became a free concert, much to the surprise of the show's financiers.

Woodstock is a giant among films, and it's the one piece of evidence which proves, after some fashion, that maybe, just maybe, the hippies were onto something. Specifically, that there was a communal way to live that didn't require lawyers and policemen and suits and jobs, and dollar bills. Because the amazing fact this film reveals is that even with 1.5 million folks, pounding rain, mud slicks and the occasional (*ahem*) recreational drug, these hippies behaved themselves. "We expected 50,000 a day, and there must have been a billion," notes one local in the picture, "and the kids were wonderful. Nobody can complain about the kids." Indeed, this isn't the dark side of the counterculture, as in *Gimme Shelter*, where a Rolling Stones concert turned ugly and violent. Instead, this is just what the film's subtitle promises: "*Three Days of Peace and Music*."

Another impressive fact about *Woodstock* (the movie, not the festival) is that director Michael Wadleigh tells two stories. One is the story of the music, of the on-stage performances. Everything about this aspect of the film is wonderful, from Joan Baez on stage by herself at night

A view from the ground at the Woodstock festival,
in the groundbreaking (and breathtaking) documentary, *Woodstock* (1970).

singing about her jailed husband (a draft dodger) to the amazing and always energetic Jimi Hendrix doing his particular brand of hard rock.

Yet, what really makes this movie special is the steady focus with which Wadleigh records every possible angle of the concert's logistics. We see the preparations in meticulous detail, and it's rather amazing. This is a film that doesn't want merely to provide shots of a teeming mass that represents the audience, it wants to reveal how they lived for those three days. It reveals how and when people slept (carving out for themselves a piece of territory and "saying goodnight" to their neighbors).

It reveals how people made the best of things when it began to rain, and the ground turned to slick, messy mud. We see folks standing in line to use a pay phone and check in with their worried parents. We learn that a baby is born there, and come to the realization that this gathering is not a "shitty mess," as one person indicates, but a full-blown city. It's got health care (forty-five doctors from Army medical teams have come in without pay to help out), it's got food, it's even got bathing facilities (meaning a place to skinny dip).

Not surprisingly, Wadleigh even arranges one sequence around toilets; portable chemical port-a-johns that service the 1.5 million-strong crowd. At the end of the film, we see people cleaning up the field, picking up what seems like a vast ocean of garbage. "Just love everybody and clean up a little garbage on the way out," one organizer suggests, "and everything's going to be just fine."

Of course, Woodstock was not without its worries. A bit of paranoia rears its ugly head as one of the revelers suggests that the Federal government has sent planes to seed the clouds and produce rain. Others have more earthly concerns, namely that the festival needs to make $2 million to break even. But talk of capitalism is quickly silenced by more humanitarian concerns. "*The point is, it's happening,*" says one festival goer, seemingly understanding that a chapter in history is being inscribed before his eyes.

There was so much footage shot on this film, that at times, Wadleigh is able to stunningly fracture the picture with split screens two-and-three strong. To his credit, he uses the technique when it is merited, as balance and counterweight, not when he's simply trying to be stylish. The result is a film that is never less than compelling.

Lewis Teague, a director in the 1980s of such Hollywood fare as *Cujo* (1983) and *Cat's Eye* (1985), worked on the post-production end of *Woodstock*. "There were two production managers," he relates. "One who was responsible for the overall production and shooting of *Woodstock*, and me. I worked on the editing. While they were shooting in New York, I was setting up the editing in California and developing liaisons with the laboratories. I wasn't at Woodstock.

"We needed special facilities to edit it because it was the first film to be shot for multiple screens, and edited on the flatbed editing machines that they started using at that time. I also needed to set up a screening room where we could project the work prints before they were optically combined on one strip of film, which meant that when we were screening the work print, sometimes there would be five projectors running," Teague describes.

"I set up a room. I had to find a facility that had enough space, because seven or eight editors were working on the project. We didn't want to go onto a studio lot because the producer and the director wanted to maintain as much independence as they could. I had to rewire the office building so we had enough power coming in to run all the equipment, and set up an editing and projecting space where at times we could run five or six film tracks simultaneously.

"We all knew that it was great," Teague notes with pride. "We didn't know that it would be as memorable as it was. But we all knew that it was great. The music was great, the performances were great, and the festival itself was really the watershed event. So while we were working on the film, the festival had already become the event of the year of 1969. So as we were making a movie, we knew the movie was going to be even better than the event. Woodstock was event of the decade, not just *the year*."

Woodstock sounds as great as it looks thanks to the performances of Joan Baez ("Swing Low, Sweet Chariot"), Crosby, Stills, and Nash ("Long Time Gone"), Joe Cocker ("With a Little Help from My Friends"), Arlo Guthrie ("Coming into Los Angeles"), The Who ("Summertime Blues"), "Jimi Hendrix ("Purple Haze"), and more.

DVD The recently released director's cut DVD adds more performances to the film, and is worth renting for those who want to know more about three days that changed a generation.

(is for *Xanadu*)

Xanadu (1980)(MUS)(SNDTRK)(ANIM)

STARRING: Olivia Newton-John (Kira); Gene Kelly (Danny McGuire); Michael Beck (Sonny Malone); James Sloyan (Simpson); Dimitra Arliss (Helen); Fred McCarren (Richie); Ren Woods (Joe); Muses (Sandahl Bergman, Melinda Phelps, Cherise Bate, Juliette Marshall, Marilyn Tokuda, Yvette Van Voorhees, Terri Beckerman):

FILM EDITOR: Dennis Virkler. DIRECTOR OF PHOTOGRAPHY: Victor J. Kemper. WRITTEN BY: Richard Christian Danus, Marc Reid Rubel. PRODUCED BY: Lawrence Gordon. OLIVIA NEWTON-JOHN'S songs: John Farrar. ELECTRIC LIGHT ORCHESTRA'S songs by: Jeff Lynne. "XANADU" by: Jeff Lynne. DIRECTED BY: Robert Greenwald. M.P.A.A. RATING: PG. RUNNING TIME: 96 minutes.

Even the tagline for this 1980 musical fantasy was confused. "Open your eyes and hear the magic!" it went. That's a mix of metaphors or something. Usually, you open your eyes and see the magic, or open your ears and hear it, but the movie's designated combo doesn't work.

Not much does in this film, frankly. It's story of Sonny Malone, a struggling rock album cover artist who is inspired by a muse to renovate an old auditorium with an aging clarinetist and re-open it as a paradise-like nightclub called Xanadu. The only problem is that along the way, things get personal for the Muse and she falls in love with Sonny, making things awkward.

This movie stars Olivia Newton-John ("the girl you loved in *Grease!*"), Michael Beck ("who thrilled you in *The Warriors!*), and Gene Kelly ("the greatest dancer of all time!") and puts them together for "ten hit songs," in a club "where time stops and the magic never ended." That's the movie's hyperbole, but it seems the production team spent more imagination on the ads than the actual screenplay, which makes no sense.

For instance, Newton-John plays a muse who has "worked" with Michelangelo, Beethoven, and Shakespeare, but the guy she falls in love with is Sonny Malone? And, why does anybody need an inspirational muse to open a new nightclub? Again, given the company this muse has kept in the past, she's really setting her sights low this time to focus on this particular guy.

Still, Gene Kelly may indeed be the best dancer of all time, and he maintains his dignity here. "*I've been known to twinkle a toe or two,*" he knowingly comments at one point, winking at the audience. The only scene that sinks this grand performer occurs about an hour in. *Xanadu* provides a lengthy montage of Kelly picking out an outfit for the club's opening night, and in one of them, this great icon of the American cinemas resembles nothing so much as a 1970s era pimp.

New Wave rock group The Tubes makes an appearance in the film for a number blending 1940s and 1980s sensibilities ("Hey, you got your Bee Gees in My Glenn Miller!"). The song they perform is called "Dancin'." You may insert your own joke about going down the tubes here.

The best part of the film is saved for last, however—the unveiling of Xanadu (to the tune, naturally, "Xanadu"). The club features a frightening array of clashing styles and

Olivia Newton-John (left) is a Greek muse celebrating the grand opening of a roller-skating, neon nightclub in *Xanadu* (1980).

events. There are mimes with painted faces throwing bowling pins, an army of roller skaters, and a wild dance floor that's lit with flashing neon lights. The dancers skate around this circular platform wearing skimpy futuristic outfits and I was tempted to shout "Renew!" in honor of the apparent homage to the Carousel death ritual in the 1976 flick, *Logan's Run*.

Besides the obligatory animated sequence (which transforms Beck and Newton-John into fish) Olivia Newton-John's muse comes alive to the strains of Electric Light Orchestra's "I'm Alive," a special effects show stopper. The film's greatest hit is her ballad (sung in the empty, pre-Xanadu auditorium), "Magic." Other tunes on the *Xanadu* soundtrack include Olivia's "Suspended in Time" and "Suddenly," as well as ELO's "The Fall," "Don't Walk Away," and "All Over the World." Hard to believe, but *Xanadu* was scheduled to be reborn as a $5 million Broadway musical in 2007.

Ⓓ Available on DVD.

(is for *Yellow Submarine*)

Year of the Horse (1997)(DOC)

STARRING: Neil Young, Frank "Pancho" Sampedo, Billy Talbot, Ralph Molina, Jim Jarmusch.

FILM EDITOR: Jay Rabinowitz. CINEMATOGRAPHERS: Jim Jarmusch, L.A. Johnson, Steve Onuska, Arthur Rosato. PRODUCED BY: L.A. Johnson. DIRECTED BY: Jim Jarmusch. M.P.A.A. RATING: PG. RUNNING TIME: 106 minutes.

Quirky director Jim Jarmusch tackles the life and times of Neil Young and Crazy Horse in this contribution to the documentary format. The film chronicles Young's 1996 tour, but also finds time to go back and gaze at his last twenty years. The film includes footage from tours in Europe and the United States that go back to the mid-1970s.

Some of the footage in *Year of the Horse* is grainy (super 8mm) but ultimately that's beside the point. The interview sections vacillate from being *Spinal Tap* funny to deadly serious, especially when the specter of drugs is raised. Young himself looks like a wreck.

Neil Young and Crazy Horse perform about a dozen or so tunes including "Tonight's the Night," "Music Arcade," and "Big Time."

ⒹⓋⒹ Available on DVD.

Yellow Submarine

(1968)(ANIM)(SNDTRK)(MUS)

STARRING (THE VOICES OF): George Harrison, John Lennon, Paul McCartney, Ringo Starr, Paul Angels, John Clive, Dick Emery, Geoff Hughes, Lance Percival.

FILM EDITOR: Brian J. Bishop. ANIMATION DESIGN BY: Jack Stokes, Robert Balser. BASED ON AN ORIGINAL STORY BY: Lee Minoff. BASED UPON A SONG BY: John Lennon, Paul McCartney. SCREENPLAY BY: Lee Minoff, Al Brodax, Jack Mendelsohn, Erich Segal. PRODUCED BY: Al Brodax. DIRECTED BY: George Dunning. M.P.A.A. RATING: G. RUNNING TIME: 89 minutes.

Billed as The Beatles' "mod odyssey," the 1968 animated fantasy *Yellow Submarine* is an 89-minute retro delight: an imaginative fairy tale girded by whimsical flights of verbal and visual imagination, and all of it featuring the terrific, timeless music of Ringo, George, John and Paul.

The film's story begins "once upon a time" in far off Pepperland, where the nice, happy (and colorful) folks living there are attacked without warning by The Blue Meanies, a bunch of killjoys armed with anti-music missiles who only "take no" for an answer. Their unprovoked attack takes the Pepperland people by surprise, and the community literally "turns blue" under the assault of Blue Meanie weaponry, which includes a guided missile called GLOVE which looks like a giant human hand with a pointed finger. The rolling green hills and lovely land of Pepper become a landscape of grimacing gray faces, all frozen in a sullen silence. Joy has been exterminated.

However, one man escapes the onslaught of the Blue

The Beatles hold up a miniature of the titular vessel from the animated fantasy masterpiece, *Yellow Submarine* (1968).

Meanies in a yellow submarine and goes in search of someone—anyone—who can restore his home to its former wondrous glory. After the opening credits, the yellow submarine arrives in the audience's reality, the UK to be exact, a brick and mortar world of factories, workers, industry, and lonely, isolated people…almost a deadly dull palette after the color and vitality of Pepperland; a feeling which is nicely accentuated by the Beatles' sad tune "Eleanor Rigby." In short order, the Beatles are recruited to save Pepperland, and begin a long journey to reach it.

On this incredible sojourn fusing music and madness, The Beatles travel through time and space and age rapidly (to the tune of "When I'm Sixty-Four"), pass through a sea of strange animals (including a walking teacup and saucer) and even encounter a "Nothing" named Jeremy, who speaks entirely in rhyme. Here, as Ringo thoughtfully decides to bring Jeremy from nowhere to somewhere, the tune "Nowhere Man" is played. Next up, The Beatles move to the "foothills of the headlands" to find the route to Pepperland (accompanied by trippy imagery and "Lucy in the Sky with Diamonds").

Finally, The Beatles arrive in Pepperland and wage a most unusual war of melody and love against the Blue Meanies. They must impersonate Pepperland's most popular group, Sgt. Pepper's Lonely Hearts Club Band, and rally the people of the land into rebellion with the return of their music. They do so quickly, restoring color and vitality to Pepperland in the process. The tunes they use in this endeavor include "All You Need Is Love," and "With a

Little Help From My Friends." There's even a genuflection to "flower power" as Jeremy casts a spell on a Blue Meanie that makes flowers bloom all over the villain's chubby body.

In all, *Yellow Submarine* is a dizzying trip loaded with unforgettable line imagery and songs (twelve of 'em, in fact). It's a bizarre exploration of inner space from the same year that gave the world *2001: A Space Odyssey*.

The movie positively springs from one silly verbal pun to another, and is packed with wall-to-wall jokes. When the Blue Meanies are defeated, for instance, one of the baddies asks where they will end up. "Argentina?" another responds questioningly, implicitly linking the Blue Meanies to the real life villains of the Nazi regime, some of whom also fled to Argentina after WWII.

The language in the film is silly and wonderful, filled with non sequitur and malapropism, yet it is the trippy imagery that remains so evocative of the late 1960s and early 1970s, a great time for world cinema. For instance, there's a vast sea of holes preceding a sea of green; and when the yellow submarine first departs England, the film cuts to a dizzying, rapid-fire montage of landscape photographs to indicate the exodus from our world to another. From an ocean of sine waves to an explicit demonstration of how long—precisely—sixty-four seconds is, the film is daring in its imagery, abstract in its jokes, and never less than entertaining.

In a sense, *Yellow Submarine* made me a little sad because I realized while watching it that even in an era when CGI can create anything—how mundane and "realistic" our movie imaginings have become. Even our most sprawling fantasies (like *Lord of the Rings*) rarely seem abstract, symbolic, weird or wonderful. Back in 1968, a fairy tale like *Yellow Submarine* was cutting edge, but also an entertainment that a child and an adult could enjoy on totally different levels. It is the result of a silly, unfettered imagination, and yet no industry executive would dare greenlight such a project today, not when movies cost so much and must return a profit on the significant investment. The result is that we don't really have movies like *Yellow Submarine* now, and thus I wonder, did the Blue Meanies win? Has grim reality, and our own creative limitations forced us to endure a world where we only take no for an answer? I don't know about you, but that's not the world I want to live in when I'm sixty-four...

(DVD) Available on DVD.

The Yoko Factor (GENRE CONVENTION) The

Sex Pistols documentary *The Filth and the Fury* (2000) reminds audiences of a simple fact. "Everyone knows when a bird starts poking her nose into a rock 'n' roll band it's suicidal. That's when you really start getting fucked up and not caring about the music."

Fairly or not, one woman carries this burden more than others: Yoko Ono, wife of the late John Lennon. In circles far and wide, she is credited (or blamed) for breaking up The Beatles, and so it's only appropriate that rock movies reflect this dynamic. In the aforementioned *The Filth and*

The Fury, the surviving Pistols blames Nancy Spungeon, a crypto-hooker, groupie and heroin junkie, for Sid Vicious' downfall. In *This Is Spinal Tap*, Jeanine Pettibone (June Chadwick) briefly breaks up the band after taking over as manager. Nigel Tufnel leaves in a huff, and David St. Hubbins claims "*we shan't work together again.*"

Over and over again in rock film, the Yoko character has been revived to destroy the all-boy's club vibe of the genre. Courtney Love, a kind of latter-day Yoko Ono is even incriminated in the death of Kurt Cobain in the documentary *Kurt & Courtney* (1998).

Despite the "Yoko Factor," all rock films shouldn't be considered misogynist, since many films (including *That Thing You Do!*, 1996, *Velvet Goldmine*, 1998, *Almost Famous*, 2000, and *Rock Star*, 2001) boast positive images of rock wives and girlfriends.

(is for *Ziggy Stardust*)

Ziggy Stardust and the Spiders from Mars (1973)(DOC)

STARRING: David Bowie, Mick Ronson, Trevor Boldon, Mick Woodmansy, Angela Bowie, Ringo Starr.

FILM EDITOR: Larry Whitehead. CINEMATOGRAPHERS: Jim Desmond, Randy Franken. PRODUCED BY: Edith Van Slyck, Tony Defries. DIRECTED BY: D.A. Pennebaker. M.P.A.A. RATING: PG. RUNNING TIME: 90 minutes.

The age of glam (or glitter rock) officially came to an end in this memorable rock documentary from *Don't Look Back* (1967) director D.A. Pennebaker, sometimes called *Bowie '73*. Here, the intrepid devotee of cinema verité records the live event that occurred on July 3, 1973, a concert by David Bowie which represents his last public appearance in the persona of space alien Ziggy Stardust.

Shot at the Hammersmith Odeon in London before an enthusiastic crowd, *Ziggy* finds twentysomething David Bowie (at this point still looking very young and very androgynous) rocking the house after announcing his decision to kill Ziggy. Pennebaker captures all the performance footage ably, and there's also some boilerplate behind-the-scenes material, but nothing that renders the enigmatic Bowie less opaque. Indeed, this failure to "reveal" the true artist behind the myth is what disappointed many critics.

"...*Ziggy* provides no cultural context," suggested film critic Richard Cromelin in the *Los Angeles Times*. "It doesn't attempt to be a personality profile like *Don't Look Back*, and it doesn't seek to illuminate a movement like

Penelope Spheeris' punk documentary *The Decline of Western Civilization*. You'd think then, it would at least transmit some of the concert's excitement, since that's all it tries to do. But the dim, poorly lit, often fuzzy images and arbitrary cuts suggest not only minimal preparation, but a lack of familiarity and rapport with the star of the show. The film gropes vainly for the heart of Bowie's performance and comes up empty."[67]

Bowie performs "Moonage Daydream," "Oh You Pretty Things," "Rock and Roll Suicide," "Space Oddity" and "Watch That Man." He also covers the Rolling Stones tune "Let's Spend the Night Together."

DVD Available on DVD.

CONCLUSION
Don't Look Back...

The late John Lennon famously declared in March 1966 that The Beatles were *"more popular than Jesus."* He also stated: *"I don't know which will go first; rock 'n' roll or Christianity,"* a thought that provides the basis of our closing statement.

It's an important question, this matter of rock's longevity. Especially given the age of such longtime rockers as Mick Jagger, or Tina Turner. When they pass (we hope not until some very, very distant date), who will replace them? Will there ever be another Elvis? Or for that matter, another Prince? Or another Sting? The music industry seems intent on grinding out pre-fab stars like the pleasant Kelly Clarkson or Justin Timberlake, but will anybody be enthusiastically attending their concerts fifty years from now?

That can't be known, one supposes.

Still, I'll go out on a limb and make the following prediction. Rock 'n' roll is here to stay.

It will never die.

Which means that in the years and decades ahead audiences can anticipate future rock movies. However, one wonders if those hypothetical enterprises will surpass the productions audiences now consider classics, titles such as *A Hard Day's Night*, *This Is Spinal Tap*, or *Tommy*. Will there ever be another film document like Wadleigh's *Woodstock*? Another fairy tale like *Yellow Submarine*?

Perhaps not, but recent films such as *Metallica: Some Kind of Monster* (2004) give audiences and rock enthusiasts reason for real hope. That Joe Berlinger/Bruce Sinofsky film is every bit the equal of any rock film on the list in the preceding paragraphs, and there's no doubt there's more to come.

One must never forget that the rock-movie format is a game for the young. So the new rock cinema of the future ages will most likely be one that old fogies like you or I will actively hate, detest, protest against, and deride. We'll be the authority that new brand rebels against.

But for rock to stay true to itself, it must again evolve.

And the great thing is, it will. What shape (fictional bands? rock operas? documentaries?) the genre will take we can only guess, but surely, the movies will be rocking around the clock for years and decades to come.

THE TOPS (AND BOTTOMS...)
of the Rock Film Genre

"Rock" films encompass so many different forms that generating a single top ten list of "best rock films" doesn't quite cut it. How can you compare a great movie about rock and roll as a "life experience" (like *Almost Famous*) with an all-singing-all-dancing rock opera like *Tommy*, or a bio-pic of an authentic rocker such as *What's Love Got to Do With It*. It's like comparing apples and oranges.

Since rock movies might be documentaries, biographies, or even films with particularly strong soundtracks, here's this author's list of the "tops" in each classification or stratification under the rock film banner.

I.

The Top Ten
ROCK FILMS OF ALL TIME:
(rock music as subject matter)

These are simply films about rock'n'roll in which ether something new about the genre is learned; or in which rock music pushes film style ahead.

This Is Spinal Tap proved such a spot-on parody of real life rockers and "road" situations that the film nearly killed off the rock documentary format permanently. It's ranked number one on this list because the observations it makes about rock music (and heavy metal rock specifically) are not merely funny, but accurate. And, those observations remain as true today as they were twenty-two years ago when the film was created.

Number two on the list, The Beatles' amazing *A Hard Day's Night,* is revolutionary both in terms of how it reveals its rock music scenes and also the manner in which it introduces the Fab Four as (manufactured or fictionalized) onscreen "characters" audiences will feel affection for. Perhaps the first pop-culture meditation on celebrity, this film could make a valid claim for being the vanguard of the music video movement.

Each film on this list pushed rock movies into fresh territory, or shed new light on this popular form of music. The exuberant, anti-establishment youth-centric power of rock is nowhere more plain than in the wild, undisciplined and joyous *Rock'n'Roll High School*.

Meanwhile, rock is treated reverently as modern-day art form via the *Citizen Kane* format in both the glam rock *Velvet Goldmine* and *Eddie and the Cruisers*. Other films concern the peripheral world of groupies (like *Almost Famous*), the almost-ran who could have been one of the most famous men in the world (*Backbeat*), the world's hardest working band (*The Commitments*), introduce to the masses a distinctly non-mainstream artist (*Purple Rain*), and examines the quandaries of a "one hit" wonder (*That Thing You Do!*).

1. *This Is Spinal Tap* (1984)

2. *A Hard Day's Night* (1964)

3. *Almost Famous* (2000)

4. *The Commitments* (1991)

5. *Rock'n'Roll High School* (1979)

6. *Purple Rain* (1984)

7. *Velvet Goldmine* (1998)

8. *Eddie and The Cruisers* (1983)

9. *Backbeat* (1994)

10. *That Thing You Do!* (1996)

II.

The Top Five
ROCK OPERAS/ROCK MUSICALS

The form of the rock opera or rock musical is one of the most challenging to do well (which is why so many of these films are genuinely terrible).

The five films below are examples of the form which—with dazzling success—combine rock music and music video–style imagery to create fantasy realms that reflect strongly on our own world. *Yellow Submarine* is potently and poetically anti-war; *Tommy* a riotous roller coaster and diatribe against the commercialism of everything from sports competitions to organized religions. Ditto the satirical *O Lucky Man!*

Pink Floyd: The Wall gazes seriously (with its trippy, disturbing imagery) about the ways childhood and adult traumas can lead a person to grow a black heart (and embrace hatred as a governing philosophy). Finally, *Hedwig and the Angry Inch* involves finding identity within, not defining oneself by a partner or lover.

1. *Yellow Submarine* (1968)

2. *Tommy* (1975)

3. *Pink Floyd: The Wall* (1982)

4. *O Lucky Man!* (1973)

5. *Hedwig and the Angry Inch* (2001)

III.

The Top Five
ROCK DOCUMENTARIES

Rock documentaries show us the world not as we might like it to be; but as it truly is. The top two selections in this list are flip sides of the same, illuminating coin. *Woodstock* reveals how the generation of peace and love could come together in vast numbers and share musical performances in relative harmony, despite bad weather and uncomfortable conditions.

Contrarily, *Gimme Shelter* is the end of the hippie utopia, a bracing wake-up revealing bad behavior, violence, and even death. To understand the rock movement of the late sixties it is perhaps necessary to watch these films one after the other.

Metallica: Some Kind of Monster is a caustic and intimate look at one of rock's greatest bands, one packed with searing revelations, interventions, fights, and unexpected character epiphanies. If any film has been able to rehabilitate the "rockumentary" after *This Is Spinal Tap*'s ribbing, Joe Berlinger and Bruce Sinofky's film did so.

Don't Look Back is an undeniable trailblazer with its cinema-verité style, lovely black-and-white photography and its strutting, pompous focal point (Bob Dylan). Finally, *The Last Waltz* by Martin Scorsese is a great concert film and perhaps the one that set the standard for future satire (again, think *Spinal Tap,* but with Rob Reiner instead of Martin Scorsese as the interviewer).

1. ***Woodstock*** (1970)

2. ***Gimme Shelter*** (1970)

3. ***Metallica: Some Kind of Monster*** (2004)

4. ***Don't Look Back*** (1965)

5. ***The Last Waltz*** (1978)

IV.

The Top Five
ROCK BIO-PICS

Bio-pics recount the "true stories" of real-life rockers, and in terms of this form, the five films below enumerate the high points. Oliver Stone's magnum opus, *The Doors* turns the disintegration of rocker Jim Morrison into the stuff of tragic opera, while *Sid and Nancy* takes a decidedly more gritty look at the fall of the self-destructive Sid Vicious.

Walk the Line (the story of Johnny Cash) is a surprisingly upbeat bio-pic (a rarity, really, in this genre), while *What's Love Got to Do With It* boasts genuine moral uplift: it's a story of Tina Turner's battle not just to achieve stardom, but independence and self-esteem. Finally, *Great Balls of Fire* (the story of Jerry Lee Lewis) is an underrated treasure from the late 1980s featuring a wild performance by Dennis Quaid.

1. ***The Doors*** (1991)

2. ***Sid and Nancy*** (1986)

3. ***Walk the Line*** (2005)

4. ***What's Love Got to Do With It*** (1993)

5. ***Great Balls of Fire*** (1989)

V.

The Top Five
ROCK SOUNDTRACK MOVIES

A great rock soundtrack can do wonders for a movie. It can complement, undercut or contrast with the imagery unfolding on screen, and thereby forever forge mental connections between a song and a scene in the minds of viewers.

The films below all achieve a delicate alchemy. You can't think of the movie *without* the rock music. *Boogie Nights* deploys cheery 1970s tunes to depict its porno "family," a world that turns ugly and cynical (along with the music) at the dawn of the cocaine-addled 1980s.

George Lucas's *American Graffiti* remembers the innocent, pre-Vietnam War era of cruising, and chronicles that time with the music of the director's youth. It's virtually impossible to think of *The Graduate* without thinking of Simon & Garfunkel, and *Easy Rider*'s soundtrack captures the freedom of an unconventional life on the road.

Finally, *The Return of the Living Dead* is the first and only "punk" zombie movie, and like that movement in rock music, is the most nihilistic horror to emerge from the Reagan Eighties. The characters in the film are Mohawked punks who meet their grim deaths while hard- driving rock blasts on the soundtrack.

1. ***Boogie Nights*** (1997)

2. ***American Graffiti*** (1973)

3. ***The Graduate*** (1968)

4. ***Easy Rider*** (1969)

5. ***Return of the Living Dead*** (1985)

VI.

The Top Five
ELVIS PRESLEY MOVIES
(either starring Elvis or
concerning Elvis)

A healthy percentage of the movies covered in this book either star Elvis, document his rise and fall, showcase his concerts, or fictionalize his life and transform him into a hero, a good father, a god, and an American icon.

By my reckoning, these are the finest silver-screen efforts with or about the King of Rock.

1. *King Creole* (1958)

2. *Bubba Ho-tep* (2002)

3. *Follow That Dream* (1962)

4. *Kid Galahad* (1962)

5. *Jailhouse Rock* (1958)

VII.

The Top Five
CHEESIEST ROCK MOVIES
(any genre) OF ALL TIME

Something really horrible happened in rock culture during the 1980s. Too many examples of the genre suddenly came off as...well, cheesy; and truth be told, bizarre. If the films below aren't the worst rock films ever made, they certainly qualify as the campiest.

Honorable mentions would include *Xanadu* (another Eighties flick) and 1978's Bee Gees fest, *Sgt. Pepper's Lonely Hearts Club Band*.

It's hard to know which film on this list is the worst, but the disco/spandex adventures of The Village People in the musical *Can't Stop the Music*, and the pseudo-religious, futurist *The Apple* are certainly contenders.

Meanwhile, rounding out the worst of the worst, Prince (*Under the Cherry Moon*), John Travolta (*Staying Alive*), and Rick Springfield (*Hard to Hold*) vie for the title of most embarrassing performance.

1. ***Can't Stop the Music*** (1980)

2. ***The Apple*** (1980)

3. ***Under the Cherry Moon*** (1983)

4. ***Staying Alive*** (1983)

5. ***Hard to Hold*** (1982)

ENDNOTES

Introduction

1. Michael Campbell and James Brody. *Rock and Roll: An Introduction*. Schirmer, 1999 page 7.

2. Michael Campbell and James Brody. *Rock and Roll: An Introduction*. Schirmer, 1999 page 7.

The Encyclopedia: A-Z

1. Louise Stanton. "Absolute Beginners." *Films in Review*. August–September 1986, page 424.

2. Wayne Robins. "AC/DC: Let There Be Rock." *Newsday*. May 25, 1982, Part II, page 20.

3. Ed Naha. *New York Post*. May 24, 1982, page 26.

4. Marc Savlov. "Airheads." *The Austin Chronicle*. August 12, 1994.
   http://austinchronicle.com/gbase/Calendar/Film/?Film=oid%3A138511

5. Mike La Salle. "Heavy Metal Airheads Actually Has Substance." *The San Francisco Chronicle*, January 13, 1995, page D-16.

6. Roger Ebert. "Alice's Restaurant." RogerEbert.com.
   http://rogerebert.suntimes.com/apps/pbcs.d11/articles?AID=/19691111/REVIEWS/911110301/1023

7. "Almost Famous." *Rolling Stone magazine*. September 28, 2000, page 64.

8. Stanley Kauffmann. "Almost Famous." *The New Republic*. September 25, 2000, page 30.

9. David Ansen. *Newsweek*. September 18, 2000, page 16.

10. Ty Burr, Glenn Kenny, Greg Kilday, Steve Simels. "The Big Pictures: America's 100 All-Time Favorite Films." *Entertainment Weekly*. April 29, 1994, page 40.

11. David Shirley. *The History of Rock and Roll*. Franklin Watts, October 1997, page 11.

12. Owen Gleiberman. "*Backbeat*." *Entertainment Weekly*. April 29, 1994.

13. Marshall Crenshaw. *Hollywood Rock*. Agincourt Press, 1994, page 27.

14. Vincent Canby. "The Buddy Holly Story." *The New York Times*. July 19, 1978, page C14.

15. Janet Maslin. "*Can't Stop The Music*."*The New York Times*, June 20, 1980, page C12.

16. Ira Mayer. *The New York Post*. February 10, 1984, page 43.

17. Wayne Robins. *Newsday*. February 10, 1984, Part II, page 7.

18. Stephanie Zacharek. "*Coyote Ugly*," *Salon.com*. August 4, 2000.
http://archive.salon.com/ent/movies/review/2000/08/04/coyote_ugly/index.html?CP=IMD&DN=110

19. Michael Musto. *Saturday Review*. May–June 1985, page 83.

20. Richard Schickel. *Time*. April 1, 1985, page 70.

21. Mike Villano. *Billboard*. August 14, 1999, page 19.

22. D.A. Pennebaker. "Liner Notes." *Don't Look Back*. Warner Reprise Video.

23. Kevin Cahillane. "Look Back in Laughter: Essential Takes on New Jersey." *The New York Times*, May 22, 2005, page NJ11.

24. Archer Winston. *The New York Post*. April 15, 1983, page 33.

25. Philip French. *Guardian Unlimited*. May 23, 2004.
http://filmguardian.co.uk/News_story/Critic_Review/Observer_Review/0,, 1222538,00.html

26. Erin Free. "Garage Days." *Hollywood Reporter*. October 21, 2002.
http://www.hollywoodreporter.com/thr/reviews/review)diplay.jsp?/no_content_id=1745460

27. Elliott Stein. *The Village Voice*, May 22–28, 2002
http://www.villagevoice.com/film/0221,stein/34973, 20.html

28. Kevin Thomas. *The Los Angeles Times*. August 8, 1983, Calendar, Page 3.

29. Patrick Goldstein. *The Los Angeles Times*. October 26, 1984, Calendar, page 10.

30. David Denby. *New York*. February 29, 1988, page 117.

31. David Sterritt. *The Christian Science Monitor*. February 26, 1988, page 22.

32. Michael Wilmington. *The Los Angeles Times*. September 30, 1988, Calendar, page 10.

33. Lynn Darling. *Newsday*. September 30, 1988, page 5.

34. Jumana Farouky. "*Hedwig and the Angry Inch*: Directed by John Cameron Mitchell." *Time International*, September 17, 2001, page 73.

35. Ben Wener. "Rock musicals don't get much better than *Hedwig*." *Orange Country Register*, January 8, 2002.

36. John Simon, "*The Hunger*," *National Review*, June 24, 1983, pages 764-765.

37. Janet Maslin, "*Idolmaker* Creates a Teen Star." *The New York Times*. November 14, 1980, page C8.

38. Michael Wilmington. *The Los Angeles Times*. October 6, 1988, Calendar page 1.

39. Julian Petley. *Monthly Film Bulletin*. November 1988, page 332.

40. Susan Wloszczyna. "The anti-conformist message of '*Josie*' misses." *U.S.A. Today*. April 11, 2001. http://www.usatoday.com/life/movies/2001-04—11-josie-and-the-pussycats-review.htm

41. David Edelstein. "Plump It Up." *Slate*. April 13, 2001. http://www.slate.com/id/104231

42. David Sterritt. *The Christian Science Monitor*. July 24, 1987, page 19.

43. Michael Buckley. *Films in Review*. October 1987, page 494.

44. Josh Goldfein. "Band of Outsiders." *The Village Voice*. April 10—16, 2002. http://www.villagevoice.com

45. Rita Kempley. "Darkness in the '*Light of Day*.'" *The Washington Post*. February 6, 1987, page 23.

46. David E. Thigpen. "The Sweet Sound of *Magnolia*: Aimee Mann's tale of romantic distress finds emotionally satisfying release on a vibrant new soundtrack." *Time*. December 19, 1999, page 108.

47. Vincent Canby. *The New York Times*. November 2, 1974, page 16.

48. Gerry Marta. *Films in Review*. October 1982, page 491.

49. David Denby. *New York*. August 23, 1982, page 88.

50. Ronnie Scheib. *Daily Variety*. September 29, 2003, page 44.

51. Carla Hay. "Director Hackford on the genius of 'Ray.'" *Billboard*, November 20, 2004, page 18.

52. Ann Marie Cruz. "Plight Unseen." *People Weekly*. May 31, 2004, page 122.

53. Aldore D. Collier. "Jamie Foxx gives awesome performance in acclaimed movie 'Ray.'" *Jet*. November 1, 2004, page 52.

54. Philip Wuntch. "'*Ray*.'" *Knight Ridder/Tribune News Service*. October 29, 2004, page K3371.

55. Janet Maslin. *The New York Times*. June 13, 1980, page C8.

56. J. Hoberman. *Village Voice*. August 6, 1985, page 56.

57. Danny Peary. *Cult Movies*. Delacorte Press, 1981, page 299.

58. Michael Wilmington. "*Satisfaction* Gets Caught in a Time Warp." *The Los Angeles Times*. February 17, 1988, page 7.

59. Joel Isaac Frady. "North Carolina State U: Film Review: '*The Singing Detective*' a topsy-turvy turn of psyche." *The America's Intelligence Wire*. November 25, 2003.

60. Dafna Lernish. "*Spice World*: constructing femininity in the popular way." *Popular Music and Society*. February 2003, page 17.

61. Dafna Lernish. "*Spice World*: constructing femininity in the popular way." *Popular Music and Society*, February 2003, page 17.

62. Harry Medved with Randy Dreyfuss. *The Fifty Worst Films of All Time*. Warner Books, 1978, page 221.

63. David Denby. *New York*. August 1, 1983, page 54.

64. Vincent Canby. "Excess, Excitement and Many Decibels." *The New York Times*. March 30, 1975, II, page 13.

65. George Meyer. "Getting Ziggy Wid'It: '*Velvet Goldmine*' is the History of Glam Rock in the Gloaming—With a Personal Twist." *Sarasota Herald Tribune*. November 27 1998, page 18.

66. Jonathan Romney. "*Velvet Goldmine*." *The New Statesman*. October 23, 1998, pages 35-36.

67. Richard Cromelin. *The Los Angeles Times*. December 23, 1983, Calendar, page 5.

SELECTED BIBLIOGRAPHY

Books

Campbell, Michael and James Brody. *Rock and Roll: An Introduction*. Schirmer, 1999.

Crenshaw, Marshall. *Hollywood Rock*. Agincourt Press, 1994.

Ehrenstein, David and Bill Reed. *Rock on Film*. G.P. Putnam's Sons, 1982.

Giannetti, Louis. *Understanding Movies, Fifth Edition*. Prentice Hall, 1990.

Grossberger, Lewis. *Turn that Down! A Hysterical History of Rock, Roll, Pop, Soul, Punk, Funk, Rap, Grunge, Mowtown, Metal, Disco, Techno and Other Forms of Musical Aggression Over the Ages*. Emmis Books, 2006.

Katz, Ephraim. *The Film Encyclopedia: The Most Comprehensive Encyclopedia of World Cinema in a Single Volume*. Harper and Row Publishers, 1979.

Mayo, Mike. *Videohound's Horror Show: 999 Hair—Raising, Hellish, and Humorous Movies*. Visible Ink Press, 1999.

Medved, Harry, with Randy Dreyfuss. *The Fifty Worst Films of All Time*. Warner Books, 1978.

Muir, John Kenneth. *Best in Show: The Films of Christopher Guest and Company*. Applause Theatre and Cinema Books, 2004.

Muir, John Kenneth. *Singing a New Tune: The Rebirth of the Modern Film Musical From Evita to De-Lovely and Beyond*. Applause Theatre and Cinema Books, 2005.

Peary, Danny. *Cult Movies*. Delacorte Press, 1981.

Sandahl, Linda J. *Rock Films: A Viewer's Guide to Three Decades of Musicals*, *Concerts, Documentaries and Soundtracks*, *1955–1986*. Facts on File Publications, 1987.

Shirley, David. *The History of Rock and Roll*. Franklin Watts, October 1977.

Taylor, John Russell. *Great Movie Moments*. Crescent Books, New York, 1987.

Wlaschin, Ken. *The Illustrated Encyclopedia of The World's Greatest Movie Stars and Their Films; From 1900 to Present Day*. Harmony Books, 1979.

Zinman, David. *Fifty Grand Movies of the 1960s & 1970s*. Crown Publishers, Inc., New York, 1986.

The Movie Book. Phaidon Press Limited, 2002.

Periodicals and Internet

Adams, Noah. "Review: Movie '*Hedwig and the Angry Inch*.'" *All Things Considered* (NPR), July 20, 2001.

Ansen, David. "A Sprinkling of *Ziggy Stardust*." *Newsweek*, November 9, 1998, page 70.

Berliner, Todd. "The Sounds of Silence: songs in Hollywood Films Since the 1960s—Critical Essay." Style, Spring 2002, pages 1–11.

Bernard, Jami. "*The Singing Detective*." *Knight Ridder/Tribune News Service*, November 3, 2003, page K2566.

Brown, Scott and Downey, Robert Jr. "Downey Fresh: Watching the *Detective*." *Entertainment Weekly*, November 7, 2003, page 53.

Bullock, Marcus. "Treasures of the earth and screen: Todd Haynes' film, *Velvet Goldmine*." *Discourse*, Fall 2002 pages 3–27.

Burr, Ty, Glenn Kenny, Greg Kilday, Steve Simels. "The Big Pictures: America's 100 All-Time Favorite Films." *Entertainment Weekly*, April 29, 1994, page 40.

Cahillane, Kevin. "Look Back in Laughter: Essential Takes on New Jersey." *The New York Times*, May 22, 2005, page NJ11.

Cocks, Jay. "Lindsay Anderson: 1923–1994; in celebration." *Film Comment*, Nov–Dec 1994, pages 7–10.

Collier, Aldore D. "Jamie Foxx gives awesome performance in acclaimed movie '*Ray*." *Jet*, November 1, 2004, page 52.

doCarmo, Stephen N. "Beyond good and evil: mass culture theorized in Todd Haynes' *Velvet Goldmine*." Journal of American and Comparative Cultures, Fall–Winter 2002, pages 395–398.

Ebert, Roger. "*Alice's Restaurant*." RogerEbert.com. http://rogerebert.suntimes.com/apps/pbcs.dll/articles?AID=/19691111/REVIEWS/911110301/1023

Edelstein, David. "*Plump It Up*." *Slate*, April 13, 2001. http://www.slate.com/id/104231

Eisner, Ken. "Seattle embraces new '*Love's*'." *Daily Variety*, May 15, 2000, page 72.

Farouky, Jumana. "*Hedwig and the Angry Inch*: Directed by John Cameron Mitchell." *Time International*, September 17, 2001, page 73.

Fleming, Michael. "Gumshoe thriller at Icon." *Daily Variety*, February 26, 2002, pages 1–2.

Fleming, Michael. "*Detective* gets its girl." *Daily Variety*, April 4, 2002, pages 1–2.

Frady, Joel Isaac. "*The Singing Detective*—a topsy-turvy turn of psyche."*America's Intelligence Wire*, November 25, 2003.

Free, Erin. "*Garage Days*." *Hollywood Reporter*. October 21, 2002.
http://www.hollywoodreporter.com/thr/reviews/review/diplay.jsp?/no_content_id=1745460

French, Philip. Guardian Unlimited. May 23, 2004.
http://filmguardian.co.uk/News_story/Critic_Review/Observer_Review/0,,1222538,00.html

Fuller, Graham. "*Moulin Rouge* gives the screen musical a make over." *Knight Ridder/Tribune News Service*, May 11, 2001 page K1622.

Gardner, Chris. "Par Classics books rights to '*Detective*.'" *Hollywood Reporter,* February 7, 2003, pages 1–2.

Gleiberman, Owen. "Backbeat." *Entertainment Weekly*, April 29, 1994.

Gleiberman, Owen. "Ballroom Blitz: In the frenetic musical *Moulin Rouge*, Nicole Kidman and Ewan McGregor look for love in a Paris gone pop." *Entertainment Weekly*, May 25, 2001, page 48.

Goldfein, Josh. "*Band of Outsiders*." *The Village Voice*, April 10–16, 2002.

Gutman, Barry. "*Hedwig and the Angry Inch*." *Video Business*, October 29, 2001, page 17.

Harvey Dennis. "*Hedwig and the Angry Inch*." *Variety*, January 29, 2001, page 48.

Hewitt, Chris. "*The Singing Detective*." *Knight Ridder/Tribune News Service*, November 6, 2003, page K4150.

Honeycutt, Kirk. "*The Singing Detective*." *Hollywood Reporter*, January 21, 2003, pages 89–90.

Kauffmann, Stanley. "*Almost Famous*." *The New Republic*. September 25, 2000, page 30.

Kinder, Marsha. "*Moulin Rouge*." *Film Quarterly*, Spring 2002, pages 52–60.

La Salle, Mike. "Heavy Metal Airheads Actually Has Substance." *The San Francisco Chronicle*, January 13, 1995, page D-16.

Maslin, Janet. "Can't Stop the Music." *The New York Times*, June 20, 1980, page C12.

Savlov, Marc. "Airheads." *The Austin Chronicle*, August 12, 1994.
http://austinchronicle.com/gbase/Calendar/Film/?Film=oid%3A138511

Simon, John. "The Hunger," *National Review*, June 24, 1983, pages 764–765.

Stein, Elliott. *The Village Voice*, May 22–28, 2002.
http://www.villagevoice.com/film/0221,stein/34973,20.html

Villano, Mike. *Billboard* magazine. August 14, 1999, page 19.

Wlosczcyna, Susan. "The anti-conformist message of 'Josie' misses," *U.S.A. Today*. April 11, 2001.

> http://www.usatoday.com/life/movies/2001-04—11-josie-and-the-pussycats-review.htm

Zacharek, Stephanie. "*Coyote Ugly*," Salon.com. August 4, 2000.

> http://archive.salon.com/ent/movies/review/2000/08/04/coyote_ugly/index.html?CP=IMD&DN=110

"*Almost Famous*." *Rolling Stone* magazine. September 28, 2000, page 64.

INDEX

ABBA: The Movie (film), 3

Absolute Beginners (film), 3–5;
and mod culture, 4;
rock, and civil rights movement, 4

"Absolute Beginners," 5

AC/DC, 147

AC/DC: Let There Be Rock (documentary), 5

Ackland, Joss, 36

Aerosmith, xviii, 52, 249, 299

Affleck, Ben, 68

Airheads (film), 5–6, 67

Alice's Restaurant (film), xiii, 6, 8, 293

Allen, Debbie, 98

Allen, Nancy, 152

"All You Need Is Love," 316

Almost Famous (film), 9–10, 99, 228, 235, 317, 323, 325; bus
trip in, 50

Alone in the Dark (film), 10

Alvarado, Trini, 243, 276

American Graffiti (film), xiv, xviii, 10–11, 13, 18, 52, 67, 152,
193, 220, 250, 329

American Hot Wax (film), 13–14, 67, 228

American Idol (television show), xiii

American Pop (film), 14–15

Americathon (film), 15, 185

Anderson, Carl, 163

Anderson, Lindsay, 199, 200

Anderson, Paul Thomas, 44, 45, 184

Andress, Ursula, 91

"Angry Inch," 144

Angus, David, 147

Anka, Paul, 119, 178

animated films, xvii

animation, 15–16

Aniston, Jennifer, 235

Annis, Francesca, 288

Ann-Margret, 277, 279, 294

"Another Brick in the Wall," 206–7

Ansara, Michael, 139

Ant, Adam, 79

Apollo Theatre, 16

The Apple (film), 16–17, 331

Armageddon (film), xviii

Apted, Michael, 46

Arkins, Robert, 59

Arkush, Allan, 229, 230, 232, 233, 293

Arquette, Rosanna, 70, 183

Ash, Leslie, 220

Ashby, Hal, 178

At Folsom Prison (recording), 296

Aubrey, Juliet, 264

authority, 107;
    as enemy, 18;
    in Elvis Presley films, 18;
    and hair, 132;
    and rock, 22;
    and Vietnam War, 293

Avalon, Frankie, 21, 24, 25, 28, 34, 52, 125, 148, 195, 202

Aykroyd, Dan, 40, 42, 43

Baby Snakes (documentary), 20, 225

Bach, Barbara, 120

Back to the Beach (film), 20–21; cameos in, 21

Backbeat (film), 21–22, 31, 325

backstage antics, 22–23

Bacon, Kevin, 107

"Bad to the Bone," 56

bad fathers, 23

Badham, John, 245

Baez, Joan, 71, 74, 305

Bakshi, Ralph, 14, 15

Baldwin, Alec, 127

Bale, Christian, 292

Bancroft, Anne, 123

The Band, 174, 175

Barty, Billy, 139

Basinger, Kim, 298

Bassett, Angela, 265, 286, 300–1

Bateman, Justine, 98, 243, 250

Bates, Alan, 240

battle of the bands competition, 23, 197

Beach Ball (film), 25

Beach Blanket Bingo (film), 25, 27, 185

Beach Boys, 27, 192

The Beach Boys: An American Band (documentary), 27–28

beach party movies, 24–25

Beach Party (film), 28

Beals, Jennifer, 46, 104

Beatlemania (film), 22, 28–29, 31

Beatles, xii, xiv, 15, 22, 29, 31–32, 60, 134, 145, 152, 153, 177, 178, 189, 249, 321;
    on *Ed Sullivan Show*, 83

The Beatniks (film), 32–33, 64

Beatty, Warren, 281

Beavis and Butthead Do America (film), 33

Beck, Michael, 16, 310, 312

Bee Gees, 245, 249, 263

Bello, Maria, 63

Belushi, John, 40, 42–43

Be My Guest (film), 24

Benton, Jerome, 214, 216, 288

Berkoff, Steven, 288

Berlinger, Joe, 186, 187

Berry, Chuck, 57, 177, 236

Big Bopper (J. P. Richardson), 49, 172

The Big Chill (film), 33–34

Bigelow, Kathryn, 265

Bikini Beach (film), 34–35

Billboard magazine, 36–37

Bill Haley and His Comets, xii, 37, 77, 228, 229;
on *Ed Sullivan Show*, 83

Bill & Ted's Bogus Journey (film), 36;
battle of the bands in, 23; *Billboard* in, 37

Bill & Ted's Excellent Adventure (film), 35–36, 99;
bad fathers in, 23

bio-pics, xvii

Bixby, Bill, 58, 92, 258

The Blackboard Jungle (film), xii, 11, 37, 39, 228

Black, Jack, xi, 23, 146, 247

Blackman, Joan, 40, 167

Blair, Linda, 238, 239

Blame It on the Night (film), 39

"Blueberry Hill," 255

Blue Hawaii (film), 40

The Blues Brothers (film), 40, 42

The Blues Brothers 2000 (film), 42–43; battle of bands in, 23

The Bodyguard (film), 43

"Bongo Rock," 4

Bon Jovi, Jon, 44, 147

Bono (Paul Hewson), 290

"Bony Maroni," 56

Boogie Nights (film), 44–45, 184, 223, 225, 239, 329

Bostwick, Barry, 238

Bowie, David, xiv, 4, 5, 45, 147, 150, 238, 319

"Brand New Key," 239

Brandon, Michael, 104

break-ups, 45–46, 275; in *The Buddy Holly Story*, 49

Breck, Peter, 32

Brennan, Eileen, 104

Breton, Michele, 204

The Bride (film), 46

Bring on the Night (documentary), 46, 265

Broomfield, Nick, 169, 170

Brown, Bruce, 96

Bubba Ho-tep (film), 47, 92, 101, 330

The Buddy Holly Story (film), 16, 45, 47, 49, 83, 172, 299

Burns, George, 249

Buscemi, Steve, 6

Busey, Gary, 49

bus trips, 50

Buttram, Pat, 241

Byrne, David, 265

Calloway, Cab, 42

Camelot, 52

cameos, xvii, 52

Campbell, Bruce, 47, 92

Canned Heat, 192

Can't Stop the Music (film), 52, 53, 55, 238, 331

Carey, Mariah, 121

Carlin, George, 35

Carney, Art, 228

Carpenter, John, 56

Carradine, John, 189, 190

Carrere, Tia, 297, 298

Carter, June, 296

Carter, Nell, 132

Carvey, Dana, 297, 298

Cash, Johnny, 71, 92, 102, 127, 296, 328

Caulfield, Maxwell, 126

Celebration at Big Sur (documentary), 55

Chadwick, June, 272, 317

Change of Habit (film), 55–56

Channing, Stockard, 125

Cheap Trick, 230

Checker, Chubby, 177

Christine (film), 56

Chuck Berry: Hail! Hail! Rock 'n' Roll (documentary), 57

circular logic, 57–58

Clambake (film), 58, 91

Clapton, Eric, 174

Clark, Candy, 11, 193

Clarkson, Kelly, 321

classics: as well-versed in, 299

Cobain, Kurt, 169, 170, 317

Cobb, Bill, 270

Coffey, Scott, 243

Coffield, Peter, 276

Collette, Toni, 292

"Come Together," 249

The Commitments (film), 59–60, 123, 261, 325

The Compleat Beatles (documentary), 60

The Concert for Bangladesh (documentary), xiv, 31, 61, 209

Conn, Didi, 125

Connors, Mike, 251

Contino, Dick, 67

Coogan, Steve, 283

Cook, Paul, 100, 101

Cook, Rachael Leigh, 165

Cooper, Alice (Vincent Damon Furnier), 52, 61–62, 147, 190, 228, 249, 297–98

Coppola, Francis Ford, 11

Corman, Roger, 229, 230

Coscarelli, Don, 47

Costner, Kevin, 33, 43, 208, 283

Country Joe & the Fish, 192

cover art, 62

Cox, Alex, 252

Coyote Ugly (film), 62–63

Critters (film), 63–64

Crowe, Cameron, 9, 10

Crudup, Billy, 9, 10

Cruise, Tom, 184

Cry-Baby (film), 64–65

"Cry, Cry, Cry," 296

Culkin, Macauley, 43

Cumming, Alan, 165, 259

Cummings, Bob, 28

Curry, Tim, 238, 276

Daddy-O (film), 67–68

Dafoe, Willem, 64, 266

Daltry, Roger, 277

dance contests, 68

"Dancing Queen," 3

D'Angelo, Beverly, 132

Daniels, Phil, 220

Danko, Rick, 58, 175

Danning, Sybil, 149

Danova, Cesare, 294

"Darling Nikki," 217

Davidson, Martin, 84, 87, 88

Davies, Ray, 4

Davis, Geena, 183

Day, Morris, 124, 214

Dazed and Confused (film), 62, 68

The Decline of Western Civilization (film), 69, 319

dee jays, 67

Deezen, Eddie, 152

Delaney, Charles, 32

De Matteo, Drea, 209

Demme, Jonathan, 265

Deneuve, Catherine, 150

De Palma, Brian, 206

Depp, Johnny, 64

Dern, Bruce, 211

Desperately Seeking Susan (film), xiv, 70, 183

Detroit Rock City (film), 71–72, 223, 254

"Devil with a Blue Dress On," 14

Diamond, Neil, 161, 162, 174

Dirty Dancing (film), xiv, 52, 72–73

Dirty Dancing 2: Havana Nights (film), 68, 73

disco, xiii

Divine, 133

Dixon, Donna, 298

Dogs in Space (film), 74

Domino, Fats, 177

Donovan, 76

Don't Knock the Rock (film), xii, 77

Don't Look Back (documentary), xii, xiii, xiv, 69, 71, 74, 76–77, 185, 189, 209, 261, 271, 327;
circular logic in, 58

The Doors, 83

The Doors (film), xvii, 45, 49, 77–78, 83, 189, 208, 223, 225, 328;
property, destruction of in, 71

Dorff, Stephen, 22, 111

Downey, Robert, Jr., 254

"Dream Weaver," 297, 299

Dreyfuss, Richard, 11, 67

Dr. John, 175

Drop Dead Rock (film), 79, 99, 138

Dylan, Bob, xviii, 58, 61, 69, 71, 74, 76, 174, 175, 177, 189, 203, 209, 261, 293

Easy Rider (film), 81, 329

Eddie and the Cruisers (film), 83, 84, 86–88, 301

Eddie and the Cruisers II: Eddie Lives! (film), 88–89, 325

The Ed Sullivan Show (television series), 83

Eegah! (film), 89–90, 147

Egan, Richard, 180

Eilber, Janet, 136

"Eleanor Rigby," 316

Electric Light Orchestra (ELO), 312

Elvis: That's the Way It Is (documentary), xvii, 92, 93–94

Elvis on Tour (film), 92–93

Empire Records (film), 94–95

The Endless Summer (film), 95–96

Entwistle, John, 130, 303

Eric Burdon and the Animals, 192

Erickson, Leif, 241

Evita (film), 183

Fabares, Shelley, 58, 117, 260

Fame (film), 98

family ties, 98–99

Fantasia (film), 15

Farina, Sandra, 249

Farr, Jamie, 39

Feldman, Corey, 261

Feldshuh, Tovah, 153

fictional bands, 99

Fields, Tony, 280

Fiennes, Ralph, 265

Fierstein, Harvey, 133

The Filth and the Fury (documentary), xviii, 62, 100–1, 129, 184, 225, 317

54 (film), 99–100

Finding Graceland (film), xviii, 92, 101–2, 123

Finley, William, 206

first marriages, 102

Fishburne, Laurence, 301

The Five Heartbeats (film), 16, 45, 62, 102–3, 185, 223, 225, 267, 301;
bad fathers in, 23;
Billboard in, 37

Flashdance (film), xiii, 103–4

FM (film), 52, 67, 104–5

Follow that Dream (film), 40, 91, 105–6, 168, 330

Fonda, Bridget, 102, 250

Fonda, Peter, 81

Footloose (film), xiii, 106–7;
    authority in, 107;
    bad fathers in, 23

Ford, Glenn, 37

Ford, Harrison, 11

Forman, Milos, 132

Forrest, Frederic, 240

Fox, James, 4, 204

Fox, Michael J., 98, 179

Foxx, Jamie, 224

Frampton, Peter, 249

Francis, Anne, 39

Francis, Connie, 236

Franklin, Aretha, 43

Fraser, Brendan, 6

Freed, Alan, 13, 67, 77, 172, 189, 236

Freeman, Joan, 241

Fubar (film), 107–8

Fugit, Patrick, 9

Fun in Acapulco (film), 91, 108–9, 185

Funicello, Annette, 21, 24, 25, 28, 34, 148, 149, 195, 202

Gaillard, Slim, 5

Gallagher, Peter, 153, 154

Gambon, Michael, 256

Garage Days (film), 111

Garber, Victor, 121

Gardenas, Elsa, 91, 108

The Gate (film), 111

Geldof, Bob, 207, 260

George, Christopher, 124

Gershon, Gina, 209, 210, 286

Get Back! (documentary), 112

Get Crazy! (film), 112–13

The Ghost in the Invisible Bikini (film), 113–14

Gibb, Barry, 125

Gibson, Mel, 254

G.I. Blues (film), 114

Gifford, Gloria, 272, 275

Giles, Sandra, 67

Gilmour, George, 16

Gimme Shelter (documentary), xii, xiv, xvii, 114–15, 117, 164, 209, 271, 285, 305, 327

Girl Happy (film), 117

Girls! Girls! Girls! (film), 40, 91, 108, 118

Girls Town (film), 118–19

Give My Regards to Broad Street (film), 31, 119–20, 225

Glitter (film), 121

Godard, Jean-Luc, 267

Godspell (film), 121, 123

Goldblum, Jeff, 269

Goldeneye (film), 286

Goodwin, Ginnifer, 296

Goodwin, Laurel, 91, 118

Gordon, Keith, 56

Gorney, Karen Lynn, 245

Graceland, 123, 275, 290

The Graduate (film), 123, 329

Graduation Day (film), 124

Graffiti Bridge (film), xviii, 124–25, 210

Graham, Gerrit, 206

Graham, Heather, 239, 251

Grant, Richard E., 260

Grease (film), xviii, 52, 65, 125

Grease 2 (film), 126

Great Balls of Fire (film), 92, 102, 123, 126–27, 223, 328;
    Billboard in, 37
"Great Balls of Fire," 4
The Great Rock 'n' Roll Swindle (film), 16, 31, 50, 100, 128–29,
    136, 184–85, 252
Grey, Jennifer, 72
Grossman, Albert, 76, 185
Guest, Christopher, 272
guitar: as sacred object, 129
Guthrie, Arlo, 8
Guttenberg, Steve, 53, 238

Hackford, Taylor, 57, 153, 154, 224
Hair (film), xviii, 132, 144, 293;
    bad fathers in, 23
Hairspray (film), 52, 68, 133–34, 138
Haley, Bill, 228
Hall, Arch, Jr., 89, 147, 303
Hall, Jerry, 178
Hanks, Tom, 183, 185, 269, 270
Happy Days (television series), 13
A Hard Day's Night (film), xii, 31, 119, 128, 134, 136, 145,
    189, 259, 321, 324;
    and backstage antics, 23;
    press conference in, 208;
    as seminal, 134
Hard to Hold (film), 136, 138, 331
Harper, Jessica, 206
Harrison, George, 29, 31, 61, 177, 209, 249, 314
Harry, Deborah, 52, 79, 138, 226, 228, 234, 243
Hart, Dolores, 91, 168, 181
Hart, Ian, 147
Harum Scarum (film), 56, 91, 138–39, 181
Hayek, Salma, 99
Haynes, Todd, 292, 293

Head (film), xiii, 52, 139, 141
Heartbreak Hotel (film), xviii, 23, 92, 101, 141–42
"Heartbreak Hotel," 90
Hedwig and the Angry Inch (film), xviii, 99, 142, 144–45, 326
Help! (film), 31, 145
Hemmings, David, 24
Hendra, Tony, 272
Hendrix, Jimi, 14, 16, 71, 130, 163, 192, 224, 307
"He's a Dream," 104
Hesseman, Howard, 15
Heston, Charlton, 298
Hetfield, James, 186
"High School Confidential," 127
High Fidelity (film), 146
Hill, Marianna, 203
Hill, Walter, 266
hip hop films, xiv
The History of Rock and Roll (Shirley), 13
Hollywood Rock (Crenshaw), 24
Hoffman, Dustin, 123
Hoffman, Philip Seymour, 9
Holly, Buddy, 49, 172
Honeymoon in Vegas (film), 92
Hopper, Dennis, 52, 81
The Horror of Party Beach (film), 146
horror rock, 147
The Hours and Times (film), 22, 31, 147–48
House (film), 148
Houston, Whitney, 43
Howard, Ron, 11, 13, 193
Howerd, Frankie, 249
The Howling (film), 149
Howling II: Your Sister Is a Werewolf (film), 149
How to Stuff a Wild Bikini (film), 148–49
Hudson, Kate, 9

Hughes, Finola, 262
The Hunger (film), xiv, xviii, 45, 150, 238
Hutchence, Michael, 74
Hutchens, Will, 58

The Idolmaker (film), 153–54, 185, 189, 228
"I Got Life," 132
Imagine: John Lennon (documentary), 154–55
"Interstellar Overdrive," 211
It Happened at the World's Fair (film), 91, 92, 93, 155–56
"It's Only Make Believe," 255
I Wanna Hold Your Hand (film), 22, 31, 83, 136, 152–53,
        189, 223
Izzard, Eddie, 185

Jack, Wolfman, 67
Jackson, Samuel L., 164
Jagger, Mick, xviii, 115, 178, 204, 209, 321
Jailhouse Rock (film), 91, 118, 158, 160, 330
"Jailhouse Rock," 158, 160
James Bond films: songs in, 160
Janis (documentary), 161
Jarmusch, Jim, 314
Jay and Silent Bob Strike Back (film), 52, 162
The Jazz Singer (film), 161–62
Jeffries, Fran, 139
Jenner, Bruce, 53
Jett, Joan, 98, 179
Jesus Christ Superstar (film), 162–63
Jimi Hendrix (documentary), 163
Jimi Plays Berkeley (documentary), 163–64
John Cafferty and the Beaver Brown Band, 87
John, Elton, 260, 277
Johnny Suede (film), 164
Jones, Carolyn, 91, 168

Jones, Christopher, 304
Jones, Steve, 100, 128
Joplin, Janis, 161
Jordan, Will, 83
Josie and the Pussycats (film), 164–65, 225
Joy Division, 284
"Jungle Love," 162

Karras, Alex, 104
Katt, William, 148
Katzman, Sam, 229
Keaton, Buster, 27, 149, 202
Keener, Catherine, 164
"Keep a Knockin'," 56
Keitel, Harvey, 101
Keith, David, 142
Kelly, Gene, 310
Kelly, Roz, 197
Kensit, Patsy, 4
Kid Galahad (film), xvii, 40, 91, 105, 167, 168, 330
Kidman, Nicole, 194
The Kids Are Alright (documentary), xv
Kiel, Richard, 89
Kiley, Richard, 39
Kilmer, Val, 78, 225, 280
King Creole (film), xii, xvii, 40, 56, 91, 105, 167–68, 330
Kirk, Tommy, 114, 202
KISS, 254
Korman, Harvey, 15
Kurt & Courtney (film), xiii, 169–70, 317

La Bamba (film), 172
Ladies and Gentlemen, the Fabulous Stains (film), 99, 172, 174
Lake, Ricki, 133
Land, Paul, 153

Landau, Martin, 10

Landis, John, 42, 43

"Landlords and Tenants," 4

Lane, Diane, 174, 266

Langdon, Sue Ann, 241

Lange, Hope, 304

Lansbury, Angels, 40

La Paglia, Anthony, 94, 95

La Rosa, Julius, 178

The Last Waltz (documentary), xiv, xvii, 69, 112, 174–75, 177, 180, 226, 299, 327; circular logic in, 58, 175

Laughton, Charles, 83

Led Zeppelin, 258

Lee, Christopher, 149

Lee, Sheryl, 22

Lehman, Michael, 6

Le Mat, Paul, 11, 193, 234

Lembeck, Harvey, 21, 24, 25, 28, 34, 114, 149, 195, 202

Leon, 102

Lennon, John, 29, 31, 60, 136, 154, 155, 177, 314, 321

Leno, Jay, 14

Lester, Richard, 112, 134, 145

Let the Good Times Roll (documentary), 177

Let It Be (documentary), 31, 60, 177–78

"Let's Go Crazy," 217

Let's Rock (film), 178

Let's Spend the Night Together (documentary), 178

Lewis, Jerry Lee, 4, 13, 92, 102, 126, 127, 296, 297, 328

Lewis, Juliette, 265, 266

Light of Day (film), 44, 45, 99, 179

"Light of Day," 179

"Light My Fire," 78, 225

lineage: of bands, 180

Linklater, Richard, 247

Lithgow, John, 23, 107

Little, Cleavon, 104

Little Richard (Richard Penniman), 77

Live and Let Die (film), 31, 98

Locane, Amy, 6, 64

Lockwood, Gary, 92, 304

Lopez, Jennifer, 104, 248

Los Lobos, 172

Loughlin, Lori, 21

Love, Courtney, 169, 317

Love's Labour's Lost (film), 5

Lewis, Jerry Lee, 4, 13, 92, 102, 126, 127, 296, 297, 328

Love Me Tender (film), 90, 158, 180–81

"Love Reign O'er Me," 220

Loving You (film), 158, 181

Lowe, Rob, 297, 298

Lucas, George, 11, 115

"Lucy in the Sky with Diamonds," 316

Luhrmann, Baz, 194, 265

Lupus, Peter, 195

Lymon, Frankie, 236

Lynde, Paul, 185

Lyne, Adrian, 103

MacLachlan, Kyle, 78

Macy, William H., 184

Madigan, Amy, 266

Mad Max: Beyond Thunderdome (film), 285

Madonna, xiv, 70, 76, 183, 281, 283

Malkin, Vicki, 139

Mancuso, Nick, 39

Mangold, James, 297

Mangoli, Albert, 214–17, 253

Magnolia (film), 44, 183–84

Mailer, Stephen, 64

Mamas and the Papas, 192

managers: in rock movies, 184–85, 275

Mann, Aimee, 44, 184

Mantegna, Joe, 6

The Man Who Fell to Earth (film), 45, 203

Martin, Steve, 249

Matthau, Walter, 168

Maynard, Ian, 79

Masekela, Hugh, 192

Maysles, Albert and David, 115

Mazursky, Paul, 37, 39

McBain, Diane, 260

McBride, Jim, 127

McCartney, Linda, 120

McCartney, Paul, 29, 31, 60, 112, 119, 120, 177, 249, 314

McConaughey, Matthew, 68

McCrea, Jody, 24, 28, 202

McDormand, Frances, 9

McDowell, Malcolm, 60, 112, 113, 199

McGregor, Ewan, 194, 292

McGuire, Kim, 64

McIntire, Tim, 13

McKean, Michael, 6, 133, 179, 225, 272

McKenzie, Scott, 192

McKern, Leo, 145

McLaren, Malcolm, 100, 128, 129, 184

Meat Loaf (Marvin Lee Aday), 15, 52, 185, 228, 238, 260

"Memo from Turner," 204

Meredith, Burgess, 262

Metallica: Some Kind of Monster (documentary), xii, xiii, xviii, 45, 130, 186–87, 290, 301, 321, 327;
    circular logic in, 58;
    rock movie clichés in, 186–87

Mewes, Jay, 162

Meyerink, Victoria, 258

Midler, Bette, 161, 240

"Midnight Radio," 144

"Minnie the Moocher," 42

Mirren, Helen, 199

Mister Rock and Roll (film), 187, 189

Mitchell, John Cameron, 144, 145

Mitchell, Joni, 8, 174

mobbed: in rock movies, 189

Mobley, Mary Ann, 139

Mol, Gretchen, 101

The Monkees (television series), 139

The Monster Club (film), 189–90

Monster Dog (film), 190

Monterey Pop (documentary), xiv, 55, 71, 130, 190, 192, 271

Montgomery, Elizabeth, 149

Moon, Keith, 71, 277, 301, 303

Moore, Joanna, 105

Moore, Julianne, 184

Moore, Mary Tyler, 55, 56

Moore, Roger, 259

Morales, Esai, 172

Moranis, Rick, 185

More American Graffiti (film), 13, 193–94, 293

Morris Day and the Time, 52, 162

Morrison, Jim, 83

Morrow, Vic, 37, 168

Moulin Rouge (film), 194–95, 265

movie soundtracks, xiv

Moyle, Allan, 94, 212

Murphy, Johnny, 59

Muscle Beach Party (film), 195

music videos, xiii

Myers, Mike, 99, 129, 297, 298

"My Generation," 192, 301

Mystery Science Theatre 3000 (television series), 33, 119

"My Way," 129, 252

"The Name of the Game," 3
Neeley, Ted, 163
Neeson, Liam, 243
Neon Maniacs (film), 23, 197
Newman, Susan Kendall, 152
Newstead, Jason, 186
Newton-John, Olivia, 16, 62, 125, 310, 312
New Year's Evil (film), 197
Nichols, Mike, 123
Nicholson, Jack, 52, 81, 141, 211, 279
"Night Fever," 245
Night of the Living Dead (film), 252
"Night Moves," 14
Northam, Jeremy, 254
Nouri, Michael, 104
"Nowhere Man," 316

Ocasek, Ric, 133
O'Connell, Eddie, 4
O'Connell, Jerry, 261
O'Donnell, Rosie, 183
Oldman, Gary, 252
Olmos, Edward James, 248
O Lucky Man (film), 199–200, 326
Ono, Yoko, 177, 317. *See also* Yoko factor
Orbach, Jerry, 72
Osbourne, Ozzy, 52, 147, 281

"Paint It Black," 158, 192
Pajama Party (film), 202
Palance, Jack, 10
Pallenberg, Anita, 204
Paltrow, Gwyneth, 251
Paradise, Hawaiian Style (film), 40, 91, 202–3

Paré, Michael, 87, 88, 89, 266
Parker, Alan, 59, 98, 206, 207
Parker, Tom, 90, 271
Pat Garrett & Billy the Kid (film), xviii, 203
Patrick, Robert, 23, 296
Patterson, Chuck, 103
Penn, Arthur, 8
Pennebaker, D. A., 74, 190, 192, 319
Penn, Robin Wright, 254
Perabo, Piper, 63
Performance (film), xviii, 158, 203–4, 293
Perkins, Millie, 304
Perrine, Valerie, 53
Petty, Tom, 208
Pfeiffer, Michelle, 126
Phantom of the Paradise (film), xiv, 204, 206, 225, 236
Phillippe, Ryan, 99
Phillips, Lou Diamond, 172
Phillips, Mackenzie, 11
Phillips, Sam, 127, 296
Phoenix, Joaquin, 71, 297
Phoenix, River, 261
Pink Floyd: The Wall (film), xii, xiv, xvii, 16, 206–7, 305, 326;
    bad fathers in, 23;
    property, destruction of in, 71
Pitt, Brad, 164
Pleasence, Donald, 10, 249
Plummer, Glenn, 265
Poitier, Sidney, 37
The Police, 264
Pop, Iggy, 234
Posey, Parker, 68, 165
The Postman (film), 208
Potter, Dennis, 255

Presley, Elvis, xii, 40, 55, 56, 58, 90–92, 105, 108–9, 114,
    117, 118, 127, 139, 155, 156, 158, 167, 168, 202, 203,
    240, 241, 258, 259, 260, 262, 270, 271, 294, 296, 297,
    303, 304, 321, 330;
    on Ed Sullivan Show, 83;
    impersonators of, 92;
    parody of, 280;
    screen debut of, 180
Presley, Priscilla, 101
press conferences, 208–9
Preston, Billy, 249
Prey for Rock & Roll (film), xiv, 99, 209–10, 286;
    genre conventions in, 210
Price, Alan, 74, 199–200
Price, Vincent, 189, 190
Prince, xiv, 124, 210, 214–17, 253, 254, 288, 321, 331
property: destruction of, 71
Prowse, Juliet, 114
Psych-Out (film), 211
Pump Up the Volume (film), 67, 212
The Punk Rock Movie (documentary), 212
"Purple Haze," 14, 16
Purple Rain (film), xii, xiv, 124, 210, 214–17, 325
"Purple Rain," 214

Quadrophenia (film), 220, 264
Quaid, Dennis, 37, 126, 328
"Queen of the Night," 43
Quinn, Aidan, 70, 183

radio concert ticket contest giveaways, 223
rags-to-riches, 223
Rainbow Bridge (documentary), 223–24
Ramones, 71, 229, 230, 232, 233
Randazzo, Teddy, 236

Ray (film), 224
Rea, Stephen, 264
reality television, xiii
The Real World (television show), xiii
record companies, 225, 275
recording studio sessions, 225, 275
Redding, Otis, 192
Reed, Lou, 234
Reed, Oliver, 277
Reeves, Keanu, 35
Reilly, John C., 184
Reiner, Rob, 228, 261, 327
"R.E.S.P.E.C.T," 43
The Return of the Living Dead (film), 226, 329
Return of the Secaucus 7 (film), 34
"Return to Sender," 118
Rey, Alejandro, 108, 109
Rhodes, Cynthia, 262
Rhys-Meyer, Jonathan, 292
Ribisi, Giovanni, 269
Richards, Keith, 57, 115, 178, 204
Richards, Michael, 6
Richardson, Ralph, 120, 199
Rickles, Don, 27, 195
Ritter, John, 15
road, 226
Roadie (film), 52, 62, 185, 226, 228
Robards, Jason, 184
Roberts, Julia, 243
Robertson, Robbie, 176, 226
Rock Around the Clock (film), xi, 228–29
"Rock Around the Clock," 11, 13, 37, 228, 229
rock: and horror, as inseparable, 147

rock movies: conventions of, xiv; and counterculture, xiii; as documentaries, xvii; as genre, xiii, xiv; as horror, xviii; rock stars in, xviii; as subject, xviii

rock music: as music, of youth, xii

rock musicals, xiv, xviii

rock operas, xiv

Rock, Rock, Rock (film), 236

rock and roll: and cinema, xii

Rock and Roll: An Introduction (Campbell and Brody), xiii

Rock 'n' Roll High School (film), 62, 223, 229–30, 232–33, 324

"Rock 'n' Roll High School," 229

"Rock 'n' Roll Is Here to Stay," 56

Rock and Roll Superhero (documentary), 129–30, 233–34

Rock and Rule (film), 234

rock soundtracks, xviii

Rock Star (film), xiv, 44, 45, 189, 209, 225, 235–36, 261, 317

Rocky Horror Picture Show (film), xiv, 185, 204, 236, 238

Roddam, Franc, 220

Roeg, Nicolas, 203

Roller Boogie (film), 68, 238, 239

roller boogie rock, 238–39

Rolling Stones, 83, 115, 178, 192, 204, 267

Ronstadt, Linda, 52

The Rose (film), xviii, 161, 223, 239–40

Ross, Katharine, 123

Rotten, Johnny (John Lydon), 100, 128, 284

Roustabout (film), 240–41

Rowlands, Gena, 179

Rudolph, Alan, 228

Rundgren, Todd, 229, 230

Rush, Richard, 211

Russell, Ken, 277, 279

Russell, Kurt, 156

The Rutles: All You Need Is Cash, 32

Ryan, Meg, 78, 225

Sade, 4

Sadler, William, 36

Saldana, Theresa, 152

Sandler, Adam, 6

San Francisco (documentary), 211

Sarandon, Susan, 150, 238

Satisfaction (film), 98, 138, 243, 250

Saturday Night Fever (film), xiii, 68, 125, 245, 247

Savage, John, 132

Schacch, Johnathan, 101, 270

Schlatter, Charlie, 141

The School of Rock (film), xi, 247–48; authority in, as enemy, 18; battle of bands in, 23

"School's Out," 62

Schultz, Dwight, 10

Scorsese, Martin, 93, 174, 175, 177, 327

Scott, Bon, 5

Scott, Tom Everett, 185, 269

Seeger, Pete, 8

Selena (film), 248

"Selling Out," 5

Sex Pistols, xviii, 16, 31, 100, 101, 128, 129, 184, 212, 225, 284

Sgt. Pepper's Lonely Hearts Club Band (film), xiii, 31, 62, 225, 248–49, 285, 331; *Billboard* in, 37

Shag: The Movie (film), 52, 68, 250

Shake, Rattle, & Rock (film), 251

Sha Na Na, 125

Shankar, Ravi, 190, 192

Sharkey, Ray, 153, 154

Shearer, Harry, 272, 275

Shigeta, James, 202

Sholder, Jack, 10

Shout! (film), 251

Sid and Nancy (film), 129, 251–52, 328

Sign 'o' the Times (documentary), 210, 253–54

"Silly Love Songs," 120

Simmons, Gene, 52, 67, 72, 147, 254, 281

Simon & Garfunkel, 123, 192, 329

Sinatra, Nancy, 258, 259

Singer, Lori, 107

The Singing Detective (film), 254–56

Slate, Jeremy, 118

Slater, Christian, 10, 67, 212

Slaves to the Underground (film), xiii, 99, 256–57

Slumber Party Massacre 2 (film), 257

Smith, Charlie Martin, 11, 193

Smith, Kevin, 63, 162

Smokler, Peter, 115, 117, 164, 272, 274

Soles, P. J., 229

Somers, Suzanne, 11

"Song to Aging Children," 8

The Song Remains the Same (documentary), 257–58

Speedway (film), 91, 92, 108, 258–59

Sperber, Wendie Jo, 152

Spheeris, Penelope, 69, 297

Spice Girls, 50, 259, 260

Spice World (film), 50, 136, 185, 259–60

Spinout (film), 260

Springfield, Rick, 136, 138, 331

Springsteen, Bruce, 57, 146, 179

Spungeon, Nancy, 101, 252, 317

stagecraft 101, 261, 275

Stallone, Sylvester, 263

Stand By Me (film), 261–62

Stanton, Harry Dean, 240

Stanwyck, Barbara, 241

Starr, Ringo, 29, 31, 120, 145, 174, 177, 208, 303, 314

Stay Away Joe (film), 262

"Stayin' Alive," 245, 263

Staying Alive (film), 247, 262–63, 331

Stevens, Stella, 91, 118

Stewart, Catherine May, 16

Stigwood, Robert, 125

Still Crazy (film), 99, 263–64

"Still Haven't Found What I'm Looking For," 290

Sting (Gordon Sumner), 46, 220, 264–65, 321

Stockwell, John, 56

Stone, Oliver, 77, 78, 79

Stop Making Sense (documentary), 265

Strange Days (film), 265–66

Strasberg, Susan, 211

Streets of Fire (film), 164, 185, 266–67

Strong, Andrew, 59

Sullivan, Ed, 83

"Sunday Bloody Sunday," 290

Sutcliffe, Stuart, 22

Sutherland, Kiefer, 261

Swayze, Patrick, 72, 73

Sympathy for the Devil (film), 267

"Sympathy for the Devil," 115, 267

Talking Heads, 265

Taylor, Lili, 146

Taylor, Mick, 115

Teague, Lewis, 307, 308

Temple, Julien, 100, 129

Terry, Joyce, 32

Thames, Byron, 39

Thank God It's Friday (film), 269

That Thing You Do! (film), 99, 180, 185, 223, 269–70, 317, 325;
 Billboard in, 37, 45
This Is Elvis (documentary), 92, 270–71
This Is Spinal Tap (film), xiv, xviii, 45, 62, 99, 123, 129, 175, 180, 184, 223, 225, 228, 261, 264, 271–72, 274–75, 299, 301, 317, 321, 324, 327;
 and backstage antics, 22; bus trip in, 50;
 circular logic in, 57;
 rock movie conventions in, 275
Thomas, Kristin Scott, 288
3,000 Miles to Graceland (film), 92, 156
Timberlake, Justin, 321
Times Square (film), 99, 174, 275–76
"The Times They Are A-Changin'," 293
"Tiny Dancer," 9, 50
Tiu, Vicki, 155
Toast of the Town. See *Ed Sullivan Show*
Tommy (film), xii, xiv, 52, 206, 220, 236, 277, 279, 285, 321, 323, 326;
 bad fathers in, 23
Top Secret (film), 279–80
Tormé, Mel, 119
Townsend, Robert, 102, 103, 266
Townshend, Pete, 71, 130, 192, 220, 301
Travis, Tony, 32
Travolta, John, 68, 125, 245, 251, 262, 263, 331
Trick or Treat (film), xviii, 52, 67, 254, 280–81
Truth or Dare (documentary), 76, 183, 281, 283
Tubes, 310
Tunney, Robin, 94, 95
Turner, Tina, 277, 285–86, 300, 301, 321, 328
24-Hour Party People (film), 283–85
Tyler, Judy, 158, 160
Tyler, Liv, 94, 95, 185, 270

Ullman, Tracey, 120
Under the Cherry Moon (film), 124, 210, 254, 288, 331
U2, 290
U2: Rattle and Hum (documentary), 27, 123, 208, 290

Valens, Ritchie, 49, 172
Valli, Frankie, 125
Van Doren, Mamie, 119, 230
Van Halen, Eddie, 35
Van Lidth, Erland, 10
Van Patten, Vincent, 229
Velvet Goldmine (film), 115, 185, 208, 292–93, 301, 317, 325
Vicious, Sid, 100, 101, 129, 212, 252, 317, 328
Vietnam War, 293
Village People, 53
Viva Las Vegas (film), 294
"Viva Las Vegas," 294
von Zerneck, Danielle, 172

Wadleigh, Michael, 305, 307
Wahlberg, Mark, 44, 225, 235, 236, 261
Walken, Christopher, 298
Walker, Nancy, 53
Walk the Line (film), 37, 49, 92, 102, 223, 296–97, 328;
 bad fathers in, 23;
 property, destruction of in, 71
Walley, Deborah, 114, 260
"Wannabe," 259
Waters, John, 64, 65, 133
Waters, Muddy, 177
Watts, Charlie, 115
Wayne's World (film), 52, 62, 69, 129, 185, 297–98
Wayne's World 2 (film), 52, 298–99
Webb, Chloe, 252

"We Belong Together," 56

Weld, Tuesday, 141, 236, 304

Wells, Tico, 102

West Side Story (film), 90

Wham! In China (documentary), 112

What's Love Got to Do With It (film), xvii, 16, 50, 223,
    285–86, 299–301, 323, 328;
    and backstage antics, 23

Wheaton, Wil, 261

"When Doves Cry," 217

"When I'm Sixty-Four," 316

White, Mike, 247

White, Vanna, 124

The Who, 192, 220, 279, 301

The Who: The Kids Are Alright (documentary), 27, 31,
    50, 130, 301, 303;
    property, destruction of in, 71

"Whole Lotta' Shakin' Goin' On," 127

"Wig in a Box," 144

Wild in the Country (film), xvii, 40, 91, 303–4

Wild Guitar (film), 303

Wild in the Streets (film), 304–5

Williams, Cindy, 11, 193

Williams, Paul, 206

Williams, Treat, 132

Wilson, Dennis, 27

Wilson, Tony, 283, 284, 285

Wings, 160

Winter, Alex, 35

Winterbottom, Michael, 283

"With a Little Help from My Friends," 316

Witherspoon, Reese, 296, 297

Wonder, Stevie, 34

Woodstock (documentary), xi, xiv, xvii, 55, 192,
    305, 307–8, 321, 327

Woronov, Mary, 229, 232

Wyman, Bill, 115

Wynn, Keenan, 34

Yagher, Jeff, 250

Yates, Cassie, 105

Year of the Horse (documentary), 314

Yellow Submarine (film), xvii, 15, 16, 29, 31, 119, 128, 145,
    314, 316–17, 321, 326

"Yesterday," 120

Yoko factor, 275, 317. *See also* Yoko Ono

Young, Gig, 167

Young, Neil, 174, 175, 314

"You Should Be Dancin'," 245

Xanadu (film), 16, 62, 238, 310, 312, 331

Zabriskie Point (film), 211

Zadora, Pia, 133

Zahn, Steve, 270

Zappa, Frank, 20, 225

Zellweger, Renée, 94, 95

Zemeckis, Robert, 152, 153

Zeta-Jones, Catherine, 146

Ziggy Stardust and the Spiders from Mars (documentary), 319

PHOTO CREDITS

p. 7   *Alice's Restaurant* © United Artists, credit: United Artists/Photofest

p. 12   *American Graffiti* © Universal Pictures, credit: Universal Pictures/Photofest

p. 26   *Beach Blanket Bingo* © American International Pictures, credit: American International/Photofest

p. 30   The Beatles © United Artists, credit: United Artists /Photofest

p. 38   *Blackboard Jungle* © MGM, credit: MGM/Photofest

p. 41   *The Blues Brothers* © NBC, credit: NBC/Photofest

p. 48   *Bubba Ho-tep* © and credit: Photofest

p. 54   *Can't Stop the Music* © and credit: Photofest

p. 75   *Don't Look Back* © Pennebaker Films, credit: Pennebaker Films/Photofest

p. 81   *Easy Rider* © Columbia Pictures, credit: Columbia Pictures/Photofest, photographer: Peter Sorel

p. 82   *The Ed Sullivan Show* © CBS, credit: CBS/Photofest

p. 85   *Eddie and the Cruisers* © Embassy Pictures, credit: Embassy Pictures/Photofest

p. 116 *Gimme Shelter* © Maysles Films, Inc. credit: Maysles Films, Inc./Photofest

p. 122 *Godspell* © Columbia Pictures, credit: Columbia Pictures/Photofest

p. 135 *A Hard Day's Night* © United Artists, credit: United Artists/Photofest

p. 137 *Hard to Hold* © Universal Pictures, credit: Universal Pictures/Photofest

p. 140 *Head* © Columbia Pictures, credit: Columbia Pictures/Photofest

p. 143   *Hedwig and the Angry Inch* © and credit: Photofest

p. 159   *Jailhouse Rock* © MGM, credit: MGM/Photofest

p. 173   *Ladies and Gentlemen, the Fabulous Stains* © Paramount Pictures, credit: Paramount Pictures/Photofest

p. 176   *The Last Waltz* © United Artists, credit: United Artists/Photofest

p. 180   *Love Me Tender* © and credit: Photofest

p. 188   *Mister Rock and Roll* © and credit: Photofest

p. 191   *Monterey Pop* © Pennebaker Associates, credit: Pennebaker Associates/Photofest

p. 205   *Phantom of the Paradise* © 20th Century Fox, credit: Twentieth Century Fox/Photofest

p. 213   The Sex Pistols © and credit: Photofest

p. 221   *Quadrophenia* © World Northal, credit: World Northal/Photofest

p. 227   *Roadie* © United Artists, credit: United Artists/Photofest

p. 231   *Rock 'n' Roll High School* © New World Pictures, credit: New World/Photofest

p. 237   *The Rocky Horror Picture Show* © 20th Century Fox, credit: 20th Century Fox/Photofest

p. 244   *Satisfaction* © 20th Century Fox, credit: 20th Century Fox/Photofest

p. 246   *Saturday Night Fever* © and credit: Photofest

p. 273   *This Is Spinal Tap* © Embassy Pictures, credit: Embassy Pictures/Photofest

p. 278   *Tommy* © Columbia Pictures, credit: Columbia Pictures/Photofest

p. 282   *Truth or Dare* © Miramax Films, credit: Miramax Films/Photofest

p. 289   *Under the Cherry Moon* © Warner Brothers, credit: Warner Brothers/Photofest

p. 302   *The Who: The Kids Are Alright* © New World Pictures/MCA Records, credit: New World Pictures/MCA Records/Photofest

p. 306   *Woodstock* © and credit: Photofest

p. 311   *Xanadu* © Universal Pictures, credit: Universal Pictures/Photofest

p. 315   *Yellow Submarine*: © MGM, credit: MGM/Photofest